TEXAS PRISONS

THE WALLS CAME TUMBLING DOWN

UNIT LOCATIONS
TEXAS DEPARTMENT OF CORRECTIONS

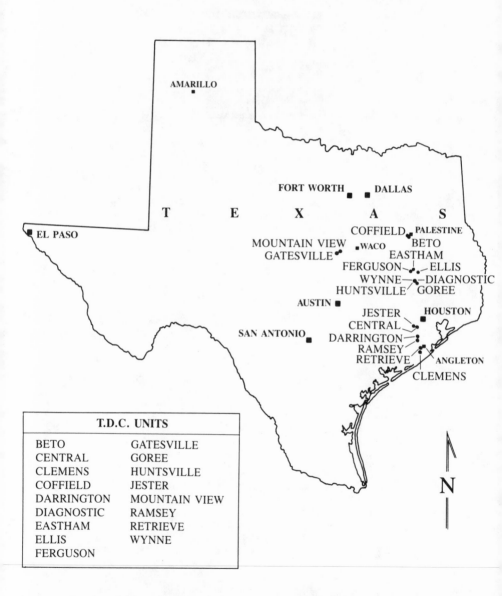

TEXAS PRISONS
THE WALLS CAME TUMBLING DOWN

BY STEVE J. MARTIN &
SHELDON EKLAND-OLSON
FOREWORD BY
HARRY M. WHITTINGTON

★

TexasMonthlyPress

Texas Monthly Press, Inc.
P.O. Box 1569
Austin, Texas 78767

       B   C   D   E   F   G   H

Library of Congress Cataloging-in-Publication Data

Martin, Steve J., 1948–
  Texas prisons.

  Bibliography: p.
  Includes index.
  1. Prisons—Texas—History. 2. Prison administration—Texas—History.
3. Prisoners—Legal status, laws, etc.—Texas—History. 4. Prison
violence—Texas—History. I. Ekland-Olson, Sheldon. II. Title.
HV9475.T4M37   365'.9764   87-7110
ISBN 0-87719-090-9

Design by David Timmons
Map design by Richard Balsam
Cover photo by Alan Pogue

To Frances Freeman Jalet Cruz, for her unwavering belief in the rule of law; to William Wayne Justice, William B. Turner, Harry M. Whittington, and Robert Gunn, who demanded that the rule of law be applied to the Texas Department of Corrections; and finally, to all the correctional officers and prisoners of TDC who believe that the rule of law is compatible with sound prison administration.

Contents

Foreword

The prison system is probably the least understood public institution in Texas. Though more than half a billion dollars are spent each year operating twenty-seven separate prisons that admit thirty thousand new inmates annually, few citizens have been interested in learning of the vast financial, legal and human problems involved. Most are also unaware that this massive effort at punishment results in the incarceration of only a very small percentage of criminals.

The more we learn of the history, politics, and legal requirements of our prison system, the more we will be able to participate in making the proper decisions about its purpose, management, cost, and value to society. Prison reform has not received as much attention as education, judicial, tax, and tort reform because the public has never been adequately informed about prisons. This book will not only be educational to those who want to know more about state government; it will also open the eyes of Texas upon a nontraditional concept of law and order, the one that applies inside the red brick walls.

Until recent years the walls of Texas prisons kept one of the state's gravest responsibilities out of sight and out of mind, allowing an agency with conglomerate business, agricultural, medical, and educational activities to escape accountability for its fiscal mismanagement, illegal operations, and the dehumanization of persons under its control.

I am deeply honored to share in the dedication of this incisive book and am grateful for the opportunity to contribute the foreword. The authors asked that I relate some of the issues and confrontations that led to my role as the first "maverick" member of the Texas Board of Corrections.

When I was appointed in June 1979, I was not only the first Republican but also the first member who had not been serving for several years under the leadership of H. H. Coffield. Appointed in 1948, Coffield had been chairman of the board for twenty-two years when he resigned in 1977 at the age of eighty-three. Coffield had also been treasurer of the state Democratic Party for many years, a position that likely led to his appointments to terms totaling thirty years by five different governors. Most board members and TDC officials would probably agree that chairman Coffield ruled with a firm hand and that the board meetings did not encourage open discussion or public involvement. When I was considering the appointment, director Estelle encouraged me to accept, assuring me that the boards meetings never were longer than one and one-half hours and that he would have me back in my office by early afternoon the day of the meeting.

Though Governor Clements had not discussed the prison system with me prior to my appointment, I thought that since he was the first Republican governor in 100 years, the citizens of Texas would be expecting his administration at least to question the past policies and practices of their state government. While serving on various corporate boards of directors for more than twenty-five years, I have always felt that a part of my responsibility to the shareholders was to question and challenge the recommendations made by management and to avoid a personal relationship with the president that would prevent me from voting for his removal. It is very difficult for a board member to properly exercise his fiduciary duty to the shareholders while cultivating friendships and fraternizing with management and other board members. It was with this background and belief that I became a member of a state board that had been dominated by one man for almost a quarter of a century.

At my first meeting on July 9, 1979, it was difficult to believe what I was hearing. In private session Estelle asked the board's approval to become affiliated with a private corporation engaged in providing security services in Middle East countries. Some of the members quickly expressed approval, noting that their friend and underpaid director deserved the opportunity to make more money on the side. I hesitated to speak until one or two other members began voicing their concerns. Following the discussion there was no doubt in my mind that a majority had clearly disapproved.

To my amazement, three months later at breakfast, Estelle told the chairman of the board and me that he was already associated with the private security firm, and if his involvement ever began to interfere with his duties as director, he would resign from one or the other position. Since the chairman, who was also present at the July meeting, made no comment, neither did I, but it was my first realization that Estelle would openly defy a majority of the board.

A few days later, while visiting with Governor Clements, I told him about Estelle's outside business involvement. Within a week I received from the governor a copy of Estelle's letter to his partners withdrawing from the business. There was no question about the governor's source of information, so from that time until Estelle left almost four years later, I knew that our personal relationship would never prevent me from voting for his removal.

During the latter part of 1979, Estelle and the board were proceeding with plans to buy a large tract of land in the Rio Grande Valley for a prison farm to house 4,000 inmates. They had been unsuccessful in gaining the approval of Governor Briscoe and attorney general Hill in April 1978, but with a new governor and a new attorney general, Estelle and most of the board members were firmly set to try again to spend $8 million for a site. In September 1979 the chairman appointed me as a member of the Site Selection Committee, and I was told that we would be visiting many large tracts of land throughout the state. I soon learned, however, that no sites except two in the Rio Grande Valley would be considered. A tract on the Mexico border was quickly identified as the choice location.

I began asking some questions about land values in the Valley as compared to other parts of the state, outstanding mineral interests and easements, and transportation costs to and from the other prisons and the Galveston hospital. I also questioned the distance that families of inmates would have to travel for visits, and the problems in separating violent and nonviolent inmates at a unit so far removed from the other prisons. The answers I received were incomplete, deceptive, or untruthful.

At a time when overcrowding was becoming a very serious problem, use of the 100,000 acres of existing prison land seemed to be the best and fastest solution for a new unit; but I was told it was state policy to have each prison unit agriculturally self-sufficient, that at least 5,000 acres would be required, and that there was no large tract of land near any existing unit that could be purchased. This was another misrepresentation, because the 7,200 acre tract adjoining the Ellis Unit in Walker County had been available for several years and was later purchased in 1981 as the site for the Ellis II Unit.

I soon realized that my opposition to the Valley site would not change any votes of other board members, particularly the seven who had been members when the decision was first made in 1977. However, since a board containing the governor and the land commissioner had to give final approval, I wrote a memorandum to Doug Brown, the governor's chief of staff, outlining my objections. Despite the urging of the governor's general counsel, a Democrat who had worked closely with Estelle while serving three years as general counsel to former Governor Briscoe, the Approval Board failed to support the purchase. With the second effort in two years to locate a prison in the Valley having failed, TDC then focused on acquiring a site in the proximity of its other facilities. Within six months 5,968 acres on the Brazos River forty miles from Huntsville were purchased with the funds that had been appropriated by the legislature three years earlier.

As I became more familiar with the care and treatment of the inmates, my differences with Estelle continued. At the January 1981 board meeting, I requested the staff to prepare recommendations for reducing the inmate population, since there were 2,000 people sleeping on the floor. One of my proposals was to study the possible transfer of approximately 2,000 mentally retarded inmates to other state institutions. Estelle responded that this idea would encounter strong opposition of families of mentally retarded persons in state institutions, who would not approve of having "convicted felons being integrated into those programs." To those of us who have been involved for years with efforts to improve the status and lives of mentally retarded citizens, this statement by Estelle was both disappointing and offensive, because it reflected not only a lack of expertise on his part, but more importantly, a callousness toward a sizable segment of offenders confined in Texas prisons. The TDC Director was one of many state officials who were uninformed about the mental deficiency which has led to so many offenders being incarcerated and then left plagued with the euphemism of "once a convict, always a convict."

At the March 1981 meeting, the staff reported that approximately 4,000 inmates (13.2%) were mentally retarded with an I.Q. of 69 or below. The staff also said that as many as 60% of the mentally retarded inmates had been convicted of nonviolent offenses. I, nevertheless, was convinced that much more should be done to provide appropriate care and treatment for the mentally retarded inmates and determined to make every effort to bring about a change in the way they had been classified and confined for many years.

Until the state's public policy could be changed to deal with offenders who have the minds of children, I felt that it was imperative for the Board of Corrections to insist that the staff carry out the legislative intent in the confinement of mentally retarded inmates. Since 1927 it has been the law in Texas that the prison system provide humane treatment and give inmates opportunity, encouragement, and training in the matter of reformation. Since 1975 it has been the law of Texas that inmates be separated and classified according to sex, age, health, corrigibility, and character of offense. It was my opinion that the mental age, as opposed to chronological age, should be controlling, and that those having the lower mental ages should be confined among themselves.

During the next year all available information on the problems of mentally retarded offenders encountered in prison was gathered. The governor had appointed a task force to examine the plight of intellectually handicapped inmates, and the Texas Legislature granted authority for TDC to contract with public and private agencies to provide care and treatment for mentally retarded inmates.

The issue before the board was whether to transfer all the mentally retarded inmates to one unit where they could be protected from other inmates, or to continue mainstreaming them throughout all prisons. TDC officials strongly favored mainstreaming, ironically on the grounds that the mentally retarded inmates should live as "normally" as possible. Studies had convinced me that humane treatment for mentally retarded persons in prison was not possible unless they are separated from the "normal" prison environment, where the physically and mentally weak are victimized.

Finally, on July 13, 1982, the board voted unanimously to discontinue mainstreaming retarded inmates and directed the staff to present alternative proposals. This action by the board was a disappointment to TDC officials, though it provided a clear direction for them to follow and came after many months of study.

Instead of accepting the new policy adopting a standard of humane treatment for mentally handicapped inmates, Estelle put the question of mainstreaming back on the agenda for the November 1982 meeting. This was another example of the director's determination to defy the board, only this time his real motivation for mainstreaming became known. An expert witness was hired to tell the board that abolishing mainstreaming would seriously affect the productivity of the industrial division where many mentally retarded inmates were employed; and, further, in the expert's opinion, if industrial revenue from the prison should be curtailed, it might lead to a state income tax. In other words, the business capabilities of the prison were paramount to humane treatment.

The vote was delayed until the May 1983 meeting. By this time those "one and one-half hour meetings" were lasting all day, and this was the only meeting during my six-year term when members of the Board of Pardons and Paroles came to offer words of advice. Estelle had requested that they attend and say that they supported mainstreaming mentally retarded inmates in prison because they would be mainstreamed while on parole. After a long debate, the board voted five to two to create a separate unit for the mentally retarded inmates.

Today the Mentally Retarded Offender Program at Beto I is providing a decent and humane environment to a large number of inmates who are unable to cope with the normal prison life in Texas, and who now have much greater hope for rehabilitation. Moreover, the TDC staff is genuinely dedicated to the program and proud of its results.

When Steve Martin came forward in 1982 from the ranks of TDC employees and courageously told the truth about the agency's deception in operating the illegal building tender system, there were very few state officials and board members who commended him for his honesty and the worthy example he set for other state employees. These same officials did not lose confidence in Estelle as general manager, because of his popularity and the personal relationships he had with so many of them. Since practically every phase of prison operations was being challenged in the class-action lawsuit, and Martin had now cast doubt upon the credibility of the entire management, it seemed appropriate for the state to conduct an honest appraisal and learn of the system's deficiencies. Instead, most politicians chose to complain about the authority of federal judges without knowing, or refusing to believe, that the conditions inside the red brick walls were substantially below standards adopted by other states. The politicians and members of the Board of Corrections all took the same oath of office to uphold the laws of Texas and the United States Constitution, yet they would not accept the fact that the Texas prison system was the largest in the nation found to be unconstitutional by the federal courts. With the substantial increase in appropriations for TDC enacted by the Legislature in 1987, the plan to begin building prisons on credit, and new laws authorizing the state to delegate to private vendors its responsibility to provide care and treatment of its inmates, there will soon be more prisons, more prisoners, more guards, and more profits to monitor, resulting in an increasingly complex prison system and even greater opportunity for corruption, mismanagement and mistreatment of inmates. Yet, there have been no structural changes in the management and oversight procedures to assist with these growing problems. The serious responsibility facing Texas as it deals with corrections is awesome, and the course we are following will be a continuing impairment to the financial stability and moral obligation of our state.

My six-year stint as a member of the board of one of our state's largest agencies was truly an eye-opening experience. I had no idea that it was possible for a state agency to operate so autonomously. Neither the legislature with its oversight committees, the state auditor with his annual financial reviews, the attorney general who is the agency's lawyer, nor the citizens who serve as board members were interested or effective in placing the TDC director and staff under proper controls and in compliance with the law.

Harry M. Whittington
Austin, Texas

Acknowledgments

As we come to the close of our research on this most interesting story, we realize our indebtedness to numerous individuals and organizations. We are grateful to the Hogg Foundation and the School of Law at the University of Texas for financial, secretarial, research, and collegial support throughout the project. In particular, Professors Mike Sharlot and Mike Churgin of the University of Texas Law School were kind enough to read and comment on early drafts when our ideas were just beginning to come together. Likewise, Professor James Jacobs of the New York University School of Law provided invaluable encouragement, advice, and assistance. Finally, we would like to thank F. Scott McCown and Harry M. Whittington for their thoughtful criticisms throughout the course of the project.

Among those who agreed to be interviewed, we are particularly thankful for the insights offered by Frances Jalet Cruz, Rick Gray, Toni Hunter, Ed Idar, Vincent Nathan, Richel Rivers, William Bennett Turner, and Harry M. Whittington. Valuable research assistance was provided by Kathy Grant, Gina Martin, Allison Supancic, and Michael Supancic. Finally, Scott Lubeck's enthusiastic response to the manuscript and subsequent editorial suggestions are greatly appreciated.

On a more personal note, we want to thank our wives, Gina and Carolyn. They were the source of much-needed support throughout the project, even when it meant listening to the latest discoveries for the fourth and fifth times. A special note of thanks for Gerard Saucier's encouragement at a time when it was especially needed.

Introduction

When we began to reconstruct the events that led petitioning inmates in Texas to the courtroom of an activist judge, and from there to a declaration that Texas prisons were unconstitutional, we knew the struggle had been long, bitter, and costly. We also knew that the court case *Ruiz* v. *Estelle* had been the major battleground. In addition, it was quite clear that *Ruiz* had implications far beyond state boundaries. The scope of the issues in the case and the eventual reforms ordered by Judge Justice were far broader than in any previous prison litigation. They were, in a sense, a high-water mark for the national prisoners' rights movement, which had begun in the early 1960s. In short, for both local and national reasons, we felt that the story of prison reform in Texas was well worth telling.

As our early research progressed, it became evident that there was a compelling and deeply human side to the picture. Tensions ran remarkably high from the beginning of the reform efforts in 1967. Prison administrators had developed a highly efficient operation. These same officials did not react favorably when confronted by a fifty-seven-year-old female volunteer attorney from New York who began, gently at first, but then with unrelenting commitment, to assist inmates in their challenges to existing practices.

From the beginning there were frequent confrontations both inside and outside the courtroom. Pressures were exerted that resulted in the volunteer attorney's being transferred and eventually losing her job. Petitioning inmates were subjected to pressures, deprivations, and sometimes quite brutal intimidations, which were not experienced by less litigious prisoners. Thus, as the litigation progressed, it became apparent that there was a dark underside to the surface efficiency in the Texas Department of Corrections. The methods that Texas prison administrators used were effective when it came to controlling prisoners. These same practices proved to be, according to the evolving constitutional standards of decency, in violation of the Eighth Amendment prohibition against cruel and unusual punishments. This finding by the court was met by defiance from those who ran the prisons, by charges that Judge Justice was hopelessly biased and ignorant of the facts of prison life, and finally, with more than a touch of irony, by the assertion that Judge Justice had little concern for the safety of either inmates or staff. At one point the personal nature of the rhetoric deteriorated to such an extent that Judge Justice's opinion in *Ruiz* was likened to a cheap dime-store novel by W. J. Estelle, then the director of the Texas Department of Corrections.

The highly tense climate began to ease when influential state leaders became convinced that the prison system was not only in violation of the federal constitution, but also in blatant violation of a state law prohibiting the use of inmates as guards, a law that had been on the books for some ten years. This acknowledgment by state leaders led to a sweeping turnover in high-level prison personnel and massive changes in the methods used to control inmates in Texas prisons.

This period of dramatic administrative transition saw an equally dramatic increase in turmoil among the inmates. Predatory gangs gained a strong foothold, evidenced most directly by their participation in an upsurge in lethal prison violence. Judge Justice and other reform-minded lawyers and state officials were accused of ruining the formerly tightly controlled Texas prison system. Counterclaims were made that the post-*Ruiz* problems of the prison system were more probably the result of administrative recalcitrance to implement transition measures that would have avoided the loss of control within the cell blocks and dormitories.

As the story began to unfold, our initial objective of documenting the specific details of prison reform in Texas was broadened to include the individual struggles of certain key players, some of whom have spent years of their professional lives involved in a single piece of litigation. We came to realize that the interpersonal dynamics of these players very often overshadowed the legal issues. We have therefore attempted, whenever possible, to preserve the human side of the story. For the broader policy and research arena, we present a case study of what happens when a relatively rigid and complex organization is confronted by an intrusive evolving moral order. In this regard, there are important comparisons to be made between prison reform and the reform of educational organizations stemming from *Brown* v. *Board of Education*, the reform of mental health institutions related to cases such as *Wyatt* v. *Stickney,* and the reform of juvenile institutions in cases such as *Morales*

v. *Turman*.

In each of these instances, institutional reform was stimulated by an evolving concern for civil rights. Less well developed is comparative empirical analysis of how the ideological agenda of the broad-based civil rights movement became operational in particular life circumstances. Much of the story we present is relevant to how public organizations, such as the Office of Equal Opportunity, meshed with private organizations, such as the NAACP and its attendant prison reform programs, through evolving interpersonal networks. It was through these interpersonal networks that the civil rights movement coalesced at certain places and points in time and around specific issues of reform. Systematic examination of this and other empirical patterns through the comparison of accounts such as our own with others, such as James Jacobs's study of Stateville in Illinois and John Irwin's account of prison reform in California, is well worth pursuing.

Similarly, comparative analysis will shed light on the course taken by the litigation process itself. In many instances courts have moved toward broad systemic relief and the prescription of policy for the administration of public institutions. This greatly complicates the political, normative, and economic impact of the decision. There is only rudimentary knowledge about how legislatures and voters have responded to judicial pressures to improve state-run institutions.

The call for systemic relief has also placed the court in social arenas where judges have traditionally had no experience. Having decided to impose changes on recalcitrant insitutions, judges have increasingly come to rely on special masters, who are given the job of moving the litigation from an adversarial posture to one of negotiation, mediation, and implementation. Some commentators have argued that instead of facilitating change, these court-appointed functionaries have prolonged the litigation process and have failed to ease the adversarial nature of the proceedings. Without more specific case studies from which to draw inferences, we are not likely to reach any informed decision on whether this charge is true, or when and under what circumstances it seems to be accentuated.

Our research suggests that much of the influence of the special master and the eventual impact of the court-ordered prison reform depends upon mediational strategies employed by the special master as well as the reaction of prison administrators and inmates. While commentary is divided on whether the prisoners' rights movement has been responsible for an increase in prison violence, we would contend that to date it is not reform per se, but the way in which people react to the process of change, that accounts for the noted upsurge in violent activity. Future comparative analysis in this area might well concentrate on the link between the opportunistic behavior of predatory inmates and the reaction of prison administrators to court-mandated change.

As we began to discover first one piece and then another of the story of prison reform in Texas, we were encouraged by the availability of a wide variety of sources through the public record. We spent many hours in the state archives, poring over historical documents. We relied heavily on trial transcripts, as well as published and unpublished court opinions. We set up interviews, sometimes with great and sometimes with little success, with many of the principal actors in the case. We had both been involved with the TDC throughout many of the reform years and frequently drew on this personal knowledge.

For one of us, Sheldon Ekland-Olson, this knowledge came from sporadic contacts with numerous prison units, first while working on the Transitional Aid Research Project (funded by the American Bar Association and the United States Department of Labor) in the mid-1970s and then while conducting research on prison violence and acting as a consulting expert for the state of Texas in portions of the *Ruiz* proceedings. For the other of us, Steve Martin, the knowledge was more continuous, detailed, and in one sense problematic, because of his status as a former TDC lawyer. For this reason, the next portion of the preface is a strictly personal account of his resolution of that conflict.

In June 1972, I became a prison guard ("Boss" Martin) at the Ellis Unit, a maximum security prison of the Texas Department of Corrections. When I started work at Ellis, I was twenty-three years old and had never been inside of a prison. The same month that I began my job as a prison "boss," a "jailhouse lawyer," David Ruiz, filed his handwritten prisoner petition claiming that the Texas prison system was oppressive, brutal, and in violation of the Eighth Amendment prohibition against cruel and unusual punishments.

My first week on the job at Ellis, I can recall how impressed I was with the clean halls and cell blocks and the long, quiet lines of orderly prisoners in white uniforms walking single file inside the green lines along the prison corridors. If I had left the Ellis Unit after my first week of work never to return, I would have dismissed David Ruiz's petition as nothing more than the hyperbolic muses of a "jailbird." Instead, I remained at Ellis for the next year. Even though I never penetrated the inner circle of the guard regime during my twelve months at Ellis, I observed enough to know that Ruiz's allegations were not without merit, and I suspected that a close examination of the TDC might reveal a long history of systematic violations supported and encouraged by prison officials.

In 1981 I returned to the Texas prison system to work in the legal affairs division, after graduating from law school. My first assignment was to assist TDC's lawyers in trying to appeal the findings of Judge Justice, who had not taken David Ruiz's petition as lightly as I would have in June 1972. For the next several years I was employed, not as a prison boss, but as a lawyer for prison bosses. During my tenure as a TDC lawyer,

I came to believe that the *Ruiz* lawsuit and the federal court intervention that it produced created such bitter controversy because of the myth, misunderstanding, and misrepresentations that surrounded the Texas prison system. I also came to believe that until a comprehensive and objective record was produced "separating the wheat from the chaff," a proper analysis of the Texas prison system during this period of revolutionary change would be impossible.

I first discussed such a project with Professor Ekland-Olson in 1983, while I was still employed as a lawyer with the TDC. He wholeheartedly embraced the idea and agreed that if the opportunity arose, we would attempt to produce a record that could be used as a resource for professionals, scholars, and public officials interested in studying the largest prisoners' rights lawsuit in the history of American jurisprudence.

In June 1985 I resigned from TDC. During the following two months, Professor Ekland-Olson and I organized the effort and secured the necessary resources to undertake this rather ambitious project. One of the first issues we addressed was the potential conflicts I would face in writing such a book since I was, in my role as a TDC attorney, routinely involved in privileged communication between TDC officials and their lawyers. Such information is normally not available to outsiders unless the holder of the privilege, the client, makes it available. After discussing the issue with a number of colleagues, most of whom are lawyers with experience as government attorneys, I resolved this issue, at least for myself. Professor Ekland-Olson and I agreed to rely wherever possible on documents and resources available through the public record. In those instances where information was deemed critical, but was privileged, we secured the information from sources other than myself.

It was impossible in all instances to maintain a strict demarcation between my role as an author and my role as a former TDC lawyer. There are those, therefore, who will question the propriety of my having coauthored the book. To those persons, who are surely entitled to raise this issue, I simply say that I have decided that the significance of the issues justifies my telling the story. Through the years, I developed a strong conviction that the story was of such importance that if Professor Ekland-Olson and I could successfully complete the project, its impact would far outweigh any criticism directed against me personally. I would add that, as a government lawyer, I represented not only TDC officials, but also the citizens of Texas who support the principle that public officials should administer social institutions in a lawful and humane fashion.

Major Events in the History of Prison Reform in Texas

•1849–1946

Prisoners in Texas are considered "slaves of the state." Large agricultural and ranching operations become hallmarks of the prison system. Widely respected prison expert declares the Texas prison system one of the worst in the country in the early 1940s.

•1947–1961

O. B. Ellis appointed as reform-minded director of Texas prisons. Broad-scale improvements made in agricultural operations, educational and vocational training programs, and housing and salaries for staff. Prison system becomes much more self-sufficient.

•1961–1966

George Beto selected as director when O. B. Ellis dies. Beto continues many of the reform programs initiated by Ellis. Texas prison system becomes nationally known for clean, orderly, and secure institutions.

U.S. Supreme Court holds in *Cooper* v. *Pate* that prisoners have right to challenge administrative practices in prison.

•1967–1970

Frances Jalet arrives in Texas as volunteer poverty attorney and makes contact with TDC prisoner Fred Cruz after article is published in Austin newspaper about her commitment to helping the poor. Through this initial contact numerous other inmates ask Jalet for assistance.

George Beto begins his effort to oust Jalet from the TDC, and she is forced to transfer from Austin to Dallas after Beto registers concern with Jalet's supervisor in Austin. Jalet contacts William Bennett Turner through Anthony Amsterdam at University of Pennsylvania Law School and NAACP Legal Defense Fund in New York.

In December 1968, Jalet is fired from her Dallas job because of problems she was causing Beto. Jalet continues her work with inmates after securing an appointment at Texas Southern University in Houston.

•1970–1971

Jalet's appointment at Texas Southern is not renewed, allegedly due to pressures exerted on state leaders by George Beto.

George Beto's prison administration is praised in *Novak* v. *Beto.* U.S. Fifth Circuit judges Elbert Tuttle and John Minor Wisdom dissent.

Entire Arkansas prison system declared unconstitutional in *Holt* v. *Sarver.*

Three inmates file suit against Frances Jalet in September 1971, with encouragement from prison administrators, charging that Jalet is fomenting revolutionary unrest in Texas prisons.

In October 1971 George Beto, in "raw exercise of power," bars Jalet from Texas prison system. A broad-based protest is heard from legal profession. In *Rocha* v. *Beto,* Fifth Circuit begins to remand Texas prison cases that had been routinely dismissed by the U.S. district courts based on the "hands-off" doctrine.

In November 1971, George Beto compromises by transferring Jalet's prisoner-clients to the "eight-hoe squad" at the Wynne Unit. Jalet's visitation rights are restored with some limitations. The "eight-hoe squad" inmates begin to develop litigation expertise that eventually paves the way for massive court intervention.

•1972

Mississippi prisons declared unconstitutional in *Gates* v. *Collier.* In June, David Ruiz files handwritten petition, while a member of eight-hoe squad, in Judge William Wayne Justice's court in Tyler, Texas. Raises issues about the Texas prison system similar to those decided in *Gates* v. *Collier.*

Citizens United for Rehabilitation of Errants (CURE) becomes active in prison reform efforts under direction of Charles and Pauline Sullivan.

In September, for the first time, U.S. District Court grants TDC prisoners broad relief, prohibiting censorship of prisoner-attorney correspondence. Beto resigns the same month censorship decision is rendered and W. J. Estelle, with Beto's support and recommendation, becomes the new director. Estelle disbands eight-hoe squad shortly after assuming directorship.

•1973

House Bill 1056, the "Building Tender Bill," is passed in May by the 63rd Legislature. This bill prohibits use of inmates in positions with supervisory and disciplinary authority over other inmates. This same month a joint legislative committee is established to study the prison system and to make recommendations for reform.

In June, the "Father's Day Incident" occurs on Retrieve Unit, wherein allegations are made of staff abuse of inmates. In November, prisoners clash with building tenders at the Ramsey Unit, increasing tension between prison officials and attorneys for the prisoners.

Judge Justice issues written opinion in August granting interim relief to plaintiffs in *Morales* v. *Turman,* a case raising questions about brutality in juvenile offender facilities in Texas.

•1974–1977

In April, Judge Justice consolidates eight separate inmate petitions into class action suit, *Ruiz* v. *Estelle.* He also asks U.S. Department of Justice to investigate the facts alleged in the prisoners' complaints and to participate with the full rights of a party to the suit. William Bennett Turner, a leading civil rights attorney with the NAACP Legal Defense Fund, is appointed as counsel of record for the plaintiffs.

Between May and July, tensions run high at the Ramsey Unit amid charges and countercharges of plots to murder unit officials and inmates.

Joint committee on prison reform issues two reports highly critical of the TDC in December, finding, among other things, that TDC continued to use inmate guards in violation of House Bill 1056.

•1975–1977

In July, Fifth Circuit Court denies state's application to prohibit Department of Justice from intervening in the case.

Judge Justice issues a series of protective orders for inmates being harassed for their involvement in prison reform efforts. Separate contempt hearings establish pattern of abusive treatment of *Ruiz* writ-writers.

Plaintiffs and defendants in *Ruiz* begin exchanging massive amounts of evidentiary documents in preparation for trial.

•1978

On October 2, *Ruiz* trial begins in Houston. Plaintiffs organize their case around five issues: 1) physical security and the right of inmates to be free from assault and fear of assault; 2) living and working conditions; 3) medical care; 4) summary punishments; and 5) access to courts.

Inmate demonstrations spread throughout the TDC as the trial begins. These come to an end when Judge Justice issues a calming statement.

In early November, shortly after disturbances are quieted, W. J. Estelle states he finds "little charity and less solace in bringing issues before a court that has no knowledge, direct or indirect, of what the real issues are and could care less that their personal social philosophy, finding its way into so-called law, jeopardizes not only our inmates' safety, but the safety of prison staff as well."

Election of Bill Clements as governor and Mark White as attorney general brings new state officials into prison administration and *Ruiz* defense.

•1979

After calling some one hundred and fifty witnesses, attorneys for the plaintiffs and the Department of Justice bring their case to a close on May 2, 1979.

Attorneys for the prison system complete their defense against the charges made in *Ruiz* on August 30.

Trial comes to an end on September 20. Judge Justice comments, "Counsel, it has been a long trial. I'm informed by the clerk that there were actually consumed 161 trial days, that 349 witnesses have testified, that approximately 1530 exhibits have been received in evidence. It's the longest trial in my experience, and may I express the hope that none of us are involved in one of this length again."

•1980

Judge Justice issues memorandum opinion in December. The opinion is organized to cover six major issues: overcrowding, security and supervision, health care, discipline, access to courts, and other conditions of confinement (fire safety, sanitation, work safety, and hygiene).

State officials begin what is eventually characterized as a "personal and unseemly campaign of vilification" against Judge Justice and special master Vincent Nathan.

•1981

Prison population tops 30,000. Roughly 3,000 inmates are sleeping on the floor.

Consent Decree is approved by Judge Justice in early March. Common ground is reached on health care, work safety, use of chemical agents, administrative segregation, and diet for inmates in solitary confinement.

Judge Justice issues broad and extremely detailed final decree on April 20. Also establishes the Office of the Special Master to oversee implementation and resolution of disputed issues.

State's attorneys file motion in June to suspend Judge Justice's sweeping orders with the prediction that the solutions would have "catastrophic consequences for TDC management and institutional security and order."

Building tender system becomes subject of First Monitor's Report from special master's office. Relations between special master and TDC officials, always a bit uneasy, become more tense. Judge Justice, the special master, and his monitors are accused of precipitating a wave of inmate violence.

In December, a member of the Board of Corrections begins to question W. J. Estelle's credibility on the building tender issue.

•1982

Mark White defeats Bill Clements for governor after a hotly contested campaign involving prison issues.

Court hearing on allegations involving building tender abuses is scheduled for March 15.

State officials prepare a motion to dismiss special master and consider having special master and his staff investigated for criminal charges.

TDC's own attorneys confirm that prison officials used a "squad" of building tenders to suppress a riot on Eastham Unit. Other incidents involving building tenders on Central, Retrieve, Ellis, and Ramsey Units are investigated.

Due to rising litigation costs and TDC's potential vulnerability on building tender issue, state senator and Board of Corrections member call for a "cease fire" and negotiated settlement in mid-March. By early April, an agreed settlement is reached on most volatile issue, the building tender system.

In May, TDC Board refuses to violate court order on overcrowding and closes prisons to new admissions. This prompts legislature to appropriate $58 million in special session for construction and staffing increases.

In June, Fifth Circuit Court affirms facts but narrows relief ordered by Judge Justice in *Ruiz*.

•1983

Ninth Monitor's Report is issued by special master's office. Claims that physical abuse of inmates continues to occur with "alarming frequency." Findings documented in over four hundred pages of appendices to main report.

Charges of mismanagement of funds by TDC officials are raised by Board of Corrections members.

W. J. Estelle announces his intention to resign shortly after Ninth Monitor's Report and just prior to having to terminate his most senior warden. Cites as reasons his inability to secure funds from the legislature and his refusal to compromise further on court-ordered charges. Resignation is accepted in October.

•1984

Large-scale turnover of high-level TDC officials. Approximately 200 disciplinary actions eventually taken against TDC officers for use-of-force violations.

Raymond Procunier hired as director of the Texas prison system in May.

•1985

Settlement agreement reached in July on wide range of issues, including crowding, visitation, staffing, construction, and classification of inmates.

Raymond Procunier resigns shortly after settlement agreement. Lane McCotter appointed new director.

•1986

William B. Turner files contempt motion, charging TDC with failure to implement major provisions of 1985 agreement.

Governor Mark White exerts influence to block settlement of contempt issues. Clements defeats White in another bitterly contested campaign including prison issues.

On December 31, Judge Justice issues opinion finding TDC in contempt of court. Threatens fines as high as $24 million per month.

•1987

Shortly before Governor-elect Clements takes office, he meets with Judge Justice in what is described by William B. Turner as an "unbelievably useful, productive exchange of views."

Governor Clements addresses 70th Legislature and states, "Let me state clearly the facts of the *Ruiz* case. The lawsuit is over. Let me state clearly the facts of the contempt citation . . . : We must get in compliance as quickly as possible. We have no choice."

Judge William Wayne Justice personally visits TDC units for the first time in the fifteen year history of the litigation, and thereafter vacates fines imposed for contempt after a hearing which establishes "remarkable progress" by state officals.

Chapter One:
Evolving Standards of Decency
and State Initiated Reform—1849–1967

A convicted felon, whom the law in its humanity punishes by confinement in the penitentiary instead of with death, is subject while undergoing that punishment, to all the laws which the Legislature in its wisdom may enact. . . . He has, as a consequence of his crime, not only forfeited his liberty, but all his personal rights except those which the law in its humanity accords to him. He is for the time being a slave of the State. He is civiliter mortuus; and his estate, if he has any is administered like that of a dead man.
Ruffin v. *Commonwealth*, 1871.

Prisoners' rights in the United States emerged as an integral part of the broader civil rights movement in the 1960s. In the process, convicted felons, who had long been declared *civiliter mortuus* and "slaves of the state" by American courts, awakened and abandoned their shackles with an intensity that transformed American prisons into institutions under constant siege from jailhouse lawyers, activist judges, reform groups, and a corps of dedicated movement attorneys. Judicial intervention into the affairs of prison life, encouraged by the proddings of lawyers who were supported by foundation and federal funds, eventually spread across all regions of the country to precipitate an avalanche of cases. As a result, inmates secured wider freedoms in the practice of religion, increased protections from severe corporal punishments, greater access to courts, lawyers, and legal materials, and expanded due process protections in disciplinary hearings. Eventually, a judicial forum was secured in which inmates could broaden their challenges from isolated conditions and practices to attack the constitutionality of an entire prison system.

This book presents a detailed case study of reform efforts directed at the Texas Department of Corrections (TDC) and how administrative expectations and practices of the past collided with evolving legal standards of the present. The struggle for control of the Texas prison system that this collision occasioned produced an intense and long-standing wall of resistance to eventual reforms. Prison officials who became immersed in this bitter and often brutal struggle were supported for years by their lawyers, high-ranking government officials, and public sentiment. Prisoners responded with an outpouring of handwritten and often inartfully drawn pleadings that proved to be effective once placed in the hands of civil rights attorneys eager to do battle with prison administrators, who until the 1960s operated prisons with near-autonomous control. These prisoners and attorneys steered their pleadings toward a receptive judicial forum that through careful orchestration ultimately produced the broadest prison reforms ever handed down by a federal judge. The mandated reforms were met with defiance, denial, and deceit. In the end, these obstructive and unlawful actions precipitated sweeping change in the highest levels of prison management, followed by a vigorous effort to implement reforms in the midst of an organization shattered by charges of corruption, brutality, and mismanagement.

The story begins in 1967, when a legal aid attorney in her mid-fifties, who had come to Texas fresh from a brief training session in poverty law at the University of Pennsylvania, was contacted by a convict known for his dedication and skill as a jailhouse lawyer. Together these two engaged in constant legal skirmishing with the administrators of a proud, autonomous, tightly controlled agency. From this unimposing beginning, a small group of writ-writing prisoners emerged. Backed by their attorney, who was inexperienced in prisoners' rights law but perservering, these prisoners began to mount legal campaigns that could no longer be suppressed by prison administrators. These encounters resulted in victories and setbacks for both sides. As the course of the litigation progressed, however, it became apparent that evolving standards in the national legal arena favored the prisoners, who quickly became all too aware that through skillful writ-writing autocratic administrators could be forced to answer to a higher authority.

The trend toward increased judicial intervention and away from the idea that prison officials were free to treat prisoners as they pleased was set solidly in motion by the Supreme Court in 1964, when an Illinois prisoner was granted the right to challenge administrative restrictions on his access to the Koran and opportunities for worship among prisoners professing the Muslim faith.[1] Shortly thereafter, with the right to take grievances against prison officials to court secured, inmates in Arkansas challenged the practice of forced physical labor, along with a variety of corporal punishments then in use. In these cases the link with a past shaped by the idea that prisoners were literally slaves of the state was quite evident. In 1965 a district court in Arkansas had no difficulty with the proposition that prison officials were in violation of constitutional protections when they knowingly compelled convicts to perform physical labor that was unduly painful, beyond the inmates' strength, or a danger to their lives or health.[2] In a related case, a court of appeals likewise had "no difficulty" in reaching the conclusion that whippings in Arkansas prisons with the strap, described in testimony as a three-and-one-half- to five-and-one-half-foot piece of leather, about four inches wide and a quarter of an inch thick, attached to a wooden handle about eight to twelve inches long, ran afoul of contemporary standards of decency, human dignity, and "precepts of civilization which we profess to possess."[3]

Revelations about life in the Arkansas prison system, which were clearly out of step with the standards of decency in the mid-1960s, added substantial emotional momentum to the prison reform movement. Support of a more practical nature came in 1969, when the Supreme Court ruled in favor of a Tennessee inmate who challenged a prison regulation prohibiting inmates from helping other inmates prepare writs or other legal materials.[4] This Tennessee case, along with subsequent litigation arising from similar allegations in California, Nebraska, and North Carolina, expanded contact among writ-writing inmates and increased the availability of law libraries and outside legal assistance.

Thus, by the late 1960s the trend toward the improved legal status of inmates was well under way. The civil rights movement had drawn attention to discrimination against minorities. Widely read books, such as Eldridge Cleaver's *Soul on Ice,* written while Cleaver was housed in California's Folsom prison, argued with eloquent conviction that discriminatory repression was vividly illustrated by the conditions of imprisonment. Activist federal judges were more than willing to demand adjustments in specific administrative practices within prisons. It remained for the efforts of a reform-minded director of prisons in Arkansas, coupled with the grievances of inmates, arguments of legal counsel, and the opinions of federal court judges, to move the prison reform movement beyond specific practices to the totality of prison conditions, first in Arkansas, Mississippi, and Alabama and, subsequently, in systems throughout the country. By the end of 1982, thirty-six states were under court order or faced with pending litigation aimed at improving the conditions of confinement.

This national trend was not readily acknowledged by those who ran the Texas prisons. There were strong feelings about the importance of states' rights. State officials could point in the late 1960s to cases that seemed to continue the tradition of judicial nonintervention. The federal courts should stay out of the business of prison administration, it was argued, not only because of states' rights but also because the administration of prisons required a special expertise, an expertise not possessed by federal judges. In the late 1960s and early 1970s a period of unrest swept across the nation's prison systems, accentuated most dramatically by the killings of guards and inmates in the San Quentin and Soledad prisons in California and Attica prison in New York. State leaders, such as then-governor of California Ronald Reagan, attributed much of the violent unrest to the revolutionary activities of political activists, including lawyers for inmates. The prisons in Texas did not experience this turmoil, a fact that Texas prison officials used to support their resistance to judicial intervention, as well as their policies of tight controls over inmates, including the denial of contact with legal counsel interested in reforming prison conditions.

Armed with tradition, some early court victories, and a private conviction that right was on their side, prison administrators in Texas repeatedly defied court orders and engaged in harassment, sometimes subtle, sometimes quite violent, of those who dared challenge their beliefs and practices. This defiance and harassment served to postpone eventual reforms. It also broadened the base of support for petitioning inmates to include nationally recognized legal talent and the resources of the United States Department of Justice. This same administrative defiance of clearly stated federal court orders eventually complicated the defense of existing conditions to such an extent that judicial remedies were broadened far beyond those originally requested by petitioning inmates. Eventually, the walls constructed from denials and defiance collapsed when influential state leaders joined the federal court in recognizing the need for broad-based reforms and precipitated a sweeping turnover in high-level administrative personnel and practice.

Although these events took place in Texas, their import reached far beyond state boundaries. Correctional officials throughout the country viewed the litigation efforts in Texas as a struggle between correctional philosophies. Admirers compared the Texas prison system to highly successful corporations and pointed to results achieved: low costs per inmate, a lack of idleness among inmates, low escape and homicide rates. As one put it, Texas prison administrators did what they were supposed to do: they kept you in, they kept you busy, and they kept you from getting killed. Detractors were quick to point to the lack of rehabilitative programs and the repressive measures used to maintain what was labeled by one nationally recognized expert as the last remaining example of slavery in the United States.

Whatever the philosophical stance on then-current practices, both detractors and admirers acknowledged that the Texas Department of Corrections had its roots in plantation slavery and had been nurtured by vast agricultural holdings, an emphasis on the work ethic, and a concern for making the prison system self-sufficient. A brief look at these early East Texas origins of the Texas Department of Corrections is a useful starting point for understanding the bitter struggle for control of the prison system in the late 1960s through the 1980s.

Many of the issues raised during these decades had clear historical precedents. Charges of staff brutality, inadequate medical facilities, and crowded, unsanitary living conditions had been heard with cadence-like regularity since the Civil War. Political maneuverings, inadequate funding, and the use of prisoners to supplement an overtaxed guard force were all familiar stories as the litigation movement in Texas gained momentum. Ironically, dramatic improvements in the 1940s through the early 1960s, which brought the Texas prison system from one of the worst in the country to what many thought was one of the best, formed the foundation for the righteous defiance that greeted those who desired further changes and who were willing to go to court to get them.

Private Profits and Slaves of the State—1849–1909

Prisoners in Texas have always been expected to pay their own way. Scarcely a year after the first prison in Huntsville opened its 225 cells to three prisoners in 1849, the state legislature launched an investigation into ways to defray the costs of incarceration through inmate labor. By 1854 there were enough inmates to justify the construction of a cotton mill. Products from this mill were sold to the public, and eventually the mill, manned by convicts from Texas, Louisiana, and Arkansas, as well as laborers from the free world, assisted the Confederacy during the Civil War. By 1865 there were 165 prisoners housed in the Huntsville prison. Continued production in the cotton mill, coupled with a decreased demand for products following the Civil War, meant that the prison's warehouse quickly filled with materials and manufactured products. As production slowed and demand for products waned, inmates were left with increased idleness while the costs for incarceration rose.

In December 1865 the Thirteenth Amendment to the United States Constitution abolished slavery throughout the nation. Prisoners, however, remained slaves of the state.[5] In Texas, as well as elsewhere, prisoners were used to help fill the labor void left by the abolition of slavery. In 1866 the Texas Legislature established the Board of Public Labor and directed its members to secure contracts with private interests for the use of inmate labor. The prison's superintendent was asked to organize prisoners to work on farms, railroads, public utilities, river channels, iron mines, and any other useful employment. The result was a cheap source of labor for plantation owners. "The greater number of persons who have incurred Penitentiary punishment for lesser offenses, since liberty was bestowed upon our uneducated population, are unfitted for other than agricultural employment, and as their periods of sentences are mostly of short duration, they cannot with profit to the lessees, be taught trades. Many of these convicts are now at work on plantations."[6] So began the use of inmates in Texas for private profit and the production of public revenues. The plantation-like nature of many Texas prison operations would be noted for years to come.

By 1871, the year inmates were officially certified as "slaves of the state" in *Ruffin* v. *Commonwealth,* the inmate population in Texas had grown to just over five hundred convicts. The prison in Huntsville was still not operating at a profit. With hopes of remedying this problem, the state leased the entire penitentiary operation to private interests. It was not long, however, before problems with this move toward "privatization" became apparent.

Transferring total responsibility of prisoners to private interests decreased costs to the state. It also meant lessened security, increased brutality, and a deteriorization of physical facilities. In response to criticism of the leasing system, a legislative commission was appointed to investigate alleged mismanagement and cruel treatment of convicts. This committee filed a report in 1875. It was noted that, by 1873, 53 cells had been added to the original 225 cells in the Huntsville Unit, also called the "Walls." In that same year 676 convicts lived within the walls of the prison. This meant that, on average, 3 inmates were housed in cells that measured seven feet two inches high, five feet wide, and seven feet long. There were 13 inmates less than 14 years old, which led Governor Richard Coke to note, "A personal visit to the Penitentiary, and an inspection of all its apartments and inmates, has impressed upon me the conviction that a serious defect exists in our prison system, in the promiscuous mingling, in this common receptacle, of children from nine years old upwards, with old, depraved and hardened criminals."[7]

The state of Kansas had received a number of military prisoner transfers from Texas. The 1875 legislative report took note of the tragic and bitter complaints lodged by the Kansas Board of Public Institutions about the evils of the leasing system in Texas: "When received they [the prisoners from Texas] were in horrible condition, from lack of proper food, and ill-treatment generally. Most of them were emaciated and sick, reminding the prison authorities more of returned Andersonville war prisoners than military prisoners, some of whom had committed only trivial offenses. . . . A few died from the effects of the inhuman treatment received. . . . They sleep in graves outside of our Penitentiary walls, the victims of the infamous lessee system, which makes men slaves of officers, often more brutal and criminal than the worst convict."[8]

In addition to these accounts of the "infamous lessee system," the 1875 legislative report contained numerous excerpts from sworn testimony by former inmates, as well as summary conclusions drawn by committee members. Sleeping arrangements were described as "decidedly filthy" and infested with vermin. Writers of the report were "at a loss for terms sufficiently strong to condemn as inhuman and unfit for the purpose, the place in the Penitentiary miscalled a hospital."

The committee was also interested in disciplinary procedures used by the private contractors. The Penal Code in effect at the time read: "The punishments to be prescribed by the Directors of the Penitentiary shall consist of closer imprisonment, confinement in irons, deprivation of privileges enjoyed by other prisoners, and punishments of like kind. Whipping shall not be resorted to, except by special order of the Directors in the particular cases, nor shall shaving the head of a convict be allowed." In fact, the committee found these prescriptions routinely violated. Whippings were frequently administered that left inmates "scarified in a most shocking manner." The "horse" was singled out for particular criticism. This device consisted of a vertical post that had slots into which a peg could be placed at various heights. An offending inmate was seated astride with his back to the post. His hands were fastened behind him, and as the peg was a sufficient distance from the ground, his feet were brought down tight and stretched until the tension became intense.

"Dark cells" were found to be seldom used, though with proper ventilation the committee found no objection to this punishment. Stocks were used routinely and were generally accepted by the committee, though it was noted that because of poor construction and surveillance, they had led to the death of at least one inmate. Finally, a number of miscellaneous punishments, such as "kicking, striking with fists, sticks, roots etc," [were] "lavishly administered by guards, and sergeants of guards, and foremen of the work, and [were] administered oftener for supposed affronts to their personal dignity, than for any real breach of prison discipline."[9]

Records during the lessee period are sketchy, but they do include tabulations for total population, escapes, and inmate deaths. During the first five years of the Board of Labor system (1866–70), the prisoner population rose from 134 to 503. By the end of the first five years of the leasing system (1872–76), there were just over 1,700 prisoners. The extent to which this growth represented a demand for more slaves from the state, as opposed to an increased crime rate, is unknown. Whatever the source of its growth, the effectiveness of the penal system during the leasing period, in terms of escapes and inmate deaths, was deteriorating. In the final full year of the Board of Labor period (1870), there were 37 escapes and 8 inmate deaths. In 1876 there were 382 escapes and 62 inmate deaths recorded.[10]

This record, along with detailed revelations of filthy conditions, cruel and frequently fatal punishments, poor medical facilities, and the indiscriminate mingling of very young "convicts" with adult offenders, led to a modification of the leasing system, wherein the state maintained control of the penitentiary and convicts but continued contracting arrangements with private interests. This contract-lease system began in 1883. In 1885 the system, in another move to increase the prison's self-sufficiency, was expanded with the purchase of the first farm in what would eventually become a very large agricultural component of the prison system.

During the early years of the farming operations there is little evidence of efficiency or profitability. Farm labor for prisoners served more as a punishment and a way to occupy inmates' time than a source of state revenue. However, records do show a decrease in inmate deaths and escapes during the contract-lease period (1884–1909). By 1909 the inmate population had risen to just under four thousand, while the number of escapes had fallen to seventy and the number of inmate deaths was reported as sixty-one.[11]

Even with these signs of improvement, there was continuing concern over disciplinary methods and prisoners' living conditions. In 1909 yet another investigating committee released a report that contained the following comments:

After witnessing with my own eyes accounts of brutality and hearing with my own ears tales of atrocious and brutal treatment at the hands of certain sergeants within the penitentiary system of this State upon convicts entrusted to their care, I cannot find it in my heart to endorse the use of an instrument by which death has been inflicted upon human beings; neither can I endorse a modification of the punishment by the strap or a bat, believing that the same should be totally abolished. . . .

Nowhere in our findings is there any report made on the State Railroad camp. I believe that the people of Texas should know something regarding this. . . . The evidence will show that the brutality of the guards and sergeants in this camp exceeded that of any other camp visited by this committee; that the convicts were poorly fed, half clothed, and that they were driven to their work with the lash, like galley slaves, from early dawn until the sombre shadows of evening put an end to their sufferings and gave them relief from the bull-whip. . . .

I state my conviction in closing this report that our whole penitentiary system needs reform; that legislation is needed to make reform; that barbarous treatment of convicts in our penitentiaries and convict farms is changed. . . . Without additional law, the Governor is powerless. He cannot inspect, for his duties confine him to his office. We do not doubt that he thought he had secured the best officers obtainable; the vice is in the system under which barbarity can be practiced with impunity.[12]

Following this commission's report, the contract-lease system was abolished and the state reestablished its total responsibility for running prison operations. However, insufficient funding and poor monitoring of prison administrative practices led to repeated charges of brutality, deplorable living conditions, and systemic impunity over the ensuing decades. As the Texas prison system moved into the twentieth century, its agricultural operations expanded, but there was little else to keep it from becoming what would eventually be characterized as one of the worst prison systems in the country.

Agricultural Expansion, Inefficiency, and Deplorable Conditions — 1910–44

From the beginning, farming operations were evaluated on the basis of whether they produced revenue for the state. Records conflict about the total amount of land owned by the prison system during the early years of the twentieth century. Estimates made by a 1913 investigating committee set the acreage at around 21,000 owned by the state, with approximately 15,000 additional acres farmed through some type of contractual arrangement. This acreage was spread over six prison units. Poor accounting procedures precluded precise financial assessments, but with the exception of the first year of World War I, when good crops and high prices yielded a profit, there was no indication that the prison system was running efficiently.

Other than a single profitable year, there was little good news coming from the prison system during the second decade of the twentieth century. State politics were in disarray. Governor Jim "Pa" Ferguson was removed from office after his impeachment and conviction in 1917. His wife, Miriam "Ma" Ferguson, was elected as his successor, but a bitter struggle for power continued. In 1911 a three-member Board of Prison Commissioners had been established to provide additional stability for the prison system. Members were to be appointed by the governor for six-year terms. The term of one of the three commissioners would expire every two years. In principle this seemed to be sound policy. In practice it resulted in a turnover of fourteen Commissioners between 1911 and 1921.

The tension between political camps over the administration of the state's prison system during this time is evident in an exchange of letters between then Governor Pat Neff and W. G. Pryor, a member of the Board of Prison Commissioners. Governor Neff asked for Pryor's resignation, charging that Pryor had been directly involved or indirectly responsible in financially corrupt purchases and practices as well as illegal and inhumane treatment of convicts. Pryor refused to resign, replying that the charges were politically motivated and that the governor's real charges were more accurately reduced to three: Pryor was an appointee of ex-Governor Ferguson; he had supported Governor Neff's opposition in the gubernatorial race; and Governor Neff wanted a vacancy to fill for some political friend.[13]

Between 1910 and 1920, five separate sets of recommendations were submitted from various legislative investigating committees. While sweeping in their scope, these proposals had little practical effect. By the mid-1920s reform efforts continued in high gear. There was interest in selling the system's agricultural and manufacturing holdings, consolidating the convict population, and moving the main location from Huntsville. No site could be agreed upon, and the Legislature established yet another commission to study the problem in 1923. Lee Simmons, who would later become a reform-minded manager of the prison system, was one of three members of this commission. In addition, the legislature authorized a "survey" of the prison system, which repeated many of the charges that had been made incessantly in the preceding decades: funding was insufficient, medical facilities and practices were extremely poor, education was all but nonexistent, working conditions were harsh, and punishments were brutal.

During the next legislative session in 1925, numerous questions were raised once again, and a joint House and Senate Committee began hearings on the conduct of prison officials. Testimony was taken from Mrs. J. E. King, a respected San Antonio pharmacist. Mrs. King testified with the assistance of a diary she had kept during her official visits to various prison units, as chairwoman of the Prison Advisory Commission. Prior to one of her visits she had received a letter from a prisoner asking for her protection, since one of the guards had threatened to kill him. Several days after receiving the letter, Mrs. King visited the unit where the inmate was being held. In her testimony she recalled, "Two guards, one of whom is F. E. Hamilton, shot that Cuban down in cold blood. Hamilton said he had killed him because he thought Chance [the inmate] was going to kill some dogs and he said he felt obliged to protect State property." King went on to testify, "I visited the Wynne farm last September where I saw filth and other things. This is the tuberculosis farm which I still think is a disgrace to the State. . . . I personally took the temperature of five men who had been working in the fields that day. All five were tubercular. . . . I went into the kitchen to see what they were being fed. They had some very thick, sour corn bread, fried mushy biscuit dough and lima beans, which were not well cooked. It is a crime against civilization to be feeding these men this food in their condition."[14]

A physician who had been a convict, and who at the time of his testimony was free on a conditional pardon granted by Governor Neff, testified about the practices of an inmate left in charge of other inmates.

Representative Irwin: Tell this committee what you know of Joe Furey, convict, who died at Huntsville, and who, the record shows, died of bladder trouble.

Dr. Boaz: I knew Furey for possibly two months before he died. He was in the cells underneath the jail where the insane were kept and a convict named Fowler was in charge of him. I carried him food when I found out that Fowler was giving him meals only once a week. He would have starved to death otherwise.

A few hours before he died, I was passing outside and saw through the window what was going on. I saw him taken from his cell, thrown into a tub of ice water, hit over the head with a stick of wood and then Fowler threw him on the floor and stamped him, jumping on his chest and abdomen several times. I went down the stairs, determined to do something about it, but then changed my mind. I was within ten feet of him when this stamping took place. He died two or three hours later. I didn't report the matter for "convicts don't talk."

The witness was then asked why he didn't tell Mrs. King or make a report of the incident. He replied, "Others were mistreated for telling Mrs. King things and I knew I would be next if I interfered in the Furey matter at the time."[15]

The day after Mrs. King testified, the committee heard from M. E. Bogle, who was employed by the comptroller, the state treasurer, and the attorney general to be "auditor of facts as well as figures of the prison system operation." Mr. Bogle's testimony centered largely around the activities of R. E. McAdams, manager of the Ferguson State Farm, and J. A. Herring, chairman of the Board of Prison Commissioners. He charged that McAdams had been caught short on cattle and ferry funds and had duplicated expense funds while manager of the Ferguson Farm. He went on to note that both Herring and McAdams owned or leased pastures near the Ferguson Farm and that markings used to identify their cattle were very similar and, in the case of Herring, identical to that used by the prison system. Bogel also testified that when some of these "irregularities" were taken before the Walker County grand jury, he was assaulted by R. E. McAdams, J. A. Herring's son, and three other men not identified.[16]

The legislature adjourned before the investigating committee could make its report. The effort was not totally lost, however, in that the three-member Board of Prison Commissioners was replaced during the next legislative session (1927) with a nine-person board to supervise the general manager of the prison system, who was to be responsible only to the board.

To further prison reform, legislators visited prisons throughout the south as well as in New York, Pennsylvania, Michigan, Minnesota, and Kansas in August 1929. In September and October there was a rash of escapes, and three buildings on the Wynne farm burned. Two weeks later W. H. Meade resigned as manager of the prison system. Lee Simmons was asked to replace Meade but refused to accept the appointment.

In January 1930, as the country entered the throes of the Depression, one hundred legislators, along with Governor Dan Moody, made a trip to investigate the prison units. Upon his return Governor Moody, noting several particulars, concluded that the prison was "not fit for a dog." By March the population had risen to a point where the prison board felt it necessary to declare a moratorium on admissions until the normal capacity of the system was reached. Many legislators responded that they would not be coerced into increased appropriations. Nevertheless, some three weeks later, prison officials refused to accept prisoners from Tarrant County in a test of the order. The next day Lee Simmons accepted the job as the new manager of the Texas prison system.

More is known about Lee Simmons than most of his predecessors, since after retiring he wrote a book, *Assignment Huntsville,*[17] detailing his tenure as prison manager as well as his early years growing up in Texas. According to this as well as other accounts, some progress was made during Simmons's tenure (1930–35) in educational programs, in lowering the number of escapes, and in medical care with the construction of a new hospital at the Huntsville Unit. At least one later investigator would point to this period as one when appropriations were actually turned back to the legislature from the prison system, which had grown to encompass just over seventy thousand acres of farm land, spread over eleven prison units centered in a two-hundred-mile corridor north and south of Huntsville in East Texas.[18]

It was during Simmons's first year as head of the prison system that he decided to improve on the prison system's reputation as a brutal, inhumane place. One strategy was to hold a prison rodeo in Huntsville. This became an instant source of pride, and in subsequent years prison administrators from across the country, state dignitaries such as Governor Hobby and Speaker of the House Coke Stevenson, along with celebrities such as Tom Mix and Will Rogers, were invited as special guests. The "Walls" Unit at Huntsville became a showpiece for the Texas prison system, and the rodeo quickly took on a larger symbolic significance.

Another source of pride for Simmons was the Cotton Pickers' Glee Club. As a farm boy Simmons had picked cotton and had spent "many a night" listening to the music of Old Harve and John. From these experiences Simmons concluded that "twenty-two hundred Negroes meant talent. I knew it was there and I meant to see it developed."[19] During the 1930s there was an official policy of racial segregation in the prison system. There were approximately 2,200 black prisoners, roughly 40 percent of the inmate population in 1933. Consistent with the slave plantation roots of the prison system, these inmates were housed almost exclusively on the farm units. When selected for the Glee Club, inmates were transferred from the farms to the "Walls" Unit in Huntsville. Once the Cotton Pickers' Glee Club was ready to perform, Simmons invited the American

Prison Conference to Texas with the promise of "some real entertainment." Part of this was to be the rodeo, the rest being furnished by the thirty-member Cotton Pickers' Glee Club. This group continued to sing at the rodeos for the remainder of Simmons's tenure as prison manager.

The routine at the beginning of these rodeo performances was for a 385-pound inmate to come into the arena driving a wagon that "contained a few old quilts and like plunder, while on the side next to the grandstand, they hung a skillet, a coffee pot and a lantern." When the wagon was about midway in front of the grandstand, the inmate would stand up in the wagon and sing "Goin' Down Dat Lonesome Road."

Such performances caught the interest of John A. Lomax, who was traveling around the country recording folk songs at the time. Lomax wanted to visit the farm units to record material from black convicts. After securing Simmons's permission, Lomax visited Central Farm, where he met "Iron Head," whom he eventually took on tour across the country.[20] Along with other tunes, Iron Head introduced Lomax to the song "Ol' Hannah," a song about the sun that convicts sang in the fields while working:

Been a great long time since Hannah went down;
Oh, Hannah, go down!
Been a great long time since Hannah went down;
Oh, Hannah go down!

She's goin' down behin' dem western hills.(etc.)

I wonder where is de Capt'in gone? (etc.)

He's gone to de house to ring de bell. (etc.)

Bullies, did you hear what de Capt'in said? (etc.)
An' if you don't I'm goin' give you hell. (etc.)

Y'oughta come on dis river in NineteenFo'.(etc.)
You'd find a dead Nigger on ev'ry turnrow.(etc.)

You orta Come on dis river in Nineteen-ten
Dey was workin' de wommens like dey was workin' de men (etc.)[21]

The fact that this song reflected more than empty lyrics about life on the prison farms is evident from Simmons's own account of two inmates on the Clemens farm who died while working in the hot sun.[22]

The conditions of the prison farms when Simmons took over were such that they were compared to the slavery camps of yesteryear: "The slave camps of olden times could not have been more unsanitary. At Camp Two, located on flat land with no drainage, the sewerage stood in the open flat. Everywhere was filth and garbage—and in consequence a set of disgruntled and rebellious prisoners."[23] In addition to the deteriorated nature of the facilities and difficult working conditions in the fields, it was common practice to whip noncooperative inmates. One officer, whom Simmons reports sanctioning, is quoted as stating, "But, Mr. Simmons, a whipping in the field once in a while does a lot of good and gets more work done."[24]

Even Lee Simmons, who was hired as a reformer and who thought of himself as such, revealed the punishment standards of the time when he opposed legislation to outlaw the "bat," a twenty-four-inch leather strap, four inches wide, with a wooden handle.

> I told my friends on the legislative committee: "Gentlemen, it's just like using spurs. You get on an old cow horse without spurs—and you can't head even a milking-pen cow; but when you've got your spurs on, the old horse will do the job." And you don't have to use the spurs, because all he needs is to know that the spurs are there. It's the same with us and the "bat." The record shows we seldom have to use it. But the boys all know it is there. The hellraiser fears nothing more than the "bat." When I was in charge he got it. Generally, after five lashes, the rebel raised his hand and cried, "That's enough; I'll behave." I saw only a very few take the full twenty.[25]

The bat was not outlawed during Simmons's term in office, but the next legislature, in response to the urgings of, in Simmons's words, "misguided and ill-informed humanitarians," forbade the use of corporal punishment.[26]

Such was the state of the Texas prison system during the early 1930s. It was governed by the Texas Prison Board, which consisted of nine members appointed by the governor. Members served for overlapping terms of six years. They elected their own chairman and were responsible for the management and control of the institutions within the prison system. They were required by law to employ a general manager, who was to carry out board policy and supervise the managers of the individual institutions. This same governing structure remained in effect into the 1980s.

The prison population increased from approximately 4,800 inmates in 1929 to approximately 5,600 in 1935. Farming continued to dominate inmate activities on eleven of the twelve units. The "Walls" Unit in Huntsville was the only unit that might be considered to have been a maximum-security unit, in that it contained individual cells and a walled perimeter. Ironically, it was used for the most part to house the "best" inmates. Housing conditions were cramped on all units. At the "Walls" Unit in 1935, where the capacity could be calculated fairly accurately, there were roughly one thousand men housed in 350 cells originally designed for one man each. The inmate population decreased during World War II, but the triple-celling of inmates reoccurred in the late 1970s, when overcrowding became the premiere issue in the landmark case *Ruiz* v. *Estelle.*[27]

Lee Simmons could point with pride to some of his accomplishments. The casual visitor to the Huntsville Unit was likely to be impressed by its cleanliness and order. The Goree Unit for women was similar. However, there was also ample evidence that many of the units were far below the standards of the day in terms of medical care, sanitary facilities, and disciplinary procedures.

The latter half of the 1930s saw an increase in the inmate population to around seven thousand inmates in 1939, followed by a decline over the course of World War II to just over three thousand inmates in 1946. The singular accomplishment in the last half of the 1930s seems to have been a limited classification program, initiated with the assistance of a group of social scientists at the University of Texas in Austin. The classification scheme consisted of six categories: young (under twenty-six years) first-time offenders, old (over twenty-six years) repeat offenders, young recidivists, old recidivists, incorrigibles, and habituals. The age dichotomy was decided on "not because of any significance of the age twenty-six, but because the prison population rather evenly divided itself into these two groups."[28]

Only white male prisoners (50 to 55 percent of the inmate population) were classified by this rather rudimentary classification procedure. In part, this restriction to the "normal white male" prisoner was due to 1927 legislation that required the segregation of white and colored prisoners. Blacks and Hispanics were segregated on separate farm units. On these units there was only one kind of housing—dormitories—and one type of work—farming. Thus, there was little use for a detailed classification scheme, even if the procedures allowed. TDC used this same basic classification scheme (age and recidivism) until a more contemporary plan was filed in 1984, pursuant to a court order in *Ruiz*.

During the late 1930s and early 1940s negative assessments of the prison system continued to surface; but given pressures from the depression and the onset of World War II, these had little practical effect. Between 1944 and 1947, however, there were a number of influential individuals and pressure groups working for change, including Governor Beauford Jester, numerous state legislators, some members of the prison board and the Texas State Council of Methodist Women. These efforts coalesced around a survey conducted by Austin MacCormick in 1944.

Substantial Improvements and Stability—1944–67

When asked by the Texas Prison Board to evaluate the Texas prison system, Austin MacCormick brought with him experience in prison evaluation surveys throughout the country dating from the early 1920s. In addition, he had served as commissioner of corrections in New York City and as assistant director of the Federal Bureau of Prisons. At the time he was asked to evaluate the Texas prison system, he was the War Department's chief consultant on penal matters, as well as the head of the Osborne Association, a nationally recognized organization based in New York established to evaluate and improve prison conditions.

Prison board members asked MacCormick to investigate three problems. First, they wanted his advice on how to make improvements in operations despite the difficulties imposed by war conditions. Second, they were concerned with disciplinary problems, most notably "escapes, perversion, assaults, self-mutilation, the bad influence of the worst prisoners on others and the frequency with which the severe punishments now used in dealing with these problems seem to result in a vicious circle of offenses and punishments." Third, in anticipation of the end of the war and an increase in the prison population, the board wanted MacCormick's ideas on plans for the future that would allow them to bring the prison system in Texas into line with "the high standards which have been demonstrated by the leading prison systems of the country to be practicable and attainable."

MacCormick's recommendations were detailed and went to the heart of the system's operations—farming. He stressed in particular the effect that his recommendations would have on the "disciplinary problems" that most concerned the board. These problems, MacCormick felt, reflected more general shortcomings, and an attack on the specific problem of discipline would be an attack on the whole problem. His report to the prison board was picked up in the press and received a good deal of publicity. In the next gubernatorial campaign, Beauford Jester ran on a promise to reform the prison system.

When he took office in 1947, Governor Jester asked Austin MacCormick to present his findings in a meeting with members of the prison board, the general manager of the prison system, and the secretary of state. The meeting was held in the governor's office on March 3, 1947. MacCormick summarized a number of his findings first presented to the board in 1944 and added some recommendations to deal with problems presented by an increased inmate population following the end of the war.

In his 1944 report MacCormick had noted that two of the major factors underlying disciplinary problems were too many prisoners on prison farms and too large a proportion of the prisoners housed in dormitories, especially of the type of the prison farm "tanks." This claim was reiterated in the meeting in the Governor's office with additional details.

The critical problems [you] have are the problems of discipline and they have reached the point to where it is almost a scandal. . . . In these tanks, which resemble the hold of a ship, you have double decked bunks. The tanks go out in wings from a central corridor in which there is a picket holding a guard. The guard is supposed to be able to see into the tanks – both upper and lower tanks – but he can't see any distance into them. The beds are crowded so that the two men in the upper bunks and the two in the lower bunks are practically sleeping together. They can crawl from one bunk to another or under the bunks so that no guard could see what is going on.

The reason behind most of your troubles is due to the whole life in the tanks, especially in rainy weather, and it results in something that is not encountered anywhere else in the country except in Georgia – self-maiming – and they claim that some ex-Texas prisoner started it there. They break their arms, cut their heel strings and there is on record cases of where men have cut off hands and feet. The usual practice is cutting the heel string. . . .

Sometimes, a man does it to get away from the farm; sometimes to get out of the tanks; sometimes because of activities of perverts; sometimes they are forced to do it by others who are going to keep the mutilations going on; sometimes, apparently a bunch draw names out of a hat and the loser has to do it. There have been as high as a hundred in the last year. And none anywhere else that I know of. It has attacked Texas like a peculiar tropical disease; it is as contagious as can be. Not only the hardened men on Retrieve but the younger men on Darrington are doing it too.

MacCormick went on to detail a "terrific amount of perversion that leads to knifings and killings," as well as an unusually high number of es-capes. As MacCormick saw it, the problem did not lie in the nature of tanks alone but also in the practice of sending the worst prisoners to farms, where housing and working conditions were the least secure. The nature of the prison farm was for MacCormick a primary reason for the "clouded reputation" of the Texas prison system.

Connecting this state of affairs with the fact that most of the prisoner population came from and would return to an urban setting, MacCormick recommended that the prison system diversify its work programs for in-mates. Such diversification could be accomplished in conjunction with the planned construction of new prison units, which he recommended be built with one-man cells instead of dormitories. Diversification and expansion with one-man-cell construction were obviously expensive propositions. MacCormick felt that if the existing law, which restricted the price of prison-made products to the cost of materials, could be changed, diver-sification would in the long run result in a profit. This profit, along with increased appropriations from the legislature, could then be used to help finance upgraded facilities and salaries for prison personnel, which Mac-Cormick saw as the third major source of the prison system's problems.

One month after the meeting in Governor Jester's office, a twenty-member legislative committee visited several of the prison units over a two-day period. Their stay at each of the units lasted little more than a couple of hours. They found the Huntsville and the Goree Units, as well as the Sugarland farm, to be clean and well run, though in the latter instance they noted an incident of a brutalized seventeen-year-old inmate. Conditions at the Darrington, Wynne, and Retrieve farms were singled out for critical comments because the committee found inadequate medical care, guard brutality, inmates exploiting other inmates, and beleaguered personnel, much in line with what had been reported by MacCormick and other critics of the system over most of the previous decades.

Historically, inspection committees such as this had filed their reports and then the matter, after receiving some publicity, would be dropped. The impotent nature of these committees was no doubt apparent to most experienced staff in the prison system. Illustrative of this was the attitude of the manager at the Retrieve farm, where the committee found brutality to be "rampant." Shortly after the members arrived at Retrieve, the farm manager told the committee that "it did not make a damn bit of difference with him what the Committee thought of how he was running the Farm, but he was Manager and would do as he damned well pleased irrespective-ble [sic] of what the Committee thought."[29] This time, however, those seeking reform would be more effective.

The Texas State Council of Methodist Women reproduced a copy of the legislative committee's report and sent it statewide with the admonition, "Write the Prison Board and give them your support. Tell them you expect and will appreciate a humane, sane, and Christian prison." These women recognized two things. First, there was a receptive prison board, and second, this board might meet opposition and need all the political support they could get. The letter-writing campaign was quite successful, as reflected in the collection of papers left by Governor Beauford Jester to the state, which contains numerous letters from church members from across the state stating their appreciation for his prison reform efforts and encouraging him to carry on.

When he took office, Governor Jester appointed four new members to the prison board who favored reform. In the first two months the new board secured the resignation of Major D. W. Stakes, the prison manager; they adopted a five-point program for reform; they established a policy that prohibited board members from interfering with the management or farm wardens; they approved a new set of personnel rules; they established a school for guards; and they approved an extensive check of business operations. Of these actions, the five-point plan and the appointment of a new prison manager would prove to be the most important.

From the beginning, O. B. Ellis, a forty-five-year-old son of a Methodist minister, former college business manager, and then manager of the Shelby County Penal Farm in Memphis, Tennessee, appears to have been the board's first choice to replace D. W. Stakes. Before recommending Ellis for the job, members of the board met with him in Houston and also visited the Shelby County Penal Farm, where the chairman of the board had been impressed "with the well being of the inmates, the efficiency of the organization and the neatness of the entire plant." In short, O. B. Ellis embodied what the board was looking for, "a man with known ability in handling prisoners, a top agriculturalist, and an industrial supervisor."

In a letter to the governor, outlining the first two months of the board's work and identifying Ellis as a possible candidate, board chairman W. C. Windsor reminded the governor of his concern for a new perspective in the prison system and his statement that it might be necessary to go outside the state for new leadership. Windsor found the historical coincidence too interesting to pass up and noted, "Sam Houston and Davey Crockett came to Texas from Tennessee and did much to advance the welfare of Texas. Mr. Ellis could also do us a great service."[30] A week after Windsor's letter to the governor, the prison board unanimously approved O. B. Ellis as the manager of the Texas Prison System.

Ellis was asked to oversee the implementation of the five-point program that the board had identified as their agenda for reform:

1. Initiate a program of rehabilitation to include religious programs and vocational training.

2. Improve living conditions for inmates, by developing a classification system and building adequate facilities with single cells.

3. Increase salaries and improve conditions for guards.

4. Modernize and mechanize farming operations.

5. Modify operations so industries would operate at a profit.

Unlike some previous periods, the years immediately following Ellis's appointment produced a great deal of continuity in both board membership and direction. Early during Ellis's tenure, the Texas Legislature increased appropriations based largely on a detailed plan of action that had been submitted by Ellis. This enabled the new director to secure the services of agricultural specialists to expand and modernize farming operations. A building program was implemented to construct new units and repair and renovate older ones. Five years into the Ellis administration, the system was generating sufficient revenues through its agriculture program to finance much of the building program.

Guard salaries were almost tripled during the Ellis administration. In addition, guards were provided room and board and barber and laundry services. Houses, duplexes, and dormitories were constructed for the guards. All construction was accomplished with inmate labor, using prison-made bricks.

Conditions for inmates also improved dramatically during the Ellis years. A prison unit was designated for the assignment of mentally disturbed inmates. An educational program offered prisoners the opportunity to attain a high school certificate. Vocational training included construction work, television repair, bricklaying, welding, auto mechanics, and carpentry. Recreational programs were implemented, including movies and television. Chapels were built and Alcoholics Anonymous programs started. A point-incentive program allowed inmates to accumulate credit for participation in various activities.

Austin MacCormick had singled out the housing conditions and discipline on the farms for special criticism. When Ellis took over, it was the practice to send troublemakers and maximum-security inmates to the Darrington and Retrieve farms. Inmates on these farms were housed in dormitories or "tanks." Shortly after his arrival, Ellis noted that escapes, stabbings, and sexual exploitation were all too frequent and beyond the control allowed by the physical facilities.[31] To remedy this problem, Ellis had an additional set of one-man cells built in the Huntsville prison. These were to be separate from the general population and reserved for inmates who posed security problems.

In addition, Ellis found that some inmates ("building tenders") were used to discipline and control other inmates in the "tanks" on the prison farms. These inmates were allowed to arm themselves with "dirks and blackjacks." Several months after Ellis took over, a building tender, using a pair of homemade knuckles, beat another inmate's head "into a pulp." When informed of the incident, Ellis issued an order that these inmates be disarmed and that they no longer be used to discipline other inmates. While this order may have been effective in the immediate situation, evidence in later years would amply demonstrate that the building tender system remained active and very much in place.

When O. B. Ellis died in 1961, George Beto was selected as his replacement. Beto had served for six years as a member of the Board of Corrections during the Ellis administration (1953–59). He was trained as an educator, serving as president of Concordia Lutheran College in Austin from 1949 to 1959. In 1959 he was appointed president of a Lutheran seminary in Illinois. While in Illinois he served as a member of the Illinois Board of Pardons and Paroles. It was during this time that he developed a close relationship with Joe Ragen, the longtime warden of Stateville Penitentiary. Beto greatly admired Ragen's administrative skills and admittedly carried many of Ragen's policies and practices with him when he returned as director of the Texas prison system.[32] Ragen's successful administration of Stateville had become nationally recognized and was a "must" on any foreign penologist's tour of United States prisons.[33]

In his book *Stateville: The Penitentiary in Mass Society*, James Jacobs described Ragen as, "a complex individual and prison administrator. He was feared and respected, beloved and despised. He inspired intense loyalty among the elite who were close to him, but many among the rank and file deeply resented his authoritarian, arbitrary leadership. Sociologists who worked at Stateville at the time remember Ragen as a strict old-style disciplinarian, while key administrators still refer to him as a penologist and a humanitarian."[34]

Ragen's authoritarian approach was the unquestioned hallmark of his administration. The stability created by this highly regimented approach had transformed Stateville into a model of efficient prison operation by then-contemporary standards. The key to Ragen's approach was freedom from outside interference. Ragen's goal of creating a stable social order at Stateville depended on gaining a large measure of economic, political, and moral autonomy. Says Jacobs, "The absence of interference by outside forces enabled him to develop his authoritarian system of internal order which reached its full elaboration by the early 1950's."[35]

With freedom from outside interference and confidence in his absolute authority, Ragen imposed an intense level of control over both prisoners and staff. He demanded personal loyalty from staff while setting out an elaborate structure of rules for prisoners. Any deviation, no matter how insignificant, could prompt immediate disciplinary action. Neither prisoners nor staff were allowed the freedom to question Ragen's policies.

Because of the high level of discipline among inmates and staff and the low number of escapes and riots, Ragen enjoyed tremendous credibility with the legislature, the press, and the public. As his credibility increased, so did his iron grip on the administration of Stateville. Through the years Stateville became an "autonomous institution accountable neither to other public agencies nor to the public at large."[36]

The desire to minimize the influence of outside forces extended by design to the courts. Through the fundamental rule prohibiting one inmate from assisting another in preparing legal work, Ragen was successful in limiting the prisoners' access to courts. Challenges to this system by jailhouse lawyers were simply not tolerated and most often resulted in punishments such as repeated transfers to restricted living quarters. This practice, coupled with a general lack of concern for prison conditions by lawyers in the community, the prevailing hands-off doctrine adhered to by the courts, and Ragen's success and credibility as warden of Stateville, produced a system basically immune to outside influence.

George Beto's administration of the Texas Department of Corrections was but a replication of Ragen's Stateville. At the time of his appointment in 1962 as director of the TDC, Beto had served on the prison board in Texas for six years and had also worked with the Illinois institutions as a parole board member. During the Ellis administration, Beto saw the restoration of order to Texas prisons. In Illinois he saw the benefits of a highly regimented institution at Stateville. He believed strongly in the Ragen approach to prisons and immediately upon his return to Texas adopted much of the Ragen philosophy.

As a member of the prison board during the Ellis administration, Beto had been very involved in the development of programs. His appointment as director enabled him to develop these further, and the priority given industry in the Ellis years began to bear fruit during the 1960s. In 1963 the legislature passed a bill that provided for the sale of prison-made products to other state agencies, which stimulated the growth of new operations in the department such as bus repair shops, brush and mattress factories, dental labs, soap and detergent plants, retreading plants, and garment factories. Like Ragen, Beto recognized the dual benefits of prison industries. First, the agency could better achieve its legislative mandate of self-sufficiency. Second, but no less important, inmates were kept busy.

The agricultural programs likewise experienced significant growth during the Beto years. The department continued to rely heavily on the inmate labor force to achieve its goals in crop production, which again served the dual interests of self-sufficiency and control. New inmates were required to spend at least six months in the field labor squads, which consisted of menial and physically demanding work. After they had become indoctrinated into the TDC philosophy of discipline and control, they were moved to better job assignments. The field force assignment became the least desirable job an inmate could have. A common punishment of the day was to be busted back to a "hoe squad."

Educational programs also began to flourish in the 1960s. In 1967 the legislature passed a bill creating an independent school district for the prison system. An adult education program had earlier been initiated, and school attendance was required for those inmates who had not achieved a fifth-grade level. To coordinate the flow of inmates into and out of the prison system better, diagnostic and prerelease centers were opened. The overall operation of the system was centralized and coordinated from a newly constructed central administration building in Huntsville.

As the growth and progress begun under O. B. Ellis was solidified, George Beto and his administration enjoyed increased autonomy. Clean and orderly institutions became a hallmark of the TDC system. The highly regimented institutions were impressive to outsiders, who seldom questioned the means by which this high state of order was achieved. Because of the rapid progress the department had made since 1948 and the resulting credibility of Ellis and Beto, legislative and executive oversight

diminished to a point where Beto ruled with little interference from outside forces.

The authoritarian regime used so successfully at Stateville was implemented systemwide at TDC during the Beto years. Like Ragen, Beto
demanded absolute loyalty from employees. It is noteworthy that Ragen's
policy on staff loyalty, which appeared in the Stateville officer's Rule
book, was reprinted on the first page of the TDC employees manual.[37]

Loyalty

"If you work for a man, in Heaven's name work for him. Speak
well of him and stand by the institution he represents. Remember
an ounce of loyalty is worth a pound of cleverness. If you must
growl, condemn, and eternally find fault, why—resign your position and when you are on the outside, damn to your heart's con-
tent. But as long as you are part of this institution do not condemn
it. If you do, the first high wind that comes along will blow you
away, and probably you will never know why."

Of course, the rewards were many for those employees who gave this
absolute loyalty. Not only did TDC provide the employee's wages, but
also his food, housing, laundry, haircuts, shoe shines, and yard service.
Among the higher-echelon staff, there were benefits that went far beyond
simple wages, such as "house boys"—black inmates assigned to be at the
constant beck and call of the warden and his family. The rural guard force
was almost totally dependent on the department for all the basic necessi-
ties of life. The formal and informal systems of wages and emoluments
produced a lifestyle that was to a significant degree cut off from the outside world.

The parochial, good-ole-boy existence became more pronounced over
the years through the TDC policy that all promotions be filled from within. The warden who had not come up through the guard ranks during
Beto's administration was rare. The self-contained nature of the TDC
community naturally facilitated a dichotomy between "us" and "them"—
"us" meaning anyone who worked for TDC, and "them" meaning anyone
who did not. It was in this environment that a separate moral order
emerged for prison officials and staff. An officer's status in the TDC community, his sense of purpose and of right and wrong, were all dependent
on approval from the authoritarian regime.

The control over inmates that unit wardens were required to maintain
was near-absolute. Staff controlled literally every aspect of an inmate's
life. Inmates were required to stay within a green stripe next to the walls
of the main corridor during any movement. They were required to remain
silent in the hallways and while eating. Punishments were swift and

severe. Special sessions for "attitude tune-ups" or "ass-whippings" were sometimes held in staff offices for disrespectful or threatening inmates. Often punishments were administered in a fashion so as to humiliate the inmate. Offending prisoners were berated with personal, family, and racial epithets and sometimes required to "stand on the wall"[38] in the main corridor for days.

At most of the TDC prisons during the Beto years, control was further enhanced by the use of inmates as both informants and enforcers. Carefully selected inmates called "building tenders," "turnkeys," and "bookkeepers" were routinely placed in key positions on the unit and expected to remain absolutely loyal to the staff. Often prisoners who were management problems ("inmate toughs") were placed in these key positions, much like Ragen had done in Stateville. A mark of TDC's immunity from outside scrutiny is that this practice was continued into the 1980s, well after a statute was passed prohibiting the practice.[39] In return, these inmates were extended privileges not afforded the general population inmates. The extent of control that these inmates exerted depended on the unit warden.

The boundary of control over inmate activities included communication with the outside world. The correspondence rules were written in ways to prohibit any criticism of the system. Staff routinely censored all prisoner correspondence. Inmates were told to "limit their letters to matters of personal interest to friends and relatives. Other inmates or institutional personnel shall not be discussed, and the letters shall not carry any institutional gossip or rumors." Outgoing or incoming letters could be rejected if they gave "false or debasing information about other inmates or prison officials and employees."[40] The concern was clearly not only for potentially dangerous contraband, but also for potentially damaging publicity. The administration knew full well that their authority depended in large measure on the absence of outside interference.

There was also an absolute prohibition on prisoners' assisting other prisoners in preparing legal documents or "writs." With this high degree of control, criticism of the system was rare and direct challenges virtually nonexistent. By the mid- to late 1960s the system had evolved into a highly predictable and stable prison environment that was the envy of many other systems that were experiencing more turbulent times.

The achievements of the Ellis and Beto administrations brought high praise from the broader correctional community. Austin MacCormick, who had been so critical of the system in the mid-1940s, visited TDC in the mid-1960s and concluded that the "Texas Prison system came up from close to the bottom of the ranking list to its present position in the top half-dozen and in many ways the top half of the top half." Between the mid-1940s and the mid-1960s the prison system had been transformed from an acknowledged blight to a centerpiece of pride for state leadership. This success laid the foundation for the idea that citizens of Texas, through their elected and appointed officials, were taking care of business when it came to the conditions of imprisonment. This history of self-imposed reforms served not only as the foundation for the administrative style and programs of George Beto but also provided a rationale for resistance when civil rights litigation eventually reopened prison administrative policies to outside scrutiny.

From the initiation of the "lease" system in the 1870s there was a periodicity to reform efforts. Every two years the legislature met. Every two years, with occasional skips in the beat, legislative committees were set up to investigate prison conditions and make recommendations for improvements. As long as these efforts were directed at increased financing and physical improvements, they were encouraged by prison officials. When they aimed at changing existing disciplinary practices and operating procedures, they met substantial resistance. The appropriate severity of punishments depends upon the moral system employed. Prison officials repeatedly claimed that "outsiders" simply did not understand the contingencies of prison life and thus dismissed procedural reform efforts as "misguided and ill-informed."

To insulate their operations from the shifting demands of reformers, the record shows that prison officials imposed harsh punishments on those who tried to "inform" the public. When information did reach the outside, it could be attributed to "lying convicts." Since thorough investigations were difficult and sometimes took place months or years after the fact, it was difficult to determine the truth. It depended in the last analysis on whom one trusted. In this situation both sides could claim bias.

The principal fact-finding mechanism for the society, the judicial forum, was inoperative until the mid-1960s. Courts had long considered the administration of prison life beyond their expertise and jurisdiction. Thus, reform depended on evolving standards of decency as applied by private groups and individuals. Unless there was a substantial public outcry, prison administrators were largely immune to effective independent scrutiny. All this began to change in the early 1960s. In 1961 the Supreme Court breathed civil life into prisoners and thereby opened the judicial forum. Prison reformers in the 1960s, while similar in many ways to those in the 1920s and 1940s, now had a formidable additional means with which to attack prison conditions. The first effective use of the judicial forum in Texas prisons came through the efforts of a remarkably persistent lawyer who first visited the Huntsville unit in 1967. Her interventions would begin a chain of events that has continued to the present.

Chapter Two:
Writ Writers and Judicial Intervention
—1967-72

*There are inherent limitations in the application of the rule of law
to a prison setting. The guards and administrators find themselves
under pressure to redefine their goals and practices, but it is easier
to resist than to adapt.*

Morris Janowitz,
(foreword to James B. Jacobs,
Stateville: The Penitentiary in Mass Society)

The Advent of Judicial Intervention

While the Texas prison system was experiencing success with its
highly autonomous and authoritarian system, the national trend
away from this style of institutional management was rapidly gaining momentum. A broad political movement, stimulated by a heightened concern for civil rights violations, gradually found its way behind prison
walls, where prisoners, with the help of attorneys and citizen action
groups, took their case to court. By the mid-1960s federal courts began
acting on the principle that prison walls did not constitute a moral "iron
curtain" between prisoners and the Eighth Amendment's ban on cruel and
unusual punishments or the Fourteenth Amendment's guarantee of due
process of law. Once established, this shift in judicial posture marked the
end to the absolute authority of prison administrators.

Prior to the 1960s judges reacted to prisoner challenges to the policies
and practices of prison administrators by adhering to the idea that courts
were "without power to supervise prison administration or to interfere
with ordinary prison rules or regulations."[1] The rationale for this judicial policy varied. Some judges cited states' rights. Others noted that
judges lacked the necessary expertise to make administrative decisions on
prison life. In addition, it was felt that judicial intervention might undermine the authority of prison administrators and thus encourage institutional unrest. Finally, there was some concern that opening up the judicial
forum to prison conditions cases would inundate the courts with frivolous
claims. It was on this legal landscape, shaped by what came to be known
as the "hands-off doctrine," that George Beto's administration, along with

other prison administrations throughout the country, had been able to consolidate their autonomy and authority.

In the early 1960s, however, the legal terrain began to change. In 1961 the Supreme Court eroded the states' rights rationale for the hands-off doctrine when it established that federal courts had jurisdiction over cases where state officials, acting under the "color of law," infringed on rights protected by the Constitution.[2] Even though this case did not involve a state prisoner claim, its logic opened a direct path for prisoners to petition federal courts about the conditions of confinement through the use of an 1871 United States civil rights statute, Article 42, Section 1983, of the United States Code.[3] More importantly, the cases filed using this statute could go directly to federal court without having to litigate first in state courts, which were usually more receptive to prison administrators than to prisoners.

This logic was explicitly extended to the claims of prisoners in 1964 when *Cooper* v. *Pate,* the watershed case that changed the course of prison management forever, was decided by the Supreme Court. Charging religious and racial discrimination, Muslim prisoners in Illinois had challenged the prison officials' practice of refusing them access to the Koran and opportunities for worship. A lower court upheld the right of prison administrators to exercise their discretion in this matter. On appeal to the Supreme Court, however, the prisoners found a more receptive audience. In a brief and narrowly drawn decision, the Supreme Court held that prisoners could challenge the practices of prison officials in federal court. By allowing prisoners to openly and formally challenge traditional prison practices and methods of control, the *Cooper* decision ended an era of prisoner isolation from the broader legal community.

This injection of judicial oversight began the diffusion of the absolute power held by administrators like Ragen and Beto. In the post-*Cooper* years, the Section 1983 suit became a much-used means for prisoners nationwide to attack conditions of confinement. In 1966, the year federal courts first reported filings of 1983 suits, only 218 cases were recorded nationwide. By 1972, this had increased to 3,348. The trend continued in subsequent years: in 1976 there were 6,958; in 1978 there were 9,730; in 1984 there were 18,477.[4] The records of the clerk of the Southern District of Texas, the district in which most of the units of TDC are located, reflect a similar pattern in conditions-of-confinement cases. In 1974, 191 prisoners' rights cases were filed in the Southern District of Texas. By 1978 this number had risen to almost five hundred. The number grew to almost one thousand in 1984 when combined with cases filed in the adjoining Eastern District of Texas, where four prisons are located.[5]

The dramatic increase, coupled with the frivolous nature of many complaints, made it difficult for meritorious complaints to be heard. This same trend made it quite easy for prison administrators to assert that prisoner claims were getting out of hand and thereby justify their rigid resistance. Prison systems with high levels of authoritarian autonomy stood to experience the greatest disruption and loss of power through court intervention. While comparative data are lacking, it would not be surprising to find that these more authoritarian regimes more vigorously opposed the activities of writ writers and activist lawyers, regardless of the merit of the claims or the prevailing law.

In the post-*Cooper* years of 1964–70, cases filed by TDC prisoners seldom reached the evidentiary hearing stage. In fact, in a number of cases the district courts continued the "hands-off" doctrine. In 1969, the Fifth Circuit Court of Appeals in *Startti* v. *Beto* concluded that federal courts would not interfere with matters of discipline and control in state prisons, since they were the sole province of the state. Curiously, the circuit court judges did not cite or address the Supreme Court's *Cooper* decision, but did cite a 1955 circuit opinion that was clearly out of step with prisoners' newly acquired access to federal court.

A review of cases filed by Texas prisoners during this period (1964–70) reflects no reported decisions at the district court level prior to 1970. The only reported case prior to 1970 was *Startti*, which read like a pre-*Cooper* decision. However, this lack of published case law is a bit misleading. By 1968 jailhouse lawyers (known as "writ-writers" in TDC), though few in number, were rapidly mastering conditions-of-confinement litigation with the support of Frances T. Freeman Jalet, the first prisoners' rights attorney to work with TDC writ-writers on a continuing basis. Outsiders like Jalet were viewed, at best, with a jaundiced eye. It was therefore anything but surprising that when this fifty-seven-year-old, female poverty-law attorney from New York started visiting prisoners who had been labeled recalcitrant malcontents, George Beto and his wardens mustered a fierce and what proved to be unlawful campaign to suppress her efforts.

Prisoners' Rights Lawyers Come to Texas

On September 14, 1967, an article entitled "Portia for the Poor Has Interest in Helping People" appeared in an Austin, Texas newspaper. The lead paragraph explained: "A chance to get justice for the poor has brought Mrs. Frances T. Freeman Jalet (pronounced as in ballet) to Austin from Cornell in New York, via the University of Pennsylvania Law School and the Office of Economic Opportunity."[6]

When Frances Jalet came to Texas she was fifty-seven years old and the mother of five children. She had degrees from Radcliffe, Columbia Teachers College, and Columbia and Georgetown Law Schools. She knew firsthand the sting of discrimination; after having received her bachelors degree from Radcliffe in 1931 and her law degree in 1939 from Columbia Law School, she could only secure a position as a law clerk and secretary. After a year in this position she quit to raise her children and eventually to work on her degree from Columbia Teachers College. In 1954 she reentered the legal profession through her own general private practice. Eventually she became a staff attorney researcher for the New York State Law Revision Commission at Cornell Law School.

In 1967 she applied for and received a fellowship funded by the Office of Economic Opportunity that allowed her to join a class of fifty talented and highly motivated young attorneys at the University of Pennsylvania Law School. For six weeks this group trained in poverty law, landlord-tenant law, juvenile courts, and processes of welfare agencies. This "Portia for the Poor" had offered to go anywhere when the six-week training session was finished. There were positions in New Mexico and Texas. She chose Texas. Her assignment was to work (for minimal salary) for the Legal Aid and Defender Society of Travis County, where the state capital is located.

Jalet's introduction to Texas prisons came as a result of the Austin news article in 1967. A TDC writ-writer, Fred Arispe Cruz, read the article and thereafter wrote to Jalet. He had earlier written attorneys with the ACLU in an attempt to secure assistance in filing his writs, but was unsuccessful. The two began corresponding and in October 1967, Jalet visited Cruz at the Ellis Unit in Huntsville, where a number of the Texas prison units are located. At the time Jalet met Fred Cruz he was fast becoming the most prodigious writ-writer in the history of TDC. He was known by TDC officials as one to resist prison regimen and "had incurred increasing disfavor of TDC officials including Dr. Beto."[7] Because Cruz was a well-known and respected writ-writer, it was not long before Jalet became acquainted with other writ-writers, who were likewise constantly at odds with prison officials. Through these contacts Jalet became interested in prisoners' rights litigation.

When Frances Jalet first visited Cruz in late 1967, the TDC may have been near its peak efficiency as a state agency. On the surface, at least, it was a highly regimented and impressive operation, as reflected in a letter from Jalet to Beto after her first visit to the Ellis Unit in October, 1967.

Dear Dr. Beto:

Thank you for your kindness in talking to me about Fred Arispe Cruz, Richard Pena and the prison generally, when I was in Huntsville last Thursday. You seem to make yourself available to outsiders, as well as to the inmates, and this I appreciate. Of course, I saw very little of the Ellis Unit when I talked with Mr. Cruz and Mr. Pena, but what I did see gave a favorable impression. The white suits the men wear surprised me. Somehow I expected gray

or tan, but white is better. And I could not resist making some
purchases from the display of the prisoners' handwork.

You said I might visit the women's unit and I would like to do
that the next time I come to Huntsville to see these two young
men. This time, however, I think I will plan to stay overnight, as I
found the trip from Austin and back in one day rather tiring.

With regards, yours sincerely,

Frances T. Freeman Jalet

Jalet's favorable first impressions of the Ellis Unit were typical of a
one-time visit to a Texas prison. Most outsiders did not threaten TDC's
autonomous operation because they rarely looked beyond the prisoners'
white uniforms or their handwork displayed in the front offices of a unit.
Jalet, however, was not like most outsiders. She began to visit TDC
prisoners routinely and became convinced that many of the conditions,
policies, and practices in force at the time were over-harsh, restrictive,
and brutal.

At the time, prisoners in Texas prisons could not possess law books or
any legal materials, including correspondence from attorneys, in their
cells. All outgoing and incoming correspondence was censored, and the
staff could refuse to forward correspondence that contained criticism of
the prison. Correspondence with the media was prohibited. There was an
absolute ban on prisoners assisting or communicating with one another
on legal matters. The number and kind of correspondents, the number of
letters that could be mailed, and even the length of such letters were
limited. Writ-writers were often confined to administrative segregation,
where they faced even more onerous restrictions. Placement in this more
restricted area of the prison could be done, and sometimes was, for what
can only be described as arbitrary reasons. Such potential for capricious
action stemmed largely from the absence of formalized placement
procedures.

These restrictions, which were enforced with unrelenting zeal, promptly evolved into outright hostilities toward attorneys and writ-writers
deemed to be the source of "conditions" litigation. Through their absolute
resistance, Texas prison administrators had created a combative environment in which jailhouse lawyers would prosper.

Justifiable or not, these restrictive policies, coupled with the national
trend of law, made the Texas prison system in the late 1960s fertile
ground for the rapidly growing number of prisoners' rights lawyers, most
of whom were supported in the early days by federal and foundation funding. This group of attorneys operated from a national perspective with
significant coordination of efforts. In general they identified with prisoners and naturally provided hope and encouragement to writ-writers who

were just learning the ways of conditions litigation.

Having very limited experience in prisoners' rights litigation, Jalet sought help from one of the attorneys involved in the national movement, Anthony Amsterdam, of the Pennsylvania Law School faculty. He referred Jalet to William Bennett Turner. At the time Turner was working as a staff attorney at the NAACP Legal Defense Fund office in New York City and was one of the few prisoners' rights attorneys with litigation experience. In the area of access to courts (prisoner-to-prisoner assistance and correspondence), he would eventually become one of the leading practitioners in America.[8] Jalet soon convinced Turner to join her efforts in assisting prisoners in the Texas prison system.

During the early period of conditions-of-confinement cases in Texas, prisoners first had to overcome procedural barriers, both judicial and institutional, before their cases could be heard. The institutional barriers centered around severe restrictions placed on correspondence and mutual legal assistance among prisoners. These restrictions made it difficult for prisoners to prepare and file their petitions with the courts.

Judicial acquiescence to administrative authority came from both the district and circuit courts. In addition to the near-absolute deference the Fifth Circuit was giving prison officials during this period,[9] at least one district court judge in the Southern District of Texas required prisoners to exhaust state remedies prior to seeking relief, concluding that it was immaterial that the procedural vehicle used was a Section 1983 suit.[10] The exhaustion requirement of this court in 1970 was contrary to the established law. Thus, while the Supreme Court had been quite clear about the rights of prisoners to be heard in federal court, institutional administrators in Texas could expect more favorable rulings closer to home.

Early Court Victories for Beto's Administration

In 1967–68, when TDC writ-writers began to file conditions-of-confinement petitions, one of the first issues to be litigated was TDC's absolute ban on prisoner mutual assistance on legal matters. In *Novak v. Beto*, prisoners Ronald Novak and Fred Cruz filed petitions attacking TDC's "jailhouse lawyer" rule. They also contended that the manner in which TDC administered solitary confinement was in violation of the Eighth Amendment's prohibition of cruel and unusual punishments. These two petitions were among the first prisoners' rights complaints in TDC to move beyond the pleading stage to an evidentiary hearing. The prisoners were, for the first time, represented by skilled civil rights attorneys, in this case William Bennett Turner and Frances Jalet.

In the *Novak* case, the district court denied all relief to the prisoner complainants. In denying relief on the "jailhouse lawyer" prohibition, the court concluded that TDC's one full-time attorney and the availability of law libraries ("writ rooms") constituted a "reasonable alternative" to prisoner-to-prisoner assistance as required in *Johnson* v. *Avery,* the first prisoners' rights case to reach the Supreme Court in the post-*Cooper* years. TDC officials had won the first round.

In making its determination on the issue of prisoners' assisting one another in case preparation, the court cited the following interchange:

Q. (By the court): Is there any particular reason why you do not want Fred Cruz assisting other prisoners in preparation of writs?

A. (By Dr. Beto): He could develop an unconscionable control over other inmates by setting himself up as a lawyer. I would like to amplify, your honor. I live in mortal fear of a convict-run prison. Earlier some attention was called to the article in the *New York Times* which described a classic example of a convict run operation.

Q. (By the court): Is that the one in reference to the Kansas penitentiary?

A. (by Dr. Beto): Yes, sir. We constantly strive against permitting that to happen. One way in which inmates develop control of an institution is by aiding other inmates writing writs.[11]

It is notable that the *New York Times* article[12] that Beto referred to did not in any way relate the disruption in that prison to writ-writers. In fact, rather ironically, the article attributed the problems of the Kansas system to the practice of using prisoners in key jobs—a practice well-entrenched in the Texas system. It is also notable that just two years after this testimony, prison officials conducted a survey, pursuant to court order in *Corpus* v. *Estelle,* in which 91 percent (32) of the states responding allowed mutual legal assistance among prisoners without experiencing substantial problems.[13]

In *Johnson* v. *Avery,* the United States Supreme Court had addressed the possibility of abuse among jailhouse lawyers and concluded that instead of prohibiting legal assistance, administrators could place "reasonable restrictions and restraints upon the acknowledged propensity of prisoners to abuse both the giving and the seeking of assistance in the preparation of application for relief."[14] Even in view of the Court's rejection in the *Johnson* case of the "unconscionable control" argument proffered by Dr. Beto and the practice of allowing prisoner legal assistance in other systems in the early 1970s, administrators in the Texas system were not to relax their prohibition on such assistance until 1975, when a district court required it as a result of litigation filed by one of Jalet's clients.[15]

With regard to the contention of Fred Cruz and Ronald Novak that the the use of solitary confinement in Texas prisons violated the Eighth Amendment, the district court concluded that the bread and water diet, among other conditions, did not offend the "evolving standards of decency" test. The court acknowledged that this policy was below the standards of other states but found it to be within the "realm of administrative discretion within which public officials must be allowed to move freely." [16] The court concluded its opinion in high praise of the TDC and George Beto, finding "that the TDC is an outstanding institution in every respect." [17]

On appeal, the Fifth Circuit Court affirmed the district court's decision concerning solitary confinement, but reversed on the prisoner assistance issue. The TDC had failed to carry its burden of proving that it provided a reasonable alternative to prisoner assistance as required by *Johnson* v. *Avery*. The circuit court also ordered the restoration of any "good time" that was lost as a result of violating the regulation against prisoner mutual assistance with legal cases. [18]

While affirming existing solitary confinement policy and practice, the circuit court referenced the strong dissent of their fellow jurist, Elbert Tuttle, and acknowledged that they were "deeply troubled" by certain conditions in solitary confinement in the Texas prisons. In finding solitary confinement to be constitutional, the circuit court appeared to rely to an extent on the reputation and credibility of Dr. Beto. Tuttle's dissent, however, offered a detailed and persuasive argument against the majority's ruling. In support of his argument, Tuttle cited the testimony of James V. Bennett, former director of the Federal Bureau of Prisons, who had provided testimony that was consistent with Tuttle's "evolving standards of decency" argument. Bennett had testified, "The use of the bread and water diet is an archaic and discredited system which has no effect except that it complicates the man's health problems." [19]

After their setback in the circuit court, Ronald Novak and Fred Cruz petitioned the circuit court for a rehearing before the entire panel of Fifth Circuit judges. [20] The motion for rehearing was denied. However, Judge Tuttle took the opportunity to reaffirm his earlier dissent. Joining Tuttle in dissent was his longtime close associate on the Fifth Circuit, Judge John Minor Wisdom. Wisdom chided his fellow jurists by suggesting the majority opinion ran counter to the trend of court decisions at the time. He believed that the imposition of solitary confinement in Texas prisons was unconstitutional because of the "lack of procedural safeguards . . . and 'overkill.' "

While Tuttle and Wisdom were in a minority in the *Novak* circuit decisions, their dissents did not go unheard. [21] After having resisted change to conditions in solitary confinement and after having successfully litigated the issue before the district court and the Fifth Circuit Court of Appeals, Beto elected to discontinue the bread and water diet in TDC. In later years, Beto acknowledged that Tuttle's dissent was a factor in his decision to discontinue the practice.[22]

Fred Cruz, the coplaintiff in *Novak,* returned to the district and circuit courts in *Cruz* v. *Beto I,* alleging that over-restrictive prison regulations, such as the prohibition on using law books or legal materials in a prisoner's cell, denied him constitutional access to courts. He also claimed that he was denied his first Amendment right to the free exercise of religion. In denying relief, the district court cited the "influence and control" argument proffered by the *Novak* district court: "There are many reasons why one prisoner should not counsel another in legal and religious matters. One which comes to mind quickly is the 'influence' and 'control' which one inmate might gain over another. Such a situation on a large scale could lead to a 'convict-run' and not a state-controlled prison system."[23] George Beto could not have said it better. The circuit court, in a *per curiam* decision, affirmed the district court's denial of relief to Fred Cruz.[24]

The Fifth Circuit Begins to Abandon the Hands-Off Doctrine

There is little question that at the time the Fifth Circuit rendered its decisions in *Cruz I* and *Novak,* Beto had the support of both the federal district courts in the Southern District of Texas and the Fifth Circuit Court of Appeals. (The Supreme Court subsequently overturned the circuit decision in *Cruz I,* citing *Cooper* v. *Pate*). Judges in the Southern District and Fifth Circuit remained reluctant to intervene, based on the stated belief that the Texas Department of Corrections was run by a first-rate administrator and that prison conditions did not go beyond the extremity of circumstances necessary to justify judicial intervention. In late 1971, however, the Fifth Circuit began to abandon its version of the hands-off policy as applied to the Texas Department of Corrections. The *Novak* decision in December 1971, according to a retrospective comment in a 1978 circuit opinion, provided "the first hint by the [Fifth Circuit] that change was in the wind."[25] However, two decisions in October 1971 actually provided the first evidence that the circuit court was lowering the threshold where circumstances became extreme enough to warrant judicial intervention.

On October 25, 1971, in *Rocha* v. *Beto,* the Fifth Circuit remanded the case to the district court. Noting their traditional reluctance and "great caution when asked to interfere in the internal operation and administration of prisoners," the judges nevertheless concluded that "interference with federally guaranteed rights may not be insulated on the basis that everything which occurs within prison walls is protected as prison administration."[26] Arturo Rocha, another client of Frances Jalet's, had filed suit, claiming that prison policy forbade him from having law books in his cell, in violation of his right to access to courts. Lawyers for the prison officials did not defend the rule but claimed that Rocha had not exhausted his administrative remedies prior to filing suit.[27] The circuit court, while not rejecting the "extreme circumstances" test for judicial intervention,[28] certainly eroded its utility as a boiler-plate basis for dismissing prisoners' rights claims. Three days later, on October 28, 1971, the circuit, in *Woolsey* v. *Beto,* remanded yet another claim to district court. Woolsey's claim that he had been given punitive work assignments and solitary confinement, with the known effect of activating his tubercular condition, had been denied by the district court as outside the scope of federal inquiry. Again, the circuit did not reject the "extreme circumstances" test but did dilute its effect by giving a more liberal construction of its scope.

Prison Officials Counterattack

Simultaneous with this transformation in the Fifth Circuit, the hostility between TDC writ-writers Frances Jalet and George Beto had escalated to a point that in October 1971, the same month *Rocha* and *Woolsey* were decided, Beto, in a "raw exercise of power,"[29] summarily barred Jalet from dealing with prisoners in the Texas prison system. This ouster came approximately one month after three TDC prisoners filed suit against Jalet, also seeking her removal from the prison system.[30] Both of these actions provide graphic examples of tactics employed by George Beto and prison wardens, with the support of co-opted prisoners, to resist those who would question their absolute authority. These tactics were important early benchmarks in the "long history of hostility" between prison administrators, writ-writers, and their attorneys. The hostility, retaliation, and punishment over the following years ranged from "overt to subtle, from the imposition of inconvenience to the perpetuation of violence."[31] Ironically, these actions set in motion forces that eventually destroyed Beto's autocratic regime, by subjecting what had become an insulated system of moral standards and punitive actions to judicial scrutiny.

There were a variety of reasons why Beto chose aggressive resistance rather than modify existing policies and practices, some of which were outdated by any applicable standard of the time. Suits were originating from society's "losers." Admitting that the prisoners' claims had merit and that existing policies, shaped from years of experience, were outdated, was difficult. The most visible lawyer during much of the early litigation, Frances Jalet, was viewed with disdain. There were early indications that resistance paid off. The *Novak* decision at the district court level was a clear victory for the TDC. On the other hand, by October 1971 there were indications that the tide might turn against then-current practices, largely through the efforts of Jalet and her clients. The system was running smoothly; there were certain risks in change, so why take the chance, especially when there was evidence in other states during this time, most notably California and New York, that disruptive violence was an ever present possibility. While convincing proof that the nation-wide rash of prison violence was affecting Texas in the late 1960s and early 1970s is lacking, it was clearly on the mind of George Beto and unit wardens as they confronted activist lawyers committed to reform of prison conditions.[32]

Eventually there was an "us" against "them" mentality. Neither convicts nor their activist attorneys would run the prisons. Fred Cruz's courtroom testimony gave an example of this mentality. Cruz claimed the Ellis Unit warden, R. M. Cousins, who in later years was terminated for ordering the beating of a prisoner, threatened him because of his association with Jalet: "I'm tired of that lawyer of yours. No lawyers are going to take over my prison. If you don't stop, I'll send you home to your mother in a pine box."[33]

This struggle, often bitter and personal, between Frances Jalet and George Beto, played out in two unusual, closely related cases: *Dreyer* v. *Jalet* and *Cruz* v. *Beto*. Ironically, it was testimony received in the *Dreyer* case in 1972 that first raised issues litigated in the prisoners' favor in subsequent class action law suits in the mid-1970s and 1980s.

Three Inmates File Suit Against Civil Rights Attorney

On September 14, 1971, exactly four years to the day after the Austin news article reporting Jalet's arrival in Texas, an article entitled "Prisoner charges lawyer disrupting prison system" appeared in a Houston newspaper.[34] This article reported the filing of a highly unusual law suit, *Dreyer* v. *Jalet,* by three inmates in the Texas prison system seeking to enjoin Jalet from "indoctrinating prisoners with revolutionary ideals" and encouraging violence in the Texas Department of Corrections. Jalet was said to be involved in a conspiracy with her prisoner-clients to have the plaintiffs beaten because they would not join them to promote unrest and violence in the TDC. According to the plaintiffs, Jalet furthered the conspiracy through some five hundred visits to prisoners with whom she had established "ostensible attorney-client relationships."

Jalet counterclaimed that the lawsuit was instigated by the plaintiffs as the result of benefits promised by prison officials, including early paroles. Jalet charged that in truth the suit was originated and manipulated by George Beto with support from the Texas attorney general's office in order to keep Jalet from representing prisoners in Texas prisons and thereby to quiet public criticism and adverse court action condemning the operations and management of the Texas prison system.

Jalet's counterclaims were not without merit. There had been a growing animosity between prison administrators and Jalet and her clients since Jalet first offered her assistance to prisoners in late 1967. Shortly after she began helping TDC writ-writers, Jalet experienced problems with her supervisor in Austin. The director of the legal aid office contended that she was acting outside the scope of her employment guidelines, which specified that she handle civil matters within the Austin metropolitan area. Eventually she was transferred to the Texas Legal Services Project in Dallas. There is evidence that George Beto influenced this involuntary move. For example, the court referred to an Austin newspaper editor, who confirmed that complaints he received about Jalet's credentials and activities had originated with Beto.

After her transfer to Dallas in March 1968, Jalet's representation of TDC prisoners continued to be an issue with her supervisors. In October 1968, Beto called Jalet's superior in Dallas, Joshua Taylor, and complained that her activities were causing unrest in numerous prison units and that she was "becoming a thorn" in his side.

During the *Dreyer* trial, Beto was questioned by one of Jalet's attorneys, William Kilgarlin (who later served as an associate justice on the Texas Supreme Court), about his contact with Taylor. Beto's response revealed his unwillingness to embrace the rule of law set out by the United States Supreme Court almost ten years earlier in *Monroe* v. *Pape* and seven years earlier in *Cooper* v. *Pate:*

Kilgarlin: Are you actually interested in prisoners bringing to the attention of the courts conditions which they do not consider fair or equitable or humane?

Beto: No, I'm not, Mr. Kilgarlin.

Kilgarlin: No. I know you are not particularly interested in that. And that really is the root of your problem with Mrs. Jalet, is it not, because she is the first attorney who has ever attempted to call to light conditions that exist within the TDC.

Beto: Well, I wouldn't put it that way.

Kilgarlin: All right. You certainly thought about it awhile, didn't you? Doctor, in regards to Mrs. Jalet, you represented to this court last night that you barred Mrs. Jalet back in 1968 because of a memora: 'am of Mr. Joshua Taylor of the Dallas Legal Services. Was that t your statement?

Beto: Yes, sir

Kilgarlin: All right. The truth of the matter is that you talked Joshua Taylor into that memorandum, did you not?

Beto: Oh, I'm not, I don't believe I'm that persuasive, Mr. Kilgarlin. I talked with him, but I don't know whether I talked him into it.

Kilgarlin: Well you talked with him about Mrs. Jalet, did you not?

Beto: Yes, sir, I did.

Kilgarlin: And you indicated to him that she was becoming a thorn in your side, did you not?

Beto: Yes, sir.

Kilgarlin: And after you talked with Mr. Taylor, and after you indicated to Mr. Taylor that Mrs. Jalet was becoming a thorn in your side, at that point Mr. Taylor issues his memorandum which says that Mrs. Jalet should not counsel with inmate clients that's true?

Beto: Yes, sir.

Based on Taylor's memorandum, Beto had Jalet removed from the approved visitors list, thus barring her from prisons in the Texas system. Jalet brought suit in December against Beto and the director of the Dallas office, which prompted termination of her employment with the Dallas Legal Services Office on December 24, 1968.

While these actions engendered bitter frustration,[35] Jalet was not deterred. After she terminated employment in Dallas, she went to work for a legal aid clinic at Texas Southern University in Houston, which allowed her to resume her work with TDC prisoners. It was not long before Beto once again wrote her superiors, but this time Jalet received support. This support lasted until February 1970, at which time her fellowship with the Reginald Heber Smith Foundation ended. Additional funds had been secured for Jalet's continued employment, but the political influence of George Beto once again surfaced.

Q. (Attorney): How about TSU? Do you have any personal knowledge of Dr. Beto's contact with either Mr. Tollet or Mr. King?

A. (Jalet): Well he was also in touch with the president of the university . . . and with the vice president . . . We had gotten a Klepper Grant, and then instead of that, my work there was terminated—I think it was the 20th of December—immediately following the *Novak* trial. . . . And he [Tollet] said that the president of the university had told him that it was not in the best interest of the university to have me continue because they would lose their funding due to pressures from Austin.[36]

Thus, when *Dreyer* was filed there was a history of tactics by George Beto to impede the work of Frances Jalet. The status of the prisoner-plaintiffs within TDC suggested that the *Dreyer* case was a continuation of these efforts. Two of the three prisoner plaintiffs were "building tenders" or inmate guards. Building tenders (BT's) were carefully selected prisoners trusted by unit officials to give allegiance to staff rather than prisoners. As we show in subsequent chapters, building tenders functioned as agents for unit officials and exercised a significant degree of power in controlling prisoners. The third plaintiff-prisoner was a "trustee," a TDC classification for prisoners who were given the greatest freedom in the prison environment and who often worked in key positions directly for the warden or assistant warden.

Testimony during the trial was presented in support of Jalet's claim that Beto and his wardens may have orchestrated the lawsuit. Plaintiff Freddie Dreyer, a well-known BT at the Ellis Unit, did not even know Jalet and was unable to provide any evidence of a conspiracy. However, Fred Cruz provided testimony that, if true, explained Dreyer's motive for filing suit against Jalet.

Q: Did he [Dreyer] have some personal feelings about Frances [Jalet] or something Frances had done?

A: Well, not necessarily against her as an individual, but because of the work that she was doing in connection with building tenders.

Q: Now, are you referring to her lawsuit attacking that system?

A: Right.

Q: Now, that lawsuit [*Jimenez* v. *Beto*], in essence, did it not, seek to destroy the building tenders?

A: Not necessarily to destroy the building tender system but to dismantle their power structure.

Q: Okay. Was it brought to your attention that Dreyer or anyone else in the TDC was upset over that lawsuit or that any inmate was upset?

A: It was brought to my attention that Dreyer and Alexander [also a BT] made some remarks to some of the prisoners in the cell blocks where they were building tenders that they were going to make every effort to bar Frances from coming into the prison because of the fact that she had filed a class action suit challenging the constitutionality of the building tender system.[37]

Another TDC prisoner from the Ellis Unit, Charles Hardin, provided evidence that implicated two TDC officials in the filing of Dreyer's suit:

> **Hardin:** I know Freddie Dreyer. In about December 1971, Dreyer told me that D. V. McKaskle [former assistant warden at Ellis and assistant director of security] had asked Dreyer to file a complaint against Mrs. Jalet, that Mrs. Jalet was causing them a lot of trouble. . . . And Dreyer asked me if I would testify on behalf of the State. . . . Assistant Warden Anderson told me if I would testify they would see I would get a good job, and they would help me get my mother back on my approved mailing list.[38]

Assistant Warden James V. "Wildcat" Anderson, who was repeatedly implicated in the harassment and mistreatment of prisoners during the 1970s, notarized Freddie Dreyer's original handwritten complaint against Jalet.

The second of the two building tender plaintiffs, Robert Slayman, was paroled during the trial and disappeared just before he was scheduled to testify, forcing the plaintiffs' attorneys to rely on his deposition. It was established during the trial that Slayman's attorney made little, if any, effort to locate him after his disappearance. One possible explanation for his disappearance was offered by one of Jalet's attorneys, again through the testimony of Fred Cruz:

> **Q:** Did you have an occasion to see him [Slayman]?
>
> **A:** Yes.
>
> **Q:** What did he say to you at that time?
>
> **A:** . . . And the only thing he told me then was that if I would tell the lawyers that were coming to see me that if they could secure some kind of protective order from the court to protect him, that he would come into court and that he would tell the whole truth about the basis of the suit and that he had been forced and pressured by the prison administration into bringing the suit against Frances but that he really didn't want to go through with it and that he wanted the case dismissed or that he wanted to tell the court what had actually—the pressure behind it. So when he told me that, at first I didn't say anything to him because I didn't know what his motivation was. And I also didn't believe him. But, at any rate, I did relate this information to the lawyers and I don't know what they did with the information.[39]

The third plaintiff, Donald Lock, who was a "trustee," testified first as a plaintiff and then recanted his testimony, claiming that TDC officials had pressured him to file suit.

While unusual, the filing of a lawsuit by prisoners against civil rights attorneys was not unprecedented in TDC, as was noted during Kilgarlin's cross-examination of Beto:

> **Q:** What about Bowen Tatum? Don't you recall him representing Guadalupe Guajardo attacking conditions in the TDC?
>
> **A:** I know that he represented Guadalupe at one time. I don't remember the nature of the suit, Mr. Kilgarlin.
>
> **Q:** Is it any significance to you, Dr. Beto, that the only two attorneys who have ever been sued by inmates seeking to bar them from TDC just coincidentally happen to be the only two attorneys who have filed suits attacking policies of the TDC?
>
> **A:** No. I didn't know that Mr. Tatum had been sued by anybody.
>
> **Q:** Yes. Well, Daniel Grunstrum and Jimmy Foster and some of the other building tenders who were either brought here as witnesses or who were subpoenaed as witnesses sued Mr. Tatum along with Mrs. Jalet, about a year ago up in the Eastern District of Texas. You think there might be some significance in that?
>
> **A:** Oh, I don't think there is any particular significance.[40]

Beto also made sure that Dreyer and his two coplaintiffs were represented by highly successful Houston trial attorneys. On at least two occasions he spoke with prominent Houston attorneys regarding their possible participation in the case.[41] Beto discussed the appointment of counsel for the plaintiffs with the presiding judge, as well. When the case went to trial, the plaintiffs were represented by seasoned trial attorneys with outstanding credentials. Tom Phillips, who represented plaintiff Slayman, was a senior trial attorney from one of the oldest and most prestigious law firms in Texas, Baker and Botts, and a past president of the State Bar of Texas. Such high-priced legal talent to represent Texas prisoners was unprecedented. Jalet was represented by six lawyer-members of the American Civil Liberties Union.

The plaintiffs attempted to prove a conspiracy to undermine the security of the inmates and to create unrest in the prison system through testimony of the three plaintiff-prisoners, as well as other building tenders, three wardens, and the introduction of two documents, the "Kirby Writ Crusade" and the "Ellis Report." The "Kirby Writ Crusade" was a document authored by Donald Lee Kirby, a TDC prisoner, in which he explained "how simple it is to get a petition in the courts and what tactics to use."[43] Kirby also made numerous references to Fred Cruz, the "Ralph Nader" of the prison system, as an example of what could be accomplished by prisoners through the courts.

Plaintiffs contended the document was part of the conspiracy by Jalet and Cruz to further the overthrow of the TDC. In tone, the document advocated lawful, nonviolent activity: "This Crusade is a silent one but very effective. The only people who hear from these revolutionaries are the courts across the country." However, the plaintiffs' attorneys placed particular emphasis on the document's reference to the establishment of a network of writ-writers in Texas prisons. Apparently it was the establishment of this network of writ-writers that Beto claimed in his testimony at trial "was a plan to create disturbances in several of the units of the department through Fred Cruz and clients of Mrs. Jalet."[44] The court concluded that the document was written independently of Jalet and Cruz and further that it did not advocate any scheme or attempt to overthrow the prison system.

The "Ellis Report" was written by Jalet (with assistance from her clients) at the request of Joshua Taylor, her superior at the Dallas Legal Services office in 1968. This report described procedures and conditions in the TDC that Jalet believed merited litigation, and it began: "The prisoners confined in TDC, more especially on the Ellis Unit, of which I can speak with personal knowledge, are deprived of their constitutional rights and subjected to a pattern of repression, harassment and even torture, that is shocking." Its intended purpose was to generate interest through distribution to strategic groups and agencies that might be willing to pursue litigation in the Texas prison system. The plaintiffs in *Dreyer* contended that the report was part of a major scheme to discredit, distort, and disrupt the TDC. The court found no evidence that this report was anything but a document intended to generate interest over Jalet's concern with existing policy and practice within the Texas prison system.

The testimony of the wardens and the three plaintiff-prisoners was, like the two reports, unconvincing. The court characterized the wardens' testimony as lacking in specifics. What became evident was the strong resentment that prison officials had for Jalet's persistence and pressure. For example, Warden R. M. Cousins testified:

Q. (Attorney): Did you ever talk to Mrs. Cruz [Frances Jalet][45] at your home in the evening?

A. (Cousins): Many times.

Q. (Attorney): What did Mrs. Cruz tell you when she called you?

A. (Cousins): Well, most of the time she'd call to complain about her clients and tell me that some of her clients was going to be brutally beaten or killed, and she had called mothers of inmates and told them that their son was going to be beaten up. . . . She'd call and tell me that she didn't get the inmates laid in properly, and she'd tell me that she wanted to see five inmates and give me the names, and next morning she'd arrive, "I want to see ten," and complain because I didn't read her mind and know to lay the rest of them in. And it was just—it was just hard for me to keep employees.[46]

Even Beto was unable through his testimony to provide any evidence that Jalet was connected to any illegal activity. Testimony was elicited from Beto, however, that revealed something of his perspective on "outsiders." Jalet's attorney had reviewed a television news piece of TDC and questioned Beto on a statement he made during the news feature:

Q: The camera scanned the line [prison work squad] there of the men, all young, I assume with smiling faces. Do you recall the words that they had you speaking there in the background as the camera was scanning?

A: No, I don't recall.

Q: The men were out there working in the field. Do you recall something to the effect that your language went: "And liberal do-gooders want to change all of this."

A: No, I didn't say that. I know what you are referring to now, and I have used that expression repeatedly, and I'll give you the background.

Q: I don't want the background. I just want the statement.

A: All right. The statement was that some do-gooders have criticized us for having too many inmates engaged in stoop labor. Actually on a given day about 3,000 inmates are engaged in what could conceivably be called stoop labor, and I pointed out that a good many taxpayers in this state who are engaged in stoop labor contribute to the financing of that operation.[47]

When questioned by one of the plaintiffs' attorneys about the first time he had misgivings about Jalet, Beto referred to a letter written by Jalet regarding her first visit to the Goree Unit for female offenders. Beto's reaction to a rather innocuous portion of this letter reflects what might be loosely termed a general paranoia toward "liberal do-gooders."

Q: When was the first time you began to have any misgivings with reference to Mrs. Jalet?

A: Well, the first misgivings I had occurred when she wrote me a letter in which she stated she had been to the Goree Unit and had been very cordially treated and been shown the unit, and she mentioned specifically some items there that she saw which pleased her, but she said, "Obviously there were some areas where they refused to take me or which they didn't show me." And that raised a question in my mind that she concluded automatically that there are places that are secretive in a prison.[48]

On cross-examination of Beto, Jalet's attorney introduced the letter into evidence:

Q: Just to read briefly with you, Dr. Beto, it's dated January 1, 1968. "My first visit to the Goree Unit for women was really remarkable. I drove up to see a group laughing and cheerful in the midst of setting up out of doors a creche with live animals. A sheep and a lamb were already in place and someone was riding a donkey, perhaps to give it a workout before having it stand quietly beside the manger. In the group it turned out was Mrs. Dobbs [Warden of Goree], who greeted me and went inside.

"She was most kind in taking me through the unit, commencing with her office, with its beautiful view. I don't need to describe it to you. You know, as I did not, that Goree is a bright, modern place, well furnished and accoutered. Not able to conceal its institutional nature, of course, more or less like a college dormitory than a prison. Whatever I saw was pleasing (though I imagine there must be some areas closed to the public not as pleasant)."

Q: Now, are you saying that that's what gave you misgivings, that language there?

A: It aroused some misgivings, yes, sir.[49]

The court found no evidence of the alleged conspiracy but did find evidence that the apparent hostility that officials had for Jalet was centered around her persistent challenges to their institutional authority through the filing of civil rights suits: "This much does stand out: The defendant [Jalet] and the authorities at TDC have become bitter antagonists over an extended period of time because the defendant represents some recidivists, recalcitrant inmates for whom lawsuits have been filed attacking the conditions, procedures, rules and regulations of the prison system. It is apparent that these so-called 'writ-writers' are strongly resented by those at the TDC, inasmuch as they challenge the status quo."[50]

During the six weeks of trial, considerable testimony was given on the conditions, practices, and policies of the TDC. The court, therefore, after entering its finding on the conspiracy allegations, commented at length in the written opinion on conditions in the Texas prison system. Even though the court's comments were no more than dicta, the commentary provided what became the road map for reform litigation later pursued by TDC writ-writers. In the preface to this section of the opinion, the court stated: "While the evidence which poured forth is in sharp conflict as to what procedures are followed and what conditions actually exist at TDC, such evidence can serve the purpose of spotlighting certain aspects of a way of life little known to those in the 'free world' as well as relating such irreconcilable factual accounts to the trend of case law in these developing areas."[51]

The first of these issues addressed by the court was the alleged brutality by guards and building tenders. Testimony detailed what was alleged as routine mistreatment of prisoners by building tenders acting in a disciplinary capacity for TDC officials. Prisoners testified that building tenders were routinely given access to pipes, bats, and clubs to administer discipline. There were even allegations that some prisoners had been beaten to death by building tenders. Testimony by George Beto about certain well-known building tenders of the time left little doubt that some of these inmate guards were indeed capable of physical mistreatment of their fellow prisoners.

Q: What about Cecil Alexander? According to inmate Carswell, Alexander and his lieutenants continuously robbed other jail prisoners, forced them to submit to homosexual acts and forced them to pay for protection. It should be noted that inmate Carswell's allegations verify numerous other reports pertaining to Cecil Alexander and his group in the Harris County Jail [Houston]. These reports were received by the Bureau of Classification sociologists, from numerous TDC inmates who were confined in the Harris County Jail during the past one and a half years. Do you think it was a mistake to make Cecil Alexander a building tender?

A: Not necessarily. It depends on the adjustment he made during the time he was there.

Q: And let's go to the best building tender of all, who has received numerous punishments for fighting, agitation, creating disturbances, making shop beer, destroying state property, cursing and abusing an employee, insubordination, stealing, self mutilation, setting an employee on fire with a bottle of lighter fluid, cutting another inmate's Achilles tendon, allegedly forcing other inmates to act as a passive partner in anal sodomy, and robbing other inmates. Subject was allegedly involved in cutting other inmates' Achilles tendons, forcing them to engage in homosexual acts, and took their commissary.

A: What was the date of that report?

Q: Well the date of that report is a few years ago, but the man is still a building tender: Jesse "Bay City" Montague, is he not?

A: (Nodding) Yes.

Q: Do you say that it might not have been a mistake to make Jesse Montague —

A: No, I don't.

Q: No?

A: I don't.

Q: One of the plaintiffs in this lawsuit, who is no longer here, Mr. Robert Slayman, was diagnosed as recently as 1969 by your psychiatrist, Dr. Sheldon, as having schizophrenic reaction, paranoid type, acute, moderately severe. That's not the type of man who should be in a building tender's position is it?

A: Well, it depends on the condition at the moment.

Q: Now, do you know anything of the reputation of Robert Barber?

A: At one time he had a bad record in the Department, yes sir.

Q: And there has been testimony in this trial by one of the plaintiffs, Donald Lock, that Robert Barber, along with Major Mote and Captain Driver, rendered him a brutal and savage beating back at the Ellis Unit in 1966. There was further testimony by Lock that when these men appeared at his solitary door and just saw Robert Barber there, he knew what was coming because of the reputation that Robert Barber had. Now, you do concede that things like this can go on, do you not?

A: No, not consistently.[52]

Barber was a well-known building tender, having worked with Warden Carl "Beartracks" McAdams almost without interruption from the time they met in the late 1950s at the Ramsey I Unit until Barber was released from prison in 1971. When McAdams took over as warden at the newly opened Ellis Unit in 1964, McAdams had Barber transferred from Ramsey to Ellis. When McAdams was transferred in 1969 from Ellis to the Wynne Unit, he once again had Barber transferred with him. In 1969 and

1970, three prisoner deaths occurred at the Wynne Unit, which cast suspicion on building tenders like Barber. One prisoner, Melvin Austin, died from a heart attack immediately after an altercation with two building tenders that began when a guard ordered the prisoner restrained by two building tenders, Tommy Carlisle and Dennis Woodbury. Austin had reached out to grab the guard's arm in the main hallway of the prison in an effort to speak with him.[53] Tommy Carlisle later submitted an affidavit admitting that he and Woodbury were aware of Austin's heart condition and during the altercation restricted his breathing by choking him. A few months prior to his death, Austin had been involved in an altercation with another building tender at Wynne, and on another occasion had been transferred from one cell block to another because of trouble he was having with the building tenders on the wing.[54]

Carlisle also submitted an affidavit on the death of another prisoner, Doyle Cole, in which he claimed to have witnessed Woodbury and Barber suffocate Cole with a pillow. TDC records note that Cole "apparently died of natural causes."

The third death at Wynne occurred on July 13, 1970, and also generated questions that remain unanswered. Harold Raymond Bunt, Jr., according to his death certificate, died from "convulsive generalized epilepsy." However, according to a former prisoner, Al Slaton, who was housed in the same cell block as Bunt at the time of his death, building tenders had assaulted Bunt and then placed him in a straitjacket, where he died shortly thereafter.[55]

The Huntsville justice of the peace, Mabel Franklow, had not ordered any investigation, autopsy, or inquiry into the deaths of either Austin or Bunt. This lack of inquiry into prisoners' deaths was also a subject of questioning during Beto's cross-examination.

Q: Now, you had a coroner's report, you say?

A: Yes, coroner, Justice of the Peace.

Q: Who is the Justice of the Peace?

A: Franklow.

Q: What is her occupation?

A: I don't know. She is Justice of the Peace.

Q: Housewife?

A: I don't know.

Q: Operates a feed store?

A: I don't know.

Q: How many employees of the TDC do you think vote in her precinct?

A: I have no idea.

Q: Do you really think that a JP there in a county that is heavily dominated by State employees is apt to come out with any sort of opinion or ruling that would in any way reflect adversely upon TDC?

A: I have a little more confidence in the integrity of people, enough confidence in the integrity to believe that they will normally faithfully perform their duties.[56]

In addition to the three prisoner deaths at the Wynne Unit, a fourth prisoner, Harvey Mayberry, was beaten to death at the Eastham Unit on May 13, 1971. This death also became the subject of testimony that linked Mayberry's death to building tenders. Mayberry had allegedly been scalded when building tenders threw hot water on him for making noise. This method of control occasionally employed by BT's was to continue until the 1980s.[57] After the scalding, Mayberry repeatedly asked for a doctor; his request was allegedly met not with treatment but with the opening of his cell door and a fatal assault by at least two building tenders.[58]

Mayberry's death certificate reflected that he died from a "blunt trauma to the abdomen." An investigation of the death resulted in a finding that Mayberry was assaulted by unknown persons.[59] A TDC employee who was on duty the night of Mayberry's death stated that unit officials worked late into the night in an effort to produce a plausible explanation for the death.[60] The officer's statement is supported in part by a disciplinary report written on the same day that Mayberry was assaulted by "unknown persons." Normally a disciplinary report, which describes the circumstances of an alleged rule infraction, is written by the charging officer on the same day that the offending prisoner violates the rule. Mayberry's disciplinary report, however, charged him with a rule violation that allegedly had occurred one month before his death.[61] The report also contained references in a summary fashion to other unrelated charges. The inclusion of such extraneous material was likewise a departure from standard practice. However, the most notable departure from the norm was the expedited processing of the report. The disciplinary report on Mayberry was typed, referred to a three-member disciplinary committee for a hearing, and thereafter reviewed and approved by the warden, all on the day that Mayberry died. Typically, such a charge would have taken at least three or four days before the final sign-off by the warden. Such expeditious processing of the report could well have kept unit officials working late into the night.

Testimony regarding these deaths was only part of the evidence in *Dreyer* regarding the use of building tenders. Even though there was considerable testimony during the trial that building tenders were routinely used to administer discipline and to supervise prisoners, TDC officials persisted in their claims that these inmates were merely used for such mundane duties as keeping the cell blocks clean.

The court went on to address such issues as disciplinary procedures, solitary confinement, censorship of prisoner mail, and prisoner access to courts. The court concluded its prophetic opinion as follows: "While the proof in this case is so extensive and so contradictory as to make impossible the reaching of any conclusion by this court in favor of either the plaintiff's or defendant's version of what transpires at the TDC, the vast amount of evidence advanced by both sides makes it perfectly apparent that neither version can be summarily dismissed and forgotten."[62]

Even though the court in the *Dreyer* case elected not to enter findings on the evidence of conditions in the Texas prison system, it did express concern that the lack of public and legal scrutiny of the prison system up to this time may have allowed prisons to operate outside the mainstream of prevailing law: "With a lack of public awareness and an absence of independent checks on prison methods, it certainly cannot be denied that the opportunity, at least, has been present for a prison system to become a law unto itself. Once such a total institutionalization emerges, its very preservation depends upon the exercise of unrestrained administrative discretion to control every facet of the lives of its inmates."[63]

In subsequent years, it became abundantly clear that the TDC writ-writers and their attorneys did anything but forget the evidence, as their vigorous pursuit of these issues was to culminate in the longest civil rights trial in the history of American jurisprudence. Each of the issues flagged by the district court in 1972 was decided in the prisoner's favor in *Ruiz v. Estelle* in December 1980.

George Beto Bars Frances Jalet From Prison System

Approximately one month after the prisoners filed their lawsuit in the *Dreyer* case, in September 1971, Beto sent the following telegram to Frances Jalet:

Your continued and frequent visits to the Department of Corrections as well as your correspondence with inmates make it impossible for me to guarantee the tranquility within the institutions and the protection of the inmates.

Accordingly, effective this date [October 14, 1971] I am requesting all wardens of the TDC to deny your admission to the institutions under my general supervision and to terminate correspondence between you and any inmate in the Texas Department of Corrections.

When Beto took this unprecedented action barring an attorney from the Texas prison system, in clear contravention to his own attorney's advice,[64] his credibility with the courts was intact.

However, once taken, his action provoked stringent efforts by members of the Texas bar as well as out-of-state attorneys to have the action reversed. One of the attorneys who appealed to Beto was Robert Webb, who like Tom Phillips was a member of the prestigious Baker and Botts law firm. When considerable concern was expressed by the Texas attorney general's office over the ouster, negotiations between NAACP Legal Defense Fund attorney Alice Daniel and Beto's representative in late October resulted in partial restoration of Jalet's visitation rights on November 5, 1971.

Beto's "compromise" position was to transfer all Jalet's prisoner-clients to one wing of the Wynne Unit, where the unit warden "Beartracks" McAdams had a reputation for working prisoners with the assistance of such BT's as Robert Barber. This transfer occurred in November, creating what became known as the "eight-hoe squad." (In TDC jargon, a hoe squad was a work detail of prisoners assigned to the agricultural fields, where almost all the work was done by hand, using farm implements such as hoes, shovels, hand saws, etc.) On November 30, 1971, Jalet and twelve of the twenty-seven prisoners assigned to the "eight-hoe squad" filed suit against George Beto, claiming he unlawfully barred Jalet and confined her prisoner-clients to a segregated cell block, where they were deprived of privileges they had formerly enjoyed in the general population. Jalet and the twelve prisoners were represented in this case, *Cruz v. Beto II,* by William Bennett Turner, Gabrielle McDonald, who was later appointed a federal district judge, and Warren Burnett, a prominent Texas trial attorney.

A number of the original twenty-seven prisoners were released from segregation when they agreed to sever their attorney-client relationship with Frances Jalet. Once transferred from the segregated hoe squad these prisoners were given desirable jobs and started receiving higher ratings for their behavior, which eventually affected their parole dates. The prisoners who remained in the squad were regularly pressured to sever their ties with Jalet.[65]

Once the prisoners were segregated from the general population, prison officials routinely subjected them to "unusually and discriminatorily harsh conditions and practices."[66] Indicative of the general harassment, beyond more direct threats and pressures, was the double-celling and integration of cells. At the time these prisoners were transferred to the Wynne Unit, TDC had a strict systemwide policy of racial segregation in the housing of prisoners. This policy extended not only to cells but also cell blocks. Once assigned to the "eight-hoe squad," however, the prisoners were routinely confined to a cell with a prisoner of a different "race." This double-celling occurred even though there were numerous cells vacant on the wing.[67]

All the prisoners had restrictions placed on their commissary privileges, recreational opportunities, and educational and rehabilitation programs.[68] They were subjected to increased strip searches, cell searches, and disciplinary actions, as well as a discriminatory denial of their opportunity to earn merit points toward parole.[69] A number of the prisoners who had heart and respiratory conditions, as well as other physical handicaps that would have normally exempted them, were routinely forced to perform manual field labor. The squad as a whole was also routinely assigned to menial, undesirable, and demeaning work not required of general population inmates, unless they were in punishment status (e.g., cleaning manure from livestock areas).

The "eight-hoe squad," with its accompanying restrictions and harassments, was maintained for Jalet's clients from November 1971 through October 1972. George Beto resigned as director on September 1, 1972, and was succeeded by W. J. Estelle, who continued the "eight-hoe" squad for the first two months of his administration.

The district court's decision in the *Cruz II* case left no doubt that the actions taken by Beto and other TDC officials were unlawful. The court concluded that, just as in the Dreyer case, there was no evidence of any conspiracy or illegal activity aimed at undermining the secure administration of prisons in the Texas prison system. The court also rejected Beto's claim that the prisoners were segregated in part because they were prone to violence. Instead the court concluded: "Defendant Beto's actions were prompted by his long-standing antagonism towards Mrs. Jalet's [*sic*] contact with TDC inmates; and they were taken primarily to discourage the prisoner-plaintiffs from exercising certain constitutional rights and to prevent Mrs. Jalet from representing TDC inmates in civil litigation."[70]

The court found that Beto's actions included "unlawful intimidation" and "unlawful punishments," and that they were "totally unrelated to consideration of proper prison administration." Because these actions were found to be unlawful and taken in bad faith, the court assessed money damages against George Beto personally and allowed each of the inmates and Frances Jalet Cruz to recover damages totaling $10,291.00.[71] The finding of personal liability against Beto and the award of money damages to the twelve prisoners and their attorney was unprecedented in the TDC.

The most damaging testimony at trial was George Beto's admission on cross-examination that he knew of no prisoner who engaged in plots against the administration, nor could he cite any correspondence that disturbed the tranquility of the Texas prison system. He also admitted that had any of the prisoners severed the attorney-client relationship with Jalet [Cruz], they would have been released from the punishment squad.

The appeals court affirmed the lower-court decision, concluding that there was "ample evidence to support the district court's finding that the sole criterion for segregating the prisoners-plaintiffs was their status as clients of [Frances] Jalet."[72] In addressing Beto's argument that prisoners did not have an absolute right to a particular attorney and that attorneys did not have unlimited right to enter prisons, the court recognized that prison officials should have broad discretion to exercise their administrative judgment. "However, not even the broadest discretion may be used to punish prisoners for the exercise of their constitutional rights to counsel and to gain access to courts."[73]

"Eight-Hoe Squad": A Writ-Writers' Consortium

Whereas the *Dreyer* case provides a graphic example of TDC officials' attempt to retain unbridled authority by attacking the credibility and motives of a threatening intruder—Frances Jalet—the *Cruz* v. *Beto II* case documents resistance of another kind. Writ-writers were denied access to their attorneys; they were placed in a separate wing with restricted privileges, less desirable job assignments, and constantly reminded that their circumstances could be improved if they simply gave up their association with Frances Jalet.

While different in their focus, actions litigated in *Dreyer* and *Cruz II* should be viewed as part of the same aggressive resistance launched by Texas prison officials, with the assistance of "building tender" inmates, against Frances Jalet and her clients. Taken together, these administrative reactions, along with the earlier political pressures of George Beto to have Frances Jalet fired or transferred from various positions, simply solidified and inspired the small group of writ-writers and their attorney, who became as deeply dedicated to reform through litigation as TDC officials were to resisting change initiated by prisoners or their attorneys.

The policy of isolation and harassment encouraged the formation of a brotherhood with a single cause—litigated reform. This single-mindedness transcended racial and cultural barriers to produce an environment in which, ironically, prisoner mutual assistance in legal matters (the very thing George Beto had resisted so vigorously in *Novak*) flourished. The "eight-hoe" prisoners spent countless hours during the eleven months of confinement improving their legal skills, strategizing and coordinating their efforts, and assisting one another in the drafting of petitions. These prisoners constituted, in retrospect, the "who's who" of TDC writ-writers. Beto, by confining all of Jalet's prisoner-clients to a single cell block, had unwittingly created a writ-writers consortium, which thereafter produced virtually all the major reform litigation in the TDC. This legacy would keep TDC under court supervision for at least the next two decades.

Moreover, Beto's action could not have been more ill-timed from the administration's standpoint, given the rapidly changing law in the Fifth Circuit Court of Appeals and the United States Supreme Court. Within two months after Beto segregated Jalet's clients, the Supreme Court rendered a decision that all but eliminated the last vestiges of the "hands-off" doctrine. Its impact on the Fifth Circuit and prisoners' rights petitions was immediate.

The Supreme Court, in *Haines* v. *Kerner,* ruled that prisoners' complaints could be held to less stringent standards than formal pleadings drafted by lawyers and that a complaint should not be dismissed unless it appeared beyond doubt that prisoners could not prove a set of facts in support of their claim. The high court also required that prisoners be given an opportunity to offer proof in support of their claims. (Stanley Bass, who worked with William Bennett Turner in the NAACP Legal Defense Fund Office in New York City and was to be involved in the early days of the *Ruiz* case, represented the prisoner-plaintiff in *Haines*.)

Prior to the *Haines* decision, it was common practice in the federal district courts of the Southern District of Texas to dismiss prisoners' petition on the pleadings alone, without receiving evidence or holding hearings. In April 1972, however, this began to change when the Fifth Circuit rendered its decision in *Campbell* v. *Beto*. Coy Campbell, one of Jalet's clients confined to the "eight-hoe squad," had filed a complaint alleging improper medical attention and that prison officials had threatened punishment if he filed further writs against TDC officials. The district court, following then-common practice, refused to allow the complaint to reach preliminary stages, by dismissing the case for failure to state a claim. The district clerk had even refused to docket the case without prepayment of costs. The circuit court, citing *Haines, Novak,* and *Woolsey* remanded the case to the district court, stating, "the courts cannot close their eyes to prison conditions which present a grave and immediate threat to health or physical well being." The court also cited the Supreme Court's rulings in two of Fred Cruz's cases, *Cruz* v. *Beto I* and *Cruz* v. *Hauck,* in which Supreme Court Justice Douglas, with regard to prepayment of costs, concluded that "in forma pauperis aid shall normally be granted as a matter of course in order to minimize courts' treatment of litigants based upon economic circumstances."

The Fifth Circuit continued to remand cases with brief decisions through 1972, citing the *Haines* decision. Two decisions reflect this trend and also the success of Jalet's clients on the "eight-hoe squad"—*Jimenez* v. *Beto* and *Bilton* v. *Beto*. In *Bilton* the prisoner claimed that he was forced to perform strenuous labor in spite of a diagnosed heart condition and was refused medical treatment while a member of the "eight-hoe squad." The district court had dismissed the suit just nineteen days after the circuit decision in *Campbell* with a finding that Bilton had failed "to allege the presence of 'exceptional circumstances' warranting interference in prison administration." The circuit court remanded the case and excused the district court for not recognizing the *Campbell* precedent, since it had just been decided.

In the *Jimenez* case, the same district court that denied Coy Campbell relief summarily dismissed Jimenez' suit filed by Frances Jalet on August 11, 1970, attacking TDC's use of building tenders.[74] The *Jimenez* case is relevant not only in the subsequent development of prisoners' rights cases in the federal courts of Texas, but also because it was the subject of testimony during the *Dreyer* trial and involved some TDC personnel who were later involved in the abusive treatment of prisoners.

Richard Jimenez alleged that on April 14, 1970, at the Ellis Unit he and several other prisoners attempted to intervene in an altercation between a fellow prisoner and three building tenders. The building tenders called for assistance and, according to Jimenez, Assistant Warden Bobby Taylor and three other officers under the direction of Warden Cousins, accompanied by approximately ten building tenders, assaulted Jimenez and his cohorts with axe handles, wood clubs, iron pipes, and blackjacks. Assistant Warden Taylor, who some three years later "sanction[ed] and encourage[d]" the beating of ten prisoners at the Retrieve Unit, also with axe handles during what came to be known as the "Father's Day Incident," submitted an affidavit verifying that he and the other officers armed themselves with clubs, but nowhere mentioned the assistance of building tenders. The alleged intervention of the BT's from other cell blocks was factually very similar to a later incident at the Ramsey I Unit, which also resulted in a suit against unit officials and building tenders.

As mentioned, the district court dismissed the *Jimenez* suit on its pleadings, and the Fifth Circuit subsequently denied Jalet leave for appeal. However, on February 22, 1972, the Supreme Court granted Jalet's petition for writ of certiorari.[76] Judgment in the case was vacated, and the case remanded to the circuit for further consideration in light of *Haines* v. *Kerner*. On October 18, 1972, the circuit vacated the district court's judgment and remanded the case for an evidentiary hearing.[77] Upon remand, during the course of trial preparation, W. J. Estelle, who had succeeded George Beto in September 1972, submitted a signed statement claiming that building tenders were used only to clean dayrooms and cell blocks and were not used for the control and supervision of other prisoners. This denial, made during the first year of his directorship, would be repeated throughout his administration in the face of mounting evidence to the contrary.

As the case neared trial, Richard Jimenez suddenly decided to drop the case, and the presiding judge dismissed the case in July 1975. Just three months prior to the formal order of dismissal, Ellis Unit officials recommended full restoration of Jimenez' lost good time. Within a few months after dismissal, warden Cousins, who was a named defendant in the suit, recommended that Jimenez receive credit for time served in disciplinary status. Good-time credit for time served in disciplinary status was rarely granted and required the approval of the director, which in this case was granted.[78] Restoration of Jimenez' good time made him eligible for parole on his life sentence for murder. On August 6, 1976, Jimenez received a favorable parole recommendation from the Board of Pardons and Paroles. According to TDC records, Jimenez was returned to TDC in January 1979 as a result of his conviction for attempted capital murder while on parole.[79]

Cases such as *Jimenez, Bilton,* and *Campbell* stimulated additional litigation from the "eight-hoe squad" consortium. In *Lamar* v. *Coffield I* (Coffield was sued in his capacity as chairman of the Board of Corrections), Allen Lamar claimed that his First Amendment rights were denied by the department's prohibition on talking in the mess hall, corridors, and during work. He also claimed that he was placed in solitary confinement without a proper hearing and was denied a proper diet while in solitary. Even though the district court denied relief, it did so through the application of the *Haines* standards.

The full effect of the Fifth Circuit's transformation and the simultaneous activity of the "eight-hoe" writ-writers was felt by the TDC administration in *Guajardo* v. *McAdams. Guajardo* was the first of a series of major class actions initiated by members of the "eight-hoe squad" that would begin in earnest the legal reform of the Texas prison system. No less than six of the "eight-hoe" prisoners (Guadalupe Guajardo, Fred Cruz, Coy Campbell, James Baker, Allen Lamar, and Lawrence Pope) were plaintiffs in suits that were later consolidated with *Guajardo.*

In *Guajardo,* the "eight-hoe" prisoners mounted a full-scale attack on TDC's correspondence rules. The district court granted, for the first time, broad relief to the prisoners in September 1972. Just six months prior to the *Guajardo* decision, "eight-hoe" prisoners Fred Cruz, Coy Campbell, and James Baker, represented by William Bennett Turner, Frances Jalet, and James DeAnda (later appointed a federal district judge), had been denied similar relief in the *Baker* v. *Beto* decision. The court in *Baker* denied relief on precedent more akin to the "hands-off doctrine" than to case law of the time.

The *Baker* v. *Beto* trial was also the subject of testimony in *Dreyer.* Fred Cruz testified that after he returned to the Ellis Unit from giving testimony in *Baker* he was assaulted by several building tenders, including Jesse "Bay City" Montague and Cecil Alexander, and warned that Warden Cousins and Assistant Warden Anderson were very upset over his testimony against prison officials.[80] Finally, it was established during the

Dreyer trial that the day after the *Baker* trial ended Beto took his action barring Jalet from TDC.[81]

As a result of the *Guajardo* decision, prisoners were allowed, for the first time, to have law books in their cells, to send uncensored letters to attorneys, and to correspond with the media. In addition, the court lifted restrictions on the number and length of letters. The *Guajardo* litigation continued well into the 1970s and 80s and had a significant impact on subsequent class-action litigation, to say nothing about its dramatic impact on the substantive rights of Texas prisoners at the time.[82]

In addition to *Guajardo,* three other major class-action lawsuits originated from the "eight-hoe" prisoners: *Lamar* v. *Coffield II, Corpus and Sellars* v. *Estelle,* and *Ruiz* v. *Estelle.* The *Lamar* v. *Coffield II* case began in 1972 when Allen Lamar brought suit to enjoin prison officials from segregating prisoners on the basis of race. Additional parties, including the United States Justice Department, were later granted leave to intervene. Two other suits were consolidated with Lamar's petition and the cases certified as a class action suit for Hispanic, black, and Caucasian prisoners.[83]

Corpus and Sellars v. *Estelle* was a continuation of the *Novak* litigation on the "jailhouse lawyer" rule. In *Novak,* the circuit court ruled that the TDC had not met the burden of showing that their legal assistance was a "reasonable alternative" to prisoner mutual assistance. Prison officials did not file a pleading in response to the circuit decision. Therefore, Julius Corpus and Calvin Sellars, represented by Turner and Jalet, filed a motion in August 1972 asking for implementation of the circuit decision. The district court held that even if prison officials had shown that permitting prisoner legal assistance would threaten prison security, their absolute ban on any such assistance was unnecessary, since regulations could be imposed to control such activity.[84] The district court also relied on a survey of other prison systems conducted by TDC officials, which showed minimal problems with prisoner mutual assistance. The court noted that almost all other systems had abandoned the prohibition. Seven years after the issue was first raised by Fred Cruz, prison administrators eliminated the "jailhouse lawyer" prohibition, but only pursuant to the district court's order.

The fourth of the major class action suits filed by "eight-hoe" prisoners, *Ruiz* v. *Estelle,* placed virtually all operational aspects of the system in litigation and became the most massive prisoners' rights suit in the history of American jurisprudence. On June 29, 1972, David Ruiz filed his handwritten petition, which was later consolidated with petitions filed by two other prisoners of the "eight-hoe squad." One of Ruiz' allegations claimed that Jalet was assisting him on an appeal to the United States Supreme Court when she was banned from the system by George Beto.

By late 1972, the insulated authoritarian administration of Texas prisons was in jeopardy. The *Guajardo* decision had ushered in the new era of prison administration. It provided very tangible evidence that TDC officials no longer had the unbridled authority to control every aspect of a prisoner's life. The *Guajardo* decision was rendered in September 1972, the same month that George Beto retired and W. J. Estelle was appointed as his successor. It was also the same month the district court rendered its decision in *Dreyer* v. *Jalet*.

Frances Jalet had been a central figure in assisting the harbingers of change—a small group of writ-writers. The actions taken by Beto and other prison officials against Jalet and the writ-writers were but an early manifestation of an entrenched mentality of resistance to change. This resistance so dominated subsequent litigation that resolution of issues, absent court intervention, became impossible. It was inevitable, once polarization had occurred, that the federal courts became the arbiters of change. The "unconscionable control" Beto feared that writ-writers would have over other prisoners had been misplaced. What he should have feared was the control that writ-writers and their attorneys would exert over TDC officials as a result of his unyielding refusal to recognize the changing social forces that had engulfed the prison environment in the 1960s and 70s.

Chapter Three:
Change in Prison Leadership and the Emergence of Prison Reform Groups—1972–74

Nobody has a more sacred obligation to obey the law than those who make and enforce it.

Sophocles

Tradition Continued but Questioned

W. J. Estelle, Jr., was appointed director of the Texas Department of Corrections in September 1972. At the time of his appointment, Estelle was forty-one years of age, with more than twenty years of experience in corrections. His first job was at Folsom State Prison in 1952 as a correctional officer. Even before his first job, he was learning about prisons. His father was a career employee of the California Department of Corrections who worked a number of years as a classification specialist and parole representative at San Quentin during Estelle's youth. Young Estelle attended school for the prison employees' children.[1]

After working for a short time at Folsom, Estelle spent five years as a parole agent in northern California. In 1960 he returned to the California prison system as a correctional officer with the rank of lieutenant. He administered a number of prison camps in northern California, took over as a program administrator, and, in 1963, became assistant superintendent of camp operations. He eventually assumed full charge of prison camp operations.

In 1970 he left the California Department of Corrections and became warden of the Montana State Prison in Deerlodge, which housed approximately three hundred prisoners. In January 1972 he resigned the warden's job in Montana to accept an appointment as assistant director of the TDC under Beto. Beto had met Estelle during a trip to Montana. Thereafter he referred Estelle to the Board of Corrections as his possible successor. Estelle's correctional philosophy was much more compatible with the practices and policies in place in the TDC than with what he saw as the "tolerance that California had for violence in its system."[2] His experience with work camps also impressed the Board, given the high priority that TDC placed on the work ethic.

Estelle was not hired as an innovator but rather for his support of the existing mode of operation. In a 1982 magazine profile of his career in Texas, he was quoted as saying, "I don't think I was brought in here to revolutionize or dramatically change a system that had already some proven success in the way of efficiency and effectiveness."[3] As Estelle saw his mandate, the citizens of Texas asked that their prison system accomplish two things: hold offenders securely, and make sure that they worked to defray the cost of their incarceration.[4] Figures were cited that suggested a low operating cost per inmate when Texas was compared with other states. Escapes and attempted escapes were relatively rare compared to other systems, as were homicides. Such comparisons led many admirers to hold a view similar to that attributed to the director of a neighboring prison system: "In Texas they do well all the things that prisons are supposed to do. They keep you in, they keep you busy, and they keep you from getting killed."[5]

Other observers felt that administrators of the Texas prison system had achieved their goals at too high a cost. John Coleman, then president of the Edna McConnell Clark Foundation, spent two weeks working as a Texas prison guard, with Estelle's permission. After this experience he reported that the controlled atmosphere in Texas prisons came from "the quiet and respectfulness of men who are completely cowed." Other experienced observers of prison life, such as William Nagel and John Conrad, were like-minded. Nagel noted, "One feels strongly a very subtle atmosphere of repression." Conrad queried, "This objective of control has never been mixed [in Texas] with that of rehabilitation. The obtrusive question that emerges from a consideration of the system is: to what end?"[6]

This controversy continued throughout Estelle's administration. The appropriateness of efficiency and safety were never at issue. Rather, it was the means by which these goals were achieved that disturbed Frances Jalet, a number of activist prisoners, and a growing number of reform-minded officials within the state.

In 1972 the TDC was composed of fourteen prison units and approximately fifteen thousand inmates. When Estelle became director he made few personnel changes, and the system continued much as it had under George Beto. While the system continued to operate with a high degree of efficiency, with an active prisoner work force, the reform movement started by Mrs. Jalet and the "eight-hoe squad" was gaining momentum. After Fred Cruz was released in June 1972, he and Frances Jalet married and established residence in Houston, where they continued their work with TDC prisoners. With Jalet's vindication in the *Dreyer* decision in

September, and the relief ordered on TDC's harsh correspondence rules in *Guajardo* (also in September), prisoners realized that TDC's authority was not absolute. With the relaxed correspondence rules, prisoners began to communicate more openly with outsiders, some of whom began to raise questions about the operation of the system. In a very short time a constant stream of correspondence to the media, the courts, legislators, and a variety of interested parties developed.

Less than eight months into Estelle's administration, events occurred that ultimately coalesced external forces from the state legislature, the media, and public interest groups. As a result of cases such as *Dreyer,* in which there were numerous charges of staff and building tender brutality, and the growing number of allegations made public through relaxed correspondence rules, concern grew among a small number of individuals that the Texas prison system was not as "lily white" as the uniforms worn by TDC prisoners.

Still, as a result of the national prominence that TDC had achieved in corrections through the Ellis and Beto reform years, the credibility of the prison system remained high. The Estelle administration continued to foster this image. A history of the department written in 1973 noted that TDC was "considered one of the best penal institutions in the nation."[7] The MacCormick pronouncement of the "worst to best" was cited in virtually every TDC publication of the time. A 1977 publication entitled *TDC: 30 Years of Progress* reprinted correspondence from MacCormick explaining the continued advancements of the agency.[8] As a result of this carefully nurtured image, TDC had become largely immune to criticism, especially since the only source of criticism up until 1973 was "lying convicts" represented by Frances Jalet Cruz, whose credibility prison officials rather clumsily attempted to destroy in the *Dreyer* litigation. However, events that occurred in May and June 1973 generated reform activity that, like Judge Bue's dicta in *Dreyer,* provided evidence that "change was in the wind."

Prison Reform Coalition Evolves

In May 1973, the 63rd Texas Legislature passed House Bill No. 1056, entitled "Supervisory or Disciplinary Authority of Inmates," and Senate Concurrent Resolution No. 87, "Joint Committee on Prison Reform." H.B. 1056 ("Building Tender Bill"), which prohibited the use of prisoners to discipline or supervise other prisoners, was the product of increasing concern over the flood of allegations coming from TDC prisoners detailing building tender (BT) abuses, which prisoners claimed were sanctioned by the administration. The graphic testimony taken in the *Dreyer* case involving prisoner deaths at the hands of building tenders was the first instance in which the issue was raised in a public forum. However, numerous cases such as the *Jimenez* case had earlier been filed by members of the "eight-hoe squad" alleging BT abuses.

H.B. 1056, along with the formation of the Joint Committee on Prison Reform, were stimulated through the efforts of such persons as Fred and Frances Jalet Cruz and Charles and Pauline Sullivan. After Fred Cruz was released from prison, both he and Frances Jalet Cruz immediately became involved in lobbying for prison reform. During this same time period, Charles and Pauline Sullivan were organizing a prison reform group called Citizens United for Rehabilitation for Errants (CURE). During the ensuing years, the Estelle administration developed the same kind of disdain for the Sullivans as the Beto administration had for Fred and Frances Cruz. It is anything but surprising that Fred and Frances Cruz and the Sullivans eventually joined efforts.

Charles and Pauline Sullivan started their prison reform work in Texas in 1971 after both had left the Catholic clergy, he as a priest, she a nun. Charles Sullivan, born in Alabama and educated at the Notre Dame Seminary in New Orleans, had entered the priesthood in 1965. After teaching in a parish school for two years, he took a leave of absence to attend University of Minnesota. While in Minnesota he met Pauline, who at the time was a nun teaching in Minneapolis. Both Charles and Pauline had become disenchanted with the theology of the Catholic Church at the time and decided to leave the church. After their marriage in 1970, they went through a period of searching for service-oriented work. Their involvement in prison reform occurred almost by happenstance.

During 1970–71, the two spent a year traveling around the country, as yet undecided on their work. These travels led them to San Antonio. They had been involved earlier in the peace movement and while in San Antonio visited a movement acquaintance who was in the San Antonio jail for distributing antiwar leaflets on an Air Force Base. As a result of his frequent visits to the jail, Charles Sullivan began hearing prisoner complaints about jail conditions. During the course of a prisoner hunger strike in the San Antonio jail, he was arrested while demonstrating outside the jail in support of the prisoners. After Charles's arrest in San Antonio, the Sullivans participated in the May Day Demonstration in 1971 in Washington, D.C., where they were arrested along with fifteen thousand other protesters.

In the fall of 1971, the two returned to San Antonio, having decided to dedicate themselves to prison reform because "no one else seemed interested in confronting the frustrating and depressing issue of poor conditions in local jails and state prisons."[9] From this time forward, the Sullivans directed their reform energies toward the conditions of prisons in Texas. In January 1972 they organized a low-cost bus service in San Antonio to transport families to Huntsville to visit TDC prisoners. Through these bus trips the Sullivans became involved with TDC prisoners and began to correspond with a number of the "eight-hoe squad" inmates. What started out as a bus service quickly evolved into a broader-based lobbying effort for prison reform.

On March 28, 1973, the Committee of Criminal Jurisprudence of the Texas House of Representatives convened to hear testimony on H.B. 1056, which had been proposed by a legislator from San Antonio. Charles Sullivan and Fred Cruz, both of whom had worked with the San Antonio legislator in preparing the proposed BT legislation, testified in favor of the bill.

Fred Cruz's testimony was detailed and addressed, among other things, the alleged routine practice of building tenders censoring prisoner mail. He also addressed the brutality issue: "If a prison guard beats up a prisoner, the prisoner has recourse through the federal courts by using the personal damage suit against the guard. If you file against another prisoner, there is not much recourse. The prison administration puts it off as just another fight between two prisoners." [10]

Charles Sullivan's testimony was based on his correspondence with prisoners and a meeting he had with W. J. Estelle on the issue: "We have brought over one thousand people to TDC, families of prisoners. With my wife, we have operated a bus service from San Antonio to the state prison. From these trips we have arranged over four thousand visits. We are now corresponding with some fifty inmates. The biggest number of complaints has been with the building tenders. I have talked with Mr. Estelle on this. We concluded, my wife and I, that Mr. Estelle thinks the bill that is presently before you *is* the policy of TDC." [11]

In testimony given before a legislative committee in 1974, Estelle affirmed Sullivan's representation: "The policy, even prior to the passage of H.B. 1056, which by the way, I supported, the internal policy at the time was that no inmate would be supervising other inmates. No inmate would administer discipline to another inmate." [12]

The legislature passed H.B. 1056 on May 19, 1973. On the same day, Guadalupe Guajardo, Jr., one of Frances Jalet's former clients in the "eight-hoe squad," filed a civil rights suit against the TDC that contained evidence in stark contrast to Estelle's testimony that TDC did not use building tenders in an administrative or supervisory capacity. Guajardo's petition alleged that a building tender, Frank Carmichael, had, under the supervision of a TDC lieutenant at the Ellis unit, assaulted Guajardo and his cellmate. [13] Just three days before filing his lawsuit, Guajardo was charged with "general agitation" and placed in solitary confinement for discussing his allegations with general population inmates. In what was to become standard practice for prison officials, including Estelle at the vanguard, each and every allegation was categorically denied in the face of substantial evidence to the contrary.

In preparing the TDC's answer to Guajardo's allegations, Carmichael submitted a signed statement that even given the most favorable reading possible, would raise doubt as to the prison officials' claims that BT's were not used in supervisory roles:

> Last night [April 21, 1973], I was reading in my cell when Lt. Hudgens came and told me to go with him. He took me to the cell where Guajardo and Thornton were housed and the lieutenant told me that he had had some homosexual activity in that cell.
>
> I told them that the lieutenant wanted them out of the cell and Guajardo began to curse and he was holding his shirt in his hand with his fist doubled up. I do not know if he was going to swing at me or not, but he did draw back his fist and I hit him. The lieutenant ordered me to stop or I would probably hit him more.
>
> The lieutenant then took both inmates from the wing and they left peacefully.[14]

This incident took place approximately one month prior to the passage of H.B. 1056. While prison officials continued their assertion that this legislation simply restated existing policy, their formal answer to Guajardo's allegations, filed one month after H.B. 1056 was passed, perhaps unwittingly admitted practices that at best bordered on violation: "Defendant [Lieutenant Hudgens] admits that he requested Frank Carmichael *to accompany him to investigate the homosexual conduct* [emphasis added]. Guajardo and Thorton refused to come out of their cell as ordered. Guajardo stepped to the door with his fist doubled up. Inmate Carmichael at this time hit Guajardo one time." Thornton then jumped up and Carmichael hit him one time.[15]

Prison officials also submitted a signed statement from an inmate nurse, John "Red" Huddleston, who had examined Guajardo for an eye injury received when Carmichael hit him. Huddleston was also considered a building tender and in later years, at another unit, achieved such authority that he routinely handcuffed inmates and had access to riot batons, which he and other building tenders were authorized to use.[16]

The implication that TDC would have been in violation of H.B. 1056, given testimony and admissions, did not escape an assistant attorney general assigned to represent TDC in the case. In an interoffice communication, dated June 15, 1973, he queried a fellow assistant attorney general about the case: "Pursuant to our telephone conversation this date, do I correctly understand that Frank Carmichael had the position of building tender and that the duties of a building tender are to keep the area in which he is assigned clean and also to assist TDC staff members in *keeping order* [emphasis added] as so requested?"[17]

The importance of this particular incident is not that the behavior of the building tender was particularly brutal. Compared to other instances discussed in later sections it was not. Rather, this case simply demonstrates that as Estelle was publicly supporting passage of H.B. 1056, prison officials were using inmate guards in supervisory roles, even for handling routine rules infractions.

Approximately two weeks before the pretrial hearing in the case, Guajardo, like Richard Jimenez had done earlier, suddenly decided to withdraw his lawsuit. In a letter to the assistant attorney general assigned to represent TDC, Guajardo asked that the necessary documents for dismissal be prepared and forwarded to Warden Cousins. Guajardo signed the stipulation prepared by the attorney but added a clause that would allow him to reinstitute his allegations upon release. Because the clause rendered the dismissal ineffective, a second stipulation was executed on February 1, 1974, that foreclosed Guajardo from refiling the lawsuit.

In November 1973, Guajardo had been denied parole consideration because he was in disciplinary status earning no good time. However, within a short time after dismissing his lawsuit, Guajardo was promoted to a good-time-earning classification and received restoration of good time credits that made him eligible for parole. Guajardo, who began serving a life sentence for murder in 1963 and was considered a problem inmate with an escape attempt on his record, suddenly found himself receiving favorable parole recommendations from Warden Cousins, and after serving twelve years on his life sentence was paroled on August 13, 1975. In correspondence advising TDC that the case had been dismissed, the attorney general's office noted that "the trial attorney did a fine job in presenting the facts to the court by way of pleadings, and the plaintiff knew that he would lose and therefore decided to dismiss the suit rather than face the judge."

The building tender legislation was clearly an outgrowth of the reform efforts of Frances Jalet, Fred Cruz, prisoner activists, and the Sullivans's reform group, CURE. This coalition of reformers also influenced the creation of the legislature's Joint Committee on Prison Reform, which in turn led to the Citizens' Advisory Committee, chaired by Charles Sullivan. With this infusion of outside groups into the prison system, TDC could no longer rely on agreed-upon dismissals to avoid inquiry into allegations such as those made by Jimenez and Guajardo.

Texas Legislators Join the Fray

The special House-Senate legislative committee on prison reform was proposed by Texas State Senator A. R. "Babe" Schwartz at the urging of Rev. C. Anderson Davis, president of the Houston chapter of the NAACP. The resolution created, in effect, an investigative committee to report on "new methods of imprisonment" and alternatives to "an atmosphere which is definitely anti-social due to the 'four walls except to work' approach." The joint study committee was to be composed of not less than five members of the Senate and five members of the House. The Texas Legislative Council was assigned the task of providing the working staff for the committee. Senator Schwartz later testified that it was his intent in proposing the resolution to "bring about an identification of the fact that we needed change and that the way to bring about change in large part was to focus attention on those deficiencies of the system for whatever reason they existed, whether it was a funding reason or whether it was a persuasive philosophical reason."[18]

Almost one month to the day after the resolution passed, an incident occurred at one of TDC's prison units south of Houston that catapulted the committee into the affairs of the prison system in dramatic fashion. What became known as the "Father's Day Incident" at the Retrieve prison unit on June 17 and 18, 1973, went to the core of TDC's management philosophy and style of operation. Moreover, it produced further evidence of the administrative strategy of denial when confronted with adverse allegations of unlawful treatment of inmates, even in the face of rather damning evidence. It also provides a further example of a pattern begun during the Beto administration that regardless of TDC's potential for culpability on a given set of facts, lawyers working for the attorney general's office acquiesced to prison administrators rather than question their policies and practices. This cooptation of attorneys in the attorney general's office persisted until the early 1980s. Finally, it illustrates Estelle's pattern of refusal to take disciplinary action against subordinates for actions that, if not clearly illegal, were contrary to acceptable standards at the time. By his refusal to take action, Estelle implicitly condoned this type of behavior, an administrative pattern that would eventually contribute to his own ouster as director of the TDC.

On June 17, 1973, warden Bobby Taylor of the Retrieve Unit ordered the agriculture prison work force (line and hoe squads) out to the fields to harvest a corn crop that was going bad because of rain-related delays in harvesting. Taylor, who had been warden at Retrieve less than six months, had worked on two other units as an assistant warden. While an assistant warden he was one of the defendant prison officials accused of beating prisoners some three years earlier on the Ellis Unit. This particular work call was unusual in that it was not only Sunday, but also Father's Day. Prisoners were rarely called on to work en masse on weekends, and Father's Day was traditionally a day of heavy visitation for TDC prisoners.

After the squads were taken to the fields, the work force head count reflected that some thirteen out of approximately three hundred prisoners had refused to turn out for work. Prison officials charged that this was directly connected to a concerted effort to disrupt the order of the prison unit. By contrast, according to testimony during subsequent hearings on the "Father's Day Incident," the prisoners' reasons for refusing to work were personal and individual in nature. All centered around having to work on Sunday, which was a religious day of rest for some, a visiting day and holiday for others. As in the *Dreyer* case, there was little, if any, evidence that these prisoners acted in concert or in a premeditated fashion.[19]

On Sunday, ten of the thirteen prisoners were charged with disciplinary offenses and placed in administrative segregation prior to their hearings. No further action was taken against the ten on Sunday. However, warden Taylor did advise director Estelle of the matter sometime on Sunday. On Monday, after turning out the regular line force, warden Taylor once again called Estelle and was told to put the ten inmates to work.[20]

Taylor assembled a group of officers with instructions to arm themselves in the event that the prisoners refused to obey the order to work. Approximately eight officers armed themselves with lead-lined rubber hoses, baseball bats, and axe handles and walked to the administrative segregation cell block. As the prisoners came out of their cells and proceeded down the cell-block run and main corridor of the prison, they were assaulted by officers positioned along their route. Prior to this action, prisoners had been locked securely in their cells and had not shown any signs of assaultiveness or posed any immediate threat to security.[21]

Several of the prisoners received lacerations and bruises as a result of the actions taken by the guards. One prisoner developed severe blisters on his feet after he was taken to the field without shoes. Some of the prisoners were taken to the field in their undershorts. One of the older prisoners collapsed in the field and was refused immediate treatment. Two of the prisoners received injuries that were severe enough that the warden in his medical judgment allowed them to receive treatment. The remaining inmates were forced to work with their injuries and without proper clothes. Evidence was offered that some of the prisoners were assaulted further on the way to the fields and after they arrived.

The prisoners claimed that Warden Taylor warned them against talking about the incident. When the prisoners returned to the cell blocks at the end of the day, the warden met with them individually and told them, "Unless they caused more trouble that there wouldn't be anything like that happen again, and I [Warden Taylor] probably said, forget, that we would forget it."[22] After these discussions the warden dropped the disciplinary actions and returned the "mutinous prisoners" to the general population the next day. In subsequent testimony during the trial of the case, W. J. Estelle, in response to queries about Warden Taylor's decision to forego disciplinary action, replied, "Those ten men were fortunate that he [Warden Taylor] was their warden, and not the Director."[23]

A number of the assaulted prisoners did anything but forget the incident. One of the ten who was assaulted, Marion McMillan, was a black activist who had received his sentence (for destruction of property) after his arrest at a Dallas food market, where he and others were boycotting the store. McMillan and his mother contacted Frances Jalet Cruz, and she subsequently filed suit on behalf of the prisoners. They also contacted Mickey Leland, a black state legislator (later a United States Congressman) from Houston who had been elected vice-chairman of the Joint Committee on Prison Reform, and Eddie Bernice Johnson, another black legislator, also on the committee. The two legislators visited the Retrieve Unit, where they met with Warden Taylor and some of the prisoners. On June 29, 1973, Estelle forwarded a memo to all members of the Board of Corrections advising them of the incident. He characterized the prisoners as "mutinous inmates" and asserted that the assault was "without provocation on the part of the staff."[24] He elected not to report the incident to the press. On July 25, 1973, state senator Chet Brooks, the chairman of the Prison Reform Committee, forwarded a letter to Estelle advising him that the committee had voted to investigate the incident. The committee had earlier issued a press release setting out a list of allegations that committee members had received from the prisoners. The press release concluded with the following statement: "We urge Governor Briscoe, Lt. Governor Hobby, Speaker Daniel, members of the legislature, and the people of the State of Texas to endorse, support, and strongly advocate the immediate undertaking of the Interim Study on any needed prison reform through the authorized Senate Concurrent Resolution No. 87."[25]

On November 15, 1973, after the incident had received a great deal of publicity, the Prison Reform Committee convened a hearing and received testimony from TDC officials and prisoners who were involved in the incident. The transcript of this hearing provides a unique glimpse into the prevailing perspective of prison officials. It also provides evidence that some TDC officials had developed a moral order that took precedence over the law.

The following are excerpts of the testimony before the committee of Lieutenant Lon Glenn, who had accompanied Major Lanham back to the cell block to assist in removing the prisoners from their cells.

Q. If the inmate continued to refuse to go to work, what force would you use to cause him to go to work?

A. That force that was necessary to effect that change.

Q. In other words, if you were to go into a cell to give an order to move—to go to work—and he continued to refuse to go to work.

A: Yes.

Q. Would you continue to hit that inmate if the inmate continued to refuse to go to work?

A. Yes.

Q. At what time would you stop hitting the inmate?

A. When he went to work.[26]

In addition to the issue of brutality, there was concern on the committee about the degrading use of racial epithets, which was without question commonplace at the time.[27] When asked about this practice, Lt. Glenn, reflecting the tendency of some staff to deny any accusations, no matter how widely known, responded as follows:

Q. Have you at any time used the term "nigger" in referring to a black inmate?

A. No sir, not only have I not used the term, abusive language is not tolerated within the TDC and is not used by officers therein.

Q. Do you have any knowledge of any of the guards or prison officials using this kind of terminology in relating to prisoners within TDC?

A. I do not have knowledge of that.[28]

In the subsequent trial of *McMillan* v. *Estelle,* Estelle testified of his approval and support of the actions taken by warden Taylor and his staff:

Q. Either warden Taylor's actions were what you wanted him to do, or they weren't. Now, which is it?

A. The fact that he [warden Taylor] received no disciplinary action was some indication of my approval of his decisions and his administration of that unit. Yes, sir.[29]

Estelle took no disciplinary action against any TDC official involved in the "Father's Day Incident."

During the trial of *McMillan* v. *Estelle* there was a great deal of graphic testimony that established that warden Taylor, Major Lanham, and Lieutenant Glenn "employed force for the purpose of summarily imposing punishment and harm upon [the prisoners] for failure to promptly obey an order."[30] The court concluded that the assaults upon the prisoners "constituted a flagrant deprivation of their civil rights."[31] The findings of the court would, in all likelihood, have been even stronger had there been a finding that the prisoners were in effect made to run through a "gauntlet" of officers on their way to the fields. Even though there was evidence of a gauntlet-like operation, the court seemed especially reluctant to conclude such.

Court: I take it you would condone inmates running through a gauntlet of officers, being beaten as they ran, in order to obey an order, as it is alleged here.

Estelle: No.

Court: You would not, would you?

Estelle: No.

Court: And I don't believe in that. I don't believe it happened.[32]

While the evidence is not conclusive, Warden Taylor's own testimony suggested that whether by design or not, something like a "gauntlet" had occurred:

Q: Now, each man had to run out of the isolation unit down the hall and out to the back gate; is that correct?

A: He had to leave isolation, go down the hall and out the back.

Q: And I believe that your testimony was that you saw some inmates struck in the hall; is that correct?

A: Yes, sir.[33]

After the court entered its findings of liability, a hearing was ordered for the purpose of assessing damages against the TDC officials. Prison officials and lawyers in the attorney general's office elected not to appeal the findings and settled the amount of damages in lieu of a further hearing. The settlement resulted in damages to seven of the ten prisoners totalling more than eleven thousand dollars, plus attorneys' fees, and was paid with state funds.

Prison Officials Clash with Another Reform Lawyer

Only days before the Prison Reform Committee convened its hearings on the "Father's Day Incident," which was receiving considerable publicity in early November 1973, a disturbance occurred at the Ramsey Unit, located in close proximity to the unit where the Father's Day Incident took place. This incident involved allegations of building tender abuses. From the beginning of its existence, the Prison Reform Committee staff maintained a prisoner correspondence log. The greatest number of prisoner complaints, aside from sentencing and parole inquiries, concerned the building tender system and alleged beatings.[34]

Naturally, an incident that was highly publicized and that had reportedly involved an altercation between eight or nine building tenders and as many prisoners prompted further investigation by the Prison Reform Committee. The committee staff had already developed information that caused them to question whether H.B. 1056 was being implemented by the TDC. Several months after the effective date (August 1973) of the building tender legislation, reform committee investigators received a copy of a TDC memo that had been posted at a prison unit, setting out the duties of a building tender. Among the "Duties and Responsibilities" listed was the following: "He shall *not* allow sex malpractice, brewing of alcoholic beverages, gambling, possession of contraband items, or fights in his wing (SHALL IMMEDIATELY REPORT ANY ILLNESS OF IN-MATES)."[35] With this evidence, which on its face suggested violations of both the spirit and letter of the law, the committee quickly ordered an investigation of the disturbance at the Ramsey I Unit and received the report the day before the hearings commenced on the "Father's Day Incident."

The Ramsey I Unit was at the time a maximum security unit, with a reputation for reliance on building tenders. Both the warden, James V. "Wildcat" Anderson, and the assistant warden, David Christian, became well-known names during much of the litigation involving TDC practices. Anderson, while an assistant warden at the Ellis Unit, had been accused of recruiting the building tender plaintiffs in the *Dreyer* case. He and Christian were also later the subjects of the plaintiffs' first motion for contempt in the *Ruiz* case. In later years Anderson was also the subject of an investigation by the attorney general's office, involving a conflict of interest arising from his personal business dealings with a TDC contractor.

Warden Christian, who was eventually fired by Estelle's successor for brutality, was often associated with the brutal treatment of prisoners. According to a prisoner who testified during the *Ruiz* trial, "Violence followed Christian like a shadow," a charge that Judge Justice in his memorandum opinion concluded was "borne out by the record."[36]

Within days after the incident, staff investigators for the Prison Reform Committee met with Anderson and Christian as well as a number of the prisoners involved in the altercation. Neither Anderson nor Christian was present on the unit when the fight broke out at approximately 10:30 AM. However, they both arrived shortly after the fight was over. They claimed in their conversations with the staff investigators that approximately eight prisoners from the administrative segregation cell block plotted to attack prisoners on the cell block immediately upon their return from the prison law library, or "writ room."[37]

Upon returning to the cell block from the writ room, one of the eight prisoners did stab a prisoner, whom Anderson described as a fifty-year-old wing barber with a medical condition. A number of prisoners on the cell block described this same inmate as a three-hundred-pound, "plenty strong," building tender. The committee's files on building tenders corroborated the prisoners' claims rather than Anderson's.

After the stabbing, building tenders on the cell block were joined by BT's from other cell blocks in fighting the eight prisoners. In addition to the stab wound suffered by the "wing barber," a number of prisoners sustained cuts, bruises, abrasions, and broken bones from the melee. Anderson concluded his remarks to the investigator by theorizing that the prisoner "assailants were out to cause trouble for the building tender system."

The prisoner assailant who did the stabbing openly admitted to the investigators that he assaulted the wing barber. He was subsequently found guilty of felony assault charges stemming from the incident. His explanation for the stabbing centered around his claims that the building tenders on his cell block had created a climate of fear as a result of recent assaults on him and others. He alleged that several days prior to the assault, several BT's, including the wing barber, had jumped him and forcibly shaved his head. He also claimed that the previous night one of his fellow prisoners had been badly beaten by two of the cell block BT's. When the prisoners gathered in the writ room the following day, they began to discuss these assaults. The discussion centered around their vulnerability when they were locked individually in their cells and eventually led to the decision that when they returned to the cell block they would "make them wup us or we wup them."

The staff investigators corroborated the prisoner-assailant's version through statements from a BT assigned to the cell block on the day of the incident. This prisoner confirmed both the forced haircutting and the assault the previous evening. During the interview, he further described, in rather laconic fashion, the dilemma of a reluctant building tender. "If I do what the Man says to do, I'm messin' on the inmates, and if I don't do like the Man wants me to do I'm going to the field."[38]

The altercation on Thursday was followed by an unexplained assault on one of the eight prisoners the following day. When asked by the investigators about this assault on Eddie James Ward, Warden Anderson explained that Ward was not injured during the Thursday altercation, but that on Friday he was found in his cell covered with blood from a number of severe head wounds. Anderson was at a loss to explain what happened. However, prisoners in the cell block claimed that three building tenders had assaulted Ward on Friday morning. He was able to get word to his attorney, Janet Stockard, about the assault, and she arrived later the same day.

Stockard was a self-defined civil rights "movement' lawyer." Her involvement with TDC, like that of the Sullivans, came through her work as a bus driver transporting friends and relatives between Austin and Huntsville for visits with prisoners. At the time she was completing work on her law degree at the University of Texas. Through these visits she established contacts with a number of inmates at the Ramsey Unit, including Eddie James Ward. Ward was serving time on a 101-year sentence that he received in 1970 for an armed robbery in Austin. At the time, Ward was "defense minister" of the Student Non-violent Coordinating Committee, an Austin-based activist organization.

Upon her arrival at the prison on Friday, Stockard's first order of business was to get medical attention for Ward, a concern prompted by her observations of his injuries. She later testified at the *Ruiz* trial that when Ward was brought out for his visit, he had a gauze bandage around his head with fresh blood running from his wounds. She immediately questioned Warden Anderson about the apparent lack of medical attention and asked Anderson if she could use the phone to call the director. Anderson refused this request, suggesting instead that she use the pay phone at a convenience store some five miles away.

Stockard left the unit, went to the pay phone, and called two members of the Prison Reform Committee, Mickey Leland and Ben Reyes. The legislators, both in Houston at the time, traveled to the Ramsey Unit and thereafter secured Ward's transfer to the prison hospital in Huntsville. Stockard's intervention on behalf of Ward was the beginning of a bitter struggle between her and Anderson and Christian that resulted in a series of court actions involving Stockard's claims of harassment and retaliation by Anderson and Christian, and counterclaims by Anderson and Christian that Stockard was disrupting their prison.[39]

Approximately one month after the November incident, Stockard filed a civil rights suit on behalf of Ward and seven other prisoners against Anderson, Christian, and the eleven building tenders who allegedly participated in the altercation.[40] The complaint claimed that Anderson and Christian, through the use of prisoners in supervisory and administrative capacities, had subjected the plaintiffs to assaults with iron pipes, knives, sticks, and other weapons. In addition, it claimed that the prisoners had been punished, threatened, and harassed for their attempts to communicate with legislators and lawyers.

Stockard's self-admitted "abrasive style,"[41] coupled with her representation of some of Ramsey's more vocal prisoners, did not endear her to the unit staff. Christian's refusal to allow Stockard the use of the unit's telephones was but one of many instances of less-than-cordial encounters. Eventually, Stockard filed a pretrial motion in May 1974 to ensure her prisoner-client's access to the courts. She claimed that unit officials were censoring all of her legal correspondence with her clients, requiring her to wait an inordinate amount of time before she could visit prisoners, denying her access to a unit telephone, and transferring her clients to other units without notification, and that they confiscated her tape recorder and refused to return it. She also charged that her clients had been placed in solitary confinement as a means of limiting her visits with them.

On May 24, 1974, the court issued a fourteen-point pretrial order intended to guarantee Stockard's clients access to the courts. Unit officials were prohibited from reading prisoner legal mail pertaining to the case, were required to provide reasonable access to the phone, had to advise Stockard of client transfers, and had to allow her use of a tape recorder. The court also approved the participation of three law students to assist Stockard in preparation for trial. Prison officials were outraged by the court's order and formally requested that it be appealed. Lawyers in the attorney general's office eventually decided not to appeal, in part because of the obvious merit of a number of Stockard's allegations.

On July 1, 1974, Stockard filed a contempt motion charging that Anderson and Christian had willfully violated the May 24, 1974, order. Stockard's motion was denied, and thereafter the court amended the May 24 order after concluding it was "a little too broad." The contempt hearing, rather than addressing Stockard's allegations, centered around expediting the original suit filed by Stockard on behalf of Ward and the other Ramsey prisoners. The suit was eventually dismissed by the court in March 1981, because the issues raised in Stockard's original complaint were addressed by court orders in the *Ruiz* and *Guajardo* cases.

While Stockard and the Ramsey administrators were engaged in their acrimonious encounters, the Prison Reform Committee was receiving reports from prisoners at Ramsey that tension was high and the unit was "ripe for a riot." After receiving these reports, the director of staff services for the committee visited Ramsey and conducted a number of interviews with prisoners. In his report to the committee, he concluded that a "potentially explosive situation at Ramsey" did indeed exist.

The allegations centered around the unit administration's harassment of "writ-writers and agitators" as well as their use of building tenders. Allegations of racial harassment were also made. The staff director had interviewed one black prisoner who had visible bruises that he sustained from altercations he had while assigned to an all-white cell block. When warden Anderson was later asked about the unusual cell block assignment, he acknowledged that it was because the prisoner was known as a "racial agitator." Another black prisoner was assigned to live with a cellmate with apparent mental problems, who had the unnerving habit of "speaking in tongues."

Warden Anderson and Assistant Warden Christian attributed much of the tension at Ramsey to plots by certain prisoners to murder unit officials. Stockard later claimed that unit officials manufactured the plot as a means to divert attention from unit abuses. She testified about one prisoner who was allegedly asked to sign a statement claiming that Stockard was involved in a plan to smuggle guns into the unit. In a statement to the press, given during a demonstration at the state capitol in Austin, Stockard charged that unit officials would use a riot as a means to retaliate against her clients. This statement gave rise to such newspaper headlines as "Officials 'Plot' Client's Murder" and "Impending Bogus Riot Allegedly Schemed to Cover Deaths."[42]

The committee report on the tension at Ramsey was forwarded to Estelle, who responded on June 17, 1974, with a seven-page letter to the committee chairman, state senator Chet Brooks. The letter attributed the tension on the unit to a "small group of inmates with avowed revolutionary aims and goals." Whether a revolutionary conspiracy was actually behind the tension on Ramsey is unclear, as Estelle did not cite any substantive evidence uncovered by unit officials.

What Estelle did address in some detail was Anderson and Christian's reputation as administrators "who can break writ-writers and agitators."

These two men have a reputation, as a matter of fact, for being fair and consistent in seeing that rules are enforced by all. There is no reason for me to believe at this time that they have any undue interest or concern about inmates involved with legal work or who are in contact with your Committee. Whatever else these gentlemen represent, they represent a group of people who recognize constituted authority and the necessity for a chain of command in a large organization; they are also quick to respond to instructions from their supervisors. One of the instructions that I have given all of our unit administrative staff, both verbally and in writing, is that inmates who are involved in litigation or who are involved in contact with the Committee on Prison Reform are to be treated no differently than other inmates, especially when it comes to administrating discipline or classification procedures.

Less than a year after Estelle wrote this letter praising Anderson and Christian, they, along with other Ramsey unit officials, were the subjects of a contempt motion in the *Ruiz* case and were later found to have subjected certain prisoners at Ramsey to "threats, intimidation, coercion, punishment, and discrimination" because of their participation in litigation.[43]

Prison Reform Committees Submit Final Reports

In December 1974 two reports were issued by the Joint Committee on Prison Reform. One report was the joint committee's *Final Report on Prison Reform* (hereafter Legislative Report), submitted to the Sixty-fourth Texas State Legislature. The second was the *Report from the Citizens Advisory Committee to the Joint Committee on Prison Reform* (hereafter Citizens Report). Both of these reports, severely critical of TDC operations, generated vigorous debate over what was rapidly becoming a controversial prison system. Many of the recommendations made by the two reports were strikingly similar to the relief that prisoners sought in the *Ruiz* case, and therefore became the subject of controversy among the attorneys during the trial of that lawsuit, approximately four years after the reports were issued.

The Legislative Report was the product of a series of working papers produced by the Committee's staff members. The staff director for the legislative committee was John Albach, a graduate of Tufts University and the University of Texas Law School. Prior to his appointment as staff director he had worked as a researcher at the Center for the Advancement of Criminal Justice at the Harvard Law School. After his work for the reform committee he became the executive director of the Texas Council on Crime and Delinquency.

In addition to Albach, the staff comprised eight researchers in addition to support staff and a group of volunteer students and faculty from the University of Texas Law School. The staff worked from a research outline that divided the study into sixteen topical areas of prison operations. The areas covered classification, custody and security, personnel, prisoners' rights, education, prison labor, medical services, treatment of mentally disturbed or retarded prisoners, and racial discrimination. Members prepared working papers on each topic based on data gathered through visits to the prison units, interviews with prisoners and TDC staff, and contacts with other public agencies in the state and federal government.

When a working paper had been completed, it was presented to the full committee, after which further hearings were held, or further information collected at the direction of committee members. Over the life of the committee, sixteen public hearings were held, and more than a thousand pages of working papers were received. The final drafts of the working papers formed the basis for recommendations for the committee's final report. Although all the recommendations were adopted by the full committee, the commentary in the final report was not intended to reflect total agreement among all committee members. The final report was signed by ten of the legislators on the committee.

The report began with a "Compilation of Recommendations" that addressed the entire spectrum of corrections, from pre-trial diversion and sentencing to prisons and parole. The compilation was followed by a detailed discussion of findings of each major area. The straightforward nature of the Legislative Report is nowhere more evident than in the section on "Discipline":

Another tool which TDC has illegally employed to maintain discipline is the so-called "building tender system". . . . TDC still maintains that building tenders do not exist in violation of the law.

Yet, a TDC inter-office communication dated December, 1973, long after the effective date of H.B. 1056, lists the duties of "wing floor tenders," and makes it clear that "wing floor tenders" exercise supervisory, administrative, and disciplinary control over inmates. . . . The staff has seen too many "incident reports" in which one of the two parties to an altercation turned out to be a building tender to believe these allegations are unfounded. The continued illegal existence of the building tender system was conceded by several unit officials in staff interviews. The Department could eliminate some of the brutality which accompanies this system where inmates have quasi-official authority over inmates by honestly investigating reports of beatings administered by "BT's" rather than denying they exist.[44]

The Committee issued equally strong findings on race relations. This section of the report began by noting that TDC had not cooperated in providing information to the committee on this subject due to pending litigation in *Lamar* v. *Coffield*. Nevertheless, some facts were not difficult to discover. In stark contrast to the prison officials' claim that racial segregation was not practiced, staff researchers found that more than 50 percent of the inmate population lived in racially or ethnically segregated cell blocks or dorms. More than half of the institutions were almost entirely segregated, not only in housing but also in work assignments. The report indicated that "most, if not all, inmates assigned to work as house boys in officials' homes are black." The report even noted one warden's comment that it was difficult to find "good house niggers now."

These data, along with staff interviews and observations, led to the following conclusion: "Discrimination, prejudice and segregation do exist in the Department of Corrections to a significant degree. Despite the fact that many department officials voice opposition to such practices and deny they exist; the evidence is overwhelming that official administrative policy of racial neutrality is not always followed. Some wardens and many employees did not even attempt to hide their prejudices from the Committee."[45]

The committee's most forceful findings dealt with medical services and treatment of mentally disturbed and retarded prisoners. The committee concluded that both staff resources and facilities were woefully inadequate and led to the routine delivery of unprofessional care. The department's routine practice of using prisoners to perform minor surgery and administer medicine was condemned. The treatment of mentally disturbed prisoners was characterized as "the worst example of TDC abuse that the committee staff found in all of the Department's operations." The treatment center for mentally disturbed prisoners was found to be no more than a solitary wing, where heavily sedated prisoners were confined without any organized treatment program.

The Legislative Report also addressed issues that were the subject of pending litigation such as correspondence rules and prisoner access to courts. Most of the committee's recommendations in these two areas were eventually implemented upon final resolution of the *Guajardo, Corpus* and *Ruiz* cases.

Of the two reports produced by the Prison Reform Committee, the Citizens Advisory Report was plainly more critical and considerably more graphic in detail. The Citizens Advisory Committee was created, and its members appointed by, the members of the legislative committee, with each legislator making two nominations. The final makeup of the citizens group included, among its twenty-five members, physicians, attorneys, clergy, teachers, ex-cons, journalists, a labor union representative, and a former member of the Texas Board of Corrections. Charles Sullivan, appointed by a San Antonio legislator, was elected chairman. The stated purpose of the Citizens Committee was to provide research assistance and a broad base of citizen input on proposed recommendations. The citizens group held hearings in Austin, Houston, Dallas/Fort Worth, San Antonio, Corpus Christi, San Angelo, and Lubbock. Committee members visited virtually every unit in the prison system and conducted interviews with guards, prisoners, and TDC officials. In the cover letter to the report, the committee chairman charged that committee members had "encountered substantial TDC opposition" in gaining access to the department, which Sullivan claimed was by design a "closed system, hidden from public view."

The Citizens Report followed the same basic format as the Legislative Report, in that findings on each major topic were discussed and then followed by recommendations. Many of the recommendations were not well received. They were criticized in particular by one member of the Legislative Committee, state senator Walter Mengden, Jr., who refused to sign the final report. Mengden was quoted by a Houston newspaper as having characterized members of the Citizens Committee as the "most grotesque collection of radical activists ever put together under one roof." If their recommendations were followed, Mengden claimed, they would cause "the greatest crime wave in the history of the world by making prison life so desirable everyone would seek incarceration."

One set of recommendations dealt with visiting privileges:

> The legislature should make provisions for the reasonable cost of transportation from the State's major population centers to TDC units; a model might be found in the bus trips currently organized by private co-operative charitable groups from Austin, Corpus Christi, El Paso, Fort Worth, Lubbock and San Antonio.
> TDC should establish weekday visiting hours.

TDC should establish an effective system to keep persons on inmate visiting lists informed as to the availability of the inmate for visitation.

TDC should eliminate the restriction of inmates' visitation lists to ten persons.

TDC should take steps to assure that visits actually last as long as provided for in the regulations.

TDC should reduce the distance that justifies a four-hour visit.

TDC should take steps to assure that visiting privileges are not arbitrarily denied to individual inmates or would-be visitors.

TDC should institute programs allowing for increased contact and privacy between inmates and visitors, including, on an experimental level, conjugal and family visiting programs, and inmate furlough programs, where consonant with the needs of security.[46]

While debatable, these recommendations could hardly be considered "radical." Perhaps the most controversial, conjugal visits, was suggested only on an experimental basis. The remainder reflected little more than contemporary practice in many other states. Prison officials did not adopt conjugal visiting, even on an experimental basis. It was not until September 1985, pursuant to court agreement in *Ruiz,* that barrier-free visitation was allowed, and then only among limited classification groups.[47]

Many of the recommendations made in the Citizens Report were remedial and merely suggested that contemporary standards be applied to TDC practices, such as those in the area of mental health:

Thorough psychological testing of every entering inmate should be a requirement before final classification is made. All available information from inmates' families, previous incarceration records, and personal interviews should be collected in a central file available for assessment by fully qualified and competent professional personnel.

TDC's Mental Health Program should be under the immediate direction of a well-trained, full-time staff psychiatrist who, with such help as needed, should promptly recommend development of a fully integrated and staffed mental health program.[48]

Again, while priorities for allocating funds to various programs might be debated, these proposals were hardly "radical." They become even less dramatic when compared to statements attributed to a former chief prison psychiatrist who resigned from TDC in May 1985, charging that psychiatric care in the TDC is "as close to hell on Earth as I've ever seen."[49] Whatever the merit of the recommendations, changes similar to those suggested in the Citizens Report were not implemented until the

1980s, and then only pursuant to agreements made in the *Ruiz* litigation.[50]

In some cases recommendations in the Citizens Report were not only factually valid and in keeping with standard correctional practices, but also compelled by prevailing law. When dealing with disciplinary practices, the committee noted that in addition to the nineteen disciplinary offenses set out in the inmate rule book, there existed an additional list of approximately one hundred offenses for which an inmate might be placed in solitary confinement. The list was not posted, distributed, or explained to prisoners. The report also noted that even when rules were available they were often "unduly vague and ambigious," a finding entered in the *Ruiz* case some six years later. To illustrate, the committee set out an example of an offense report for "agitation" that not only reflected vagueness but also a presumption that an officer's accusation was sufficient to establish guilt, a finding also eventually confirmed in *Ruiz*.

> Offense Report: The above captioned inmate agitates continuously and he has been warned repeatedly. He agitates mutiny in the wing and in the squad. He tries to agitate the officials and the custodial officers by writing letters when investigated proved to be lies.
> Although he has tried to agitate he has never actually caused any trouble by his actions, but is constantly stirring up trouble through other inmates.

The report noted that this particular prisoner spent thirteen days in solitary confinement for the above offense.

Although both committee reports were submitted to the 1975 legislative session with some 160 recommendations, only one of the recommendations was directly acted upon by the legislature. The legislature had passed a statute in 1927 that required segregation in Texas prisons: "White and Colored prisoners shall be segregated in separate living quarters, workshops, and hospitals." The committee recommended the repeal of the statute and called for legislation prohibiting discrimination against prisoners based on race. The legislature deleted the archaic phrase and passed legislation prohibiting discrimination in the prison system. Even this change was not prompted entirely by the committee's recommendation, as the *Lamar* litigation was also active at this time.

By late 1974, TDC was no longer a "closed sytem hidden from public view." During the first two years of his administration, W. J. Estelle, had emerged as a more-than-adequate spokesman for the preservation of the authoritarian work-ethic approach to prison administration. However, unlike his predecessor, Estelle did not enjoy unfettered authority. What had started out as a small group of prisoners with virtually no credibility had evolved during the Beto administration into a substantial group of legislators and citizens who demanded accountability from the prison system.

As a result of inquiries and investigations, TDC officials were suddenly asked to defend their policies and methods of operation before legislative committees and reform groups. From the outset, prison officials adopted a strategy of simply denying any wrongdoing regardless of the evidence to the contrary. After passage of the building tender legislation, TDC officials, including Estelle, categorically denied that building tenders were used for any purpose other than their janitorial-like duties. As evidence continued to mount over the ensuing years establishing the routine use of BT's in violation of H.B. 1056, agency officials became inextricably wed to this posture of denial. To accept evidence in direct conflict with longstanding denials was to risk the credibility that agency officials had acquired during the Ellis and Beto years. When denial defied reason and logic, reformers were asked to defer to the expertise and judgment of prison officials. When deference was not forthcoming, prison administrators and some of their supporters relied increasingly on rhetoric to cast reformers and prisoners as a grotesque group of radicals or revolutionaries engaged in murderous plots against the administration.

The conspiracy that officials alleged was taking place on the Ramsey Unit with the participation of Janet Stockard and her clients, was similar in many respects to the charges leveled earlier in the George Beto administration against Frances Jalet Cruz and her clients. While charges of revolutionary activities backed by plots to murder prison staff with the assistance of legal counsel may seem rather extreme more than a decade after the fact, it is important to note that prison administrators in Texas were not alone in their assertions.

Such respected prison reformists as Austin MacCormick and traditional advocates of treatment rather than punishment, such as Walter Dunbar, moved closer to the punitive approach in corrections during this time in part as a response to criticisms and activities of "radicals."[51] This movement toward an increased emphasis on control was accompanied by an expanded definition of the opposition: "The custodial faction moved back into power with a revised ideology. To their old punitive philosophy, in which prisoners were worthless and untrustworthy, they added new categories for the prisoners and outsiders who were criticizing prisons and guards and participating in the prison movement activities. The outsiders were dirty, hairy, hippie freaks or seditious, traitorous communists, and the prisoners who sided with them were a new type of vicious psychopathic opportunist."[52]

The "custodial" approach to incarceration had always been the philosophy in Texas. The national trend during this period simply reaffirmed existing beliefs and practices among Texas prison administrators. Just as important, if not more so, the national trend added credence to the idea that resistance to misguided reformers, whether prisoners, citizens, legislators, or judicial personnel, was not only reasonable but positively required by an allegiance to a higher set of values. It is with such values in mind that officials could condone actions like those taken in the "Father's Day Incident," even to the point of suggesting that prisoners should literally be beaten into submission.

Even though the reform movement had gained momentum during these years, the TDC and W. J. Estelle, in particular, retained a high degree of credibility. The credibility was such that agency officials enjoyed unqualified support from lawyers in the attorney general's office, who time and again deferred to prison officials rather than question their policies and practices. TDC's strategy of denial was successful during this time in part because prison officials were able to limit access to the system. Reform groups found it difficult to move forward with allegations of wrongdoing without a fact-finding process. Even though prison reform committee reports later proved to be highly credible documents, they had no official force or effect at the time. However, with a potentially sweeping prison conditions case like *Ruiz,* the fact-finding mechanism was available and TDC could no longer ward off allegations by mere denial of wrongdoing. The *Ruiz* case began to take shape in 1974. From the very beginning, TDC's strategy of denial escalated to outright defiance and unlawful behavior by prison officials. This defiance would so dominate the early development of the case that judicial intervention on a massive scale was inevitable.

Chapter Four:
Ruiz v. Estelle:
The Beginnings of Guerilla Warfare—
1974–78

Though we may be dealing here with some of the most incorrigible members of our society (although not solely), how we treat these particular individuals determines to a large extent, the moral fibre of our society as a whole and if we trespass beyond the bounds of decency, such excesses become an affront to the sensibility of each of us.

Circuit Judge Tuttle, Novak v. Beto

The First Step: A Receptive Judicial Forum

By 1974 writ-writers, reform groups, and the Texas Legislature, all with increasing support from the courts, had produced such pressures on the internal operations of TDC that the once-stable prison system was showing signs of turmoil and unrest. Amidst this increasing unrest, David Ruiz's handwritten complaint began its transformation from an individual prisoner petition to a massive prison conditions case, which was to be dominated by personalities and ideologies rather than efforts to settle the substantive issues of the case.

Ruiz's petition alleged that he was subject to unconstitutional confinement due to a variety of conditions and practices routinely employed at TDC. By 1974 this type of pleading had already resulted in affirmed court decisions declaring two southern prison systems unconstitutional. In *Holt v. Sarver II*, a federal district court declared unconstitutional the entire Arkansas State Penitentiary System, which consisted primarily of the "Cummins Farm," a nine-thousand-acre farm that housed about one thousand inmates. This decision, rendered in 1970 and affirmed in 1971, was the first to rely on the Eighth Amendment to declare the operation of an entire prison system unconstitutional.

The Arkansas prison system was typical of many southern prisons in its reliance on farming operations and the use of inmates in supervisory and administrative roles. Prisoners on the Cummins Farm worked six days a week, often engaged in stoop labor, such as picking cotton, fruits, and vegetables. While working in the fields prisoners were guarded by armed inmates or "trusties." The court concluded that inmates virtually ran the prison, a condition that "bred hatred, mistrust and violence." The court also concluded that physical and sexual assaults were routine, that isolation cells were repulsively filthy, and that there were absolutely no rehabilitation or training programs available in the prison. In addressing the trusty system in Arkansas, the court commented on the criteria used to select trusties, criteria that seemed to echo those testified to by George Beto in the *Dreyer* case: "Actually, few, if any, objective criteria are used in selecting trusties; that a man is a bad man, or a dangerous man, or that he has a bad criminal record is by no means a disqualification; on the contrary, it may be a recommendation."[1]

Holt v. *Sarver* was an important watershed case because rather than declaring any single condition unconstitutional, the Court based its finding on the cumulative effect of conditions of confinement and thereby provided a means for broadscale remedies to correct fundamental deficiencies in the system. *Holt* was followed by an avalanche of decisions in which massive structural relief was the order of the day.

One of the first systems to come under a *Holt*-like attack again involved a southern prison system dominated by agriculture and dependent upon trusties for many supervisory and administrative tasks. In *Gates* v. *Collier* the district court found that the Mississippi State Penitentiary had failed to provide prisoners adequate protection against physical assaults, abuses, indignities, and cruelties of other inmates, by placing excessive numbers of inmates in barracks without adequate classification or supervision and by assigning custodial responsibility to incompetent and untrained inmates.

The issues litigated in *Gates* were strikingly similar to those raised in David Ruiz's original petition. In *Gates* prisoners claimed that they were routinely subjected to abuses by inmate guards, denied proper medical care, placed in solitary confinement without procedural safeguards, and had all correspondence censored. In describing the use of trusties, the court noted that they performed administrative duties such as distributing mail and medicine, maintaining prison files, recommending punishment for fellow prisoners, and enforcing discipline in the cell blocks. The court found that the "evidence is replete with instances of inhumanities, illegal conduct and other indignities visited by inmates who exercise authority over their fellow prisoners." In finding the prison unconstitutional, the court entered an order that included both immediate and long-range relief.[2]

The State of Mississippi did not appeal the court's findings of fact or conclusion of law but did challenge the nature and extent of the relief granted. The governor of Mississippi had earlier conceded the existence of constitutional violations in the prison and all but asked the court to enter such findings. Judge Tuttle, who had delivered the strong dissent in the *Novak* case, wrote the circuit opinion in *Gates* affirming the district court's orders. The state's argument that implementation of the court's orders within the required time frames was impossible due to lack of financial resources was rejected. Also rejected was the state's claim that because of their good faith reform efforts and the state officials' stated desire to improve the prison, an extensive court order was unnecessary. The circuit court recognized that improvements were under way but also noted that they had not been undertaken until after the suit was filed.

The door for judicial review of prisoner complaints about prison conditions had been opened in the early 1960s. In the following decade, courts considered only the constitutionality of the treatment of a particular inmate or the operation of specific practices. The importance of *Holt* and *Gates,* beyond the improvements they brought in the Arkansas and Mississippi prison systems, was the seminal effect they had on broadening judicial review to include the systemic nature of prison conditions. The concern for systemic conditions dramatically complicated the court's task when it came to specifying remedies and making sure these remedies were implemented.

The willingness to evaluate the totality of conditions of confinement had the inevitable result of moving the courts firmly into an era of prescribing policy for the administration of public institutions, an era that had its genesis in *Brown* v. *Board of Education.* From the beginning this judicial "activism" was the subject of heated debate.[3]

In the early 1970s activist judges were more the exception than the rule.[4] During this period, finding a receptive judicial forum became the key ingredient to initiating broadscale institutional reform. The fortuitous presence of a receptive judge in the judicial district in which a prison was located determined whether the *pro se* litigants would receive more than a cursory review of their often inartfully pleaded handwritten petitions.

A judge's known willingness to review prisoner petitions often determined whether prisoners would continue their efforts to litigate prison conditions. In a 1979 law review article, William Bennett Turner commented on the importance of receptive federal judges: "The 'liberal' decisions and reputations of individual judges appear to encourage prisoner suits. These judges act as magnets for prison cases. Some lawyers with considerable experience in handling prison litigation believe that the presence of a well known liberal judge is the most important factor encouraging prisoner filings."[5]

A judge willing to exercise the full powers of his or her office could readily orchestrate an institutional reform case due to the ability to shape, organize, and facilitate the litigation. The financial resources and technical expertise required to litigate institutional reform cases successfully could not be borne by prisoners and attorneys alone. Intervenors, additional attorneys, and *amici* could be invited by the judge to join the case, which provided the writ-writer with substantial resources that he could not otherwise muster. In the court of a receptive activist judge a *pro se* petitioner, who would otherwise have to rely on his own limited skills, could suddenly find himself represented by government organizations such as the Department of Justice and attorneys with highly refined prison litigation expertise.

When David Ruiz filed his petition in June 1972, an activist federal district judge in Tyler, Texas, William Wayne Justice, was turning his attention from enforcing school desegregation in East Texas to prisoners' rights. Through his liberal decisions on school desegregation in a deeply conservative region of the state, he had acquired a reputation as a judicial activist in just three years on the federal bench. While Ruiz's petition was receiving little more than routine procedural attention from mid-1972 to early 1974, Judge Justice was presiding over his first large-scale reform case involving state institutions in Texas. In *Morales* v. *Turman,* which involved state facilities for delinquent youth, Judge Justice placed the state on notice that judicial activism had arrived in Texas. In addition to the youth facilities, both the prisons and mental health facilities in Texas would eventually undergo major reforms at the hands of this strong-willed, liberal judge from the small East Texas community of Athens.

William Wayne Justice: Judicial Activism in Texas

Judge Justice was nominated to the federal bench by Texas's liberal United States Senator Ralph Yarborough, a longtime family friend. Justice was among the last of Lyndon Johnson's appointments confirmed by the Senate in 1968. At the time of his appointment, Justice was the United States attorney for the Eastern District of Texas, an appointment also secured by Senator Yarborough. While U.S. attorney he lived in a small town—Athens, Texas—just outside Tyler, where he had grown up. His father, Will Justice, was a well-known attorney, much admired by his son. In a televised interview Judge Justice recalled how his father had placed his name on the firm's stationary and office signs when Justice was but seven years of age.[6] Due in part to this encouragement and devout admiration for his father, Justice attended the University of Texas Law School and thereafter joined his father's firm. By the time he accepted the appointment as federal judge he was not only well schooled in the law but also acutely aware of the cultural pride and prejudice that would generate deep and longstanding resentment for many of his decisions.

From the very outset, Judge Justice's court seemed to draw controversial cases. Within his first two years on the bench, he presided over four cases involving local schools, three of which involved racial discrimination issues. In 1969 he ordered the integration of an East Texas school district that had openly refused to desegregate.[7] That same year he took control of desegregation in the Tyler schools, which later resulted in a local furor over his order requiring a Tyler high school to hold a cheer-leader election with proportionate representation from the black student enrollment.[8] In another case, involving Robert E. Lee High School in Tyler, he ordered the school to abandon its confederate theme song, "Dixie," as well as its use of the rebel flag.[9] Addressing a different type of discrimination, Justice ordered a local junior college to admit students who had been denied admission because of their long hair.[10]

Such decisions went to the core of the fears and biases of many local residents, who stood powerless to stop this liberal judge daring to challenge their way of life. Emotional responses prevailed over reasoned assessment of existing law and evidence. Justice's decision in the hair code case was met with such dire predictions as, "This will destroy the college."[11] Justice later recalled that it "was as if I had gotten out in the middle of the public square and announced I was a communist or some-thing, or in favor of peddling dope."[12] Citizens readily held this native son personally responsible for imposing unwanted change on institutions that had become outdated as a result of the civil rights movement of the 1960s.

In 1978 a popular magazine with statewide circulation ran a major fea-ture on Judge Justice entitled "The Real Governor of Texas."[13] The arti-cle, which appeared before Judge Justice had rendered his decision or any remedial orders in *Ruiz,* began with the forceful proposition that "No one cast a single vote for him, but everyone in Texas lives beneath the power of a solitary judge in Tyler." Like Judge Frank Johnson, who brought re-form to Alabama's major state institutions, Judge Justice was an ar-chetypal judicial activist who was undeterred by political demagoguery, personal affronts, or emotional appeals to sacred ideologies.

His actions generated such controversy that on one occasion, following his ruling dealing with the state's juvenile institutions, a bill directing the Texas Youth Council to build a halfway house next door to Judge Justice's residence in Tyler was passed out of the State Affairs Committee of the Texas Senate by a nine-to-two vote. The author of the bill commented, "Up to this point Judge Justice has put these halfway houses in low and middle income areas, but he has escaped putting one next to his house. . . . This will give William Wayne Justice fair and equal treat-ment to what he has dished out to the hardworking, God-fearing people of this state."[14] While the bill was never passed into law, it did provide a rhetorical outlet for legislators who were incensed by what they consi-dered the intrusion of a federal judge into matters belonging to state law-makers.

Closer to home, some ten thousand of Tyler's sixty-five thousand resi-dents signed petitions calling for his impeachment after his decisions af-fecting the administration of local schools.[15] His wife was forced to travel outside Tyler to have her hair done when local beauticians refused her service.[16] On another occasion a local repairman walked off a job at the judge's residence when he found out whose home it was.[17] There were even bumper stickers that read "Will Rogers never met Judge Justice."[18]

While Justice was the subject of severe and ongoing criticism from school officials, local residents, and politicians, as well as the broader conservative elements of East Texas, his bold moves in these early cases quickly established his reputation with aspiring reform-oriented litigants as a judge "willing to address constitutional issues with broad ramifications and to consider the full range of equitable powers possessed by a federal judge."[19] It was this reputation, combined with astute forum shopping, that brought the Texas juvenile justice system into Justice's court in 1971, where it remained throughout the 1970s while undergoing major reforms.

In *Morales* v. *Turman* attorneys filed a class-action suit in Justice's court on behalf of juvenile offenders confined to Texas Youth Council (TYC) facilities, alleging that TYC officials denied attorneys private access to their juvenile clients. At the time there were five major institutions for some twenty-five hundred delinquent youths. The executive director had been in office for almost fifteen years, and the chairman of the council had held his post for eleven years. During this time TYC had become an isolated state agency with little accountability to anyone. Two years prior to the suit, the state legislature authorized funding for a professional evaluation of TYC, but according to a state senator, the executive director, James Turman, "got with the House leadership and torpedoed it."[20]

In the subsequent hearing before Judge Justice on the attorney visitation issues, two basic problems emerged that turned the hearing into a mere prelude to future litigation. First, it became apparent that there were a substantial number of juveniles who had been denied basic rights at their commitment hearings. Second, there were few if any written policies to guide TYC staff in their treatment of inmates. In this sense, the "operation of the system seemed lawless."[21] Judge Justice's initial order was limited to the requirement that TYC officials permit private consultation. However, this was only the beginning. Justice had acquired jurisdiction over TYC, and the case soon mushroomed into a frontal assault on statewide commitment procedures and the administration of the entire TYC system.

The frontal assault on TYC was due in large part to Justice's willingness to assume an affirmative role in the aftermath of the initial skirmish in *Morales*. Broadbased reform required that significant organizational resources be made available to the *Morales* attorneys. In May 1972, Justice invited the United States to participate as a party through the Civil Rights Division of the Department of Justice. According to one commentator, this invitation was preceded by a telephone call to a Justice Department lawyer in which Judge Justice let it be known that he was receptive to further reform efforts directed at the TYC.[22] Not long after that, attorneys for the TYC inmates broadened their lawsuit, which now included intervention by the Department of Justice. The Justice Department provided a corps of experienced attorneys, support personnel, and FBI agents to collect data on all aspects of institutional conditions. They also brought the expertise of other federal agencies and nationally recognized authorities.

In addition to the Department of Justice, Peter Sandman of the Youth Law Center of San Francisco and later William Bennett Turner's law partner, joined the case, as did attorneys who represented other public interest groups. What had started out as litigation seeking relief on a single, rather narrow issue with representation by local counsel had by design mushroomed into a class-action lawsuit that would prompt major reform of the TYC. Judge Justice's orchestration efforts left little doubt that he was willing to bring the full force of his court to bear on the operation of TYC facilities.

In August 1973, Judge Justice conducted hearings on the plaintiffs' motion for emergency relief regarding certain conditions and practices routinely employed at TYC facilities in violation of constitutional rights. On August 31, 1973, Justice issued a written opinion granting interim relief to the plaintiffs. This interim order almost overnight thrust TYC and Justice to the forefront of public controversy in the state. The factual findings revealed that inmates at the TYC facilities, many of whom were "status offenders," were routinely subjected to physical punishments and psychologically damaging treatment.

Justice found that correctional officers at Mountain View (TYC's maximum security facility) routinely administered various forms of physical abuse such as slapping, punching, and kicking. One form of this physical abuse, referred to as "racking," consisted of requiring the inmate to stand against the wall with his hands in his pockets while he was struck a number of times by blows from the fists of officers. The evidence also showed that TYC officials were too quick to use tear gas. For instance, one prisoner was gassed for fleeing from a beating he was receiving, while another was gassed while locked securely in his cell for failure to work. Prisoners who were labelled homosexuals by untrained staff found themselves confined in "punk dorms." Other prisoners were forced to engage in "make-work tasks, such as pulling grass without bending their knees."

Justice entered a detailed interim order limiting the use of physical force and solitary confinement and imposing conditions under which youths could be confined at Mountain View, a facility characterized as having a reputation of "brutality and repression." Justice also appointed the chief of casework services at Mountain View as an ombudsman and required him to file reports with the court on violations.

Within a matter of days after Justice issued his interim order, residents at Mountain View and one other facility created disturbances that TYC officials charged were "riot situations" caused by the posting of Justice's orders at TYC facilities. These disturbances received a wave of publicity both statewide and nationally with such headlines as "TYC Blames 'Riots' on United States Court Order."[23] The TYC officials who blamed the disturbances on the court order were not the first to point the finger at outside interference, nor would they be the last.[24]

TYC director Turman, while laying blame on the court, unwittingly demonstrated his own administration's ineptness and culpability in the disturbances. Reportedly, when Turman asked the Texas attorney general, John Hill, to get relief from the court order "so we can keep control," Hill asked if the order had been explained to the prisoners, to which Turman replied that "we would be in contempt of court if we did that."[25] The court order, of course, had no such restriction. To the contrary, it required "conspicuous" posting of the order for inmates to read. Moreover, the order did not prohibit lawful use of force or the imposition of appropriate punishments as Turman and other TYC officials claimed.

Given the official response to Justice's order and the subsequent disturbances, reports later emerged suggesting that TYC staff "had actually encouraged the riot to embarass the court."[26] During one disturbance, in which sixty boys were shouting and throwing trash in one of the security wings at the reception center, Turman said he would not "risk human life by sending anybody in there to quell those boys."[27] Another report provided some evidence that TYC officials almost literally threw up their hands instead of taking action to avoid the spread of what started out as an isolated disturbance.[28]

The disclosures of mistreatment made public in Justice's order, coupled with the disorganized staff response, prompted the resignations of Turman and Robert Kneebone, chairman of the Texas Youth Council. The new chairman, Forrest Smith, who seconded his own nomination for the chairmanship, recognized and supported the need for change in the agency. The newly aligned council quickly appointed a new executive director, Ron Jackson, who was at the time superintendent of what was "widely recognized as the most progressive of the TYC institutions."[29] Jackson, only thirty-two years old at the time of his appointment, had grown up with the agency as a teenage orphan who had been adopted by a superintendent of a TYC institution. With strong support from the new chairman, Jackson moved quickly to implement the court's interim order along with his own new programs, which lessened the emphasis on security.[30]

Judge Justice's interim order thus served as a catalyst for sweeping change in the administration of TYC. Even though the state would resent Justice's continuing efforts to direct specific changes, there was general recognition that changes were needed. The new chairman of the TYC board typified the state's posture. "The court did a good deed in helping to expose many things which ought never to have happened. But it's one thing for the court to tell us we can't beat the hell out of kids anymore — we've stopped that by now — and it's a wholly different thing for him to tell us how to run the agency."[31]

Within a few months after the interim order, a governor's task force was created to establish a master plan for youth services. The TYC administration continued to implement new programs and to eliminate clearly unlawful practices. This progress served as a basis for the state's attempt to reopen the case. Judge Justice refused, however, and in August 1974 he issued an extremely detailed decision in which every aspect of institutional life was addressed.[32] The extent of Judge Justice's willingness to make administrative decisions for TYC officials was reflected by his finding "that two TYC institutions, Gatesville State School for Boys and Mountain View State School for Boys, are places where the delivery of effective rehabilitation treatment is impossible, and that they must not be utilized any longer than is absolutely necessary as facilities for juvenile delinquents."[33]

Judge Justice also commented on the TYC's use of co-opted prisoners, a practice he would later encounter in a more pronounced fashion when he heard evidence regarding the administration of the state's adult prison facilities and the use of building tenders: "Correctional Officers single out certain inmates as 'office boys'; these inmates act both as informers and as enforcers, using threats and violence on other inmates at the direction or with the encouragement of the officers."[34] Some of these same "office boys" would go on to become building tenders in the Texas Department of Corrections.

In the *Morales* case, Judge Justice had succeeded in prompting much-needed reforms. However, he was unable to implement the specific reforms detailed in his three-hundred-page opinion. While state officials acknowledged the need for change, they did not wish to surrender their prerogative to direct and implement new programs and thus appealed Justice's decision, arguing that the added deliberation and procedural protection provided by a three-judge court was warranted when such broadscale reform was at issue. While the United States Supreme Court eventually rejected this argument, the strategy worked to the state's advantage in that officials were able to "put their own house in order" while the appeal was processed. Without specific plans against which to gauge compliance with his order, Justice was limited in his supervision of TYC. Having recognized the need for change, state officials were able to establish their ability to run state institutions without ongoing and direct supervision by a federal judge. Had they resisted the need for change, the litigation could have been expanded substantially. It is just such resistance that Judge

Justice encountered when litigation involving reform of a proud state prison system began to take shape. The experience he gained in *Morales* would prove to be quite useful. From the outset of *Ruiz* v. *Estelle* it was evident that Justice had benefitted from the *Morales* experience. He would have every opportunity in the next ten years to apply his newly acquired expertise in the administration of institutional reform cases.

Ruiz v. Estelle: A Lesson in Judicial Orchestration

When David Ruiz filed his handwritten petition while confined to the "eight-hoe squad" at the Wynne Unit in 1972, it was but one of several hundred petitions filed that year by TDC prisoners. At the time there were thirteen Texas prisons with more than fifteen thousand inmates. Ruiz's petition had two characteristics that distinguished it from most of the others. First and most important, it was filed in the Eastern District of Texas. Eleven of the thirteen Texas prisons were located in the multijudge Southern District. The vast majority of prisoner petitions were filed in the Houston Division Court, which had a host of federal judges, some of whom were less than receptive to prisoner claims. The fate of a petition was therefore often subject to the vagaries of court docketing. More often than not, the "luck of the draw" determined whether the prisoner's claims would move beyond the filing stage.

However, the two remaining units in TDC were located in the much smaller Eastern District. One of these prisons, the Eastham Unit, was a maximum security prison with a reputation for handling problem inmates. Eastham also had a reputation for heavy reliance on building tenders. A number of the "eight-hoe squad" had been confined at Eastham prior to their transfer to Wynne, including David Ruiz. Because Ruiz chose to attack the conditions of his confinement while at Eastham, he filed his petition in the Eastern District Court in Tyler, Texas, which had a single resident judge at the time, William Wayne Justice. In addition to finding its way into a receptive judicial forum, David Ruiz's petition raised a variety of issues that went to the core of the operation of the Texas Department of Corrections: the unlawful use of building tenders, inadequate medical care, harassment by TDC officials for legal activities, and unlawful confinement in punitive segregation. Thus, Ruiz's petition set out a series of allegations that had the potential, through artful amended pleading, to support a broadbased conditions suit.

In addition to the Ruiz petition, seven other prisoner petitions were filed in the Eastern District, that had the cumulative effect of raising issues which touched on virtually every aspect of TDC's operation.[35] Because these petitions encompassed such a broad area of TDC operations, their selection from hundreds of others reflects a reasoned effort by Judge Justice to create a single suit that would provide the framework for a

Holt-like conditions case.

On April 12, 1974, Judge Justice consolidated six of these prisoner petitions with Ruiz's original petition and ordered the United States Department of Justice to appear as *amicus curiae,* "in order to investigate fully the facts alleged in the prisoners' complaints to participate in such civil action with the full rights of a party thereto, and to advise [the] Court at all stages of the proceeding as to any actions deemed appropriate by it." [36] With this simple two-page order of consolidation, Judge Justice had taken the first major step toward organizing eight handwritten prisoner petitions into a class-action conditions case that would keep TDC under the superintendence of his court through at least two decades, five directors, four attorneys general, and four governors.

Justice's appointment of the United States as *amicus curiae* left little doubt that he was willing to extend his authority to the outer limits of his judgeship to ensure the *Ruiz* plaintiffs adequate representation. Historically, an *amicus curiae* is appointed to assist the court in an advisory or investigatory role. However, Justice gave the United States full rights of a party to the litigation, which for all practical purposes made the United States an intervenor from the outset. This type of *amici* appointment was later the subject of an appeal in a similar prison conditions case in which the appeals court concluded that the status of the United States as a full party to the litigation was "more than the usual participation for *amici.*" [37] When the state appealed the broad discretion and power placed in the hands of Justice Department attorneys, Texas attorney general John Hill charged that Judge Justice was simply attempting "to cause to be conducted a wide ranging investigation into the Texas prison system for which he could fashion precise remedies. Judge Justice seeks to abandon his role as a jurist hearing complaints of parties who appear before him, and becomes an active pursuer of the petitioner using the Justice Department as his sword and shield." [38]

Shortly after Justice entered his order of consolidation, he appointed Stanley Bass of the NAACP Legal Defense Fund (Inc. Fund) as counsel of record for the prisoners. Although unknown to attorneys for TDC at the time, Bass was appointed as interim counsel until William Bennett Turner could accept the appointment. Judge Justice and Turner first met in 1972 at a prisoners' rights conference in Dallas, where they served on the same discussion panel. Justice was familiar with Turner's growing national reputation as a highly capable prisoners' rights attorney and also knew of his familiarity with the Texas prison system through his participation in *Novak* v. *Beto.* Thus, when it came time to appoint counsel for the prisoners, Justice extended his judicial authority to one of the more remote regions on earth, the Himalayas. He had attempted to contact Turner at the Inc. Fund office in New York City and was told that Turner was on sabbatical in Nepal. Justice contacted Turner there and asked if he would accept the appointment as counsel for the *Ruiz* plaintiffs.

By 1974 Turner was a seasoned and highly successful prisoners' rights attorney, who, once assigned as lead counsel in *Ruiz,* would be seen by prison officials as an "eastern establishment do-gooder." Turner, although raised and educated in the north, was actually a native of Fort Worth. He completed his undergraduate degree at Northwestern and thereafter attended Harvard Law School, where he received his degree in 1963. After his graduation from law school, he received a Fulbright Scholarship and studied in Europe. In 1967 he joined the Inc. Fund and almost immediately became involved in prisoners' rights litigation.

The Inc. Fund was a nonprofit organization established in 1939 and headed by Thurgood Marshall to develop and pursue legal strategies on racial discrimination throughout the United States. Under the direction of Marshall, the Inc. Fund successfully litigated the *Brown* v. *Board of Education* case in 1954. It was one of Marshall's protégés, Jack Greenberg, who hired Turner. Under Greenberg's direction the Inc. Fund expanded beyond its desegregation efforts and moved into arenas such as prisons and jails. Through its engagement in civil rights litigation, the Inc. Fund had evolved into a powerful, nationally based organization with the financial backing and legal expertise to engage in long-term social reform litigation. With the interim appointment of Stanley Bass, the *Ruiz* plaintiffs had the organizational backing of both the Department of Justice and the Inc. Fund. With these substantial bases for operations, attorneys for the plaintiffs almost immediately began to expand the case.

In October 1974 the plaintiffs were given leave to file an amended complaint on behalf of David Ruiz and his coplaintiffs.[39] To avoid a trial before a jury, the amended petition did not seek any money damages. Judge Justice would be the sole trier of fact. The plaintiffs also moved to have the suit certified as a class action to include all fifteen prisons of the Texas system, rather than just those located in Justice's Eastern District.

Within a month after Bass filed the amended complaint, Turner had returned from his sabbatical and was appointed as counsel of record. The first court hearing in the case was in December 1974, at which time Justice severed all damage claims and granted the Department of Justice's motion to intervene in the case. Within a matter of days after the hearing, Justice issued an order certifying the suit as a class action. What had started out as a single handwritten petition was within a thirty-day period expanded to a major class-action conditions suit in which a fleet of Justice Department and Inc. Fund attorneys were seeking broadscale relief for all fifteen thousand prisoners in the Texas prison system. The state complained that "eight prisoner-petitioners in the Eastern District is a far cry from the present posture of the case wherein the court has allowed amended pleadings by the plaintiffs which have expanded the scope of the action into a major class action."[40]

From this point forward the attorneys, the court, and TDC officials would engage in a bitter struggle to protect their respective interests. Within the first six months the state would mount a major effort to remove the Department of Justice from the case, while at the same time defending a major contempt motion brought by Turner, charging TDC officials with subjecting the *Ruiz* plaintiffs to "threats, intimidation, coercion, punishment and discrimination."[41] These first two legal skirmishes were clear victories for the plaintiffs and marked the beginning of a pattern of denial of wrongdoing by prison officials, coupled with rhetoric intended to shift the blame to a federal judge who was said to be biased and overindulgent of "pathologically maladapted inmates" and their attorneys.[42]

State's Attorneys Charge Justice with Flagrant Abuse of Judicial Power

In December 1974, after Judge Justice expanded the case to include all TDC prisons, the state attorney general's office began to centralize responsibility for the case. On February 10, 1975, a hearing on pending motions in the case was held at which Justice denied the state's motion to dismiss the United States as plaintiff-intervenors, as well as their motion to stay the *Ruiz* proceedings pending the outcome of *Lamar* v. *Coffield*, a class-action racial discrimination suit against prison officials in which the United States had also intervened. The following day, the division chief for civil rights cases briefed the attorney general, John Hill, on the hearing and requested that formal responsibility for the case be assigned to a senior assistant attorney general.

Even though the case was still in its formative stages, the attorney general's office was already "thoroughly disgusted" with how Judge Justice was handling the case. Ed Idar, who would repeatedly complain of Justice's biases in favor of the plaintiffs over the next eight years, was officially designated as lead counsel for the case. He was given an assistant on an as-needed basis. While Idar and his assistant were to continue their other duties, they were instructed to give the case high priority. Neither Idar nor his assistant had much special expertise in prison conditions cases at the time. Over the next several years, however, there would be ample opportunity to refine their skills.

When Ed Idar joined the attorney general's staff in October 1973, at the age of fifty-three, he was one of the more experienced staff attorneys in a division overrun with recent law school graduates, who traditionally used the attorney general's office as a training ground for private practice. In later years, the *Ruiz* trial team would be composed almost exclusively of recent law graduates with no prisoners' rights litigation experience and limited, if any, trial experience. At least four of the nine members of the

trial team had virtually no courtroom experience when the *Ruiz* trial commenced in October 1978. Three of these were admitted to the state bar
after the trial began.

Idar began to practice law at age thirty-six after graduating from the
University of Texas Law School in 1956. He was born and raised in
Laredo, Texas, and after graduation returned to his native city to open his
own practice. After less than two years in Laredo, he closed his office
and joined a small firm in McAllen, Texas, where he remained until 1962.
In 1962 he left the McAllen firm to open an office in San Angelo, Texas.
In 1966, while still engaged in private practice in San Angelo, he worked
part time for the Office of Economic Opportunity as an inspector of
federal programs. In 1968 he closed his practice and went to work full
time as an OEO inspector. In 1970 Idar joined the Mexican American
Defense and Educational Fund (MALDEF) and was assigned to the San
Antonio office, where he worked with a team of attorneys litigating a
Texas legislative redistricting plan.[43] These reapportionment cases were
heard by a three-judge federal district court, which included William
Wayne Justice.

Idar left the MALDEF office in 1973, due in part to a disagreement
over the type of litigation taken on by the office. One of these disagree-
ments centered around Idar's refusal to pursue prisoners' rights litigation
on behalf of Mexican Americans incarcerated in TDC prisons. After he
joined the attorney general's office, his primary caseload consisted of
defending the state in prisoners' rights cases. In one such case, *Lamar* v.
Coffield, he became acquainted with the same Justice Department attorneys who would later represent the plaintiffs in *Ruiz*. Either because of
Idar's "somewhat abrasive" nature,[45] or because of the actions of the
"unreasonable people"[46] who made up the Justice Department's litigation
team, animosity quickly developed between attorneys for the state and the
plaintiffs. These strained relations influenced legal strategies throughout
the trial. At one point during the discovery process, long before the trial
of the case, Judge Justice convened a meeting with the *Ruiz* attorneys to
address his concern over the "increasingly bitter correspondence exchanged between counsel in this case."[47] While Justice's efforts may
have had a temporary calming effect, they certainly fell short of producing a lasting peace.[48]

Charges of inappropriate behavior were not restricted to the exchange
of letters between attorneys. Within ten days after the February 10 hearing, the state filed a petition to the Fifth Circuit Court of Appeals contending that Judge Justice had abused his discretion by permitting the United
States to intervene in *Ruiz* and by allowing their participation as *amicus
curiae* with full rights of a party to the litigation. The petition charged that
Judge Justice had violated fundamental principles involving federal-state
relations by allowing "the U.S. to rampage through the Texas prison sys-

tem in the hope of finding unconstitutional activities." It was this type of rhetoric, characterized by Turner in his response to the petition as "inflammatory and quite silly," that state attorneys used to divert attention from agency practices even in the face of reports such as those produced by the legislature's Joint Committee on Prison Reform.

In the same month in which the state filed its petition seeking to oust the United States from the case, an Austin newspaper reported testimony from various members of the Joint Committee on the claims brought by the prisoners in the lawsuit.[49] One committee member testified that "the unconstitutional practices alleged in [the] federal suit pending against the TDC have largely been substantiated already by the legislature's own Joint Committee on Prison Reform." A Dallas news article had earlier suggested legislative action could "reduce the severity of any [court] decision by showing that it is making a goodfaith effort to improve weaknesses in the prison system."[50] However, this same article also noted that with the exception of an admission that TDC could upgrade medical services, all other charges were categorically denied by prison officials.

The state's petition was full of trenchant language directed at Judge Justice and left no doubt that the state would vigorously contest his intervention in the affairs of the prison system. It charged that Justice had "flagrantly abused" his judicial power by acting as an "investigator and prosecutor of state institutions." In asking the circuit court to order Justice to "refrain from any further attempts to conduct on its own motion investigation into the activities of state institutions," the petition asserted that Justice's actions thus far were such that "a grosser misuse of judicial power cannot be imagined."

In response, Turner outlined the "practical effect of participation by the U.S." and argued that their ouster would "preclude inquiry into [TDC's] questionable prison conditions and hide these conditions from judicial scrutiny." From Turner's vantage point, the Justice Department was not "rampaging" through the Texas prison system, as attorneys for the prison system contended, but simply gathering evidence in the same manner as Turner would if he had the resources. Turner had accepted the court's appointment on an uncompensated basis without available funding for costs and expenses in litigating the case. He asserted that attorneys for the State of Texas were attempting to overreach his available manpower by scheduling depositions in Denver, Austin, Chicago, New York, Maryland, San Antonio, and Washington, D.C., so that at least three attorneys would be needed. In summary, Turner felt the financial burden of representing TDC prisoners in *Ruiz* would be enormous and next to impossible without the intervention of the United States.

On July 24, 1975, the Fifth Circuit Court denied the state's application to prohibit the intervention of the United States in the case. Two of the three judges on the circuit panel issued written opinions. Judge Tuttle, who had by now become very familiar with TDC litigation, rejected the state's argument that the participation of the United States would result in burdensome and expensive discovery. According to Tuttle, Justice Department's "rampaging" was "no more than the full and vigorous discovery that a large, systemwide class action anticipates." Turner's contention that he had the "identical right, though possibly not the same means and manpower," to gather evidence as the United States was attempting to do through discovery, was also affirmed.

After the Fifth Circuit ruling, the state filed a petition for writ of *certiorari* to the Supreme Court.[51] This request fell one vote short of the four votes necessary for a hearing. In a somewhat unusual departure for denial of *cert,* the three justices who voted in the state's favor issued a written dissent.[52] The dissent, authored by Justice Rehnquist, supported through implication the state's position that Justice had violated the "delicate area of federal-state relations" by [pitting] the U.S., as a virtually involuntary coplaintiff, alongside the inmate plaintiffs and against correctional officials. Rehnquist characterized the course of the litigation up to the time of appeal as "really extraordinary" and thereby justified the state's attempt at "forestalling the intrusion of the federal judiciary."

Even though the state had exhausted all avenues of appeal and lost in their attempt to oust the Justice Department, the narrow denial of *cert* provided some air of legitimacy to their claim that Judge Justice was overreaching his authority. However, this air of legitimacy was soon tainted by the actions of certain TDC officials who in May 1975 became the subject of a contempt proceeding that was initiated by the plaintiffs exactly two months after the state petitioned the Fifth Circuit to deny the intervention of the United States.

Plaintiffs Charge Prison Officials with Campaign of Retaliation and Harassment

The contempt motion filed by Turner on April 28, 1975, set the stage for the first hearing in *Ruiz* at which live testimony was taken from both inmates and TDC officials. Turner charged that TDC officials had engaged in a campaign of retaliation, punishment, and harassment against David Ruiz and Ernesto Montana (two of the named plaintiffs in the class-action suit) as well as others for their participation in the litigation.[53] The hearing in turn prompted the state's second trip to the Fifth Circuit to appeal a Judge Justice ruling. In contrast to the state's credible appeal of Justice's procedural ruling on intervention by the United States, the next trip to the circuit court reflected an obvious lapse in legal judgment on the part of the attorney general's office, which resulted in a totally uncontested factual record of harassment and intimidation by TDC officials of the plaintiff-prisoners and their attorneys.

Two months after the order of consolidation, prison officials entered into a consent order allowing confidential communication, by mail and in person, between Inc. Fund attorneys and the named *Ruiz* plaintiffs. In addition, the consent order restrained TDC officials from taking any retaliatory actions against the plaintiff-prisoners. This order was not precipitated by any hearings or even any formal allegations of retaliation. Approximately six months later, a second protective order was agreed to, in which the named plaintiffs were to have access to law libraries, receipt of legal mail, reasonable cell searches, and possession of certain legal materials in their cells. This second order was precipitated by Turner's recurring complaints that officials at the Ramsey I prison, where David Ruiz and Ernesto Montana were confined, were interfering with case-related activities.

At the time these two protective orders were entered, the Ramsey I prison officials were already embroiled in a struggle with another activist attorney, Janet Stockard, in *Ward* v. *Estelle*. At the center of Turner's contempt motion were Warden James V. Anderson and Assistant Warden David Christian, both of whom were also the subject of numerous harassment allegations made by Stockard. The first of the two *Ruiz* protective orders came just one month after a similar, though more controversial, order had been issued in *Ward* v. *Estelle*. The *Ruiz* order, just as the one entered in *Ward,* simply served to single out the *Ruiz* plaintiffs to be "treated as a special class of inmates" by the Ramsey officials.[54]

Confronted with court orders governing the treatment of inmates, prison officials reacted with something less than full compliance with either the spirit or the letter of the orders. Turner's contempt motion charged that Warden Anderson failed to even advise his staff of the June order and that central administration officials failed to give Anderson notice of the January 20 order until February 12. In addition, it was charged that when Ruiz and Montana returned to Ramsey after the December 1974 hearing granting the United States's motion to intervene, they were deprived of their underwear, shoes, hygiene supplies, and legal materials. Thereafter, Turner claimed, they were placed in segregation, where they were triple-celled in two-man cells while adjacent cell vacancies existed. It was alleged that they were repeatedly placed in solitary confinement where they could not communicate with counsel. When not in solitary, they were forced to go to the law library at early morning hours, where they were locked in a small adjoining room without access to law library materials. Finally, it was charged that following and preceding their trips to the law library, Ruiz and Montana were subjected to strip searches, including digital rectal exams, not used in similar situations on other Ramsey prisoners.

Beginning on May 22, 1975, testimony was taken over a two day period from ten inmates, including three of the named plaintiffs, and

seven officials and officers from the Ramsey staff. Montana, the first inmate to testify, provided highly detailed testimony on actions by prison
officials that seemed intended to impede, punish, and discourage him
from litigation activities. Included was his account of an incident wherein
an officer sprayed him with Mace because he had questioned a guard
about some legal mail he had received. Typical of the allegations suggesting that TDC officials had an almost obsessive concern with writ-writer
activity was Montana's testimony regarding an interchange he had with
assistant warden Christian over the possession of a "law book":

Q. [Turner] Was there any discussion about law books?

A. [Montana] Yes sir. I was going to the writ room during the
time, and I had brought down a law book that wasn't classified as a
law book by Sgt. Robertson. I had told him that I had four law
books of my own in the cell and I showed it to him, and I asked
him if he would please take a look at it to see whether he would
classify it as a law book and he [assistant warden Christian] said,
"Well, I don't consider this a lawbook." I was permitted to take it
to my cell, and Mr. Christian, when he found it, just because it
had something on prisons on the front, asked me what it was
about, and I told him, "Well, I haven't read the book," but I had
just glanced through it, and I told him, "It's on the penology field."
And he said, "Well, it talks about prison doesn't it?" And I said,
"Yes, sir." He [Assistant Warden Christian] said, "Well, it's a law
book."

Montana was charged with possession of contraband, taken before a disciplinary committee chaired by Christian, and placed in solitary confinement for possession of the book.

David Ruiz was the second prisoner to testify and, like Montana, gave
highly specific testimony. Ruiz related an instance of being gassed by a
unit official (Assistant Warden Christian) while securely locked in his
segregation cell. The gassing occurred when Ruiz refused to allow a correctional officer to read a letter he had written to the Joint Committee on
Prison Reform. He further testified that he had been subjected to
numerous rectal searches when going to and from the unit's law library.
Ruiz corroborated much of Montana's testimony regarding loss of
property such as underwear, shoes, and hygiene articles, triple-celling
when vacant cells were available, placement in solitary confinement, and
being forced to go to the law library at odd hours.

The third named plaintiff to testify, O.D. Johnson, claimed that
officials at the Coffield Unit had searched his cell and destroyed some of
his property. When he attempted to lodge a complaint with one of the

officers, he was threatened. In a subsequent interview with the unit warden, Don Costilow, who was later removed as warden for willful violations of *Ruiz* court orders, Johnson claimed he was told, "It was nothing and that his officers wouldn't do anything to harm him."

On December 30, 1975, Judge Justice issued his factual findings, along with a detailed set of orders granting substantial relief to the prisoners. In the opening paragraphs of the order, Judge Justice complained of the difficulty of "ascertaining the truth of the plaintiff's allegations without adequate outside investigation." This obvious reference to the state's motion seeking to prevent intervention by the United States reflected Justice's belief that their participation was necessary in order to investigate allegations such as those made in Turner's contempt motion, to say nothing of the more complicated issues raised in the class-action suit itself. While Justice may have had difficulty in weighing the evidence, he eventually came down on the side of those making the allegations of harassment and intimidation.

He found that Ramsey officials had deprived the plaintiffs of their underwear in December 1974 and that the official policy justifying this action was not adopted until a week before the contempt hearing. Similarly, he found that a policy permitting removal of the plaintiff's shoes in December was not formalized until the following April, again just before the contempt hearings. In addition, he found that the policy had been applied unevenly, in that non-*Ruiz* prisoners were allowed to keep their shoes. Regarding the triple-celling of Ruiz and Montana, Justice found this was done even though there were nearby vacancies. Justice felt that the evidence confirmed that both Ruiz and Montana had been subjected to repeated cell searches, at which time their correspondence with the Department of Justice and the Joint Committee on Prison Reform had been seized; the prisoners thereafter were placed in solitary where they could not communicate with their attorneys. Likewise, the charges of arbitrary rectal searches, the gassing of both Ruiz and Montana, and their required trips to the law library, where they were locked in a small adjoining room with no access to the library law books, were all confirmed.

Justice concluded his findings with a thirty-point set of orders regarding the handling of legal correspondence, the use of the law library, possession of legal materials, cell searches, rectal searches, the use of gas (Mace), triple-celling, possession of personal property items, and conditions and placement proceedings for solitary confinement.[55] Given the highly damaging factual findings entered by Justice, which supported virtually all the allegations made by Turner and his clients, and the resulting broadscale and specific relief ordered in this first hearing on specific prisoner allegations, a vigorous appeal was in all likelihood anticipated by the court and the parties to the litigation. Instead, the state appealed only two of the more than thirty specific remedial orders and did not attack any of the damaging factual findings in its seven-page brief.[56]

On April 7, 1972, the Fifth Circuit later issued a one-page *per curiam* decision affirming Justice's orders. The circuit court was careful to note that "a review of the record (which was undisputed by TDC) reveals that as a result of their instigation of and participation in this litigation, these named plaintiffs have been subjected during its pendency to threats, intimidation, coercion, punishment and discrimination."[57] Judge Justice would cite this case in future orders, as would the plaintiffs when seeking further protective orders.

With the December 30 order, TDC was now subject to three separate witness protection orders, all issued within an eighteen-month period.[58] The second and third orders were generated by violations of the first. This self-perpetuating series of witness protection orders was to continue into 1976 due to further violations by the Ramsey administration. Less than five months after the December order, Turner filed yet another motion charging that at least four of the *Ruiz* witnesses had repeatedly been subjected to invalid disciplinary proceedings resulting in long-term confinement in solitary.[59] For example, Ernesto Montana had on four different occasions been charged with refusal to work while he was confined to administrative segregation, even though such inmates were not allowed out of their cells for work. TDC was also charged with repeatedly locking Montana in a small room next to the law library, in clear violation of the December 30 order.

Another prisoner was placed in solitary confinement without lighting when an officer allegedly demanded to read his legal mail and the prisoner refused.[60] Ramsey officials were charged with continuing their improper censoring of legal correspondence, as well as their refusal to deliver legal mail to prisoners in solitary confinement. Turner further claimed that some of the *Ruiz* prisoners were forced to remain in the law library for the full two hours, even though they had gone to the library only to receive their legal mail. Finally, Turner charged that virtually all disciplinary proceedings involving the *Ruiz* witnesses ended in periods of solitary confinement, while lesser punishments were never imposed.

On July 15, Judge Justice once again convened a hearing on alleged violations of his orders. At the beginning of the hearing, the parties advised Judge Justice that they had entered into a fourth witness protection agreement. TDC officials agreed to expunge many of the disciplinary actions taken against Montana, Ruiz, and others, all of which had been initiated after the December 30 order. They further agreed to provide lighting in solitary confinement during normal daylight hours as well as to deliver legal correspondence to prisoners confined to solitary. TDC also agreed to reprimand the officer or officers responsible for locking Montana in the small room next to the law library. Estelle issued the written reprimand to assistant warden Christian. He also reprimanded himself for his failure to make clear all the provisions of the December order.[61]

While the December 30 order clearly prohibited the practice of locking Montana in a separate room without written certification from Estelle,[62] the letter of reprimand all but exonerated Christian from any wrongdoing: "In regards to what appears to be a violation of this provision regarding inmate Montana, I am pleased that you have already made the correction. You and I both had a shared responsibility in this matter and, while I realize there was no more intent on your part than mine to violate any of the court's Order, I know we will renew efforts to see that such violation does not occur again. Consider us both reprimanded by this document. /s/ W. J. Estelle, Jr."[63]

Even though the parties had resolved a number of the issues with the fourth agreement, Judge Justice allowed two days of testimony on the remaining charges. Testimony was taken from six *Ruiz* prisoners and six Ramsey officials, including warden Anderson and warden Christian. For the first time in a *Ruiz* hearing, TDC also called prisoners to testify in their behalf. Of the five prisoners called, four were building tenders, all of whom were reluctant to admit that fact during cross examination by Turner. They did, however, describe duties that were those typically performed by building tenders. They also each gave remarkably similar testimony supporting the Ramsey officials.[64]

The continuing animosity between the parties and the chronic nature of harassment was evident at the conclusion of the two-day hearing when TDC attorneys unwisely requested that Judge Justice instruct the six *Ruiz* prisoners to extend "courtesy and respect" to the TDC guards who would transport them back to prison. The request backfired when Turner suggested that if the guards wanted respect they should behave in a less denigrating manner.

> **Harry Walsh** [assistant attorney general]: Your Honor, one final request that has been relayed to us by the TDC. Our clients have asked if the court will remind the plaintiffs [attorneys] or ask the plaintiffs if they would treat the officers who are going to have to carry them back this evening with a certain amount of courtesy and respect.

> **Bill Turner:** I think that's an outrageous request, your Honor. I don't see any basis for it. There's certainly no evidentiary basis for it, but I have no objection to it if the court would equally admonish the officers to treat the prisoners with the same amount of respect.

> **Judge Justice:** Well, that's what I was going to suggest. Bring the guards in, and I'm going to admonish both sides to show courtesy and respect to the other.

Bill Turner: Your Honor, my clients have advised me that on the way up here they were handcuffed together the entire trip from the units to the courthouse in a way that's never been done before that is very uncomfortable, and they believe it is a form of harassment for being brought to this court. They have gone to other hearings, and this has never been done before.

Judge Justice: I'm going to leave it to the attorneys and to the officials of TDC to see that the prisoners are transported in the ordinary way, unless there is some justification, and if so, bring it to the attention of the court.[65]

Whether lawyers for the prison officials believed the allegations of harassment is not clear. However, by July 1976 the Ramsey prison officials had been the subject of three court hearings at which evidence clearly established repeated violations of protective orders. Moreover, it was clear that this self-perpetuating cycle of order-violations-order had the effect of increasing the level of judicial scrutiny early in the case. The state's reluctance to appeal factual findings, coupled with their agreement to additional orders, reflected more than a modicum of culpability by TDC officials. Nevertheless, the only disciplinary action initiated was done so at the insistence of the plaintiffs' attorneys. Even this resulted in no more than a nominal letter of reprimand. Rather than having subjected themselves to disciplinary action by repeatedly and willfully violating *Ruiz* orders, Warden Anderson and Assistant Warden Christian if anything enhanced their standing with Estelle, as both were promoted within twelve months of the July hearing. Anderson was promoted to assistant director and named warden of the year. Christian was promoted to warden of the Retrieve Unit, where he would be the subject of repeated accusations of brutality in the years to come.

Emergence of the State's Legal Strategy

When the July 1976 hearing concluded, Judge Justice asked that the attorneys try to resolve among themselves numerous pending discovery motions such as the appointment of experts to conduct inspections of TDC facilities. The state's two appeals to the Fifth Circuit on intervention and the December 30, 1975, protective order had caused substantial delays in preparing the case for trial. Judge Justice was becoming increasingly concerned about the delays and the number of hearings he was having to conduct on procedural matters. By July 1976 it had been almost two years since the case was consolidated and certified a class action and four years since the original petition was filed, yet the case was nowhere near to a trial setting.

Nevertheless, the state continued to file procedural motions that resulted in repeated delays and hearings right up to the time of trial. Discovery by the Department of Justice had been delayed for approximately one year, pending the Fifth Circuit Court's decision on the intervention issue. Shortly after the circuit ruling, the Justice Department attorneys renewed their request to inspect all TDC facilities. The TDC attorneys immediately filed objections to any such inspections and attempted to limit the scope of the inspections as well as access to prison personnel. Less than a month later, however, the state entered into an agreement with the United States that allowed experts for the plaintiffs to inspect prison facilities in the areas of medicine, industrial hygiene, industrial and safety engineering, sanitation, security, and nutrition. The agreement provided for joint inspections to be conducted by experts for both sides.

While these inspections were conducted over the next twelve months, the discovery process continued and was marked by a constant barrage of motions, objections, and periodic hearings. Since the plaintiffs had prevailed in the three major hearings before Judge Justice and the Fifth Circuit Court in 1975 and 1976, Turner filed a motion for an award of attorneys fees in November 1976, which was of course contested by the state. During the hearing on his motion, in December 1976, an interchange occurred between Judge Justice and Ed Idar that not only reflected the growing rancor between the Judge and the state's lead attorney but also illustrated the contentious and not always coordinated efforts of attorneys for the state.

Idar: Your Honor, before proceeding, I would indicate to the court, as Ms. Rivers [an assistant attorney general] indicated, we are not prepared to cross examine Mr. Turner [on attorneys fees] today. We will ask the court for leave to consider the matter and discuss it among ourselves, and take Mr. Turner's deposition, if we deem it proper.

Justice: Oh, now, I've indulged you gentlemen, the counsel for the State, to the maximum extent. I cannot believe that you were not aware that Mr. Turner was going to be here today and give testimony, and I cannot believe that you are not capable of crossexamining an attorney as to the amount of time that he has spent in relation to a case. Your motion is overruled. There's such a thing as going too far.

Idar: Can I have the record reflect our objection?

Justice: Yes, sir, you may have the record reflect, and I ask that you not indulge in these kind of objections. This is entirely out of bounds. You were given full notice that this hearing was going to be held.

Idar: Your Honor, I again except to the statement of the court that we received full and adequate notice. Please the court, I would like Ms. Rivers to simply dictate for the record what she was advised.

Justice: All right, and I will put my law clerk on as a witness to give her version of it also.

Ms. Rivers: Your Honor, I have no quarrel with the court or the law clerk of the nature of the notice we had. I am fully aware and was fully notified that we were going to have a hearing today on the issue of attorneys' fees.[66]

In February 1977 the plaintiffs and defendants began filing their inspection reports. The parties' respective experts on security filed reports that were in stark contrast to one another. These reports, more than any documents filed to this point in the litigation, clearly reflected the differing philosophical positions of the two sides.[67] The plaintiffs' expert, Arnold Pontesso, was a former director of corrections in Oklahoma and administrator for the Federal Bureau of Prisons. He began his report with the statement that TDC was "overcrowded, understaffed, and personnel were absorbed by custody and work production." In a section titled "Confinement Conditions," Pontesso likened TDC's "work ethic" approach to corrections, which had always been at the very core of TDC's style of management, to that of plantation slavery:

A visitor to the Texas prison for the first time comes away with many impressions, even if the visit was brief. Residents are orderly, cleanliness of both buildings and persons is evident, and food appears to be wholesome and plentiful. The most overpowering impression is the immense size of the facility and the well kept farms of thousands of acres. The venerable institution of slavery still exists in Texas with huge plantations operated by the State and made bountiful by the unpaid labor of thousands of convicted felons. One gets the strong feeling that the TDC exists not for the protection of society, not to punish offenders or deter others from committing crimes, not to rehabilitate criminals, but to perpetuate the plantation as the largest agri-business in the State.[68]

Ironically, the so-called work ethic that guided prison policy was never at issue in the pleadings of the case.

Pontesso went on to describe the field labor force, again in terms of his plantation analogy.

Prior to the 13th Amendment to the United States Constitution, slaves were transported to the fields in mule-drawn wagons. Today,

TDC inmates are transported in wagon trailers (with rubber tires) by tractors. One tractor will pull five or six of these trailers crammed with human cargo, followed and flanked by the high rider and his armed assistants. Staked out near the work site is the dog boy and his passel of hounds. The hounds are tracking dogs, not guard dogs, and the dog boy is an inmate. If the field hand escapes, the dog sergeant, assisted by a dog boy takes charge. Incidentally, the dogs are kept in the shade of a nearby tree, or if none is available, under a canvas shelter. Dogs are also given more space in a kennel than is usually alloted each inmate in a dormitory. How the field hands envy these pampered dogs!

Each squad of 20 or 30 inmates has an armed guard responsible for the custody of the group. The only supervision on the ground is provided by inmates. The leader and assistant leader of each squad are called "lead row" and "tail row." Theoretically the "tail row" sees that all men in the squad keep up with the "lead row" by assisting the laggards. In practice, it is my opinion, that the "tail row" is more of an enforcer than a helper.[69]

Fred Wilkinson, the state's expert on security, was also a former Federal Bureau of Prisons administrator. While he and Pontesso had toured together, Wilkinson's report was in many ways the antithesis of Pontesso's observations and conclusions. Wilkinson began his report with a statement that "the TDC is superior to other state systems in physical facilities, quality of personnel and operational programs." He made repeated references to TDC's highly favorable statistics on escapes, assaults, and prison homicides. He was very impressed with the agency's staff training program and the overall curriculum of the training academy.

Unlike Pontesso, Wilkinson found no evidence that building tenders were supervising other prisoners. He had interviewed building tenders at many of the fifteen prisons he inspected and concluded that "in no case did [building tenders] admit to nor was there any indication that they received special privileges or that they exercised supervision over inmates." Based on these interviews, he further concluded that "under no circumstances are they ever used to 'supervise' other inmates."

Like so many visitors before him, Wilkinson was most impressed with the "general appearance" of TDC prisons. He opined that "many experienced correctional officials feel that the general appearance from a standpoint of sanitation, cleanliness, and upkeep of an institution is indicative of its overall management and related thereto the general 'climate' of the inmate population. In 38 years of correctional experience at all levels, I have not seen any system or individual units that equal the level of cleanliness and presentability of the institutions in TDC."

The experts' inspection reports continued to stream in through mid-1977. As the exchange of massive amounts of evidentiary documents and information continued in preparation for trial, hearings became more frequent and were usually convened to resolve pending discovery matters. Attorneys for the state continued the pattern of vigorously filing objections, most often directed at the Justice Department attorneys, who were just as vigorously collecting reams of information from all fifteen prisons in Texas. The resentment toward the Justice Department's intervention in the case, along with the perception that the court was biased in favor of the plaintiffs, continued to build with each successive demand made by Justice Department attorneys. The resulting frustration quite often surfaced during the course of hearings on routine discovery issues.

Idar: Your Honor, the court gave the United States leave months ago to use FBI agents, to use paralegals, to use attorneys [to assist in its discovery efforts]. We objected strenuously. We were overruled. Two years ago they had all this authority, and here they come now and say it's going to take another three months before they will know what witnesses they are going to rely on. It's entirely unreasonable at this stage of the game, Your Honor, that we should be restricted to three months when they had over three years to prepare this case. I don't think they know yet what this case is all about.[70]

At an earlier hearing, attorneys presented arguments to Judge Justice regarding the state's discovery request for information from the Department of Justice on some two thousand alleged incidents of mistreatment of prisoners by TDC guards and officials. Contrary to Idar's hyperbolic assertion that the Justice Department attorneys did not "know yet what this case is all about," their discovery requests reflected a highly coordinated effort to gather evidence that would show systemic constitutional violations. Knowing that all of the two thousand allegations would not be offered into evidence by the United States, Justice queried Idar as to why the state wanted specific details on each one of the incidents. Idar's response provided an early glimpse into what was to become an argument that the defense would use until the close of trial:

Idar: [This] is a case in my humble opinion I think the United States is going to have the burden of showing a system-wide pattern and practice in regard to various issues it seeks to litigate. I do not think they will be able to prove up a case of cruel and unusual punishment, and that's what they are basing their case on and will have to—a few selected incidents that could occur over a given period of time.[71]

The state, relying on *Rizzo* v. *Goode* (a Supreme Court decision rendered in January 1976 that found that twenty incidents of police misconduct over a twelve-month period in a city of some three million inhabitants did not establish a pattern of misconduct), would contend that any misconduct proved up by the plaintiffs reflected nothing more than "isolated incidents" or "occasional abuses" rather than a systemwide "pattern or practice." Moreover, the state would argue that such incidents, when compared to the total number of prisoners in TDC, reflected no more than a level of abuse that "is genuinely inevitable in a state prison."[72] Finally, the state would argue that Judge Justice was powerless to remedy the alleged violations in that there was no "affirmative link" between the incidents and the director, wardens, and other administrators in the Texas prison system.

As the case began to move toward trial, the plaintiffs would continue to mount evidence that they would argue reflected a level of abuse far in excess of the "inevitable" and clearly linked to prison officials through knowledge, tolerance, encouragement, and participation. On January 6, 1978, Judge Justice set a trial date in early March. The state immediately filed a motion for continuance, which Justice granted; he reset the trial for six months later in September. He also advised that no further continuances would be granted. By this time the parties had been engaged in discovery for three years, had participated in numerous hearings before Justice, and had been to the Fifth Circuit Court of Appeals on three occasions. As a result, the case had developed into a lengthy and complex legal proceeding with a substantial procedural history. Not withstanding this complexity and the specialized knowledge that Judge Justice had built up, the State mounted one final effort at avoiding a trial before this jurist, whom they felt was irretrievably biased against their case.

On February 3, 1978, almost four years after Judge Justice had expanded the case to encompass all fifteen TDC prisons (thirteen of which were located in a judicial district other than his own), the state filed a motion for change of venue from the Eastern to the Southern District of Texas. This attempt to transfer the case from Justice's court was yet another legal manuever that backfired on the state when Justice granted the motion and the chief judge of the Southern District assigned Justice to hear the case in Houston.

The state argued that because the vast bulk of inmate witnesses were located in the thirteen prisons in the Southern District, the Houston location would minimize the logistical burdens of transportation. In addition, the jail facilities in Houston provided better security for the prisoners than the much smaller facility in Tyler. Finally, since the case was broadened to include all TDC prisoners in 1975, venue was more proper in the Southern District, where all but two of the prisons were located. This argument, which had obvious merit, gave rise to the question of why the state had waited for three years before attempting to get the location of the trial changed. During these years the complexity of the case had escalated to such an extent that assignment of a new judge would mean another substantial delay. This fact did not go unnoticed by the Justice Department attorneys, who, in their response to the state's motion, charged that "the defendants delayed the filing of their motion for years, filing it two months after the court had set a trial date, after the court granted their motion for continuance and on the eve of a pretrial conference." If the primary objective was to avoid a trial before Judge Justice, a tactical error may have been made some years earlier when the class-action proceedings were just getting under way. Had the state filed its motion immediately after class-action certification and before the complex procedural history had developed over a four-year period, assignment to a new judge in the Southern District would have been more likely.

Justice granted the change of venue on May 30, 1978. Three days later, then–chief judge of the Southern District, Reynaldo G. Garza, assigned Justice to the case, noting Justice's willingness to preside in the Southern District, and the fact that Justice had been "handling the case in the Eastern District for approximately four years." In view of the anticipated length of the trial, the complexity of the suit, the heavy docket in the Southern District at the time, and the authority of Justice to hear cases in the Southern District, Judge Garza's decision was anything but surprising.

Nevertheless, within the next month the state mounted one more effort to remove Justice from the case by attacking Judge Garza's order of assignment. In an unusual pleading to all the judges of the Southern District, attorneys for the state filed a motion to vacate Judge Garza's assignment and also asked for a hearing on the question of "whether the Honorable Judge Justice has not abused his judicial discretion in this cause and whether his impartiality may not be reasonably questioned." The motion further charged that Judge Justice agreed to the change of venue "only after he was satisfied that he would be designated to continue with the case." Finally, it was claimed that Judge Justice had issued discovery orders favoring the Department of Justice attorneys, such as improperly appointing experts for the plaintiffs who had been previously contacted by the state to perform research on overcrowding in TDC. Attorneys for the Justice Department countercharged that the state had "opposed, objected to, and curtailed discovery efforts at every opportunity." It was also noted that the state had refused to permit FBI agents to fully conduct criminal investigations and to photograph or measure typical TDC housing areas.

Within a week after the state's motion, chief judge Garza issued a memorandum and order in which he denied the state's motion "as being wholly without merit." He also warned the attorney general's office that "he [did] not need to be lectured by a Special Assistant Attorney General of the State of Texas on what his power, duties and responsibilities as Chief Judge are."[73] On the day Judge Garza's response was issued, Judge Justice moved the trial date from September to October 2, 1978.

When Judge Justice set the case for an October trial, it had been just over six years since David Ruiz had filed his original handwritten petition. The state's attorneys had been extremely successful at delaying the proceedings. However, these delays proved to be counterproductive when it eventually became necessary to defend the totality of conditions in the Texas prison system. Where the TYC had taken advantage of procedural delays in *Morales* v. *Turman* to improve dramatically the conditions of the state's youth facilities by depopulation, the delays in *Ruiz* had exactly the opposite effect. In 1972 the TDC prison population was approximately 15,000.[75] By the time of trial, the population was fast approaching 25,000 and would exceed 26,000 by the end of trial, with more than one thousand prisoners triple-celled in forty-five-square-foot cells, creating such crowded conditions that the third prisoner in a cell slept on the floor with his head next to a toilet. The overcrowding issue, which had arisen while the six-year procedural battle was waged by the state, would become the preeminent issue in the suit, and more than any other issue provided the basis for broadscale systemic relief to the TDC prisoners.

Chapter Five:
The Ruiz Trial Runs Its Course—
1978–79

Going into Justice's courtroom is like playing poker in a strange town without a clean deck.

W. J. Estelle, Jr.,
Speech before the Texas Associated Press Broadcasters,
February 20, 1982.

In the months just prior to trial, prison officials and their attorneys could claim only limited success. They had seen the *Ruiz* case grow from a single prisoner's petition to a systemwide class-action suit. They had been unable to prevent the intervention of the Department of Justice. They were confronted with a skilled civil rights attorney who was familiar with the Texas prison system and well schooled in prison conditions litigation. After repeated attempts, attorneys for the state had been unable to rid the case of a judge whom they perceived to be hopelessly biased. A factual record had begun to accumulate that was damaging to the their case. The state's only success had come through procedural delays. Ironically, these delays proved to be counterproductive in that while the case wound its way through a series of hearings and appeals a dramatic growth in the inmate population compounded administrative difficulties and complicated the defense of existing conditions.

Regardless of these setbacks, prison officials remained firm in their belief that they had much to be proud of. Their primary responsibility was to the public, and as they saw it, the public in Texas asked only that offenders be held securely and that they work to defray the cost of their incarceration. It was widely acknowledged that TDC accomplished these tasks, perhaps better than any prison system in the country. Homicide, suicide, and escape rates were low compared to most other large prison systems. Units were clean and orderly, and the Texas system had remained relatively free from the type of collective violence that had received so much publicity in California and New York. While no claim was made for an extensive set of "rehabilitation" programs, officials could point with pride to the fully accredited Windham School District. This program, initiated during the administration of George Beto, had developed into one of the most comprehensive correctional educational programs in the country.[1] Thus, when Judge Justice set the case for an October trial date, prison officials and their attorneys continued to express confidence that TDC's overall record was strong enough to prevail against any charge that the alleged shortcomings were the result of systemic pattern and practice.

Last-Minute Attempts to Settle

On June 16, 1978, about a month before the October trial date was set, Justice Department attorneys attempted to initiate settlement discussions. They suggested certain issues, such as work conditions and sanitation, as the most likely candidates for firm settlement proposals. Attorneys for the state viewed working conditions and sanitation as among TDC's strongest issues. They felt further that settlement of these issues would result in an unbalanced picture of the system when the more difficult issues were tried.[2] In addition, state and prison officials continued to resent any intrusion by the Justice Department and thus were in no mood to be accommodating. Whatever the reasons, Idar summarily dismissed the settlement overture, claiming that the Texas prison system was free of any substantial systemic constitutional violations.

In the week following Idar's refusal to engage in settlement negotiations, the United States and the attorneys for the plaintiffs filed a joint motion for the appointment of a special master to conduct and direct pretrial settlement discussions. This strategy broke down when the parties could not agree on any mutually acceptable candidates. One final attempt to get settlement negotiations started was made in a pretrial conference the week before trial. Once again, however, the state's attorneys felt that plaintiffs and the United States wanted to dispose of issues on which they were weak before discussing those that the attorney general's office would find difficult to defend.[3] As a result, this last-minute settlement attempt was at best perfunctory.

The *Ruiz* v. *Estelle* Trial Begins

On October 2, 1978, the trial began. A small demonstration was held outside the federal building in Houston with some twenty-five demonstrators carrying signs reading "Prisons are Concentration Camps for the Poor," "Brutality Does Not Rehabilitate," "W. J. Estelle is a Slave Master."[4] Inside the courtroom Judge Justice announced the case and asked if the named plaintiffs and the plaintiff-intervenor were ready to proceed. William Bennett Turner for the plaintiffs and David Vanderhoof for the United States responded that they were. When Justice turned to the defense, Ed Idar replied, "Could I address the court on that matter?" Idar went on to state that the defense would be happy to proceed if they could be assured of an additional sixty or ninety days to prepare once the plaintiffs and the United States rested. Now that the case was finally under way, after more than four years of legal maneuvering, Judge Justice was not about to grant this request. Nor was Ed Idar ready to give in.

> **The Court:** Mr. Idar, make an announcement. Are you ready or not ready to proceed.
>
> **Mr. Idar:** I am not ready, Your Honor, under the record before this court.
>
> **The Court:** All right, the court concludes that you have adequate opportunity to be prepared, and if you are not prepared, it is not through any fault of the court.[5]

After this rather rocky beginning, Justice asked for opening statements. Before the plaintiffs could begin, Idar broke in to restate motions entered a week earlier concerning the admission of evidence from the Joint Committee on Prison Reform. In addition, he expressed concern over the number of attorneys that would be able to cross-examine witnesses. Since there would be as many as three attorneys for the plaintiffs conducting cross-examinations, Idar felt it only fair that the state be granted the right to use more than one.

> **The Court:** I have no objection to more than one person conducting examination. However, there should not be more than one attorney representing the State cross-examine any one witness.
>
> **Mr. Idar:** Well, that's my point, Your Honor. The other side is going to have three people that will be examining . . . .
>
> **The Court:** Mr. Idar, I have made my ruling. I ask that you respect it.[6]

These initial interruptions and irritated responses were not the first less-than-cordial exchanges between Ed Idar and Judge Justice, nor would they be the last. Relations between the judge and attorneys for the state would reach a point during the trial when direct accusations of bias would be made, cross-examinations would be terminated, and contempt of court would be threatened.[7]

When the opening statements were finally heard, William Bennett Turner began by summarizing the plaintiffs' case, which would attack the totality of conditions in the Texas prison system.[8] The case would be organized into five clusters of issues. These clusters encompassed virtually all aspects of prison life in Texas.

- *Physical security and the right of inmates to be free from assault and the fear of assault:* Turner stated that the plaintiffs would show that TDC had a staff-to-inmate ratio less than one-half of the national average. Because of this, officers relied, to an unnecessary degree, on physical force and fear to maintain order. In addition, and contrary to state law, TDC utilized "building tenders" in positions of authority. Since the existence of the building tender system was illegal, prison officials denied its very existence. Nevertheless, Turner suggested that his evidence would show what the building tenders' special privileges were, as well as the inevitable abuses that accompanied their power. He promised to produce testimony about assaults by building tenders, including the rape at knifepoint of one of his witnesses.

- *Living and working conditions:* The prisons in Texas, Turner asserted, were confronted by "unspeakable overcrowding of stacking a lot of these prisoners wherever they'll fit." This crowded condition, it was charged, contributed to and was made worse by unhealthy, unsanitary living conditions and unsafe working conditions.

- *Medical care:* Turner charged that TDC facilities were substandard, that there were too few trained personnel, and that inmates were used to perform many medical services, ranging from the dispensing of drugs to taking X-rays and performing minor surgery. The evidence would reveal, Turner asserted, "inadequate care, needless injuries, careless administration of potent and debilitating drugs like Thorazine." The plaintiffs would also offer evidence of "deliberate indifference by security staff to the medical problems of prisoners, for example forcing them to work when they're medically unable to do so."

- *Summary punishments:* In addition to evidence related to unofficial beatings, Turner promised to reveal an official system of punishments involving solitary confinement and the deprivation of good time that was guided by vague rules and illegal procedures.

- *Access to courts:* TDC officials would be charged with interfering with the inmates' right to obtain an attorney, with attorney-client confidential correspondence, and with prisoner efforts at self-help. This interference, it was asserted, often took the form of punishment both "subtle and not so subtle, for prisoners who resort to the legal system as a means of complaining about mistreatment."

Having outlined his clients' case, Turner promised to keep his presentation short by calling only about two dozen witnesses to illustrate the general patterns described. He would rely on the Justice Department and its resources for systemwide patterns that affected these issues. When all the evidence was in, he felt the court would conclude "that while corrections in Texas may be cheap in some senses, the System exacts intolerable costs to the human rights of the citizens in its custody and its unlawful practices must be remedied."

David Vanderhoof for the Justice Department was the next to speak. The United States had been called into the case by Judge Justice as *amicus curiae* to thoroughly investigate the allegations made by the plaintiffs. Not surprisingly, Vanderhoof announced that the investigations had been conducted and that the allegations had been found to be meritorious. The presentation by the plaintiff-intervenors would be organized the same as that outlined by Turner. Approximately twenty experts would be called to the stand, along with more than one hundred additional witnesses drawn from the inmate population and former employees.

Less predictable was the parallel that Vanderhoof went on to draw between current prison conditions and those noted by an investigating committee in 1924. Repeatedly, Vanderhoof read excerpts from the 1924 investigation and suggested that few improvements had been made during the fifty-four intervening years. This charge was in stark contrast to two publications produced by TDC in the four years preceding trial that detailed reasons for the widely heralded claim that the Texas prison system had risen from one of the worst to one of the best in the country during this same time. Thus, if taken seriously, Vanderhoof's comments must have left prison officials incredulous and firm in their belief that the Justice Department investigations were biased and seriously flawed.

Whatever the response, Vanderhoof went on to read from a number of TDC incident reports that he believed illustrated systemic problems, which he promised to document further over the course of the trial. These related to the use of inmates in positions of authority, the abusive use of force by TDC personnel, the insensitive treatment of inmates with special needs, and the concern for operating the prison system at a profit, regardless of the "cost to human suffering." He closed his statement with a personal note: "I have a very good friend in Virginia. He's a uniformed officer. He has the responsibility of supervising his charges. He has more training than many of the TDC guards. His charges are permitted daily exercise. His charges are housed in an area greater than many prisoners. In fact, in some places in Texas we have three prisoners housed in a space less than the size of this table that counsel is sitting at, but my friend's charges are housed in greater space. He is an animal warden, a dog catcher in Fairfax, Virginia."

Where Vanderhoof ended with a personal statement, Ed Idar began with one. Conditions in TDC were not close to those he had seen in 1954 as a member of a team set up to study conditions among illegal immigrants along the Texas border near El Paso. Nor were they as bad as those he had encountered in World War II.

> I think that I have a frame of reference about experience in human affairs that goes way beyond that of opposing counsel. I can weigh what I see from a frame of reference that goes back to World War II to the conditions that we served then in troop ships, to the conditions that we trained under where I trained in a camp for medical basic training in hutments that had been condemned for general prisoners of war. I have seen conditions in TDC, despite what opposing counsel says, that are far superior to what I was required to submit to as a Serviceman for this country. I cannot be as easily shocked, consequently, because of some of the things that may go on in TDC.

From this personal recollection Idar argued that prison conditions in Texas failed to reach a level that would shock the public conscience and therefore were not in this sense cruel and unusual. Nor were the acknowledged problems the result of deliberate indifference. Contrary to claims made in Vanderhoof's opening statement, substantial improvements had been made in the conditions of confinement during the administrations of Ellis, Beto, and Estelle. Idar argued that problems among inmates and staff were "isolated instances" and not part of a pattern and practice condoned or encouraged by prison officials. Persons running the prisons were doing a commendable job in the face of very difficult circumstances.

By the time of trial, there had been substantial discussion around "some real philosophical differences as to what a prison system should do or should be." Comparisons would show, Idar argued, that TDC's work ethic coupled with strict discipline guaranteed the health and safety of the inmate population to a far greater extent than systems, such as California's, where the atmosphere was thought to be more "relaxed." Prison officials were well aware of the shortcomings in medical care. They knew they needed a new hospital. In fact, Idar pointed out, it was TDC officials who had asked the Texas Hospital Association for an evaluation in 1968 and 1969. In subsequent years, TDC officials had gone repeatedly to the legislature "seeking funds for a new hospital for a better medical facility, and we hope to show that the last Legislature at long last did appropriate funds for the creation of a special facility at the John Sealy Hospital in Galveston."

In addition to the acknowledged shortcomings in medical care, the problems inherent in a rapidly expanding inmate population were the second set of issues that prison officials recognized. As with medical care, the defense would argue that substantial efforts were being made to deal with these problems. New units were planned. The tension producing influence of crowded conditions was being dealt with, Idar argued, by having inmates work in the fields or participate in other educational, vocational, and industrial activities. The point was that inmates were not spending all their time in crowded cells and therefore "the totality of circumstances under which people in TDC have to serve their time" did not involve constitutional violations.

In closing, Idar made reference to Judge Justice's experience with the Texas Youth Commission and expressed the hope that this experience would not bias his opinion when evaluating the nature of conditions in the Texas Department of Corrections. Indeed, Idar suggested, "Your Honor, I think the evidence is going to show that Mr. Ruiz, Mr. Johnson, and Mr. Hilliard [plaintiffs present in the courtroom], these people who are so concerned about due process, but did not accord their victims due process, are far safer in TDC than they are walking in the barrios of San Antonio and Houston or Dallas."

After quieting the laughter that accompanied this closing comparison and ordering that anyone who did not remain quiet be ejected from the courtroom, Judge Justice called for the first witness. Before the first witness was called, the plaintiffs entered nearly one hundred exhibits, most of which were objected to by attorneys for the state, objections that were, with few exceptions, overruled.

The Plaintiffs' Case in Chief

Finally, during the afternoon of October 2, some eight years after David Ruiz had filed his original handwritten petition, the first of thirty-four witnesses called to the stand by lawyers for the plaintiffs began his testimony. The first to testify was Lawrence Pope, a sixty-year-old inmate who had been in the Texas Department of Corrections since March 1970. Virtually from the day he arrived Pope was identified as a "writ-writer" and therefore an inmate to watch. He had been one of the inmates affected when George Beto segregated the clients of Frances Jalet in 1971 to form what became known as the "eight-hoe squad." As a member of this group of writ-writers, Pope was well versed in the history of conditions litigation directed against TDC and had himself filed numerous cases. On the first day of trial he proved to be an articulate witness for the plaintiffs and their concern with the building tender system, abuses of that system, and the harassment of inmates who challenged TDC in the courts.

The Building Tender System When it came to the building tender system, there was never any question that inmates could be used to take care of or "tend" the buildings. The complaints made by the plaintiffs were twofold. First, contrary to state law, inmates were being used in supervisory and disciplinary roles throughout many institutions in the TDC. Second, acting in these roles, with the knowledge and encouragement of the administration and staff, building tenders frequently engaged in the abusive use of force. Much of the testimony received from Turner's thirty-four witnesses centered on these two issues.

This testimony ranged from rather mundane assertions that building tenders acted as auxiliary guards to direct accounts of brutal and even fatal assaults. Lawrence Pope provided an example of the former on the first day of trial:

Q: Mr. Pope, at a couple of places in your testimony, you have mentioned building tenders. What is a building tender?

A: A building tender gives orders to the inmates. He orders them to rack up . . . to go to their cell and the door is then closed on them. He orders them to go in the dayroom. He gives orders for them to go to various places within the unit, for instance, the writ room or the gym or E and R, wherever he might be called . . . .

Q: Do they have any function with regard to the television?

A: Yes, they operate the television and only they can operate it. They select programs that they want to see. Sometimes, occasionally, they will put it to a vote as to what programs the inmates in the dayroom want, but if the building tenders happen to want another program, they override the vote and go ahead and put the one they want on it.

Q: Do they have any function with regard to inmate traffic from place to place?

A: Yes, they have a different category, that of turnkeys out in the hall, and they act in the same capacity as a building tender in that they order the inmates to go places, to walk on the other side of the green line . . . .

Q: Tell us what that means.

A: There's a green line, a tape, placed along both sides of the hall, and the inmates are supposed to walk on the outside of that green line toward the wall. The center portion is reserved for officers and building tenders and turnkeys and such as that. If you step over the green line, you are possibly subject to disciplinary action. The building tenders, or rather, the turnkeys, check you when you go in the hospital. You have to have your scrip there or a pass in there, and they stand there and check it to see that you do have your scrip. They will tell you to shut up if you happen to be talking in the hall. When you are in the hospital, you have a hospital turnkey who orders five or more men up to the pill window.

Through Pope's testimony, as well as that of other inmates testifying during this early phase of the trial, it became evident that the "building tender system" was just that, a system. It was a system in which inmates performed a wide range of duties in the cell blocks and dorms, in the hallways between wings in the prison, in the hospital and infirmaries, and in the fields. It was also evident that this system was organized into a hierarchy and that there were inmates considered "head building tenders" who exercised substantial control and influence within the cell blocks. The plaintiffs hoped to show not only that building tenders exercised supervisory and disciplinary powers throughout TDC but also that their authority was derived from the administration and staff.

In part this link was established through testimony that suggested that the extent and type of supervision exercised by building tenders varied from institution to institution and from warden to warden. Several days after Pope's testimony another inmate, testifying about conditions on the Ramsey Unit, asserted that the number of building tenders, as well as the extent of brutality, had changed from one warden to the next.

Q: Now, when you say after Anderson took over at Ramsey that the building tender system became more notorious, what was the system like under Lanier then?

A: Well, under Lanier, like in the cell block I was in, there was no brutality by the convict guards. We never saw that in there. It wasn't until—you saw some of it in the other cell blocks, but it wasn't as bad as it got after (assistant) Warden Christian and Warden Anderson got there. They started segregating what they termed as potential trouble makers or something like that, and the beatings began all over the place.[10]

Many testifying inmates linked the beatings and brutality by building tenders to the special privileges that BT's enjoyed. In particular, the BTs' activities were less restricted than other inmate's. They participated in the assignment of cells. Their cells were often left open, and they were given access to other inmates' cells. In addition, it was alleged that these inmate guards had ready access to various types of weapons. Throughout this early testimony it was claimed that the privileges and power enjoyed by building tenders were associated with various forms of abuses, some not accepted by the prison staff and administration, some apparently accepted by administrators and staff as a natural outcome of supervisory duties, and some not only known and accepted, but actively encouraged.

One example of abuse associated with the increased freedom enjoyed by building tenders involved a rape. Turner had promised in his opening statement to present testimony regarding a recent rape at knifepoint of one of the witnesses by a building tender. This testimony was received in the second week of trial. The alleged event had occurred just under four months earlier, on July 1, 1978. The assailant was a building tender whom a warden would later describe as a well-known "assaultive, violent person."[11] The victim, a known homosexual, was originally assigned by an inmate book-keeper to the cell of his assailant but was subsequently reassigned to another cell, where he resided at the time of the rape. Turner asked him to describe what happened on the day of the rape.

> A: Approximately 5:30 P.M. Robertson came to my cell on 4 row of A-1 and told me that I had better come down to 1 row at 6:00 o'clock when the doors were open for dayroom time, told me if I didn't come out, he would kill me, and I had no reason to doubt that's what he would do.
>
> Q: Why?
>
> A: Well Charley Robertson had killed an inmate by the name of Bill Keys in 1974.

After some objections related to this inmate's lack of direct knowledge of inmate Key's death, testimony continued.

> Q: After you had this conversation with Robertson, what did you do next?
>
> A: Then when the doors were opened at 6:00 o'clock for dayroom time, I went downstairs, and Charley Robertson was waiting at the bottom of the stairs for me. He told me to go back to the end of 1 Row and go into one of the open cells down there, and he followed me shortly thereafter.
>
> Q: Was it his cell?
>
> A: No, sir, it belonged to one of the major's bookkeepers on the Wynne farm.
>
> Q: So you went back to the cell where he told you to go to?
>
> A: Yes, sir.
>
> Q: What happened there?

A: Charley Robertson came in there and started performing fellatio on me, continued for about thirty minutes during which time I failed to achieve any more than a partial erection, and he became angry and told me if I wasn't going to give him his pleasure that way, he would find his pleasure in other ways.

Q: So what did he do then?

A: He then told me to turn around and bend over the sink and the toilet, and I told him no and started struggling with him. He hit me several times in the chest and knocked me back on the toilet, and he was struggling with me and pulled a homemade knife out of his pocket.

Q: What did it look like?

A: It was made from a toothbrush and razor blades imbedded in the side.

Q: What did he do with that?

A: He placed it against my neck and forced me to bend over the toilet, pulled my pants down and continued to rape me.

Following this incident the victim, on advice from his cell partner, reported the rape to a prison officer and subsequently filed a civil rights suit against several prison officials for neglecting their supervisory duties. Ironically, he further testified that while working on this suit he was written up for "damaging or destroying state property" when his rough draft was found written on paper issued by the college program. Finally, he testified that he had been told by a building major and sergeant that he could "look for a good whipping" when he got back from the testimony he was then giving.

The victim did not know what happened to Charles Robertson. Later testimony by the warden at the Wynne Unit revealed that no disciplinary action was taken. Instead, Robertson was transferred to the treatment center at the "Walls" Unit in Huntsville because he was "apparently disturbed" and in need of some kind of psychological treatment. When queried by Judge Justice about this decision, the warden reported that "his talk was erratic. He would make a statement, and then in a few minutes turn around and contradict his previous statement. His moods would change. His talk just didn't make a whole lot of sense, really." [12]

As far as the plaintiffs' case in *Ruiz* was concerned, the circumstances surrounding the rape supported charges that inmates known for their violent tendencies were often appointed to the position of building tender, that these inmates were often given greater freedom than other inmates, that these freedoms frequently resulted in abusive practices, and that building tenders were not disciplined with the same set of rules used for other inmates. There was no implication that this incident was condoned by prison officials. Testimony given by other witnesses related incidents more directly connected to abusive practices of building tenders while pursuing their supervisory duties.

One such incident involved a fight between an inmate and a building tender, where once again it was alleged that no disciplinary action was taken against the building tender.

> The building tender, Barnes, ordered inmate Gunn to get to his cell when he just had returned to the hospital after breakfast sick call, and he started up the stairs and the building tender ordered him in harsh words to get going down to his cell or he would put him in his cell . . . that if he wasn't going to get down to his cell that he was going to carry him, so they got into a fight, and they fought for a little bit, and a Sgt. Rodriguez and Building Tender Rose and about four turnkeys come up there and the Sgt. took his hand and twisted it to his back and that inmate building tender hit him again and they took him out towards the steps . . .
>
> Q: Did you see the guard restrain the building tender from hitting Mr. Gunn?
>
> A: No, sir, they locked the inmate Gunn in isolation and the building tender was still working. Nothing happened to him.

While this incident involved a rather spontaneous confrontation between an inmate and a building tender, other witnesses testified about more premeditated attacks and the participation of TDC personnnel. It was repeatedly charged that building tenders were allowed to keep weapons for control and intimidation. Testifying about his experiences on the Eastham Unit, an inmate was asked if he had ever observed any building tenders in the possession of items that could be used as a weapon. He replied that he had and described these as "a free world hunting knife approximately a foot long with a stainless steel blade about three inches wide and a bone handle," "two mop handles taped together," and "pipes and pieces of 'tracer chain.' "

There was no question in this inmate's mind that the staff knew about these weapons, in that they were frequently carried in plain sight. He also testified that they were used, in some instances, just for intimidation. As an example, he related his own experience of how his arms were beaten black and blue from the shoulder to the elbow with a piece of sawed-off baseball bat, while being told that such treatment was "customary to see how tough I was." In addition to his own experience, this inmate testified that he had seen another inmate beaten by the same building tenders, Butch Ainsworth and Charles Robertson, with a piece of pipe and chain over an apparent disagreement about a package of cigarettes.

Testimony about intimidation was not limited to the independent actions of building tenders. One inmate who had been a witness to the alleged mistreatment of Eddie Ward (see Chapter 3) testified about how he was threatened by warden David Christian. Christian first asked him about his signature on an affidavit regarding the mistreatment of inmate Ward and then stated, "Well, I think it would be best for you if you forgot about that, don't you?" The inmate replied, "No, sir, I don't think it would be best." After the implied warning and reply were each repeated once, the warden left. About fifteen minutes later three building tenders, whose job it was "to run the lockup wing," returned and entered the witness's cell with pieces of broomsticks, about two feet long, taped on one end for gripping. "They used these clubs to beat me with. After they beat me and told me that their warden had asked me to drop that lawsuit and being a witness for Eddie Ward, and what did I think now . . . I told them, 'Yeah, I think I'm about ready to drop it now,' so they left my cell."

The "Ward Incident" had taken place in 1973. The defense could argue that while the building tender system might have been more prevalent in the early 1970s, prison administrators had successfully limited its influence in more recent years. To counter this defense and to establish a continuing deliberate pattern and practice, the plaintiffs attempted to show how the BT system had flourished not only in the past, with testimony about such incidents as those involving Eddie Ward and the death of Melvin Austin, but also how it continued with active administrative encouragement well beyond the enactment of legislation outlawing the practice.

For example, testimony was received about an incident that occurred in February 1975, involving an inmate who had difficulty speaking and understanding English. He had experienced some trouble getting his medicine and had also had a number of problems with the warden, David Christian. When asked to describe the incident in question, the witness recalled that an officer, along with two "convict guards," opened Julio Nieto's cell door, went in the cell, and began to beat inmate Nieto. Shortly thereafter, the officer came out of the cell, stood up against the wall, and watched as the beating continued. Finally he told the two convict guards, "That's enough."

Testimony by one of Turner's last witnesses served to underscore the contention that the BT system was thriving right up to the time of trial. The incident allegedly occurred sometime in July 1978 on the Retrieve Unit. After identifying the "head row tender" and his "assistants," as well as the victim, the witness related an example of the plaintiffs' contention that building tenders asserted their authority through force and how it was sometimes unclear who was taking orders from whom.

A: He [the victim] had went to the noon meal and supposedly had failed to come back and check in on the wing, so a count board could be changed to go to the piddling shop . . . The 1:00 o'clock count occurred and the board supposedly was messed up, so as soon as the count cleared, [head row tender] sent another turnkey — another building tender, to go get [victim] in the piddling shop and bring him back to the wing . . . . The minute [victim] stepped in the wing door from the hall [the two building tenders got him under the arms] and they walked him past my cell. My cell is 2 cell on A row and took him to front of 4 and 5 cell, between that area next to the windows, and began beating on him, and [head BT] made a comment something to the effect that he was tired of that shit and he wasn't going to have it any more on his wing, and after they knocked him around for three or four minutes, [head BT] went to the picket boss, the officer in the picket, and told him to open the man's cell and to lock him down when he got in there and "don't let him out for anything."

Dramatic testimony of active administrative participation in building tender abuses was given by a former BT, who testified that he had been asked to scare one of the writ-writers involved with David Ruiz. He had been approached first in 1975 when he was the cellmate of building tender Charles Robertson. In the course of a conversation, a building major had said he would help the witness get back to Colorado if the witness would help him scare some writ-writers out of the *Ruiz* case. Several days later the witness moved into another cell and was eventually joined by the inmate he was to intimidate. In his testimony this former building tender recalled,

About 4:00 o'clock that afternoon Inmate Steve Blanchard was moved into my cell, and the building tender that was taking care of that area down there, Charlie Rodriguez, brought a knife to me, and he said, "Here you go," and I said, "All right, thank you." And it was about 7:00 o'clock that I cut Steve Blanchard. I cut him on both sides of the neck and both arms, and he was calling for the guard, and the guard came, and Major Maples came down there and numerous turnkeys came running down there. They took him out of the cell, and Major Maples smiled at me and said, "Later."

While Inmate Blanchard was not called to testify, documents entered into evidence noted that Blanchard had told the medical assistant that he had been cut by another inmate. By contrast, an interoffice communication from Major Maples to Warden J. V. Anderson suggested that the incident had actually been an instance of self-mutilation, somehow connected with Blanchard's involvement with David Ruiz and their "revolutionary cause." At the close of Major Maples's testimony he was asked by Judge Justice, "Do I understand from your testimony that you deny that there was ever any such conversation [related to the harassment of Inmate Blanchard] of any type?" Maples responded, "Definitely so." The correctional officer, who was apparently the first to arrive at the cell where the cutting took place, wrote in his report of the incident that he had heard a moaning sound and had gone to check: "Upon my arrival to 16-cell on 1 row, I observed the subject lying on his back on the floor. I saw Inmate Ulmer, Jerry #242909 sitting in a straddle position across the subject's stomach. Inmate Ulmer was holding the subject inmate's right arm. It appeared as though Inmate Ulmer was attempting to hold the subject's arm away from his (subject's) body." There was no disciplinary action taken against Inmate Ulmer. Ulmer's account, coupled with the conflicting official documents and the ambiguous incident report, no doubt contributed to Judge Justice's eventual conclusion that "the attendant circumstances warrant the believability of the testimony of former building tender, Jerry Ben Ulmer."[13]

By the end of the first two weeks of trial, witnesses had alleged that the building tender system had been operating for some years and that it was firmly in place at the time of trial. Descriptions given indicated that this system involved inmates in supervisory and disciplinary roles and that these inmates were used to varying degrees and purposes by different wardens and cell block officers. Inmates testified about many instances at numerous institutions throughout the TDC when building tenders engaged in brutal treatment of other inmates with the full knowledge and even encouragement of prison wardens and cell block officers. However, the testimony also alleged that not all brutality was delegated to building tenders. Officers themselves were charged with direct participation in various types of questionable practices directed against inmates, ranging from harassment to summary beatings.

Harassment and Staff Brutality Many of the witnesses called to the stand by Turner during the first two weeks of trial were well-known writ-writers. Most of these inmates related experiences of being harassed in one way or another over their law-related activities. Mail was read and delayed, it was difficult to get documents notarized, and use of the law library was made difficult. These prisoners testified that they were given undesirable job assignments and were subjected to unusual searches (e.g., repeated digital rectal exams), and disciplinary procedures. In addition, they offered testimony of more physical abuse, including being Maced and beaten.

Much of this testimony was familiar to Judge Justice through earlier proceedings surrounding the contempt motions and protective orders issued in 1975 and 1976. For example, Ernesto Montana, a named plaintiff in the *Ruiz* case, simply adopted his testimony from the previous hearings, along with that given in *Cruz* v. *Beto.* He was out of prison, living in San Antonio and working in his family's wholesale produce business. Judge Justice took note of Montana's changed appearance since leaving prison and asked him about his weight. Montana weighed 118 pounds when he left prison and gained some 70 pounds after his release.

Testimony received from other witnesses was more extensive. Some of this testimony alleged continuing harassment of trial witnesses by prison staff. David Ruiz testified about the unusual method of handcuffing used while transporting witnesses, even after Judge Justice had requested that prisoners be transported in the "ordinary way." Another inmate testified about an implied threat as he was boarding the bus at Ramsey I to come and testify. A major asked him if he was going to testify. When the inmate said he was, the major replied, "Well, you will be back." Several inmates related how cell assignments were used as a means of harassment. For example, a black or Hispanic inmate might be assigned to an all-white cell block. One of the witnesses charged that several mental patients had been put in his cell intentionally to harass and provoke him into a fight.

Taken by themselves, these instances of harassment might not have been viewed as terribly serious. However, when combined with other more serious charges, they became part of the pattern and practice that the plaintiffs hoped to establish. For example, it was charged in some reports of staff brutality that petty harassment had led to more serious confrontations. One witness recalled an incident in which he and another inmate were talking "rather loud" while waiting in line for dinner.

Lt. Maples told us to hit the hallway that we had a case . . . That means to go out and stand on the wall until he gets ready to talk to us and we were under arrest for disciplinary . . . When we got into the hallway, he told John Forbes to catch the wall, and he told me catch lockup, and I said, "Why are you locking me up?" He said, "Just go to lockup, Simonton," and I said, "Yes, sir." I turned around and started walking down the hallway to lockup, and he stepped on my heels with his feet, and I looked over my shoulder, and I said, "Lt. Maples, would you stay off my heels, please?" and he pushed me in my shoulder blades and told me, "Go on to lockup, you old tall thing, before you really get into trouble." I said, "Yes, sir," and I started walking again, and I got five or six more feet, and then he started stepping on my heels again, and I was getting kind of angry at this time, so I stopped and turned around and said, "Lt. Maples, please stay off my heels. I'm going to lockup. It's not necessary."

He said, "You better get your ass on down to lockup," so I took a deep breath and turned around and started walking to lockup again. I got right to the crossover door between 3 and 4 wings, and he stepped on my heels again. I stopped and turned around and said, "Stay off my heels," and he started hitting me. I grabbed him and pushed him up against the wall, and at this time a lot of other inmates, turnkeys in the hallway, building tenders in 3 and 4 Wing and the officers in center hall, they all started running down there. I had a couple of inmates grab me and a couple of officers and other inmates grab me on the other side, and they started hitting me, and I tried to pull away from them, and I was hollering, and they just kept hitting me.

Then I seen Lt. Maples' hand coming at me, and I couldn't move to get out of the way, and I seen that he had some kind of metal in it . . . I seen it coming at my forehead, and I felt it when it hit me here (indicating), and that's the last thing I remember until I woke up in the hospital feeling my head sore.

Q: Where are you referring to, what part of your body?

A: My forehead here where this big scar is where my head is sunk in.

This inmate went on to testify that, after spending four or five days in the Ramsey infirmary, he was returned to lockup for approximately two weeks, even though he reportedly did not receive any additional disciplinary sentence for the altercation with Lieutenant Maples. He testified that while he was in solitary confinement Lieutenant Maples and warden Christian came to see him, and Christian said, "Well, I know we had a little trouble out of you in the past behind litigation . . . I want you to sign me another statement stating that you had a seizure [the inmate had epilepsy] and fell in the hallway and hit your head on the bars, and that's how you came with the scar on your forehead. I want you to exonerate Lt. Maples of all blame for this . . . You want to do that for me, or do you want to talk to my boys?" After this conversation, the witness testified, he agreed to sign the statement.

Officer Maples would later recall the events somewhat differently in his own testimony. According to Maples, the problem had started at the noon meal when there was a shortage of officers. Two inmates did not stop their "horse-play" when ordered, and so Maples told them to go to the center hall. One inmate complied, but Simonton did not. After further verbal exchanges in the hallway, Simonton was ordered to lockup. On the way to lockup they had to pass through a narrow doorway, where without provocation Simonton turned and attempted to strike Maples. He missed, and Maples responded by hitting Simonton one time in "the head area."

This knocked Simonton into the bars. He bounced off and hit the floor unconscious. From there Simonton was taken to the unit infirmary. About two weeks later Simonton apologized for the incident. Maples felt that Simonton had been punished enough and, after conferring with Warden Christian, decided not to file a charge for assaulting an officer.

In other testimony an inmate related how his jaw had been broken when Captain Robert Lawson hit him after his hands had been cuffed behind his back. The incident allegedly took place in the officer's office and was reportedly precipitated when the witness failed to furnish information about an incident of which he claimed to be ignorant. When Lawson testified several months later, he acknowledged that the inmate's jaw had been broken but recalled that this had happened when the inmate broke away and ran into another inmate. "They were rounding the corner right there. It's a blind corner right here, and they both—they were coming and they just ran into him, and at that time they both fell. Inmate Diaz hit the left side of his head on a steel security gate back there."

Another incident was apparently triggered when a field major on Ramsey took exception to the way a gay inmate was relieving himself in the field. "The major just jumped off his horse and started beating on this prisoner. He kept screaming that he didn't need to squat down to take a piss, and the prisoner was determined to do just that, and he kept beating him and beating him and he never did get up." The officer charged was not called to testify.

Several witnesses offered testimony about being maced while securely locked in their cells. In one incident, an inmate, who at the time of the macing was confined in the Treatment Center in Huntsville, was asked on cross-examination by the state's attorney why the officer sprayed Mace in his cell. The testifying inmate replied, "Well, on the first occasion he came by my cell, and he said, 'Oh, Old Crosson, how do you like the Treatment Center now?' I said, 'I don't like it a bit.' He reached in his back pocket and sprayed me with Mace and said, 'You're going to like it less when I get through with you.' " In a second instance, an epileptic inmate, who had trouble testifying because of his broken English, stated that he was maced in his cell after asking warden Christian for his medicine on November 29, 1975. When asked how he remembered the November 29 date so accurately, the witness replied, "Because Thanksgiving, that was the day my mother died."

When Warden Christian took the stand in May 1979, attorneys for the state questioned him about the macing charges, including those involving David Ruiz. Much of this testimony had been heard in earlier contempt hearings, and Judge Justice had already entered findings of fact favoring the plaintiff's charges. Nevertheless, attorneys for the state, over objections from Turner, wanted to reopen the issue to point out inconsistencies in the previous testimony and to clear up who was telling the truth. Justice

George Beto, Director of TDC, 1962–1972

Field labor

"Hoe Squad"

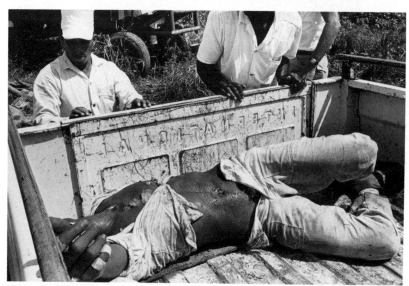

Heat exhaustion

TDC writ-writer, Fred Cruz lecturing prison reform group after his release from prison

Prisoners' rights attorney,
Frances Jalet Cruz

David Ruiz (*far left*) and fellow writ-writers preparing for trial

Prisoners' rights attorney (*center*) William Bennett Turner on first day of *Ruiz* trial with co-counsel and members of prison reform group CURE (*standing next to Turner*, Charles Sullivan; *far right*, Pauline Sullivan)

W. J. Estelle, Jr., Director of TDC, 1972–1983

"Building Tender"

William Wayne Justice, Chief U.S. District Judge, Eastern District, Texas

Mike George

Judge Justice visits TDC prison (*left to right,* Special Master, Vincent M. Nathan; William Bennett Turner; Assistant Attorney General, F. Scott McCown; Judge William Wayne Justice; Eastham Prison Warden, George Waldron; U.S. Department of Justice Attorney, Daniel S. Jacobs)

"Dog Boy"

"Hoe Squads" and "High Riders"

allowed Christian's testimony with the statement, "I have a very good idea about who's telling the truth about it, but go ahead."[14] Warden Christian acknowledged that he had maced Ruiz. He was not questioned about the details of the situation, other than what happened after the macing. He responded, "He [Ruiz] was taken out of his cell after a confrontation where he hit me. We was forced to subdue him. He was taken on out to what is known as the solitary building and placed in administrative segregation status in that building." The Thanksgiving Day incident was not pursued.

Much of the reported staff harassment and brutality centered around instances of medical and psychiatric problems and perceptions by the staff that inmates were faking their condition. One such instance, which occurred in February 1978, involved a suicidal inmate. The inmate had been placed in solitary confinement and had been yelling "in both English and in Spanish, asking to be let out, to have his door open, asking for someone to come back there he could talk to, asking for some type of help, just more or less on a regular basis around the clock for approximately two or three days prior to him being found hung." At one point the disturbed inmate was visited by a Mexican-American guard. The witness reported hearing the guard tell some building tenders as he left the cell, "I have really got that Mexican fucked up now. He doesn't know whether he is coming or going." About three hours later the inmate was found hung in his cell.

The most detailed testimony during the first two weeks of trial alleging the mistreatment of an inmate with special medical needs and the accompanying countercharge that the inmate was putting on an act came from a witness who entered the courtroom in a wheelchair on the next-to-last day of Turner's presentation of witnesses. This witness had injured his back by slipping on a soapy floor that he was mopping and hitting his back on the mop bucket. This happened on February 4, 1977, on the Retrieve Unit. After having some difficulty obtaining a medical exam, the inmate wrote his mother, who contacted TDC's head physician, who in turn saw the inmate about a month and a half after his accident. At that time, the doctor gave his opinion that the inmate probably had a herniated disc and that he "should be moved to the Walls hospital as soon as possible in an ambulance." After further tests and X-rays at the Huntsville hospital, the doctor again diagnosed the problem as a herniated disc and tried to get an appointment for the inmate at John Sealy Hospital in Galveston. This appointment, however, was not until June 10. From mid-March to June 10, the inmate was housed at the Huntsville hospital.

The inmate testified that between mid-March and mid-April he gradually lost the use of his legs and that he began using a cane to help himself get around. He recalled that on April 17 he was seen by an inmate nurse who was accompanied by another inmate nurse just learning the routine.

He [the experienced inmate nurse] was going around to each bed, telling this new inmate nurse what was the problem with each patient. When he got back to mine, he told him that I had a lower back injury, and he thought he should maybe give me a massage and show him how I should be massaged . . .

Q: Was the doctor with them, supervising the instruction?

A: No, no doctor, M.T.A. or pill pusher or anything else of that kind.

Q: I believe you said that there was a comment with regard to your lower back problem. Did anything occur then?

A: Well, he told me to roll over and that he would give me a massage, so knowing the problem if you didn't do what most of them told you to do up there, I complied and rolled over. He then began giving me a back massage, and after he had been massaging it a few minutes, and telling this other inmate nurse how it should be done, he said, "Hell, I see what the problem is with you. You've got a disc out of place," and with saying that, he took the flat palm of his hand and hit me squarely in the small part of the back a very resounding, loud, hard blow, which caused me a considerable amount of pain at the time. I screamed and told him to get away from me, that he was hurting me, and so he quickly, with the other inmate nurse, turned me back over and said, "That's all right. You'll be Okay. Maybe you haven't got a dislocated disc after all."

The impact of this recollection in the courtroom was visibly apparent on Judge Justice, who reportedly winced when the above testimony was given.[15] The witness went on to relate how a few days later he lost complete use of his legs, and how on the night he realized he could not use his legs he "messed" on himself before he could be taken to the commode. It was late in the afternoon when this testimony was given. On several previous occasions Judge Justice had admonished counsel, especially Ed Idar, for long and inefficient questioning of witnesses. To compensate, he had been extending the court day by beginning at 8:00 in the morning instead of the customary 9:00. On this particular day, however, he decided to adjourn the court a bit early with the compliment, "Compared to what has gone on in the past, all counsel have done well."

The following morning testimony began with the same witness and his account of his appointment with the doctors at John Sealy Hospital on June 10, 1977. On that day the TDC's representative at the hospital approached the witness and asked him about his prior record of escaping from jail. The representative then went into the clinic. The first thing the witness was reportedly asked by the doctor when he was seen in the clinic was, "Are you sure there's anything wrong with you? You're not just down here trying to fake it so you can run, are you?" The witness later learned that this doctor reported that the patient was considered "a malingerer," because someone had seen him move while lying on the gantry in the hall.

During his appointment the next month he underwent a series of tests that revealed a "voluntary reflex" and a subsequent muscle spasm in his leg. The witness reported, however, that the next visit in August, as well as another in October, revealed no further such movements, nor did they reveal the underlying cause of his paralysis. The recommendation of the doctor seen in August was that the patient see a neuropsychiatrist, which he did in September. The diagnosis on this occasion was that the witness's condition was psychosomatic, and the suggestion was made that he receive further psychiatric examination. This exam took place in the Huntsville hospital. The examining doctor concluded that the paralysis was not "hysterical paralysis" and suggested further tests. By December 1977 there was no final cause, physical or psychological, identified, and the decision was made to move the inmate from the Huntsville hospital to the Retrieve Unit.

When the witness arrived at Retrieve, the unit psychologist indicated that "they were going to have to run some tests that might be very painful and severe," but if the witness was willing to do it, they could probably come up with the cause for his paralysis. The inmate agreed, but the tests were never run. "I told them whatever they wanted to do I was willing to do because I didn't enjoy being the way I was . . . I took one little written test of about 120 questions, not in the presence of anyone, but just locked in the hospital cell back there . . . and that's the last time I ever saw or heard from either one of those psychologists, and there has been no follow-up on it."

Prison administrators had apparently been convinced for some time that the paralysis was all an act. At one point the Huntsville Unit staff denied the witness use of his wheelchair. When it came time for his transfer to Retrieve, he had to move from his cell to a cell in the "transient wing" in another part of the prison, but first he had to go to the "bull ring" to get his cell assignment.

Q: Did you request the use of a wheelchair?

A: Yes, sir, I requested the wheelchair, and I was told to get my ass out of that cell and to get to the bull ring any way I could . . .

Q: How long did it take to get from the lockup cells to the bull ring at the administration building?

A: Approximately an hour and a half to an hour and forty-five minutes. After I got there, I was required to turn around and go back . . . to the transient row building . . .

Q: Were you escorted during this time?

Q: Oh, yes. I had two to three officers, not only regular CO-2 officers, but captains and lieutenants around me all the way, and different inmates stopped and asked if they could help. I had two bags that had my personal property in it that I had to drag them forward and then get past them and drag them again and then scoot up past them. They asked if they could at least carry my bags over to the bull ring or help me get over to the bull ring, and they were told if they touched me or touched my bags in any way, they would be given disciplinary action . . .

Q: What is the surface of that area?

A: It's rough asphalt surface.

This witness went on to testify that when he got to the bull ring he was handed a piece of paper and told to go to his assigned cell in the transient wing, which was back across the compound, further away than he had already come. His return trip to his new cell was interrupted while he was scooting back across the compound, when the hospital administrator sent down a wheelchair and told the officers to bring the witness to his office. When the witness arrived at the administrator's office, the witness was allegedly told to keep quiet and just listen. "He told me he was tired of my crap. He didn't want me contacting the doctors anymore trying to keep from being pulled off the chain [being transferred to Retrieve]. He told me that if I ever pulled another stunt like that again, he would make sure that things were taken care of."

After this conversation, the inmate was placed in administrative lock-up, where he stayed from December 8 to December 12. On December 12, at two o'clock in the morning, the witness testified that he was told to get up and catch the chain bus to the Retrieve Unit. The bus was not scheduled to arrive until much later that morning. The inmate was required to start more than three and a half hours early because he was once again asked to travel out of the cell block and across the yard without the assistance of a wheelchair or fellow inmates. The temperature on this morning was reported to be in the high thirties or low forties. Once again the inmate traversed the distance by scooting, with the exception of one ramp, which he was able to slide down after an officer sprayed the ramp with water. The entire trip took about three and a half hours.

Once at Retrieve, he was assigned to a cell. His cell was not equipped with any support bars to help him get from his bunk to the commode, or for support when using the sink. He was asked several questions by counsel and then by Judge Justice about how he managed to move about in the cell when taking care of basic hygienic needs. The maneuvers necessary to use the commode were described in great detail. They were difficult but possible with some care. Use of the sink, however, was a different matter. The witness testified that he could not use the sink and balance himself at the same time. Judge Justice inquired, "Well, how are you supplied with water?" The witness replied, "The inmate row tenders or building crew, whenever I need water, I have to ask one of them to bring me water from the mop room, which is next to my cell. Sometimes I get water; sometimes I don't, Your Honor."

When asked how he showered and kept himself clean, he answered that from the time of his arrival on Retrieve, on December 12, until January 10, 1978, he had been allowed to shower with the assistance of other inmates three times. After that he was told by a lieutenant and sergeant that if he wanted a shower he could get there himself. He went on to testify, "From January 10th to May 12th, I neither had a shower nor tub bath that full length of time, and I was given a small metal pan and a torn-up sheet with which to bathe myself. There was a pan of hot water or a plastic jug of hot water brought to me and poured through the cell door into the pan, and this is what I had to use to bathe with."

When this witness first arrived on Retrieve, the facilities for physical therapy were next to nonexistent. Between May 1978 and his appearance at trial in October, however, some improvements had been made, and he had been receiving help from a Captain Jenkins at Retrieve. As a result of this assistance, he had gained approximately thirty pounds and had become physically more fit. There had even been some discussion of getting leg braces for walking and standing. This same captain had also been instrumental in helping secure a wheelchair for the witness so he could travel back and forth to the hospital for therapy.

This inmate ended his testimony on October 17, the last day of Turner's presentation of witnesses, and just over two weeks after the trial began. During these two weeks, inmates had presented in graphic detail their experiences with and perspectives on prison life. The trial had been receiving substantial publicity throughout the state. Thus, inmates had an effective public forum, which until this time had not existed. To reach this point, a small group of writ-writing inmates had endured institutional rules that hampered their attempts to file cases; they had been denied access to their attorney and had confronted with numerous legal delays as well as personal harassment in various forms. For these inmates, the significance of this public airing of grievances could hardly be overestimated. Nor was the significance of the publicity surrounding the trial lost on TDC inmates less directly involved in the trial.

Inmate Demonstrations Prompt News Blackout by TDC

Texas prison administrators had been proud for many years of the orderly nature of their institutions and the almost total absence of inmate disturbances. From the beginning of court intervention they had expressed the fear that much of this order would be disturbed. In the first two weeks of the *Ruiz* trial, it appeared that these fears might be realized.

On the first day of trial, there was a small demonstration outside the courthouse in Houston, organized in part by former TDC inmates. Inside the courtroom Ed Idar interrupted Turner's presentation of his first witness to note the demonstration, as well as the publicity the trial was receiving. He went on to inform the court "that night before last at the Clemens Unit we had three rounds of a .38 caliber pistol shot [allegedly by someone outside the prison] at a picket officer on duty." The reason Idar was bringing up the demonstration, publicity, and shooting incident was to ask the court "to admonish or at least explain to the people in the audience and to counsel that we would appreciate it if we could try this case in the courtroom and refrain from demonstrating and so forth." Judge Justice replied that he was in no position to tell people they could not exercise their First Amendment rights, and he asked Turner to proceed with his case.

Within several TDC institutions there were rumors of a sitdown strike. The *Houston Post* published an article on October 2 predicting that Ellis Unit inmates would engage in a work stoppage in support of the plaintiffs' case. This prediction proved to be accurate when two days later nine inmates in the field quit work and attempted to get other inmates to join them. While this attempt was initially unsuccessful, the following day approximately one hundred and forty inmates sat down inside the turn-out gate and refused to go to the fields after the noon meal. Shortly thereafter, the remainder of this field force "defied all orders to go to work." When they returned to the cell block, approximately one hundred inmates refused orders to go to their cells and sat down in the dayroom. Eventually these inmates were asked to join the hundred and forty inmates who were staging the sitdown strike outside. "To avoid damaging the building and violence, these inmates were permitted to go outside where the group then built-up to a total of 408 inmates."[16] The next day these inmates presented the warden with a petition that restated many of the issues then before Judge Justice, including removal of all building tenders from the wings, better medication and meaningful medical exams, "no more trumped-up charges in disciplinary hearings," and complete access to the courts.

At about the time the Ellis inmates began their demonstration on October 5, 209 inmates stopped work in the field on the Darrington Unit. After a short period, they began moving back toward the unit after one inmate reportedly said, "They can't shoot all of us, let's go to the building and eat lunch."[17] The assistant warden ordered the advancing inmates to stop. When they refused, a warning shot was fired into the air. A second shot was fired to the side of the inmates, who were by this time making "hostile comments," as they got within fifty yards of the assistant warden. The inmates finally stopped when a third shot was fired in front of them and 3 inmates were slightly injured, by either pellets or ricocheting gravel. After the shots, the field force was permitted to move back to the buildings in "small orderly groups of thirty inmates."[18]

When asked about these events by the news media, TDC officials issued a statement that characterized both incidents as minor with "no resultant injuries to either inmates or officials."[19] In addition, they allowed a longtime observer of the prison system from the local newspaper to interview some inmates on the Ellis Unit. After expressing their disappointment about the media representative, the inmates stated their grievances and their support of the *Ruiz* suit. When asked what triggered the work stoppage by the group, one inmate was quoted as saying, "The *Ruiz* case . . . now is our chance to get some recognition."[20]

On the day following the Ellis and Darrington work stoppages, 339 inmates refused to work on Ramsey I Unit, again with the stated purpose of supporting the *Ruiz* case. The timing of the trial and demonstrations was in one way fortuitous if the inmates wanted to draw public attention to their grievances. The prison system's yearly rodeo was held in October, and there would be an unusual number of public visitors to the Huntsville area on the weekend of October 7 and 8. On Sunday, October 8, media attention to the strike was increased when prison officials acknowledged that their initial denial of any injuries to inmates was wrong and that indeed there had been a shooting incident on the Darrington Unit. Monday, October 9, inmates were not required to work because of a holiday. However, on Tuesday it was apparent that the strike was continuing to grow.

Nearly two hundred inmates on Ramsey II and about a hundred and thirty inmates on Eastham joined the strike on Tuesday. The most intense confrontation developed on the Coffield Unit, where official reports initially indicated that "several hundred" inmates had joined the strike. A week after the incident, in a closed conference in Judge Justice's chambers, it was learned that on the afternoon of October 10 approximately one hundred and thirty inmates assigned to the field sat down between the building and the gate. Later that same afternoon about fifteen hundred inmates barricaded themselves in the cell block areas, where they reportedly began making weapons out of TV benches, mop and broom handles, and "anything available in the unit." When officials ordered the inmates back to their cells and asked them to stop destroying property, they were reportedly told, "You're going to have to come in and get us." In the ensuing altercation, gas was used and several inmates and officers were injured. One officer suffered a broken hand, and several officers were treated for minor injuries. Five inmates were transferred to the Huntsville hospital for treatment of head wounds, one inmate suffered a broken clavical and ribs and received treatment at John Sealy Hospital. In addition, twenty-eight inmates received treatment at Coffield for such injuries as broken fingers, broken noses and head lacerations.[21]

The day following this incident, a news blackout was imposed with the following statement from Estelle:

> The actions of inmates over the past several days to focus attention on the case litigation styled *Ruiz* v. *Estelle* have been substantially diminished. While there remain problems and potential for problems, the situation appears to be easing and significantly improved.
>
> Throughout this time, the department has attempted to show its concern for the public's right to know by actively responding to press inquiries. However, it is the department's feeling that our primary responsibility to insure institutional order and the safety of inmates and staff has not been aided by our willingness to respond in detail to the various inquiries that have been made. Therefore, the department will make no further statements regarding attempts by inmates to disrupt the programs and activities of the institutions until such time that those actions have been curtailed.

This statement was issued on Wednesday, October 11, 1978. There were immediate protests from the media, the ACLU, and various action groups for the remainder of the week.

On Monday, October 16, Ed Idar, at the request of W. J. Estelle, asked for a closed conference in Judge Justice's chambers to discuss the disturbances and to request that Justice make a public statement discouraging any further protests. In this conference Idar, along with Robert DeLong, general counsel for TDC, reviewed the sequence of events and described the current situation as "very volatile," noting that wardens at two institutions were "highly concerned that a more serious and drastic situation would break out at any moment." If things got out of hand, Idar asserted, "the thing can be resolved, but force will have to be used, and hopefully that is what everybody is trying to avoid. We don't want another Attica or anything of that sort in Texas if it can be helped." DeLong concluded his statement with the observation, "It is the consensus of the wardens who have talked to the inmates on a continuing basis that the way to relieve the tension is to have something from the court saying it does not condone disobedience of orders and disruption of routine on the units and this sort of conduct is hazardous, volatile and not helping the case."

After hearing generally supportive statements from attorneys for the Justice Department and attorneys for the plaintiffs, Judge Justice adjourned the conference and about an hour later reconvened hearings in open court. Before hearing additional testimony he expressed his own concern about the disturbances: "The court is greatly concerned for the safety of both inmates and guards and what is described as a volatile situation in two of the units. At this time, the court is seeking to determine the issues in this litigation in a deliberate and impartial manner. Now, orderly progress of the trial could be impeded if violence and disruption continue. It is my hope that they cease."

This statement was widely published in news media. By October 18, the demonstrations and work stoppages were all but completely over and the news blackout was lifted. The one exception was the report that just over two hundred inmates on the Ellis Unit were continuing their protest, albeit peacefully. This report was disputed in open court on November 1, when a letter from the Ellis inmates was presented to Judge Justice. The letter charged that the Ellis inmates were willing to return to work but were being prevented by the prison's warden.[22] After receiving the letter, Judge Justice asked that the Ellis situation be investigated. On November 3, 1978, David Vanderhoof reported to Judge Justice that "the Ellis Unit appears to be functioning in a normal manner and is free of tension. The likelihood of a violent confrontation between inmates and staff has subsided."[23]

Demonstrations that spread throughout the Texas prison system were almost unheard of, and prison officials were quick to lay blame on the intrusion of a biased federal court that they contended had neither the right nor the requisite knowledge to judge the internal affairs of the Texas prison system. This assessment was expressed quite openly by W. J. Estelle before a meeting of the Houston Chapter of the Public Relations Society of America shortly after the demonstrations had subsided: "I find little charity and less solace in bringing issues before a court that has no knowledge, direct or indirect, of what the real issues are and could care less that their personal social philosophy, finding its way into so-called law, jeopardizes not only our inmates' safety, but the safety of prison staff as well."[24]

The charge that "so-called law" was being shaped from ignorance and insensitivity in Judge Justice's courtroom reflected the lack of legitimacy and respect that prison officials afforded the proceedings as the Justice Department began presenting witnesses on October 18, 1979. This posture would be maintained for several years to come.

The Plaintiff-Intervenor's Case in Chief

Justice Department attorneys called almost a hundred witnesses to the stand between October 18 and the holiday break on December 21, 1978. An additional thirty-three witnesses were presented when proceedings resumed on April 2 until the close of the plaintiff-intervenor's case on May 2, 1979. Whereas William Bennett Turner had relied on inmates and former inmates, Jutice Department attorneys presented information, not only from these sources, but also from numerous expert witnesses, FBI investigations, legislators, and former employees.

Crowding and Staffing Levels   Substantial portions of this testimony dealt with the extent and impact of crowded prison conditions. Like much of the rest of the country, Texas experienced a rapid increase in its inmate population, beginning in the mid-1970s.[25] W. J. Estelle had testified before the state legislature in 1977 that crowding had reached "severe" levels. At the time of trial it was worse. The majority of inmates were housed two to a cell in approximately nine thousand cells that measured nine feet long, five feet wide, and seven feet high. When allowances were made for the two stacked bunks, toilet, and sink, there was approximately 22.5 square feet, or just over 11 square feet of usable floor space per inmate. Conditions were even more cramped for the several hundred inmates housed three to a cell. Most of the remaining inmates were housed in dormitories. There was substantial variation across dormitory units, but estimates of spacial density ranged from under 17 to around 60 square feet of floor space per inmate. In all, approximately one thousand inmates were sleeping "on the floor," either in dorms or cells at the time of trial.

Witnesses for the Justice Department noted that the amount of space available was substantially below standards such as those suggested by the American Correctional Association (60 square feet of cell floor space per prisoner), which were equal to or lower than standards set by other similar organizations.[26] In addition, it was noted that the conditions of crowding in the TDC were worse than those in other state prison systems, and in particular worse than those in prison systems that had already been found in violation of the Constitution such as Oklahoma and Alabama.

Attorneys for the state acknowledged that the levels of crowding in the TDC were higher than in other states, but they attempted to show through cross-examination that no scientifically derived data existed that linked the amount of space available per inmate to levels of stress or violence. In addition, witnesses for the state later testified that, despite high levels of crowding, rates of homicide and suicide were relatively low in the Texas prison system when compared to other large prison systems such as California. These same witnesses testified that disciplinary and assault rates appeared to be only weakly related to levels of crowding within various TDC institutions.

At the time of trial, systematic studies of prison crowding in other settings were scarce. The ones that did exist revealed inconsistent findings when it came to the relationship between the amount of space available and various indicators of stress, such as blood pressure. At the same time, it was apparent that these studies had been done in settings with less crowding than Texas prisons were then experiencing. Tentative data from Stateville, Illinois, where space levels more closely approximated those in Texas, suggested that there might be a threshold below which the amount of space available became an important contributor to psychological stress. While suggestive, even these data were acknowledged by researchers to be open to criticism.

Inmates who testified about personal experiences in crowded cells left less room for doubt. Few would disagree that psychological stress was produced in the conditions detailed by one witness who had been triple-celled on the Wynne Unit in 1977 and 1978 and for a time was one of four inmates sharing a cell. When reviewing the types of problems created by such close quarters, the witness was questioned by Judge Justice:

The Court: I take it that when someone urinated, there were particular problems.

The Witness: Yes, sir, it'd splash on his hands and so forth.

Q: Was there ever an occasion when someone in the cells with you or yourself might have been ill, sick?

A: Yes sir, two of the men that was in the cell were ill and one of them was unassigned for medical problems and the other one, he was working, but he was still ill, you know. He had a lung problem and he coughed all night long. You just had to get so tired that you just passed out before sometimes you could sleep because of the irritation of the noise of four men in a cell and this created a lot of problems.

Q: How about reading or studying?

A: That was impossible to do that. The radios would stay up so high that they'd almost knock your eardrums out and then they had the television in the dayroom, which was packed, men sitting on the floor . . . It was just so many people could get in there and that would be it and the rest of them would have to go back to their cells. They wouldn't get no recreation.

Cramped living quarters with the accompanying inconveniences, noise, and lack of privacy were immediately felt consequences of a ballooning inmate population. Decreased staff-to-inmate ratios and overburdened medical facilities were others. W. J. Estelle testified that the uniformed staff-to-inmate ratio in Texas had been consistently the lowest in the nation during most of his years as director. At the time of trial it was one uniformed staff member for twelve inmates, whereas the national average was approximately one to five. This situation was complicated further by a 60- to 70-percent yearly turnover rate among low-level officers. This meant that vacancies in an already strained work force were created before replacements could be trained. It also meant that in some instances background checks on new officers were suspended.

Estelle testified that he had asked the legislature for improved funding for staff positions. In the most recent instance he had requested funding for a one-to-ten ratio but had been turned down. In his testimony about this decision he recalled, "I thought we were being slightly penalized for good management. I think they were impressesed by the fact that our security problems are as low or minimal as they seem to be, and they are, and if we were managing with that ratio, why, they would continue that ratio." Part of the successful management, Estelle contended, involved an extensive work program, which prevented inmates from just milling around. In addition, it had long been the practice in Texas prisons to use inmates as a supplement to the guard force. When questioned about this practice, Estelle admitted that it would be difficult to run the prisons, given current staffing patterns, without the assistance of inmates in positions such as "turnkey."

Witnesses for the Justice Department took a less charitable view of these management strategies. They claimed that inmates were routinely used as substitute officers in supervisory and disciplinary roles and that these inmates were chosen because of their long sentences and physical prowess, which often meant that they had been involved in very violent offenses. The claim that inmates were routinely used as substitute officers in supervisory roles was supported not only by charges made by plaintiff witnesses but also on occasion through testimony given by the state's witnesses.

In one such instance, a field captain at the Eastham Unit, who had worked for TDC for almost twenty-one years, testified about policies in the field, where officers were to stay mounted on their horses some fifteen to twenty yards away from the squad. If a fight broke out, officers were instructed to call selected inmates out by name to break up the fight. In other testimony, a building captain acknowledged that due to staff shortages some inmates were used to help escort inmates from one location to another; but this practice, the officer claimed, was limited to routine matters in the center hall of the prison and was not employed when escorting troublesome inmates to lockup. A disciplinary report was presented that read, "Due to Adams' behavior and also the shortage of officers, I instructed Inmate Combs and two inmate night workers named Henry Richard and John Maddox to accompany Adams and myself to 2 Wing East [lockup]." On further questioning, the testifying officer admitted that such practices had occurred. Another officer, testifying about a particularly brutal attack by one inmate on another with two pipes, noted that no officer had been on the cell block at the time.

Q: Your statement, though, in this report was that there was no officer there, and my question was, on all too frequent occasions it is an inmate, a building tender or a turnkey who allows other inmates out of the cell and out into the hall without an officer approving that particular action. Is that yes or no?

A. At times that's true, yes, sir.

The potential for outrageously bad consequences of crowded cell blocks and low staffing levels were also revealed in testimony elicited from prison officials. Three examples were eventually summarized in Judge Justice's memorandum opinion.[27] One of these incidents occurred in December 1978, while the trial was in progress. The victim was an eighteen-year-old offender who had been sentenced to prison on "shock probation." When he arrived at the Ferguson Unit, officials were not made aware of this special status, and he was assigned to a cell with two other inmates, one of whom had an extensive disciplinary record, including a serious assault on another inmate. The other had been involved in the sexual abuse of fellow inmates. Over a three-day period, these cellmates repeatedly raped and beat the young offender. He was forced to remain naked much of the time, burned with cigarettes, and prevented from going to meals. When the picket officer made his rounds, the cellmates simply forced the victim to face the cell urinal so the officer could not observe his injured condition.

The situation was finally brought to the attention of officers by an inmate "porter." No disciplinary action was taken against officers for failure to notice the situation, since their superiors felt that they were fulfilling their assigned duties. One of the aggressor inmates was prosecuted and received a seven-year sentence. The other lost accumulated good time but within five months had received it all back and had been promoted to the highest good-time earning status.

Witnesses for the Justice Department repeatedly claimed that low staffing levels and a reliance on inmate assistance often meant that cell blocks were left unattended and that inmates given the task of "taking care" of the cell block could do much as they pleased. Large portions of the relevant testimony centered around a group of inmates who were allegedly left in charge of "K line," also known as Ku Klux Klan, on the Eastham Unit. Two of the building tenders were Charles Robertson and Butch Ainsworth.

In his recollection of a particularly egregious instance, an inmate witness, who was himself a building tender at the time of the incident, testified:

A: I saw Building Tenders Charley Robertson and Butch Ainsworth, who were sniffing paint thinner, lacquer thinner, and were foaming at the mouth. They tortured Inmate Gilbert and caused him to submit to Inmate Ainsworth, who was a building tender.

Q: What do you mean they tortured him?

A: They wrapped a wet blanket around him first, plugged an extension cord into a socket. The ends of the extension cord were uninsulated, and they stuck this energized electric cord to this wet blanket.

Q: Did that work?

A: This wasn't getting the results that they wanted, so they unwrapped Inmate Gilbert, made him stand up in the commode in Ainsworth's cell and then placed the electric wires to his body and into the water.

Q: What kind of physical effect did this have on Gilbert?

A: This caused Inmate Gilbert to scream from extreme pain, to begin to tremble, even to cry, and to submit to the homosexual acts.

Q: Did they want anything from Gilbert other than sex?

A: Yes, they wanted him to sign up for a commissary book. On numerous occasions Inmate Gilbert had been—his commissary had been taken away from him by Building Tender Robertson and Ainsworth, so he refused to even sign up for commissary any more rather than have it taken away from him. He just wouldn't even sign up. They made him sign a withdrawal slip for a commissary book.

Staff Misconduct and the Building Tender System   Prison officials were quite aware of the potential for harm inherent in crowded cell blocks and an overextended staff. However, they repeatedly countered that instances such as those involving Ainsworth and Robertson were isolated, and that more generally conditions had been kept in check by dedicated correctional officers and tight managerial controls on the inmate population. The plaintiffs contended that these tight controls often meant the arbitrary enforcement of vague disciplinary rules, harassment, brutality, and as a consequence a pervasive climate of fear. The two perspectives were brought together on the issue of escapes. Prison officials accurately reported that the escape rate from the TDC was far below that of any other comparable prison system. Justice Department attorneys introduced dramatic evidence on the treatment of those who tried to escape and failed.

An inmate involved testified that he and another prisoner had attempted to escape from the Eastham Unit on a foggy morning in September 1977.

> Well, we were finishing up a cut that we had started. We were working next to a river. As the boss had told us to pick up and go to another cut, why they turned their backs on us and we jumped the fence and attempted to run off . . .
>
> When we jumped the fence the bosses that was near us didn't see us. It was some officer from another squad and he hollered out. Right as we got to the bottom of the creek, well, they'd already got up to the fence and started shooting. When they started shooting, David took a left and he crossed the creek and I continued on up the creek around brush where I could stay out of the line of fire from their guns. I come to where I had to cross and I was going up the far side of the river bank and I slipped and they supposedly fired eleven shots at me. I was hit once in the scrotum.

Shortly thereafter the field captain caught up with the inmate, where-upon he "hollered back at the dog boy to go back and get the dogs." The inmate surrendered and told the captain that he had been shot, and asked to be taken to the prison. The captain allegedly replied, "Well, you've done made two kind of liars out of me today, so you'll just wait here and fight the dogs when they get here." After some discussion, the captain agreed to let the inmate climb a tree but told the inmate that when the dogs arrived he would either come down out of the tree and fight the dogs or be shot. When the dogs arrived, the inmate related,

> Captain Shipper, he goes to waving his pistol, and says, "Come on out or I'm going to shoot you out," so I pulled my shirt off and come on out of the tree. When I got down, they motioned me out in the open part of the creek bank, the bottom, and the dogs were all around me. None of them had tried to attack me. They was just all—I was surrounded. There was ten dogs.

The dogs didn't attack, the inmate testified, until he was hit on the back with a bullwhip. Then he started fighting the dogs. "I hit them with my shirt, my fist, kicked them, even after—they got pretty rough on my legs." While this was happening, the "dog sergeant" came up behind the inmate and, using the handle of his whip, "[He] hit me once right above my ear and hit me again on my neck." Once the dogs were called off, the inmate was ordered back to the trailers with the rest of the field inmates. When he was on his way back, the dogs allegedly continued to nip at his legs as he ran.

When testifying about the same incident several months later, the field captain recalled the events somewhat differently. He agreed that the inmate had been shot while trying to escape and that he had surrendered peacefully. However, the captain denied seeing any use of a whip, other than as a signal to the dogs, nor did he see the dogs bite the inmate. Instead he recalled that the inmate had been treed by the dogs and that the dogs had been called off before the inmate came down to be handcuffed. The inmate's wounds, the officer speculated, might have been suffered when "he went over a four-barbed wire or five-barbed wire fence and ran through a thorn patch."

After the incident, the inmate was seen by a doctor. In his trial testimony, the doctor recalled treating the inmate for a gunshot wound to his testicle and for "a tremendous number of puncture wounds where something had bitten him, and welts were bleeding across his back and buttocks." The welts were consistent with the assertion that the patient had been beaten with a bullwhip. It was, the doctor summarized, the worst example of brutality he had seen. This latter assertion suggested the possibility that the doctor had been witness to other instances of brutality. When asked if this were the case, he replied that he had seen "hundreds" of cases where "it happened to be obvious that another human being or more than one had inflicted the injuries," and that in many of these he was told that the inmate had fallen off a bunk or slipped in the shower.

Just as Turner's witnesses had done earlier, witnesses for the Justice Department continued to appear before the court with repetitive claims that prison officials were guilty of harassment and summary punishments and that the disciplinary system was characterized by vague rules that were applied in an arbitrary manner.[28] These claims were, with equal fervor, repeatedly denied once the state began to present its case in May 1979.

In many instances the denials were all-encompassing, as illustrated by the testimony of a six-year veteran of TDC, who would have been in a position to witness staff brutality as a captain on the Eastham Unit, where many of the alleged altercations had taken place. When asked if he had "ever personally observed a correctional officer physically abuse or harass another inmate," the officer simply replied, "No, sir, I haven't."[29] In other instances the denials were more detailed, as with the field captain who denied the charges of unleashing the dogs on the escaping inmate, the lieutenant who denied charges of harassing and then beating an inmate following a confrontation in the dining hall, and the building captain who detailed how an inmate's jaw was broken, not by a blow the captain had delivered but when the inmate bumped into another prisoner while rounding a blind corner on the run.[30]

In most instances Judge Justice had to decide who was telling the truth. In one case it was quite clear how he perceived the situation, when he all but accused the witness for the state of lying about the treatment of writ-writers.[31] In another, he expressed extreme indignation when informed of how his earlier protective orders had been violated in a disciplinary hearing involving David Ruiz.

The witness, D. V. McKaskle, was the assistant director for special services for the TDC. One of his duties was to review and then approve or modify all state disciplinary reports. In this particular instance, Ruiz had been denied the right to call witnesses and had been punished with the loss of thirty days' good time. This penalty subsequently played a role in the denial of his parole in November 1978. When queried by the judge, McKaskle admitted that while he had been briefed on the protective order, he had not read it. When Idar attempted to justify the actions, Justice abruptly responded, "Well, I'm very interested that that's your opinion about the thing. That is the most outrageous opinion that I have ever heard of . . . Let's get off on something else. I find the position of the Texas Department of Corrections in that proceeding arbitrary, tyrannical and any other word that you want to apply to it."

Behind this harsh assessment was the long-standing concern that prisoners who dared to challenge prison officials were very likely to be harassed in a number of ways. As the trial progressed, a substantial number of inmate witnesses wrote Justice Department attorneys about "being beaten or otherwise punished." When informed of this, Judge Justice asked that the matter be investigated. In December 1978 FBI agents were assigned to the investigation. While no immediate action was taken, by July 1979 negotiations were conducted for the transfer of inmates who had either testified or been scheduled for testimony to federal prison facilities. On the last day of the trial, in September, Judge Justice ordered that such transfers be allowed at the discretion of the prisoners. On October 16 and 17, 1979, approximately eighty prisoners accepted the offer and were transferred to various federal institutions.

On the same day that the FBI investigation was announced, in December 1978, further charges of harassment were raised when David Ruiz was indicted on a charge that he attempted to sexually abuse a prisoner, initially identified only as a sixteen-year-old Mexican alien charged with murder, while housed at the Harris County Rehabilitation Center during the trial proceedings. This charge came just a month after the denial of parole to Ruiz based on the disciplinary proceedings that had so troubled Judge Justice. Given the juxtaposition of these circumstances, questions were raised about the legitimacy of the rape charges. Even the sheriff in charge of a jail where Ruiz once spent a short time was quoted as saying, "Unfortunately, in law enforcement, many people are sometimes told to try and make a case for some reason. Not that I know anything definite about this one, but you see what I mean."[32]

Further questions were raised when it was learned that Jack Heard, the sheriff in charge of the Harris County Rehabilitation Center, was a former high-ranking TDC official. In addition, the district attorney's office in Houston had originally been reluctant to take the case because of the lack of evidence. At first there was only one witness, the victim, who might have been involved in a "setup" to help his own chances at trial. Eventually a second witness appeared, but this witness turned out to be a former TDC building tender. It was reported that the district attorney's office did not even have the knife allegedly used in the assault. When asked about this, the prosecutor in charge of the case was quoted as saying, "Not that particular knife, no, but we have another one. But I can't discuss it. The defense doesn't know yet, and I want to keep it a secret for a while."[33] As shaky as the case might have seemed, it eventually had an impact on the *Ruiz* proceedings when the former building tender who claimed to be a witness to the alleged rape, and who had originally testified for the Justice Department, changed his testimony and became one of the state's first witnesses when the defense began to present its case on May 2, 1979.

Fabricated charges, staff brutality, and harassment were only part of the climate of fear that Justice Department attorneys promised to reveal. The improper use of inmates as enforcers was the other. When it came to the building tender system, witnesses for the Justice Department simply underscored many of the points made early in the trial. Building tenders enjoyed special privileges, including longer out-of-cell time and access to other inmates' cells. They ran "inmate stores" that were "stocked" by coercively obtained commissary. They engaged in homosexual exploitation. They brutalized other inmates. They had ready access to weapons and were frequently called upon to support staff in stopping fights, quelling disruptive behavior, and administering discipline.[34]

The position taken by witnesses for the state was that building tenders were treated like everyone else. When they were abusive or when they disobeyed the rules, they were punished. They often helped break up fights, but so did other inmates. Some had extensive records of violence, but no more so than the general population on the units where they worked. And most importantly, officials claimed, they were not placed in positions where they were asked to exercise authority over other inmates.[35]

These charges and denials of staff brutality and use of inmates as enforcers would eventually coalesce in an altercation on the Retrieve Unit on October 23, 1979, which resulted in the death of a prisoner, Gus Feist. Feist was the third inmate connected with the *Ruiz* trial to die in the space of three months as the trial drew to a close. The first, Julio Nieto, died on July 29, 1979. He had testified in October 1978 about being maced and being denied medication by warden Christian. The listed cause of death was complications from diabetes. At the time of his death, however, one "federal source" was quoted as saying that the death appeared to be "particularly suspicious."[36] No negligence or other foul play was ever proven.

The second inmate witness to die was Carl Reed. Inmate Reed died on the Ellis Unit on October 5, 1979, when his throat was cut by another inmate with a homemade knife fashioned from razor blades and ice cream sticks. Reed had long participated in the barrage of charges launched against the TDC's building tender system. He had repeatedly written the FBI as early as March 1975, charging that his life was in danger and eventually stating that he had been the victim of a brutal beating conducted by the unit's . . . building tenders, and authorized by the unit's assistant warden."[37] When he testified in November 1978, he alleged that he was beaten by building tenders to such an extent that he had to be taken to the hospital, where the bones in the left side of his face were wired back together. The officer in charge of investigating these altercations was Robert Lawson. In trial testimony, Lawson indicated that Reed had precipitated both fights, in one instance by pushing the building tender to the floor for not waking him up to meet a visitor, and in the other by striking a building tender after he was told that "he wasn't supposed to be out of his cell for recreation."

Because of his testimony, Reed was one of the prisoners given the option of transferring out of TDC. In a letter to David Vanderhoof dated September 24, 1979, accepting the transfer offer, Reed wrote, "I definitely want to be transferred out of this sorry system . . . Yes, I want to go bad."[38] Close to two weeks after Reed's death, two reporters for the *Dallas Times Herald* wrote that they had interviewed Reed's half-brother, who had received a letter from Reed charging that he "had been beaten by three Ellis unit officials who wanted him to drop his charges against the TDC." Reed asked that his half-brother visit him as soon as possible. The visit was planned for October 6 or 7, a day or two after Reed was killed, and ten days before the testifying inmates were transferred to federal facilities.[39] Just over a week after Reed's death, the FBI announced an investigation amid complaints from the Justice Department that prison officials were not providing adequate protection. Charges were never proven.

The third inmate connected with the *Ruiz* trial to die was Gus Feist. Feist had volunteered to be a witness in the *Ruiz* trial and was listed for appearance but was never called. In addition, he had been charged by Robert Lawson, who at this time had been promoted to major, and assistant warden G. H. Stricklin as being one of the "ringleaders" of the October disturbances that accompanied the beginning of trial.[40] At the time of his death, Feist was housed on the Retrieve Unit, where David Christian and Robert Lawson, two officials who had been central actors in much of the trial testimony, worked. Feist had been an active writ-writer for some time, and just over two weeks before his death he had written to United States marshals in Houston about harassment by Christian and Lawson.[41]

Feist died as the result of an altercation that took place on October 23, 1979. The official account of the incident indicated that as Feist was walking through the center hall of the Retrieve Unit with a squad of inmates returning from the peanut fields when he passed an inmate, Roy Melancon, and began cursing him. A fight ensued, whereupon the squad of inmates stopped, thus creating a "very explosive" situation. However, "Due to Major Lawson's quick reactions the entire incident did not last over approximately thirty seconds."[42] As a result of this brief fight, inmate Feist was transferred via ambulance to John Sealy Hospital, where he died from "brain stem hemorrhage, cerebral hemorrhages and contusions, and trauma,"[43] which were suffered, according to official accounts, when his head struck the cement floor. Statements taken from inmates in the hall at the time of the altercation basically supported this official account.

Shortly after Feist's death, however, contradictory reports began to emerge. When FBI agents interviewed inmate witnesses to the incident, they were informed that instead of a brief fight between Feist and Melancon, the incident had actually involved an attack by several "prisoner-guards" armed with weapons and that Major Lawson had participated in the beating. This account was consistent with the extensive injuries revealed on the certificate of death, as well as impressions of those who saw photos taken of Feist's body. Given the additional information, Judge Justice ordered a United States attorney to conduct an independent investigation of the incident in November 1979.[44]

In April 1980 a wrongful death action was filed by Feist's parents in the United States District Court in Galveston, naming Warden Christian, Major Lawson, Roy Melancon, and the Texas Department of Corrections as defendants. Inmate Melancon was accused of acting as a "convict guard" or enforcer as the request of Major Lawson and Warden Christian, who, it was alleged, had asked Melancon to elicit the help of other building tenders to take actions that Warden Christian and Major Lawson could not "officially" take. The suit included charges of responsibility for the fatal assault as well as participation in a subsequent conspiracy to cover up the incident.

In particular, it was alleged that when the work squad returned to the building, a "gang of convict guards were waiting for [Feist] led by defendant Melancon." Feist was "grabbed and pulled into the unit hospital, where the gang [of building tenders] beat him with their fists and an iron pipe." Feist managed to break away and ran back into the hall where the rest of the work squad had gathered. There, [Feist's] head was repeatedly slammed into the concrete floor and Defendant Major Lawson stomped upon [Feist's] head as he lay on the concrete floor. This abuse occurred until [Feist] was unconscious."

It was further alleged that, immediately following the attack, a conspiracy emerged wherein inmates were induced, with threats and promised privileges, to sign statements supporting the official story. Those inmates who refused were placed in solitary confinement, allegedly "for their own protection." In addition, officials were charged with fabricating the story that the fight had lasted only a short time and that it had involved only Melancon and Feist. The conspiracy involved a further change in the official account that Feist's injuries had been suffered in a "fall" to an account wherein Feist had "flipped" over when struck by Melancon and had thereby hit the floor with greater force than a fall alone would cause. Finally, it was charged that the named defendants were guilty of providing false information to the treating physicians and pathologist as well as to "officials and investigating authorities."[45]

On July 23, 1982, after some two years of legal maneuverings, W. J. Estelle authorized settlement of the case for more than $18,000. By settling the case, TDC was able to avoid a trial in which building tenders and charges of guard brutality would once again be central issues, since most of the prisoners involved in the death of Gus Feist allegedly were well-known building tenders. TDC had, just months previously, been embroiled in a controversial court report on building tenders, in which prison officials had denied all allegations of building tender abuses. Also, at about the same time, the prison system had been subjected to adverse publicity over the capital murder trial of a TDC prisoner, Eroy Brown, whose claim that he killed a TDC warden and farm manager in self-defense had resulted in a hung jury.[46] Finally, the attorney general's office was concerned that even if the state could overcome the building tender issue at trial, there was other potentially damaging evidence pointing to gross negligence, such as the inexplicable fact that it took the unit ambulance more than twenty minutes to travel less than a quarter of a mile to the unit infirmary after they received the emergency call to transport Feist to the prison hospital in Galveston.

In addition to being the focus of the civil rights case brought by Gus Feist's parents, David Christian's and Robert Lawson's participation in this incident was investigated by a federal grand jury. A well-known attorney, Richard "Racehorse" Haynes, was paid a flat fee of $10,000 by TDC for "professional services" rendered in their defense.[47] While criminal responsibility was never proven in this particular incident, Lawson and Christian were repeatedly implicated in charges of brutality throughout the *Ruiz* trial, and both were subsequently fired for incidents involving brutality that occurred after the trial. Eventually, Lawson was convicted and sentenced to prison on a charge of beating an inmate who attempted to escape.

Medical Care and Special-Needs Inmates   Attorneys for the state had long recognized that TDC was vulnerable when it came to medical care and meeting the needs of physically handicapped and mentally retarded inmates. In February 1979, during the three-and-a-half-month trial recess, the possibility of settling the case was again pursued. Medical care, according to TDC's lawyer, Ed Idar, was the prison system's worst issue when Judge Justice had originally consolidated the case in May 1974. However, in what would prove to be an overoptimistic assessment of improvements since that time, Idar claimed that this issue had been eliminated to a large extent over the intervening years. Problems that remained, according to Idar, included difficulties in hiring enough qualified medical personnel such as physicians, psychologists, and psychiatrists. To supplement the medical staff, TDC made extensive use of paramedical personnel, both convicts and civilians, a practice Idar believed would have to be limited substantially. In addition, Idar acknowledged that TDC did have problems in their record-keeping practices, but that this issue could probably be resolved if officials were willing to take the necessary steps to improve their practices.

Since TDC was not in compliance with federal regulations intended to ensure equal access for handicapped persons,[48] Idar felt that the state might be asked to make modifications throughout the prison system at substantial cost. Less costly, but no less important, Idar noted, was the fact that TDC was vulnerable when it came to the treatment of mentally retarded inmates. There was no screening system that allowed prison officials to identify mentally retarded individuals when they entered the system. Instead, in what Idar characterized as a rather hit-or-miss operation, these individuals might or might not be identified at some later point. Once identified, there was a continuing problem of tracking these same inmates as they transferred from one unit to another.

These acknowledged problems were quite consistent with what Turner had promised to prove in his opening statements to the court. In addition, Turner had promised to establish that the problems created by inadequate facilities, poor classification procedures, and the extensive use of inmates to supplement medical professionals were compounded by "deliberate indifference by security staff to the medical problems of prisoners, for example forcing them to work when they're medically unable to do so." On the issue of staff and building tender abuse, prison officials had been able to attribute many of the charges to "lying convicts." When it came to medical care, the most damning testimony came from expert witnesses and was confirmed by former nurses and currently employed physicians, including the head of the TDC medical staff.

One of the first witnesses put on the stand by the Justice Department was a former director of the national Joint Commission on Accreditation of Hospitals. Members of this commission were appointed by the American Medical Association, the American College of Surgeons, the American College of Physicians, and the American Hospital Association. This witness had made inspection visits of TDC medical facilities for the Justice Department in 1976 and 1978 and had concluded that the medical care system did not meet minimal standards. He was particularly disturbed by what he had seen and heard while visiting the Diagnostic Unit, where entry examinations and medical classifications, which determined work assignments, treatment programs, and unit of assignment, were conducted.

I was absolutely astounded at what I saw and heard and verified . . . They bring in Monday through Friday an average of better than fifty patients a day . . . The doctor is there an average of one and a half to two hours. Giving him the the [sic] doubt of two hours means . . . that each physical examination consisted of an average of 2.4 minutes . . . This doctor, besides having to examine and do the physical examination on these fifty prisoners, must interpret fifty X-rays. He must also make the assignment of these fifty men for their capabilities to do physical work . . . Also, if there were sick cases . . . he had to give them special attention . . . All diabetics, epileptics and heart cases must also receive special attention. This [was] all done in a two-hour period at my last examination [1978] . . . In 1976 it was practically the same thing, if not worse, because the doctor was only there three days of the week.

A second expert witness had likewise inspected TDC's medical care system in 1976 and 1978, which he found to be "woefully inadequate." He was asked specifically about the Huntsville "hospital."

General housekeeping at the Huntsville Hospital was very, very poor. Basic sanitation, cleaning were lacking. This was obvious on my first visit and obvious on my second visit . . . On my second visit, after I had been in clinical medicine in the civilian world for approximately a year, I was in a sense really overwhelmed by what I saw on some of the wards and at one point had to leave. Crowded, dirty, people dying on the ward with not the basic amenities, just a very, very shoddy situation.

These conditions, many of which could have been easily remedied, were compounded, according to this same witness, by a general lack of space.

There was a lack of administrative space. There was a lack of office space for conducting examinations. There was a lack of laboratory space. There was a lack of waiting space. There was a lack of toilets and sinks and spaces for personal hygiene on the wards, storage space. They were just lax in almost every area of the hospital.

Nor did the witness feel that the hospital was safe in case of an emergency. There was one major entrance to the hospital on the first floor. There was a "very narrow" staircase, and there was an elevator that provided vertical access to the second floor, where many paraplegics were housed. In case of an emergency, the witness felt, there would be "no way to get people out of there quickly, and in a safe way."

Much of the testimony given by these experts was corroborated by former nurses who had worked at the Huntsville hospital.[49] One testified that while he was employed from 1974 to 1977, there had been no backup generator, which meant on one occasion that the physician had had to perform an appendectomy with a flashlight. A second nurse, who had worked at the the hospital between 1975 and 1977, testified that the elevator had "frequently" gone out of service and that, combined with poorly maintained emergency equipment, this had contributed to the death of an inmate.

I had a patient at First Aid who was complaining of chest pain. I had gone to the Pharmacy to get some medication to give him. While I was in the Pharmacy one of the inmate nurses came back to me and said that the patient had passed out and had arrested. When I went to First Aid what he told me was true. My inmate nurses had to run up by the stairs to the fourth floor and bodily carry the crash cart and the defibrillator back to First Aid . . .

Q: When they arrived with the crash cart, did you find it intact?

A: No, I did not.

Q: What was missing?

A: I went to get suction to use. There was a suction machine there, but the bottle was missing from the suction machine. I went to get the laryngoscope. I found the blade, but the handle was missing. There were no needles or syringes on the crash cart.

Q: Where were the needles and syringes?

A: The needles and syringes are kept under lock and key in the Pharmacy . . .

Q: What happened to the patient?

A: The patient died.

Q: Did anyone try cardiopulmonary resuscitation?

A: We tried to do C.P.R., but at the time the man had vomitus and had an obstructed airway, and we could not maintain the airway.

This former TDC nurse went on to testify that many of the problems were discussed in several meetings with the hospital administrator and physicians, but that nothing was done.

After one particularly egregious incident in 1977, two nurses at the Huntsville hospital threatened to resign. Their supervisor convinced them to wait a little longer while he tried to get things "straightened out." He then called an official with the Texas Board of Nursing Examiners. This conversation was recalled in the nurse's testimony.

She said, "Well, did you talk to your hospital administrator?"
I said, "Yes, to my feeling, that's part of the problem."
She said, "Well, did you check your procedure manual?"
I said, "We don't have a procedure manual."
She went right down the line. She said, "Well, did you talk to your nursing supervisor?"
I said, "I am the nursing supervisor," and then she said, "Well it looks like to me you need to get the hell out of there."

The supervising nurse then went to TDC's head physician to inform him of the threatened resignations and the impossibility of functioning without the help. He asked the doctor if there was "any relief in sight in the near future." The physician replied that he did not see "in the near future anything getting better." Shortly thereafter, the supervising nurse joined the other two nurses in turning in their resignations.

The head physician was later called to testify as a witness for the state, and during cross-examination he agreed with the statement that the Huntsville hospital was "really very inadequate" and "totally out of date which it has been for over twenty years." There were plans at the time of trial to greatly expand the medical facilities at John Sealy Hospital in Galveston, but the doctor expressed continuing frustration about the low priority given to medical care over the years.

Q: Have you ever found it discouraging the percentage of time that the Board spends, as reflected in [their] minutes, devoted to

agriculture and livestock and land acquisition and industrial sales
and arrangements for the upcoming rodeo?

A: I have appeared before the Prison Board I would say ten or
twelve times since I have been Director, usually for a specific
item.

Q: Have you had reason, though, to note the relative amount of
time the Board spends on medical care, as opposed to other activities I have listed?

A: I am well aware.

Q: Do you find it discouraging?

A: Yes, I do.

Through cross-examinations such as this, as well as through testimony
from their own witnesses, attorneys for the Justice Department and the
plaintiffs attempted to demonstrate that TDC's medical care system had
been allowed to fall far below constitutional standards. The problems, it
was charged, could be traced to deliberate indifference, poor staffing
levels, too heavy a reliance on inmates to supplement medical staff, inadequate training programs, low levels of competence, incomplete and
misleading record-keeping practices, a general lack of organization, and,
perhaps most importantly, to a set of priorities that placed medical needs
well below security and an almost obsessive concern for having inmates
work.[50]

Much of this testimony would eventually be summarized in footnotes
in Judge Justice's memorandum opinion.[51] The problems with hiring,
training, and keeping competent medical staff were similar to those encountered with security staff. While the number of physicians had risen
from one to the equivalent of just less than thirteen between 1974 and
1978, there was a concern with the competence of these physicians. Testimony was directed to one occasion in July 1976, when a physician attempted to perform an appendectomy. "After about two hours of futile
bungling around" by the doctor, the nurse in charge of the anesthesia
demanded that someone call another physician. The initial doctor had
been unable to find the appendix and, in the process of looking, had split
the cecum, which resulted in fecal material and hemorrhage in the abdominal cavity.

Finding competent physicians was not the only problem. There was
also a shortage of registered nurses. To fill the gaps, inmates were assigned medical tasks for which they had little training. This often meant
that entries on medical records were erroneous and that even simple instructions were not followed correctly. One example involved an inmate

nurse who was asked to take out half the sutures following an abdominal surgery. Instead of taking out every other one, the inmate took out all the stitches on the top half of the incision.

Nor was competence the only problem. Priorities were such that concerns for security often came in conflict with good medical practice. One instance was detailed in testimony by an inmate who had been assigned to the Huntsville hospital after returning from John Sealy Hospital. While at John Sealy, he had been catheterized and instructed to drink plenty of water and to empty his urine bag regularly. When the inmate got up to empty his bag just after ten o'clock "lights out," he was confronted by the sergeant on duty and told to return to his bed. The sergeant allegedly did not want to hear any explanations, and after a brief verbal exchange, the captain was called for assistance, along with several additional officers. Recalling the incident, the inmate testified: "Captain Scott walks up to me and tells me, 'What's your problem?' and I say, 'Well I tried to explain to Sergeant Ritters my reasons for being off the bed.' He stops me and he says, 'Whenever my officers tell you something, right or wrong, you do it.' " After a brief argument, a struggle began, about which the inmate testified, "So they grabbed me and started hitting me in the side and one of them got hold of the catheter that I had in me and yanked it out. From that I was bleeding badly." When the bleeding started, the inmate became hysterical, and the struggle continued, wherein "Someone stomped my finger, you know, and broke it and I let out a loud scream, and so he tell me to shut up that screaming and he hit me in the mouth and busted my lip."

During his subsequent testimony, the captain involved in the incident described in general terms how he talked to the inmate in an attempt to calm him down. When this was unsuccessful, a struggle started and everyone fell to the floor, whereupon the inmate stated, "I give." The officer did not remember seeing a catheter after the inmate was subdued. Nor did he see any "mess" on the floor. However, since it was dark, he acknowledged that he might not have noticed. He was unsure about the rules prohibiting inmates from getting out of bed after ten o'clock except to go to the bathroom or to get a drink of water. He did not know how the inmate's lip was cut. Other officers involved in the struggle were not called to testify.

Testimony questioning judgments involved in the care of inmates with special problems was not restricted to physical ailments. One instance involved an inmate, James Elton Batts, who, according to official records, had been in four state hospitals for mental treatment at the time of his admission to prison. After about a month undergoing various screening procedures at the Diagnostic Unit, Batts was admitted to the Huntsville Comprehensive Treatment Center (CTC) in February 1977, due to his long history of mental problems. Upon his arrival, official records show, he was "restless with extreme insomnia and suicidal ideas." After some seven months, it was felt that the "patient [had] obtained maximum benefit from CTC and [was] ready for unit assignment." His discharge diagnosis was schizophrenia, simple type, with depressive symptomalogy. His medications were to consist of Prolixin, Cogentin, and Elavil.

He was assigned to the Eastham Unit on September 15, 1977. Two days later, he attempted to hang himself in his cell. Records indicate that he would have succeeded if his belt had not broken. He was found by an inmate cleaning the wing, who informed two building tenders, who then resuscitated the inmate and called the guards and medical officer. Two days later, Batts was seen by the unit psychologist, who recommended that Batts be returned to his cell and that he work with close supervision "for manipulative suicidal attempt." The psychologist felt that the suicide attempt was Batts's "means of extracting himself from a difficult situation." Ironically, on that same day, the Unit Disciplinary Committee punished Batts with solitary confinement ("probated") and forfeited thirty days of the inmate's good time.

At around nine o'clock the next morning, Batts once again attempted to hang himself. On this occasion the same building tender who resuscitated him after the first try found Batts before he lost consciousness. Batts was then seen by the unit's physician, who pronounced the inmate "able and fit for work." Approximately forty-five minutes after his attempt to hang himself, Batts was taken to the fields. However, following the lunch break he refused to work on four separate occasions. Each time, the field captain would later recall in his trial testimony, Batts was talked into going back to work. That night Batts was assigned to stay "on the wall" at the searcher's desk instead of in his cell.

Accounts differ as to the specific events that took place during the night and the early hours of the morning. All witnesses agreed, however, that by around 6:30 A.M. Batts was in poor physical and mental shape. He wandered, stumbled, and repeatedly slumped to the floor. At one point, officers handcuffed Batts to keep him from interfering with inmates passing through the hall. Sometime shortly after breakfast (around 6:30), he was taken to the unit infirmary, where a cut on his head was sutured. Thereafter he was certified ready for normal duty and was taken back out to the fields.

This day he refused work completely and was handcuffed to a ladder on one of the cotton wagons. At one point he maneuvered his body into a position where the cuffs were cutting off circulation to his hands, and the officers had to readjust them. At noon, when the work force returned from the fields, Batts was taken to the infirmary because he was hyperventilating. After being treated for hyperventilation, he was given salt tablets, water, and two miligrams of Cogentin, which he had been taking regularly. The medical assistant would later testify that he was unaware that one of the side effects of this drug was the depression of perspiration, and that standard medical reference sources recommended against its use by "those who do manual labor in a hot environment." Following this treatment and medication, Batts was released for normal work with his prognosis marked "good." About fifteen minutes later, Batts died while sitting in front of the searcher's desk.

An autopsy was ordered and performed the next day. It was the examiner's opinion that Batts had died "as a result of massive cerebral edema following asphyxia due to hanging—Suicide."[52] Given the surrounding circumstances, this assessment raised immediate questions about the legitimacy of the autopsy. One inmate wrote letters to the District Court in Tyler and to Senator Lloyd Bentsen the night of Batts's death, claiming that Batts had died of mistreatment and beatings over a three-day period. Just over a month later, the FBI began an investigation at the request of Batts's uncle. When questioned by reporters about the apparent discrepancies between accounts of the death and her official autopsy report, the medical examiner said she had been told that Batts had never left the hospital after his suicide and that her report had been made under that assumption. Her assessment of the cause of death, "massive cerebral endema," was also consistent with the consequences associated with heatstroke.

In January 1978 a federal grand jury was convened to investigate possible criminal prosecution of TDC officers involved in Batts's death. Even though there existed damning evidence that TDC officials had kept Batts chained to cotton ladders for an extended period of time in the hot sun, after he had attempted suicide and sustained numerous head injuries over a two-day period, no indictments were ever issued.

In September 1978, however, almost exactly a year after Batts's death, a civil rights action was filed in the Eastern District of Texas by Batts's uncle, alleging wrongful death due to negligence and medical and psychiatric malpractice. Numerous postponements resulted in the case's dragging on until January 1984, when Judge Justice refused to grant any further delays. By this time attorneys for the state were well aware that Justice had referenced the Batts case in his memorandum opinion in *Ruiz*[53] and that the chances for successfully defending the officials charged were determined to be slim to none. As a consequence, on February 13, 1984, TDC and the state settled the case for $17,500.

Just as William Bennett Turner had done at the close of his presentation, Justice Department attorneys ended their presentation of witnesses by calling a paralyzed inmate, who entered the courtroom in a wheelchair on May 2, 1979. This witness testified in detail about the lack of training provided physically handicapped inmates and the general lack of facilities for recreation. In addition, he testified about difficulties associated with maintaining personal hygiene such as showering and using the toilet without the benefit of handrails. On one occasion, a paralyzed inmate had been set in the shower and was scalded when the water became too hot and he couldn't reach the faucet. Numerous inmates in the hospital ward for the physically handicapped had bed sores. Through inattention, some of these sores had been allowed to become quite severe. One inmate's sore had grown to be several inches wide and several inches deep; another's had penetrated to the bone. In a third case, the witness recalled, the sore had become so infected that the inmate's groin had become severely swollen, and a "green and yellow substance" was coming from the sore.

This graphic testimony would later be called to the attention of an expert witness, who was herself a paraplegic as the result of an auto accident. This witness suggested that with relatively minor innovations in the physical design of shower and toilet facilities, combined with standard hygiene training for the handicapped inmates, most of the cited problems could be done away with. In combination, these inmate and expert witnesses were used to paint a picture of TDC's medical care that would shock the public conscience, practices that were allegedly the result of deliberate indifference.

TDC's Defense

The basic outline of TDC's defense was revealed in the draft of a letter written by TDC's general counsel, Robert E. DeLong, to "Fellow Employees" and distributed with the TDC's employees' newsletter in December 1978. DeLong indicated that the approach would be a simple one. By presenting the "unvarnished truth, warts and all," the court would be given an "education about the realities of operating a prison that it thus far has not received."

DeLong noted that the plaintiffs and the Justice Department had spent five years and millions of tax dollars "trying to find all the bad stories they could about TDC." Many of the problems reflected in these stories were well known to TDC officials, who, DeLong noted, had initiated reforms without the necessity of a federal court order. The bulk of the testimony against TDC had come from prisoners characterized by DeLong as the "most pathologically maladapted inmates in the entire system." Much of the remaining testimony represented the opinions of experts who "often imposed impossibly high standards." It would be the goal of the defense team to "add a sense of proportion to the record of the trial."

This would be accomplished by showing, for example, that while medical care was not perfect, TDC officials had "responded to developing community standards progressively and energetically with an expanding and improving medical care service." In addition, by presenting aggregate death, health, and industrial accident statistics, it would be shown that TDC compared quite favorably with other prison systems as well as with the broader free community. Similarly, the data on homicide, suicide, and escapes would be shown to compare quite favorably with other prison systems, as well as with the free world. Thus, while the level of crowding was something no one liked, the defense would establish that it had not resulted in "severe and measurable harm to inmates." In conclusion, DeLong promised the employees the court would be shown that TDC was run by "a motivated and talented staff who perform their duties in a humane and concerned manner."

The success of the defense depended heavily on being able to show that much of the testimony against prison officials, policies, and practices came from "lying convicts." One of the first witnesses to testify for the state on May 3, 1979, was a former building tender who had allegedly seen David Ruiz sexually assault a young inmate while being held in Houston awaiting his trial testimony. This witness had originally testified for the plaintiffs but had since changed his mind. After being warned of the penalties for perjury, the witness indicated that he wanted to testify anyway. It was important, he said, because after David Ruiz raped the young offender, "I made up my mind that he ain't doing nothing but to hurt TDC. He ain't trying to help nobody. He's for David Ruiz."

Along with recanting much of his earlier testimony, the witness related how inmates would sit around and construct what they were going to say in court. One example he cited was the case of the inmate who claimed to have been beaten with a whip and forced to fight the dogs. This, the witness claimed, was a put-up story. "Michael Ellis told us that he actually added this to his testimony, that it was a lie. He actually said that the captain never put the dogs on him, but he wanted to add it into his testimony, so it would be better."

This, of course, was inconsistent with the testimony of the inmate who had been attacked, as well as with the medical reports and the testimony of the field captain who had agreed that the inmate had surrendered peacefully before the dogs attacked. Further credibility problems with this changed testimony would eventually emerge on January 6, 1981, when the trial on Ruiz's assault of the young inmate began. The victim of the alleged assault, amidst accusations and counter-accusations of threatened reprisals, testified that no rape had occurred and that someone with "official connections" at the Harris County Detention Center had offered him freedom in exchange for his lies about the assault. The sexual assault charges were dropped the next day.

Following the changed testimony, the next witness called characterized himself as a former "writ-writer." After being warned about the possibility of perjury charges, this inmate recounted how he and other writ-writers would "try to frame officials. We spread them out. We discussed them at pretrial conferrences. I had a negative attitude then." It was true, the witness stated, that conditions were crowded and that inmates had to sleep on the floor, but officials rotated the assignments so as to be fairer to everybody. In addition, the witness felt that guards were now more polite than they once were. "It's changed a lot. They might call you mister. Depends on the officer. Now they're more considerate. Twenty years ago, it was unheard of for an officer to say, 'How you been doing?' Now it's an everyday occurrence." When asked why he had changed his attitude toward prison and prison officials, the witness indicated that it had occurred when he found out he had a son. Having a son changed his values and had spurred his efforts to start a new life. He was eligible for parole in 1980.

Revised testimony and allegations that many of the charges had been fabricated was only one prong of the defense's attack on the veracity of the plaintiffs' evidence. Denials by prison officials was another. In many instances the only witnesses to various altercations between guards and inmates were those immediately involved. It was simply a matter of whose story seemed to be most believable. The third method used to undercut the plaintiffs' case was to establish that the testimony simply reflected isolated instances of "all the bad stories" the plaintiffs could find. Prison officials recognized that life in a sprawling complex prison system such as TDC would never be perfect. However, if the court would look at the total picture and compare the Texas prison system with prisons in other states, it would find one of the best operations in existence.

At times this became a battle of experts. Where the plaintiffs' experts had characterized prison conditions in Texas as woefully inadequate, reflective of a slavery mentality, experts for the defense referred to the Texas prison system as a model toward which other states should strive. A former institutional planner for the California prison system claimed the TDC was far superior to systems in most other states and that in most instances it was like "comparing the General Motors Corporation with a local department of welfare." It was, the expert asserted, a system "without obvious tension or harassment . . . a businesslike operation, like a well-run factory on the outside." Three medical experts, one from the Federal Bureau of Prisons and two from the California Department of Corrections, while more restrained in their praise, testified that there was nothing shocking or barbarous about medical or psychiatric care in the Texas prisons. When it came to security, a former deputy director of the United States Bureau of Prisons testified that TDC had "a remarkable record for safekeeping. They have the best record of any system in the United States and some countries in regard to assaults and escapes."

Much of this expert opinion was buttressed by having prison officials come to court simply to describe how they carried out their assigned tasks. It was hoped that this would "educate" Judge Justice, who W. J.

Estelle had accused of being ignorant about the realities of running a prison. Just as important, it would inform the public and thereby counterbalance some of the "horror stories" that had received so much media attention during the early phases of the trial. Attorneys for the state had promised TDC employees that they would have a chance to defend themselves against the numerous allegations and in the end that it would be established that prisons in Texas were run by a "motivated and talented staff who perform their duties in a humane and concerned manner." Toward this end, the state's attorneys had opposed moving the trial from Houston to Tyler following the holiday break in December 1978, in part because Tyler was not a major media center and they felt their side of the case would not receive press coverage comparable to that of the plaintiffs.[54]

Ironically, the attempt to educate Judge Justice and the public about the high quality of TDC employees and their sincere and energetic pursuit of improvement in prison conditions came close to producing a contempt citation. By June 1979, relations between Judge Justice and Ed Idar had developed a stormy history. The trial was dragging on longer than anyone had predicted. Cross-examinations by both state and Justice Department attorneys had been prematurely terminated by Judge Justice. On June 7, 1979, many of these tensions came close to erupting.

Ed Idar called a witness to testify about education courses available to inmates through a local junior college. Bill Turner objected to the testimony as irrelevant to the issues raised in the case. Failing this objection, Turner indicated that he was willing to stipulate to the truth of the witness's testimony, and requested for the sake of everyone's time that the witness not be called.

Idar replied that the testimony was relevant, in that the plaintiffs were "basically contesting that the Department of Corrections in the year of 1979 is hardly any different from 1924" and that they had "sought to show that there has been little or no change in some of the basic issues underlying this whole case." It was important to establish that there had been "substantial efforts to improve not only the living conditions, but the rehabilitative efforts to try to improve training schools, professional schools, vocational schools for the inmates."

Judge Justice agreed that the testimony might be relevant, but he could not understand why, since it was uncontested, it could not simply be taken by depositions. After several heated exchanges, Idar charged Judge Justice with changing the rules of the trial and stated that he wanted the record to reflect his belief that the court was committing reversible error in its actions.

The Court: I don't think any rule requires the court to sit and listen to testimony that is uncontested that's not going to be denied.

Mr. Idar: That may be so, Your Honor, but I think we are entitled to put on our case, and I think we are entitled to have the court observe the demeanor of the witness.

The Court: If it's uncontested, what is there—what credibility choice is to be made if it is uncontested?

Mr. Idar: Sir, there's still—the court still has to assess—I have gathered the impression from the beginning of the trial, quite frankly, Your Honor, that we have been adjudged guilty—.

The Court: Counsel, I'm going to hold you in contempt of court if you keep up in this vein, and I advise you to apologize to the court immediately.

Mr. Idar: Well sir, I did not intend to be in contempt of court. I simply am expressing my opinions as an attorney, and I feel that we have our First Amendment rights to respectfully address the court in this line.

The Court: I would suggest that you apologize to the court at this point.

Mr. Idar: I will state again, Your Honor, I did not intend to be in contempt of court.

The Court: I said I seek an apology.

Mr. Idar: In that event, sir, I do apologize then. The court has misconstrued my remarks.

Following this exchange the witness was sworn and did testify.

On August 29–30, 1979, the defense called Bruce Jackson as its final witness to testify about improvements made in the Texas prison system. Jackson was a widely published author and former member of the Society of Fellows at Harvard University. He was, at the time of his testimony, the director of the Center for Studies in American Culture at the State University of New York at Buffalo. He had first visited the Texas prison system in 1964 in pursuit of his research interests in prisons and black folklore. He was aware that John Lomax had done some of his research in the 1930s on black music in the Texas prison system. He had also read the report prepared by Austin MacCormick for the Osborne Foundation in the early 1940s. He approached George Beto in 1964 as a member of the Society of Fellows with his idea of doing some follow-up research on these earlier findings. Between 1964 and 1971, and especially between 1965 and 1967, he made repeated visits while working on several publications. He had not visited the prison system under the direction of W. J.

Estelle until the year preceding trial, when he was invited to Sam Houston University as a distinguished lecturer.

In general, Jackson testified he found the "institution of prison" to be "terrible," an "abominable place to live in." However, given their presence in society, he found the institutions in Texas to be safer and in most ways superior to other systems he had visited. In personal terms, Jackson stated that if his seventeen-year-old son ever got into enough trouble to be locked in an institution, he "would much rather that [his son] be locked in TDC than in any of the other state prisons that I have visited. I would not want him to go to any prison . . . but I would feel if he went to TDC his chances of surviving without physical harm would be greater than any other place I know."

Jackson found TDC's disciplinary policies to be strict but functional. Based on his observations of disciplinary hearings, he found the process to be neither cruel nor arbitrary. Based on figures he had gathered and observations he had made, he felt TDC's strict regime had produced a virtual absence of gang dominance, such as that experienced in California, as well as a very low homicide rate compared to such states as California, Colorado, Missouri, Oklahoma, New York, and the Federal Penitentiary in Atlanta. Given these observations and conclusions, Jackson counseled great caution if any attempt were made to restructure the disciplinary process: "To relax the strictures without knowing what's going into its place is something I would be very careful about, simply because those dangers are real. They're not hypothetical. They're not literary. They're not things that are in a sociological journal. Real people die in there."

Based on his years of observing the Texas prison system, Jackson believed that the power of the building tenders had decreased considerably. They were no longer used by the staff to administer "summary justice." More generally, it was his impression that there was no "systematic pattern and practice on the part of the TDC administration to encourage inmates to exercise supervision over other inmates." He did feel, however, that these inmates performed an important function as "bilateral carriers of information." They might be told about planned suicides, homicides, or problems among inmates in situations where staff would remain ignorant. In those situations, Jackson felt, building tenders fulfilled an "enormously valuable" function.

When asked to summarize his fifteen-year perspective on the Texas prison system, Jackson opined: "I think the pressure in the fields is less. I think the pressure in the buildings is less. The institutions are more relaxed than they were. I don't know how to quantify that. That's simply a qualitative statement that is more like how I feel. The educational programs, the industrial programs have expanded enormously, I think to everyone's benefit. The prison has become far more crowded, I think to everyone's disadvantage . . . In addition, Jackson noted that he had seen an increase in the educational level of correctional officers, as well as an improvement in their ethnic diversity. He had never seen any verbal or physical abuse of inmates in his initial visits to the prisons in the 1960s, nor had he seen any in more recent years. He had never seen an officer carry a whip while riding horseback in the fields; again, this was true throughout the time of his visits. He did have the "qualitative impression," however, that the fear of "arbitrary administrative manipulation" had gone down.

Throughout much of his summary, Jackson was careful to note that many of his conclusions about changes over the years were based on his impressions rather than on quantifiable facts. William Bennett Turner picked up on this distinction when he began his cross-examination.

Q: Mr Jackson, . . . one of the ground rules for the questions I will ask you deals with the proposition that belief and facts are not the same thing. That's a proposition you can subscribe to, isn't it?

A: That belief and facts are not the same thing?

Q: Yes.

A: Yes.

Q: If it's true that scholars are prisoners of their facts and that lawyers are prisoners of their lust to win, I take it you prefer the scholar's law?

A: Yes, I do.

Once established, this proposition was used repeatedly in an attempt to undercut Jackson's testimony. In one instance Jackson had testified that an inmate who had been rumored to be dead came back to the prison the next day. Jackson was asked if he was quite sure of this.

A: Well, I was told that. I didn't see that.

Q: You did state that as a fact though, didn't you?

A: Yes, I did.

Q: As a matter of fact, it was a matter of belief?

A: Yes, it was.

In other instances, Jackson was much less willing to agree that his conclusions were based solely on belief rather than on fact. The one exception revolved around some critical comments he had written about the way Judge Justice was conducting the *Ruiz* trial.

Q: And you also wrote that the TDC wouldn't be able to prepare for specific testimony, because the judge wouldn't make the Justice Department turn over certain information. Where did you get that information?

A: One of the attorneys in the case told me that.

The Court: Who told you that?

A: I don't remember.

The Court: I would like to know.

A: I don't remember that.

Q: And you also wrote that the government has interfered on some occasions with TDC witnesses, didn't you?

A: Yes, I did . . .

Q: You mentioned Norman Carlson [Director of the Federal Bureau of Prisons], didn't you?

A: Yes, I did.

Q: Where did you get that information?

A: I think I got that story from [Warden] McMillan [one of the original defendants in the *Ruiz* case.]

Q: And you also wrote that the Justice Department ordered Carlson to stay home, didn't you? Where did you get that information?

A: That's the same story.

Q: You didn't check with anybody on the plaintiffs' side of the case before writing that, did you? . . .

A: About those facts, no I didn't.

Q: Is that consistent with your view that scholars are prisoners of their facts? You only get one side of it before you write something?

A: I think I behaved irresponsibly in that article.

Turner: I have no further questions.

The defense rested after Bruce Jackson's testimony on August 30, 1979. Additional rebuttal witnesses were called by both sides over the next three weeks until September 20, 1979, when the trial finally drew to a close. After the final witness was heard, there were some last-minute "housecleaning" chores on evidence and previous motions before the court. Judge Justice signed an agreement allowing inmates who had testified in the trial to transfer to federal facilities, and then at 11:13 A.M. Judge Justice concluded: "Counsel, it has been a long trial. I'm informed by the clerk that there were actually consumed 161 trial days, that 349 witnesses have testified, that approximately 1,530 exhibits have been received in evidence. It's the longest trial in my experience, and may I express the hope that none of us are involved in one of this length again. The court is adjourned." With these words Judge Justice "strode from the courtroom, lawyers whooped and marshalls ushered the inmate plaintiffs back to the Harris County detention center."[55]

Chapter Six:
Reform, Rhetoric and Resistance—
1980-82

*It is that the relationship between the courts and jailors, and the
relationship between jailors and prisoners are ones in which there
is an attempt to coerce virtue as defined by the coercer. Even if we
were of one mind about the functions of prisons, it is hard to imagine a more inefficient system of administration than the coercion
of unwilling people over whom one has authority.*

Judge Irving R. Kaufman,
"Prison: The Judge's Dilemma,"
Fordham Law Review, 1973

Judge Justice Orders Massive Reforms

The *Ruiz* trial had been long and arduous. Once the courtroom
drama was over, a new phase in the bitter contest over who was
to control the state's prison system began. On December 10, 1980, more
than a year after adjournment, Judge Justice issued his memorandum
opinion detailing his factual conclusions and ordering specific relief. For
their part, prison and state officials remained far from willing to accept
either the legitimacy or the wisdom of Justice's conclusions and remedies.

The memorandum opinion was divided into six major sections: overcrowding, security and supervision, health care, discipline, access to
courts, and other conditions of confinement. Although considered
separately, many of the factual findings were inextricably linked. This
overlap was nowhere more apparent than with the analysis of "overcrowding." Justice concluded, in what would become perhaps the most
widely cited phrase of the opinion, "Overcrowding at TDC exercises a
malignant effect on all aspects of inmate life."

In support of this damning conclusion, Justice offered factual findings
that were detailed in graphic terms.

Crowded two or three to a cell or in closely packed dormitories,
inmates sleep with the knowledge that they may be molested or assaulted by their fellows at any time. Their incremental exposure to
disease and infection from other inmates in such narrow confinement cannot be avoided. They must urinate and defecate, un-
screened, in the presence of others. Inmates in cells must live and

sleep inches away from toilets; many in dormitories face the same situation. There is little respite from these conditions, for the salient fact of existence in TDC prisons is that inmates have wholly inadequate opportunities to escape the overcrowding in their living quarters. The environment outside the housing areas is similarly strained by the demands of the increased prison population and can offer no substantial relief from the pressures and harms generated by living in such close proximity.

On the positive side, Justice found TDC institutions to be "generally quite clean and well maintained." Unlike prisons described in other "conditions" lawsuits, the prisons in Texas could not be characterized as "filthy and dilapidated." Cleaning materials were widely available and frequently used. However, even in the cleanest of conditions, Justice felt that the confinement of two or three persons to forty-five-square-foot cells was "inhumane."

It was true, Justice acknowledged, that the Supreme Court had found no "one man, one cell principle lurking in the Due Process Clause," but it was also true that each prison system was to be judged according to specific facts presented. In the case of the Texas prison system, space levels fell far below recommended minimums. Prison officials themselves acknowledged that crowding was a problem. While "detailed scientifically exact proof" of concrete injuries caused by crowded conditions was lacking, there was ample testimony, received from "dozens of inmates and TDC employees (whose descriptions of the overcrowded conditions did not substantially vary), and also from a large number of extremely well qualified experts," that supported the conclusions drawn.

When it came to security and supervision, Justice organized his findings around two propositions. First, prisoners are entitled to physical safety. Second, physical safety in prison is largely dependent upon the prison staff—their training, their number, their deployment, and the duties assigned to them. Analyzed on these bases, Justice found "serious inadequacies" in TDC's staff. Staffing levels were among the worst, if not the worst, in the nation, less than half the national average. During the day, "it is not uncommon for one guard to be responsible for supervising two to four cell blocks [each cell block consisted of three tiers, with twenty or thirty cells on each tier] or dormitories." Guards were ordinarily stationed outside the cell area and never within the dormitory, where they would not enter unless summoned. Given these staffing levels and deployment patterns, Judge Justice concluded that it was inevitable that "inmate activities within the housing areas are almost entirely unsupervised by civilian personnel." As a result, "aggressive and predatory inmates are free to do as they wish in the living areas, and their victims can be threatened, extorted, beaten, or raped, in the absence of protection from civilian personnel."

It was further concluded that, contrary to statutory prohibitions, "TDC compensated for its chronic shortages of civilian security personnel by using inmates to perform security functions." Justice believed that these prisoners, often known as building tenders, were unofficially given "such specific powers as issuing orders to other inmates, assisting in taking daily counts of the population, keeping track of inmate movements, escorting inmates to different destinations within the prison, and distributing correspondence and commissary scrip." The close working relationship between these inmates and guards gave them "several significant advantages," which, Justice thought, they might readily abuse. Primary among the privileges were increased mobility throughout the prison and "the fact that building tenders are often allowed to carry weapons, which are employed to threaten and discipline other inmates." In short, Judge Justice concluded, "TDC officials have not adequately controlled the unlawfully maintained building tender system, and they have directly and indirectly permitted its abuses to be visited on the inmates in Texas prisons."

In addition to poor staffing levels and the use of inmates in positions of authority, Justice cited staff brutality as a third major area involving inmate safety. Staff brutality, Justice found, was "widespread" and "nothing short of routine." The record was "replete with credible evidence of inmates being unreasonably and unmercifully beaten with fists and clubs, kicked, and maced by the officers whose ostensible duty includes protecting them from harm." While brutality was against state law and formal departmental policy, Justice concluded that "TDC's systemic operations encourage staff brutality in two significant ways. First, TDC officials rarely investigate reports of violence and brutality involving civilian staff, and commonly fail to take corrective disciplinary action against officers whom they know to have brutalized inmates. Second, TDC's training program for guards fails to instruct the officers in the proper and reasonable use of limited physical force to quell inmate disturbances."

When the effects of poor staffing levels, inmates in positions of authority, and staff brutality were combined, Justice found the plaintiffs' case compelling: "The climate in TDC is one of fear and trepidation, engendered by the occurrence of frequent physical and sexual assaults, intimidation, bribery, and rule by threats and violence." Having thus concluded, Justice then required, among other things, a significant increase in the quantity of civilian guards, improvements in selection and training procedures for security officials, the complete elimination of the building tender system, and the cessation of staff brutality toward prison inmates.

The issue of health care was divided into three discrete areas: medical care, psychiatric care, and "special needs inmates." In all three areas Justice's assessment was damning. Major problems pervaded "all aspects of the medical care provided by TDC to its inmates." Personnel were unqualified, too few in number, and deficiently supervised. The "meager" medical facilities were, with the noted exception of the John Sealy facility in Galveston, inadequately equipped and poorly maintained and did not meet state licensing requirements. Procedures were "unsound and faulty at all levels of care." Proper medical treatment and practice was often "sacrificed to exaggerated concerns about security." Medical records were poorly maintained, incomplete, and inaccurate. Finally, Justice characterized the entire medical care system as being marked by "an absence of any organizational structure, plan, or written procedures for the delivery of medical care or for the instruction, supervision, and review of the personnel putatively providing it."

The evidence was quite sufficient, in Justice's opinion, to meet existing standards for showing systemwide deliberate indifference, and thereby a violation of the Eighth Amendment. First, there was a pattern of individual incidents involving inadequate medical care. Second, there were systemic deficiencies in the delivery of medical care that made unnecessary suffering inevitable. Having found both standards satisfied, Justice ordered that TDC increase staffing for all medical personnel. They were to restrict "the use of inmates to perform medical and pharmacological functions." The unit infirmary facilities were to be improved, and the Huntsville hospital was to be either substantially renovated or downgraded to an infirmary. In addition, it was mandated that "TDC establish diagnostic and sick call procedures which eliminate non-medical interferences with the provision of medical care, as well as medically sound procedures for making job assignments." Finally, TDC was ordered to remedy "the deficiencies in pharmaceutical operations, record-keeping, and overall organization of medical care delivery services.

In the area of psychiatric care, Justice found that professional treatment personnel were virtually nonexistent on the separate units. "Treatment" on these units consisted "almost exclusively of the administration of medications, usually psychotropic drugs." There was a lack of systematic procedures for determining the general mental health of the prison population. Procedures that did exist were poorly administered and evaluated and thus "did not provide useful treatment recommendations." There was "no program whatever for the identification, treatment, or supervision of inmates with suicidal tendencies." The Treatment Center in Huntsville had been described in 1978 by the defendants themselves as "an overcrowded, totally inadequate cell block." Justice felt that, as the Treatment Center was then operated, it was "little more than a warehouse for inmates with serious mental disorders." Taken together, these conditions closely resembled those found unconstitutional in Alabama.

Relying on the parallels with judicial precedent, expert testimony, and the application of "principles for minimally adequate care," Justice ordered that TDC develop a "systematic program for screening and evaluating inmates in order to identify those who require mental health treatment." Treatment programs were to include more than segregation and close supervision and were to be run by trained mental health professionals in "sufficient numbers to identify and treat in an individualized manner those treatable inmates suffering from serious mental disorders." "Accurate, complete, and confidential" records were to be maintained. The "prescription and administration of behavior-altering medications in dangerous amounts, by dangerous methods, or without appropriate supervision and periodic evaluation" were not to be considered an acceptable method of treatment. The revised mental health treatment program was to include "the identification, treatment, and supervision of inmates with suicidal tendencies." Finally, TDC was to provide "minimal procedural protections," as set forth in *Vitek* v. *Jones*, before imposing an involuntary transfer to a mental hospital.

When it came to the "large number of persons whose physical and mental handicaps severely limited their ability to adequately cope with prison conditions," Justice found practices to be "contrary to reason and common sense." Given cell assignments to handicapped prisoners on upper tiers, the lack of adequate space to accommodate wheelchairs, and the lack of supportive handrails around toilets, sinks, and showers, the daily routine of mobility-impaired inmates became "a dangerous exercise in gymnastics." Justice concluded that "in this area as in so many others, unit officials are apparently so severely inhibited by their own allegiance to uniformity and inflexibility that they are unable to deal humanely with persons in need of individualized, special considerations." For the 10 to 15 percent of the TDC inmates who were mentally retarded, TDC offered no programs to assist them "with the day-to-day problems they must grapple with in their attempts to function in the general inmate population."

Recognizing the special needs of the mentally and physically handicapped, Justice found that "unusual accommodations," such as greater attention to helping mentally retarded prisoners understand rules and proceedings and efforts to remove physical barriers for the physically handicapped, might be necessary so as to avoid the denial of Eighth-Amendment rights to these prisoners. It was not acceptable to force these individuals into "a mold constructed for persons of average intelligence and physical mobility." The evolving standards of decency as reflected in the Rehabilitation Act of 1973 and the Architectural Barriers Act of 1968, as well as the Texas Architectural Barriers Act and the Texas Mentally Retarded Persons Act, made it clear that there should be special attention given to "the misfortunes of those who are physically and mentally handicapped." TDC's failure to make even "minor adjustments" subjected these inmates to cruel and unusual punishment. Justice thus ordered TDC to "provide minimally adequate living conditions, protection, and medical treatment to all physically handicapped and mentally retarded inmates," in accordance with the Eighth-Amendment principles he outlined.

The issue of prison discipline was subdivided into hearing procedures, solitary confinement, and administrative segregation. Judge Justice had entered a preliminary injunction in 1975 based on specific findings that TDC had violated hearing procedures as set forth in *Wolff* v. *McDonnell* [418 U.S. 539(1974)] with respect to the named plaintiffs in *Ruiz*. During the trial it was "plainly apparent that the order had little impact upon TDC." Given this evidence, which was elicited from "testimony of virtually all TDC officers, including high ranking officials," Justice concluded that the requirements of *Wolff* were "either misunderstood or totally ignored" and that the state's own written regulations and procedures were "cynically disregarded."

On a personal level, Judge Justice found much that was undesirable about TDC's solitary confinement. While TDC had voluntarily improved on the bread and water diet diet described in *Novak* v. *Beto,* Justice felt that prison officials continued to attempt "to starve its most troublesome inmates into abject submission." He also felt that the evidence supported the conclusion that conditions of solitary confinement in other state prison systems were "generally much less severe than in TDC." However, he also recognized that "due deference" should be given to the *Novak* decision, which had upheld TDC's practices, and therefore "reluctantly concluded that the general conditions of solitary confinement at TDC" did not constitute cruel and unusual punisment.

Justice did find that, contrary to TDC directives, solitary confinement was often arbitrary and "commonly wreaked upon inmates in disfavor with TDC officials, including those who have pursued their constitutional rights by filing lawsuits against TDC." In addition, evidence indicated that "a number of inmates" had been placed in solitary confinement, despite medical defects that according to TDC regulations should have prevented the punishment. With this in mind, Justice ordered that "TDC must hereafter scrupulously follow its own rules regarding the administration of solitary confinement."

Much of Justice's analysis of administrative segregation paralleled the problems raised about general disciplinary decisionmaking procedures in TDC. The rules were poorly specified and often disregarded. TDC was once again ordered to bring its policies and practices into line with prevailing law. In addition, TDC was ordered to institute a regular exercise program for inmates who were confined to administrative segregation for more than three days. Some latitude was given prison officials concerning the specifics of the recreation, but they were to allow administrative segregation prisoners to leave their cells daily with the "opportunity for strenuous and active physical movement, for at least an hour, on each occasion." Litigation over access to courts and the harassment of writ-writers had a long-standing history by the time Justice wrote his memorandum opinion. Justice had found it necessary to issue five separate protective orders designed to minimize harassment of witnesses and the named plaintiffs by prison officials. The evidence presented at trial suggested that in many instances these orders were simply disregarded. Justice found that prison officials continued to hamper inmates' access to courts through the enforcement of restrictive rules and regulations. They also continued to engage in various forms of harassment, some subtle, some violent. In calling for the development of a "closely monitored" order of relief, Justice promised to take note of both the "type and degree of intransigence" officials had exhibited in the past.

In the section, "Other Conditions of Confinement," Justice reviewed fire safety, sanitation, work safety and hygiene. Throughout this section Justice noted some violations of state codes, but also took note of efforts to correct the deficiencies. TDC was commended for the cleanliness of its housing units, as well as for the practice of issuing inmates a set of clean clothes daily. In conclusion, Justice felt that some of the problems noted were well on their way to being remedied, and that those that remained resulted in part from the long-standing "misconception" that TDC was exempt from state health and safety laws. Having determined the applicability of state laws, Justice felt that the remaining problems could in all likelihood be handled by inspections from the appropriate state agencies. If not, the court would consider making arrangements for other forms of regulation and oversight. The one exception to this general conclusion was fire safety, where the guidelines of state law were inadequate. In this area, Justice ordered that TDC be brought into line with the standards of the Life Safety Code (1976) of the National Fire Protection Association.

Justice recognized that many of the mandated changes were going to be difficult to implement. He believed the task was made impossible by the size, design, and location of prison units. The size and complexity of the units resulted in ineffective and unresponsive management practices. Justice concluded, therefore, that "TDC units must be broken down into much smaller organizational entities . . . and each new component must have its own manageable supervisory structure." More specific changes would be specified in a subsequent order.

Justice felt that the remote location of prison units was largely responsible for the lack of qualified professionals and paraprofessionals. Without the skills and experience of these individuals, the prison system could not comply with constitutional standards. Therefore, Justice held that TDC

would be "precluded from locating any new unit far from a large population center, unless it is able to establish satisfactorily its ability to recruit
and maintain adequate numbers of qualified professionals and paraprofessionals in all disciplines necessary to the effective functioning of
such unit in a constitutional manner."

Judge Justice wrote in the concluding portion of his memorandum opinion that in "marked contrast" to prison cases in other states, TDC officials
"refused to concede that any aspect of their operations were unconstitutional, and vigorously contested the allegations of the inmate class on
every issue." Through much of the case's eight-year history, the contest
had indeed been "vigorous." However, following the publication of the
memorandum opinion, state officials, with W. J. Estelle at the vanguard,
moved beyond the vigorous contesting of issues and embarked on what
was characterized as "a personal and unseemly campaign of
vilification"[1] against Judge Justice and Vincent Nathan, the special
master appointed to oversee compliance with the court's orders.

For fifteen months following the memorandum opinion, there was outright defiance of Justice's orders, openly hostile rhetoric intended to deni-
grate Justice personally, and a spurious, costly, and unsuccessful legal
attack against the special master. Ironically, it was the attack on the special master that prompted the intervention of highly placed state officials,
who aligned themselves with Nathan after evidence emerged implicating
prison officials in the very same "outright misconduct" charged to Nathan
and his staff. It was this intervention that eventually destroyed TDC's substantial credibility, which had been so masterfully nurtured by O. B.
Ellis, George Beto, and W. J. Estelle.

During the months following the opinion, Estelle repeatedly made comments to the press that reflected his displeasure with Justice's opinion and
served to heighten the already pervasive divisiveness between prison personnel, prisoners, competing attorneys, and court officials. Within a few
days after the opinion was made public, Estelle made oblique reference
to Justice's lack of judicial skills when he noted that he "was glad that the
Supreme Court has raised the pay of federal judges," which, he suggested, would "encourage the appointment of competent jurists."[2]
Estelle denied that the remark was directed at Justice, but the implication
was nonetheless present. At the same news conference, Estelle indignantly charged that Justice "vilified one of the finest prison staffs in the
U.S." and flatly denied the court's findings of guard brutality and building
tender abuses.[3]

As severe as Estelle's comments were in the immediate aftermath of the
decision, his remarks in the ensuing months clearly reflected what could
only be perceived by TDC staff and prisoners as his utter contempt for
Justice. When speaking of the opinion, Estelle said, "It read like a cheap
dime store novel. I think he overused the adjective aspect of his diction-

ary. It did not read like a legal opinion and it did not even make interesting reading as far as I'm concerned."[4] Noting the opinion's bias, Estelle also critized Justice for believing "lying inmates" and discounting officer testimony.[5] On another occasion, Estelle relied just as heavily on the "adjective aspect" of his own dictionary in a speech before a meeting of the Texas Associated Press Broadcasters, when he suggested that Justice's ruling evidenced a "crass, gross, almost incredible lack of literary skills."[6]

The appellate and remedial phases of the case began in this highly charged environment. From the very beginning of the remedial phase of the litigation, it was evident that Judge Justice had gained invaluable experience in managing institutional reform cases as a result of the *Morales* litigation, which by this time was in its closing stages. Justice's 1974 order in *Morales* detailing unconstitutional practices in TYC was not accompanied by specific remedial action.[7] Judge Justice withheld specific relief and allowed the parties to confer for months on a remedial plan. As a consequence, a final remedial order was never entered. Delays in the development of a remedial plan allowed the state time to appeal portions of the judgment, which left only the interim order in effect. After the state prevailed on the three-judge court issue in 1977, TYC officials even expelled the court's compliance monitor. When the case returned to the Fifth Circuit after the Supreme Court upheld Judge Justice on the three-judge court issue,[8] the Fifth Circuit ruled that "since extensive changes appeared to have taken place in the Youth Council," a new hearing was necessary to determine whether a remedial order was necessary.[9] By this time, TYC had largely eliminated unconstitutional practices, thus minimizing Justice's role as an agency decisionmaker.

To what extent state officials relied on the *Morales* experience in the development of *Ruiz* legal strategies is not clear. An appeal of Justice's findings was a foregone conclusion. However, TDC officials were not nearly as receptive to change as the newly installed administration at TYC had been. Given TDC's demonstrated intransigence on key issues and his experience in *Morales*, Judge Justice recognized the importance of specific remedial orders if he was to retain control over reluctant state and prison officials.

Accompanying Justice's memorandum opinion was a brief two-page order that provided at least partial notice that Justice would enter a final remedial decree within a short time after issuance of the opinion, unlike what he had done in *Morales*. He ordered the parties to confer on a final remedial decree, which was to be submitted within sixty days of the order. Justice also asked that the parties submit names for the court's appointment of one or more special masters "to supervise and monitor compliance with the terms of the judgment to be entered herein."

It would become evident within a few months of this order that the

Judge Justice in *Ruiz* was different from the Judge Justice in *Morales*. The remedial orders issued in *Ruiz* would be more timely, precise, and enforceable. Justice had learned his lessons well. Although he would attempt to exercise substantial control over TDC through these orders, prison officials would not acquiesce to this legal state of affairs until they were ordered to do so by a coalition of high-ranking state officials, who recognized that continued defiance was both costly and futile in the face of mounting evidence that Justice's opinion was something more than a "cheap dime store novel."

In accordance with Justice's order, attorneys for both sides met to discuss possible settlement areas prior to the court's final decree. Earlier attempts to settle had proven futile, in large measure due to the state's "settle all or settle nothing" posture. Once the trial had concluded, the major rationale for this posture, that a balanced picture of TDC be presented, was no longer operable. At the first of these meetings it was evident that the state was now willing to negotiate certain areas of the case, such as medical health care and overcrowding.

By 1981 TDC's population had reached 30,000, or twice what the system had housed when the first of the eight original *Ruiz* petitions was filed. The number of prisoners sleeping on the floor had increased to roughly three thousand. More important, the rapidly rising population showed no signs of abating. With Justice having made overcrowding the centerpiece of his opinion due to its aggravating impact on the other issues in the case, it was easily the preeminent problem facing TDC, both operationally and legally. Unable to reach agreement on the crowding issue, the state elected to appeal this issue. TDC was willing to do no more than eliminate the some three thousand prisoners sleeping on the floor and to provide thirty square feet per prisoner in dormitory housing. This left the prison system in the position of double-celling the vast majority of inmates or housing them in dormitory settings at levels unacceptable to the plaintiffs. The negotiations were complicated further by the constant expansion of the inmate population, which, from all available indicators, was likely to continue into the foreseeable future.

The two sides were closer together when it came to the next most costly issue in the case, medical care. Prison officials had long recognized the need to improve medical care and were willing to make sizable commitments to eliminate many of the woefully inadequate practices and conditions set out in the court's opinion. On this issue, prison and state officials were willing to make commitments that according to the state, exceeded constitutional minimums. When final agreement was reached in mid-February, state officials had committed themselves to the development of an elaborate health-care program that would require huge appropriations from the state legislature. In addition, they agreed to submit plans in the areas of work safety, use of chemical agents, and administrative segregation. And, at literally the last hour of negotiations, they had agreed to serve prisoners in solitary confinement the same food as general-population prisoners received.

The agreement to serve full rations to solitary prisoners, which in later years would be repeatedly cited by TDC officials as removing the sting from solitary confinement and thereby rendering solitary ineffective as a disciplinary tool,[10] was remarkably offered to the plaintiffs by Estelle and then–attorney general Mark White for some minor word changes in the introductory paragraphs of the agreement. The restricted diet served in solitary had been vigorously contested by prisoners since the *Novak* case in the late 1960s. In his memorandum opinion, Justice "reluctantly concluded that the general conditions of solitary confinement at TDC [did] not constitute cruel and unusual punishment."

Even though Justice did not personally condone the conditions in solitary confinement, he acknowledged that he was bound by *Novak* and could not give the plaintiffs relief on this issue. Given the state's victory on the issue, one of the few favorable court decisions in TDC's long history of conditions litigation, Estelle and White's decision to concede the restricted diet in return for minor word changes is difficult to explain. Whatever the reasons, the ease with which the offer was made is a bit puzzling, in that the plaintiffs' lead counsel, Bill Turner, was in no position to make demands on TDC to alter the diet in view of Justice's decision; and therefore Estelle and White might have held out for more of a return on their concession. The vast majority of TDC administrators would later bemoan this agreement as the start of the breakdown of discipline among prisoners in TDC. It was used as one among many examples of how the *Ruiz* so-called reforms had actually made prison life worse.

In later years, Turner wrote a letter to the editor of *Texas Monthly* in response to an article that charged he had been responsible for the breakdown in discipline through his unreasonable demands for changes in the conditions of solitary confinement.

Reavis [author of the article] also argues that Judge Justice and "reformers" like me crippled the TDC's disciplinary system by making solitary confinement too comfortable. One of his major factual goofs is his description of how, in the *Ruiz* litigation, the revised but still restricted solitary diet was abandoned and prisoners in solitary began receiving the same food as all the other prisoners. He asserts that, despite our having lost the issue before Judge Justice, "when the [Ruiz] settlement talks began" I "demanded that the State make concessions," including providing a regular diet to prisoners in solitary. That is untrue. We went to Austin to attempt to negotiate an order that gave prisoners the required relief and that the TDC could live with. We discussed with Mark White, then attorney general, and the state's lawyers a complete proposed consent decree, disposing of all the issues involved in Judge Justice's decision. It included no provision on the solitary confinement diet. On February 17, 1981, Mark White telephoned me and asked that we agree to a cosmetic language change at the beginning of the decree. The "trade off" he offered, to my utter amazement, was full ration meals in solitary confinement, an issue never before discussed in the negotiations. The agreement was promptly concluded. I don't know how Mr. Reavis came up with the fictional version of the solitary issue that he published.

/s/ William Bennett Turner.

Turner's recitation of the matter proved to be entirely correct.

The consent decree, as approved by Judge Justice on March 3, 1981, failed to address in any manner such crucial issues as overcrowding, the continued use of building tenders, staffing, and disciplinary procedings. In return for the major concessions made in the agreement by Estelle and Mark White, the state received little, if anything, in return. The remaining issues would be resolved by Judge Justice, which was more than acceptable to the plaintiffs, since they anticipated broadscale relief from Judge Justice.

After the consent decree was filed with the court, the parties filed separate proposals for the final decree. The state, rather than submit a comprehensive remedial plan, used the pleading largely to place Justice on notice that any relief ordered on the remaining issues would be appealed. The state's proposal did include an end to triple-celling and a commitment to close the old prison hospital facility in Huntsville to acute care once the new prison hospital in Galveston was completed. In addition, the state filed plans in the areas of use of force, fire safety, and disciplinary procedures.

The plaintiffs' proposed decree was adopted by Judge Justice, with few minor modifications. He issued his final decree on April 20, 1981. The amended decree (Justice amended the April 20 decree on May 1, 1981, to reflect both typographical and substantive changes) was exceedingly detailed and broad in its scope, with specific time frames for implementation and compliance. The first section addressed overcrowding and was almost verbatim a recitation of the plaintiffs' proposed remedies. Prison officials were ordered to reduce the prisoner population by expanding work furlough and community programs, reviewing the good time awards, and further reviewing parole eligibility factors for all prisoners. The decree also set out a schedule of maximum population limits. By November 1, 1981, the prisoner population was to be reduced "to a figure equal to twice the number of general population cells, plus the number of prisoners who [could] be housed in dormitories at forty square feet per prisoner." After November 1, 1981, TDC was prohibited from receiving "any prisoners whose confinement would cause the population to exceed such a figure." The following year, the prisoner population was to be reduced to a figure 1.5 times the number of general population cells, plus dormitory housing allowing for sixty square feet per inmate. By November 1, 1983, all prisoners in TDC were to be housed in single cells.

The second section of the decree addressed security and staffing issues, and once again Justice set out a precise schedule of implementation, which by November 1, 1982, would require one uniformed staff member for every six prisoners. With the rise in prison population since trial, TDC was operating, by April 1981, with a 1:12 staff-prisoner ratio, which was the highest in the nation.[12] The court also set out minimal staffing patterns, which required the deployment of officers inside the cell blocks and dormitories. This was of critical importance with the court's concomitant order to "eliminate the building tender system." Justice's order on the building tender system, which was to become the most volatile issue in the remedial phase of the case, was simply a recodification of the state law that had been in force since 1973.

Prison officials were ordered to file a classification plan by August 1, 1981, which ensured that only minimum security prisoners be assigned to live in dormitories. Justice also set out highly detailed procedures regarding TDC's disciplinary practices. Among the procedures ordered by Justice was a requirement that counsel substitutes be appointed to represent certain classes of prisoners charged with disciplinary offenses. He also ordered that disciplinary proceedings be recorded in order to provide a verbatim record to prisoners who wished to contest the findings of the hearing. This section of the decree also declared a number of disciplinary offenses, such as "agitation" and "laziness," to be unconstitutionally vague.

Due to a long and now well-established history of interference with writ-writers, Justice also set out detailed guidelines on prisoners' access to courts, including censorship of legal correspondence, legal visitation, and law library services. Much of the relief ordered in this section was intended to prevent abuses that had been documented in the earlier contempt hearings involving some of the original plaintiffs and the Ramsey Unit officials.

The last two sections of the amended decree addressed the size and location of future TDC prisons and the management and reorganization of existing units. Future units would be structured in such a manner that each organizational unit or subunit within a facility would not exceed five hundred prisoners and would be located within fifty miles of a metropolitan area, unless it could be shown that qualified professionals could be recruited to work in rural areas. For existing units having more than five hundred prisoners, TDC officials were required to submit a reorganization plan by November 1, 1981, that would ensure that no warden of any unit would be responsible for more than five hundred prisoners and that existing units would be retrofitted to create these subunits of five hundred prisoners or less.

There could be no doubt, given the specific detail of the amended decree, that Judge Justice had moved firmly into the arena of prison management. This detail, coupled with the amended decree's scope, which was "infinitely broader than that encountered in any other example of correctional litigation," made the appointment of a special master with broad authority to monitor compliance critically important. Judge Justice had noted in his memorandum opinion that one important factor supporting the appointment of a special master was the "defendant's record of intransigence toward previous court orders requiring changes in TDC's practices and conditions." In addition, Justice noted that dealings between the parties [were] not likely to improve, and a special master could facilitate communication and the resolution of disputed matters. Consequently, Justice issued an order of reference contemporaneously with the amended decree establishing the Office of the Special Master. Rather than resolve disputed matters in the case, the special master's office would, over the next nine months, become the subject of the most bitterly contested dispute in the long history of the case.

By 1980 the use of special masters in institutional reform litigation was, although not routine, a mechanism gaining in popularity among activist judges engaged in large-scale reform efforts. The concept of masters was well established in the equity tradition of the federal courts as a pretrial fact-finder in complex litigation.[14] However, with the institutional reform litigation of the 1960s and 1970s, courts began to use masters in postdecree implementation functions. The duties of the special master were outlined in a leading case in this era, *Taylor* v. *Perini:* "The special master [is] to supervise compliance with the Court's order . . . . to assume primary responsibility for implementing, coordinating, evaluating, and reporting on the progress of all institutional efforts to effectuate said order. . . . [He will] hold the necessary hearings to keep pressure upon the defendant to do the the things still undone, and to evaluate the results of the things which have been done."[15]

This use of the special master has been described as "extraordinarily broad and intrusive."[16] It is also much like the role given the special master in *Ruiz,* where the enumerated powers included "unlimited access" to all TDC facilities, records, files, and papers maintained by TDC. The special master in *Ruiz* was also empowered to conduct confidential interviews with both staff and prisoners, as well as to require written reports from any staff member. In addition to compliance monitoring, the special master also had full power to order and conduct hearings on TDC's state of compliance. To assist the special master, Judge Justice authorized the appointment of several monitors who were to report their factual observations of compliance. These monitors' reports would become the basic tool used to measure TDC's compliance.

Vincent M. Nathan, a forty-four-year-old Ohio attorney, former law professor, and experienced court master, was selected by Justice to serve as the special master. Justice had allowed the plaintiffs and Justice Department attorneys to nominate five names each, while the state was allowed ten nominees. Nathan was the only nominee submitted by plaintiffs' attorney William Bennett Turner and the top nominee submitted by the Justice Department. Of the state's top two nominees, for what would be the most complex and extensive mastership in the history of institutional reform litigation, one was a sociology professor with no experience as a court master and limited practical experience in corrections, and the other a close associate of W. J. Estelle and director of a lawyer referral service for prisoners. Neither of these two nominees was an attorney, and neither had any demonstrated expertise in prison administration. Both, however, had close ties with the TDC, which seemed inconsistent with the state's request that Justice select a person "free from any taint of a prior partisan position in [the] lawsuit." [17]

Nathan was a native Texan. He had spent his early years in Tyler and Dallas, leaving the state to attend college. At the time of his appointment, Nathan was a skilled administrator and mediator whose experience at three other beleaguered prisons around the country had earned him the reputation as a "master's master." [18] His first experience as a court master came in 1975, when he was appointed as special master in *Taylor* v. *Perini,* a conditions case involving the Marion Correctional Institution in Marion, Ohio. At the time of his appointment in *Taylor,* he was a law professor at the University of Toledo School of Law with no previous experience in corrections.

From this point forward, however, Nathan would quickly achieve national prominence in corrections through his successive appointments as a court master. Following his appointment in *Taylor,* Nathan was appointed by the same judge as special master in *Jones* v. *Wittenberg,* litigation relating to the Lucas County Jail in Toledo. His demonstrated success in these two cases prompted his appointment in 1979 to serve as special monitor in *Gutherie* v. *Evans,* litigation involving the Georgia State Prison in Riedsville.

In addition to his experience with three separate masterships by 1979, Nathan had also written a well-received law review article, on "The Use of Masters in Institutional Reform Litigation," published in the *Toledo Law Review*[19] and reprinted by the Federal Judicial Center. Justice, in the order of reference, noted that Nathan had served as a consultant for the National Institute of Corrections and was an "acknowledged expert in the field of implementation of judicial decrees in a correctional setting." In 1979 Nathan left the Toledo Law School to join a Toledo law firm, and in 1983 he opened his own law office in Toledo.

When Nathan accepted his appointment in *Ruiz*, he had had no prior exposure to the operations of the TDC, nor was he acquainted with Estelle or other prison officials. Two days after his appointment on April 20, 1981, Nathan met with Estelle and his attorneys.[20] In his opening remarks, Nathan stated his desire to perform his responsibilities as master in the most "unintrusive [manner] possible." From his experience as a master and from his limited knowledge of TDC operations and officials, he was sensitive to how the presence of a master could be viewed as a threat to the authority of prison officials. In his writings on the subject he cited the problem of intrusiveness as a major "drawback" of masterships: "The first and most obvious [drawback] is the judicial intrusion into the affairs of a state agency that may be necessitated by a reference [mastership]. . . . Unless the [special master] conducts himself with the utmost circumspection, his presence may undercut the authority and standing of administration officials. Responding to this concern, some courts have made careful efforts to minimize the degree of intrusion by limiting the authority of the master. Even at a minimum level, however, the involvement of a master is likely to be resented by defendants."[21]

Even though Nathan was sensitive to this "drawback," nothing in his experience prepared him for the level of resentment and perceived intrusiveness he would experience in the first year of his mastership in Texas. The first meeting with Estelle and the TDC attorneys, however, was cordial. Nathan was informed that TDC would contest the imposition of the mastership on appeal, but otherwise there was little hint of the acrimonious resistance that would eventually develop.[22]

More substantial indications were not long in coming. Just less than two months later, Nathan had a second meeting with Estelle and the TDC attorneys. Early in the meeting, Nathan noted the "rigidity" that was emerging between TDC and his office, which he was "finding difficult and troublesome." Estelle responded with rather oblique sarcasm.

Estelle: You beat your schedule by I think seven days.

Nathan: I beat what?

Estelle: You beat your schedule.

Nathan: How so?

Estelle: I gave you sixty days on your original outline of how you were going to operate. I said in sixty days he'll be back to change that schedule and procedures — so you beat it by seven days, which doesn't surprise me.[23]

Over the next six months, the perceived intrusiveness and rigidity noted by Nathan in the July 14 meeting was to become a constant problem and would eventually culminate in a "vituperative motion"[24] filed by a prestigious Houston law firm to discharge Nathan and his entire staff.

State Retains Outside Counsel to Assist in Appeal Effort

The attorney general's office wasted no time in attacking the massive reforms ordered by Justice in his April 20 amended decree. On June 5, 1981, Ed Idar filed a 108-page motion to suspend the execution of virtually all the "sweeping and exacting changes" imposed on TDC by Justice. The state's legal argument began with the dire prediction that Justice's proposed "solutions [would] have catastrophic consequences for TDC management and institutional security and order." The state's attorneys denied that they were "asking for the sky" in seeking the stay. Rather, they were attempting to avoid "the expenditure of millions of dollars, the severe undermining of security, and in some cases the jeopardizing of inmate life and safety."

The first of Justice's remedies attacked in the motion involved overcrowding. The state recognized that overcrowding was "perhaps the single most important issue involved in [the] lawsuit," due to Justice's finding that it exercised a "malignant effect on all aspects of inmate life." The state contended, however, that the evidentiary record showing actual harm was nonexistent and asked that all the overcrowding sanctions except those forbidding triple- and quadruple-celling be stayed. In their brief opposition to the stay, the plaintiffs' attorneys were quick to point out TDC's lack of success in eliminating triple-celling, which had increased threefold since the trial.

A second issue on which the attorneys for the state sought relief was that concerning the use of building tenders. They advised the court that they were not requesting a stay on Justice's prohibition of using prisoners in a "position to exercise administrative or supervisory authority over another prisoner." This was hardly a concession by the state, since the prohibition was a simple restatement of the building tender statute passed by the Texas Legislature in 1973, which Estelle had testified at trial merely reflected a long-standing TDC policy. The state did object to the requirement that prisoners assigned janitorial duties be rotated once every thirty days. The state also argued that the elimination of the building tender system would "threaten the very integrity of the TDC prison institutions," in addition to costing the state millions of dollars for increased security staff.

Finally, the state's attorneys asked the Fifth Circuit Court to vacate the mastership, contending that there was no history of demonstrable intransigence toward previous court orders, and therefore no special master was necessary to monitor compliance with the court's order. The record of substantial violations of protective orders was simply ignored by the state's attorneys, who contended that TDC officials had "freely consented" to all except one of the protective orders. While TDC may have consented in court, the record showed that orders were ignored in prison.

On June 26, 1981, the Fifth Circuit Court issued its ruling on the stay motion, granting TDC relief on the crowding issues, such as single-celling. The court also stayed provisions of Justice's order on the reorganization and centralization of prison units and their location. In addition, the court found that Justice's order requiring the thirty-day rotation of prisoners assigned to certain jobs was "an undue interference with the details of prison administration." All other requested relief was denied, though the door was opened for a second stay motion at such time as the state could show "undue hardship" caused by implementation of the court's order.[25]

After this stay motion was filed in June, the TDC Board of Corrections elected to retain outside counsel to assist the attorney general's office in preparing the state's appeal. At the time, the chairman of the board, T. Louis Austin, estimated that "retaining outside counsel would cost no more than $200,000."[26] For the next thirty-six months, TDC would pay outside counsel more than $2 million with monthly billings frequently exceeding $200,000. For one nine-month period during the thirty-six months, TDC paid almost $60,000 for printing and copying costs alone.[27] For the previous eight years, Idar and his six-to-eight-member staff of mostly young law school graduates had provided all the state's representation. During the next three years, more than fifty different attorneys would be employed, with hourly rates ranging from $75 to $165.[28]

The decision to retain outside counsel grew from the voiced concerns of Estelle and the Board of Corrections that the appeal of Justice's massive reforms would require an equally massive brief to the Fifth Circuit Court of Appeals. Fulbright and Jaworski, a prestigious Houston law firm that had gained widespread publicity when a senior partner, Leon Jaworski, became special prosecutor during the Watergate investigations, was selected by the Board of Corrections in July 1981. Pike Powers, head of the Austin office of Fulbright and Jaworski and a former state legislator and close associate of Mark White's, took charge of the litigation.

Almost immediately, a fleet of Fulbright and Jaworski attorneys began to review the voluminous trial record. While Ed Idar continued to carry the designation of lead counsel, he increasingly assumed more of an advisory role and formation resource to Pike Powers and the Fulbright and Jaworski attorneys. None of the Fulbright and Jaworski attorneys assigned to the case had any expertise in correctional law, and therefore they had to spend considerable time reviewing the body of relevant case law in addition to the massive court record. The trial transcripts alone filled five standard-size filing cabinets.

The next four and one-half months were spent preparing the State's case. This effort culminated in a 124-page brief, which cost some $15,000 for printing alone and almost $600,000 in attorney's fees.[29] The brief began by noting that TDC administered "the largest prison system in the U.S." and that "the eighteen separate prison units operated by TDC [were] among the best penal facilities in the country."

The appeal of the overcrowding reforms was centered around the Supreme Court's June 1981 decision in *Rhodes* v. *Chapman,* which upheld the practice of double-celling at the Southern Ohio Correctional Facility, a maximum-security state prison in Lucasville, Ohio. *Rhodes* was rendered approximately six weeks after Justice had issued his decree and was repeatedly cited in the state's brief as the case most directly relevant to the facts in *Ruiz.*

[*Rhodes*] is "one of those rare occasions" when this Court is able to say, "we are favored with a recent dispositive case that gives us guidance that the trial court did not enjoy." A central message in *Rhodes* is that the Eighth Amendment does not proscribe prison conditions that do not, directly or indirectly, result in the infliction of actual, physical pain. Mere discomfort, frustration, or distress are not, in this context, matters of constitutional moment. "To the extent that [prison] conditions are restrictive and even harsh, they are part of the penalty that criminal offenders pay for their offenses against society.[30]

The brief took full advantage of the *Rhodes* decision to once again articulate the argument that Judge Justice was imposing his own personal standards rather than those mandated by the Constitution. "At least in large measure, the district judge appeared to be testing the State's prison system not against an objective constitutional standard but against his own intuitive notions of what prison life should be like. . . . [Justice's] preconceived normative standards for life in prison [have] no relation to the applicable Eighth Amendment standard."

The appeal of the overcrowding issue constituted almost half of the brief. Thereafter the state addressed the findings on staff brutality and building tender abuses. Citing Estelle as the source, attorneys for the state simply argued, "building tenders never exercise[d] any authority or control over fellow inmates" and that their "assignments are of a purely custodial and janitorial nature," which seemed to contradict the state's claim that elimination of the building tender system would "threaten the very integrity of the prison institutions." The brief also cited Estelle's summary of the basic duties of building tenders and his categorical statement that "there has certainly not been a systematic or foreknowledge abuse of it:" "[They] see that [the] place is kept clean by much of their own efforts and to keep clean those areas of traffic and congestion, to see that there are adequate lavatory supplies available. They also maintain the general cleanliness of the dayroom areas. They act as runners from officer to officer on occasion with either documents [or] supplies."

Justice's "damning assertion that building tenders 'are often permitted to carry weapons' " was also attacked in the brief. Relying on testimony of warden Christian, the state rather indignantly countered that "building tenders most emphatically are not permitted to carry weapons of any kind." With the filing of the brief, TDC's long-standing denial of building tender abuses had now been elevated by the Fulbright and Jaworski lawyers to an artful pleading pointing out the substantial benefits of the system, interlaced with rather esoteric characterizations, such as describing the building tender's informant role as the "bilateral carrier of information" rather than the more commonly used prison term, "snitch." The same month the appeal brief was filed, the special master's office filed its first compliance report, which was replete with evidence in stark contrast to the claims made in the state's brief.

The next section of the brief on staff brutality was equally indignant in tone and no less categorical in denial. In response to Justice's finding that "brutality against inmates [was] nothing short of routine in Texas prisons," the state claimed that "TDC's staff followed the rules against excessive use of force conscientiously and systematically, with only occasional exceptions." The "overwhelming evidence" to which the state referred to show that excessive force was a "rarity" was in part based on the testimony of a captain who had served at the Eastham Unit for almost five years, who claimed that he had never observed a correctional officer physically abusing or harrassing another inmate.

This type of unequivocal testimony was typical of that repeatedly cited in the state's brief and that in some instances, including the staff brutality issue, was later shown to be the very antithesis of the truth. For example, a researcher who was employed as a guard and worked with the Eastham captain later reported that prisoners at Eastham "were roughed up daily as a matter of course." He also reported that within a two-month period at Eastham, he observed more than thirty separate instances of guards using physical force against inmates and that many of these involved "tune-ups" and "attitude adjustments," both euphemisms for unauthorized force routinely employed at Eastham.[31] In later years the captain was transferred to the internal affairs division of TDC, where he investigated "tune-ups" and "attitude adjustments" at Eastham and during the course of these investigations openly acknowledged that such control techniques were routinely employed by certain staff at Eastham.

In an attempt to show that some of Justice's specific findings on brutality were "clearly erroneous," the brief attacked Justice's "inexplicable" finding that TDC officers still used summary physical punishments such as requiring prisoners to "stand on the wall" for long periods. The brief boldly stated that the trial record "unmistakably" showed that this form of punishment had not been used for some six years in TDC. Not only was this form of punishment still routinely used at certain prisons, but it continued even after Justice's findings. Approximately two months after the state filed its brief, a prisoner at the Darrington Unit, where David Christian was warden, was required to "stand on the wall," handcuffed, and left without shoes in the main hallway. He was given a gallon bucket in which to defecate, with instructions to remain motionless. He "stood on the wall" without interruption for twenty-six hours.[32]

The strongest denial was suprisingly reserved for the one issue on which a clear record of abuse had already been established at the circuit court level—harassment of writ-writers. The Fulbright and Jaworski attorneys contended that "there was utterly no basis for the district court's suggestion that TDC maintains practices or has adopted policies directed at the harassment or intimidation of litigious inmates." Relying on the *Rizzo* argument, the pleading noted that if such incidents took place, they were isolated and unauthorized and did not provide a basis for system-wide relief.

Having denied what was soon to become the undeniable, the state's attorneys set out in their "Conclusion and Prayer" the objection to Justice that had pervaded the case from the beginning: "Although Defendants cannot fault his lack of prescience, we respectfully submit that the trial judge's most pervasive and persistent error was in elevating his view of the ideal prison into a *constitutional* standard by which to judge the TDC."

This arguably legitimate position, which had been used somewhat successfully to divert attention from the substantive weaknesses in the prison system, would begin to crumble in the very month the $600,000 brief was filed with the Fifth Circuit Court of Appeals.

Allegations of Systemwide Building Tender Abuses Denied by TDC

By October 1981 the mastership was less than six months into operation. Nathan had moved quickly in this early developmental stage to appoint four monitors, who began to visit the prisons to develop compliance data. In accordance with Justice's order of reference, the monitors were to file reports of "factual observations" with Nathan, who in turn was to submit findings of fact to Justice on TDC's state of compliance.

One of these four monitors, David Arnold, was assigned the task of monitoring TDC's compliance with the building tender issue, potentially the most volatile issue in the case, not only because of TDC's long-standing denials, but more importantly due to the critical role that such prisoners played as an adjunct to the security-oriented staff. Arnold began to collect information in July 1981. His efforts included hundreds of visits and interviews with prisoners and staff over the next three months.

On October 16, 1981, Arnold submitted his report, which was the first filed by Nathan's office. The eighty-five-page report, supported by 463 pages of appendices, represented the first detailed investigation by a neutral third party of the inner workings of the "building tender system," which the Texas Legislature had outlawed some eight years earlier and Justice had ordered dismantled, and which prison officials along with their attorneys had long denied existed. Up to this point, prison officials had steadfastly presented the system as no more than custodial and janitorial in nature. Given the eventual revelations to the contrary, prison officials were remarkably successful at concealing the noncustodial aspects of the building tender system from its own attorneys, some of whom (including then–attorney general Mark White) had by this time been involved in the *Ruiz* litigation for years.

Arnold had made thirty-two visits to thirteen units over a three-month period. He had reviewed literally thousands of documents, including seven hundred letters received by the master's office alleging building tender abuses. In addition, numerous investigations conducted by Nathan's staff and directed by Arnold were incorporated into the report.[33] He mentioned early in the report a number of obstacles he had encountered during his monitoring, one of which he described as the "palpable fear on the part of inmates that cooperation would lead to retaliation." This fear, Arnold reported, was not totally unjustified, since he had himself routinely experienced surveillance by building tenders while visiting the various units.

Put mildly, Arnold's report suggested something more than an inmate janitorial and custodial system, just as the evidence at trial had done. His "observed evidence" reflected inmates' possessing a level of authority and control that in many instances exceeded that of the typical TDC guard. He presented evidence that building tenders administered disciplinary beatings, controlled access to restricted areas, had access to sensitive documents on other prisoners, possessed security keys that they used at their own discretion, and possessed and used weapons with the full knowledge of security personnel. Arnold also documented an elaborate system of special privileges, such as open cells, choice of cell partners, special clothing, and liberal property rules, which some building tenders took advantage of to run "inmate stores."

Much of Arnold's evidence was provided by building tenders who had been given a promise of strict confidentiality. These inmates confirmed that they were allowed to possess a wide array of weapons, such as knives, lead pipes, and chains. At the Ramsey I prison, which had been the subject of building tender allegations for years, Arnold learned that building tenders were even given access to riot batons. One of the prisoner affidavits recounted an incident at Ramsey, three months after Justice's order, where three building tenders armed with riot batons accompanied a guard as he entered a cell block to quell a disturbance. Nor did Arnold find this to be an isolated instance. Instead, "literally dozens of inmates alleged that [BT's] regularly arrived at the scene of an altercation with riot batons." In addition, there were reports that inmates were brought under control by building tenders and that building tenders were routinely allowed to handcuff other prisoners arriving and leaving Ramsey on the "chain bus."

In support of his conclusion that BT's routinely had access to restricted areas, Arnold cited two especially egregious incidents that were clearly documented by TDC's own records. In each instance a building tender had secured a key from a guard that provided access to a secluded area. In the first instance, three BT's unlocked a door to a secure area, where they raped a prisoner. In the second, a BT allowed two inmates to engage in sex after having unlocked the door for them. A third incident was cited, again supported by TDC's own documents, where a building tender had kept a cell door open while two other prisoners entered the cell to commit a rape.

Several of the incidents alleged by prisoners were corroborated by independent investigation and demonstrated in graphic detail the control exercised by building tenders. One such incident was set out as follows:

[The inmate] was placed in solitary confinement for a rule infraction to which he pleaded guilty.

One of the more notorious [building tenders] on that unit, a countboy for the Major, came into his supposedly secure solitary cell and demanded sexual intercourse; this occurred on his first day in solitary confinement.

[The inmate] refused, whereupon the countboy pointed out that his good friend, the solitary porter with whom he worked on the building crew, and who had let the countboy into the inmate's solitary cell, could make the inmate's stay in solitary very difficult.

[The inmate] submitted to the homosexual encounter.

For the next several days, without his requesting it, [the inmate] was provided extra food and commissary items by the solitary porter.

Almost immediately after Arnold filed his report with the special master, it was released to the press. It was widely reported in various news stories before TDC officials and their attorneys had even received the report.[35] Relations between Nathan's office and TDC were already strained with constant bickering, primarily over the manner of Nathan's compliance monitoring. The premature news release only further increased the already substantial tension.

Because Arnold's report, if unrebutted, could provide the basis for further sanctions by Justice, it could not be summarily dismissed as easily as the Joint Committee on Prison Reform Report had been in 1974. A TDC agency lawyer, Steve Martin, was assigned the task of coordinating the development of evidence to counter the charges made by Arnold. Martin was a thirty-two-year-old recent law school graduate who had worked as a guard almost ten years earlier at the Ellis Unit, which at the time had a number of the well-known building tenders who had been the subject of testimony in the *Dreyer* case. Martin had seen firsthand the prominent role that BT's played in daily prison operations, in that much of his early job training was provided by such prisoners.

During his twelve-month tenure at Ellis, Martin had observed on a daily basis the wide variety of supervisory controls exercised by inmates and reported by Arnold almost ten years later. While Arnold had provided numerous examples of supervisory control, his observations remained those of an outsider. He was not able to document such common patterns as building tenders' routinely converging to the scene of a disturbance once a "fight" was announced in the center hallway. More than once, Martin had been left holding the cell-block keys while the "turnkey" left the cell block to support other building tenders in handling a troublesome prisoner. On one such occasion, Martin had observed eight to ten building tenders converge on a prisoner who had been beaten out into the hallway after striking an officer. Once in the hallway, the "turnkeys" finished the job while literally leaving a trail of blood down the hallway. The offending prisoner was then taken to the unit infirmary, where he was sutured without a deadening agent by an inmate orderly who ten years later was assigned to Ramsey and was one of the inmates identified as assisting guards while in possession of a riot baton and handcuffs.

Arnold was also unable to fully capture the near total control that BT's extended inside the cell blocks, since his visits were limited and usually announced. Had he been able to make observations without these limitations, he might have observed BT's actually giving new prisoners an orientation to their expected behavior while on the cell block. However, such inmate control was not plainly apparent, even to guards, unless they had achieved some rank or unless their job assignment facilitated observation. On one occasion, over a two-day period, Martin had observed an example of just such control when a group of troublesome prisoners had been transferred to Ellis after having created a disturbance at another unit. After spending two days "standing on the wall," a number of the prisoners were assigned to a cell block on which Martin was working. There he witnessed three BT's provide a rather forceful introduction of the prisoners into the cell block, which included a demonstration of their physical control on one of the more defiant prisoners.

When Martin returned to TDC in September 1981, he was assigned to work with the Fulbright and Jaworski attorneys on a stay motion to the Fifth Circuit. This assignment required visits to several TDC prisons in order to collect affidavits from prison officials. During one such visit to Ellis, just a few weeks prior to Arnold's report, Martin visited with a turnkey whom he had befriended some ten years earlier. When asked what effect Justice's orders were having at the Ellis prison, the turnkey replied that he and his fellow building tenders still "took care of business" but were having to "ride a lot of heat from the Master's office."[36] During a visit to Ramsey in this same period, Martin visited with the inmate orderly whom he had observed suture the prisoner without a deadening agent. The orderly was now working as the major's bookkeeper and would in a subsequent encounter, several months later, actually show Martin his key to a box of riot batons in the major's office.

As a result of these visits, having witnessed a system that seemed to have changed little in his years of absence, Martin advised one of the Fulbright and Jaworski attorneys that Arnold's report could not be dismissed by agency officials as merely a product of "lying convicts." Over the next couple of weeks, Martin made a number of discreet inquiries of correctional officers whom he had known years earlier. Through these contacts he was told that prisoners at some units did indeed have access to weapons. He also confirmed that selected prisoners at Ramsey were allowed to handcuff other prisoners.

While Martin continued to investigate the charges made in Arnold's report and to provide status briefings to agency officials on his increasing concern that many of Arnold's allegations had substance, a series of events occurred in October and November that momentarily diverted attention from Arnold's findings. On October 1, 1981, an altercation (which would later have bearing on the resolution of Arnold's report) occurred between a Hispanic prisoner and seven building tenders during the noon meal at the Retrieve Unit. This altercation quickly erupted into a major prisonwide disturbance when prisoners, acting in support of the Hispanic inmate, refused to work and started destroying property inside the cell blocks. The disturbance continued a second day, whereupon the unit staff dispersed large amounts of tear gas into many of the cell blocks. An internal investigation of this incident several months later revealed an extremely egregious example of clearly illegal behavior on the part of unit officials and building tenders.

Several days after this incident, Dr. Robert Cohen, a New York physician retained by Nathan, filed a report detailing a number of prisoner deaths related to "serious shortcomings" in medical care at TDC.[37] This report, like Arnold's, was widely reported in the press.[38] Also during this time, a major work stoppage involving approximately one hundred and sixty inmates at Ellis was likewise reported in the press.[39] In mid-October area newspapers also published excerpts from correspondence between Nathan and TDC that "point[ed] to a growing friction between the prison and federal investigators" and the special master's office.[40]

Fatal prison stabbings on the first two days in November, coupled with the continuing work stoppage at Ellis, which on November 13 developed into a direct confrontation with injuries to both inmates and guards, kept TDC in the news through mid-December.[41] Five days after the Ellis disturbance, a major disturbance, involving some five hundred prisoners who set fires, broke windows, and fought guards, occurred at the Darrington Unit. Warden Christian, in the incident report filed with Estelle, reported that the disturbance began when an officer mistakenly opened an entire row of cell doors on a segregation wing of the unit. Two days after the Darrington riot, 275 prisoners, housed in tents at the Eastham Unit,[42] began to set fires to tents and to break cell block windows. According to the incident report filed by Warden E. H. Turner, officers using tear gas entered the tent compound and quelled the disturbance.

On November 20, attorneys for the state and prisoners met with Nathan to discuss procedures to be followed regarding hearings on monitors' reports. Just as the meeting was getting under way, TDC attorneys were advised of the Eastham riot. Two of the state's attorneys, Ed Idar and Gerald Fall, TDC's general counsel, left the meeting and returned to Huntsville. Steve Martin and a Fulbright and Jaworski attorney, Brian Greig, remained behind to continue the meetings. Due to the rash of disturbances, the attorneys and Nathan agreed to prepare a joint statement to the press appealing "to everyone to do all in their power to preserve an orderly and safe environment and to permit the resolution of issues in the *Ruiz* suit through the legal process." Even though the statement's concluding sentence called for "lawful behavior" and denounced "violence and property destruction," attorney general Mark White refused to sign the statement the following week claiming, "It did not urge Texas inmates to obey TDC rules."[43] White's refusal to join in the statement was more than perplexing, given that it had actually been drafted by his own attorneys and read to him on the telephone for his tentative approval.

Rather than make such an appeal, White exacerbated the already highly tense atmosphere by issuing an emotional press statement laying blame for the recent wave of violence on Nathan and Judge Justice. "The increased level of violence cannot be attributed to anything other than the special master and the way the lawsuit has been handled. [The federal court has given prisoners] the mistaken notion that they do not need to obey the rules and regulations of the prison system."[44]

This was one among a barrage of statements made by White and Governor Clements, who were soon to be bitter rivals in the 1982 gubernatorial campaign. Governor Clements, not to be outdone by White, charged Nathan with causing the disturbances by "playing father confessor to the inmates."[45] In one news story, which carried the straightforward headline, "State Officials Blame Judge for Prison Riots," White, referring to the complaining prisoners in somewhat less than a statesmanlike manner, stated that he was "sick and tired of hearing from the little whining devils."[46]

The strongly worded accusations leveled at Nathan by White and Clements prompted equally strong rebuttals from Nathan and the plaintiffs' lead counsel, Bill Turner. Nathan was "shocked" that the state's governor and attorney general blamed him for the wave of violence. He characterized their charges as "irresponsible," since his office obviously had neither caused nor condoned the violence.[47] Turner countercharged that TDC had been "thumbing its nose" at Justice's orders, such as the prohibition on building tender abuses, and that, "If [TDC] won't act like a law-abiding citizen, the prisoners don't see why they should."[48]

While Governor Clements and attorney general Mark White were attacking Nathan and Justice in the press (similar to what state officials had done some ten years earlier following *Morales*), negotiations between the Department of Justice and Fulbright and Jaworski attorneys were focusing on removing the Justice Department from the suit prior to the state's appeal to the Fifth Circuit. Governor Clements's ties (he had served as deputy secretary of defense under Presidents Nixon and Ford) with the Reagan administration gave state officials some hope that they now faced a more easily satisfied Justice Department. The newly appointed head of the department's Civil Rights Division, William Bradford Reynolds (whose later nomination for deputy attorney general was rejected by the Senate because of his record on civil rights litigation),[49] let it be known through Governor Clements's office that he was amenable to settlement if TDC was willing to make movement on such fundamental issues as building tenders, classification, staffing, and crowding. While Reynolds was clearly more receptive to reaching middle ground, such as increased out-of-cell time rather than the strict "one-man-one-cell" rule, certain issues, such as the court's finding that "building tenders run the prisons with a 'reign of terror,' " had to be resolved before he would withdraw from the suit.[50]

The basis for the settlement discussions that took place in November and December 1981 was a "position statement" prepared by TDC's staff attorneys. The section on building tenders, drafted just a matter of days before Arnold's report was filed, began by noting the department's continuing commitment to the state law prohibiting the use of BT's to administer disciplinary action to other inmates. TDC's positions on other issues, such as classification and staffing, were likewise little more than restatements of earlier positions with some cosmetic concessions thrown in. After reviewing the document, Bradford Reynolds, not surprisingly, requested more detailed information. Knowing that Reynolds remained optimistic about settlement, Governor Clements urged the Board of Corrections "to explore every possible ground of agreement with the DOJ." Clements felt that timely action was critical, in that the opportunity for settlement might be lost once oral arguments on the state's appeal to the Fifth Circuit began, little more than two weeks away.

A Crack Appears in Estelle's Credibility

On December 11, 1981, a meeting was held in Austin to review the details of a supplement to TDC's earlier position statement, which was to be discussed three days later with Reynolds. Among those attending were Governor Clements, attorney general Mark White, W. J. Estelle, Pike Powers, T. Louis Austin (chairman of the TDC board), and seven of the remaining eight board members.[51] Although this meeting did not produce sufficient movement by TDC to reach agreement with the Justice Department, it would nonetheless become pivotal because questions were asked and answers given that created, for the first time, serious credibility problems for director Estelle. A single board member would leave this meeting with enough doubt to start making serious and detailed inquiries into Estelle's heretofore unquestioned representations to the Board of Corrections that building tenders were nothing more than janitors. Board member Harry Whittington, a prominent Austin attorney and businessman, was a conservative Republican appointed in 1979 by Governor Clements.

Even though the December 11 meeting centered around a broad range of issues, the building tender allegations made by Arnold prompted repeated inquiry by Whittington. Whittington was the only attorney on the board and was therefore the board liaison with the state's attorneys. Having been advised by Fulbright and Jaworski counsel that some of the allegations made by Arnold might prove true, he questioned Estelle at length about the issue.

Whittington: One other thing too, is under the law no inmate is to have any kind of authority over the others. That's state law, right?

Estelle: Yes, sir.

Whittington: A lot of these things they've alleged in here (Arnold's report) indicate that some inmates in our system do have authority over the others like putting handcuffs on some of them. Are those things that actually happen, Jim? I can see how that's authority, putting handcuffs on a man.

Estelle: If an inmate has put handcuffs on another inmate, I number one don't know about it and number two it's an exception to the rule, practice and policy.

Throughout the course of questioning on this issue, Estelle denied that building tenders were as a matter of practice used in positions of authority and contended that the master's office was "hanging us by the exception." Earlier in the meeting Estelle had unwittingly created some doubt when responding to Whittington about the use of BT's as communication links with the administration: "We have many inmates who, for one reason or another, have been frightened to a degree by some of the predators in that population. If you go to the Man [prison official], you're going to walk away with a knife between your ribs. So he's scared to go to the man, but he will go to another convict. Usually they'll go to one of those support service inmates [BT's] who has frequent contact with the man."

This response caused Whittington considerable concern, due to its implication that some inmates, those who had "frequent contact with the man," might very well be used as agents for the administration and as such possess some degree of informal authority.[52] In Whittington's words, Estelle's response "brought to focus for the first time that BT's were an administrative tool for prison officials."[53]

Even though Whittington had pressed Estelle during the meeting and had had questions raised in his own mind, the exchanges had little further impact on Estelle's credibility at the time. Attorney general Mark White typified the posture of most of those present. In response to Governor Clements's suggestion to create an investigative division in TDC, White stated, "These are my clients. If they tell me they're doing it, I believe they're doing it. They're my clients, I'm defending them. I'm not questioning them."[54] Approximately two months later, after being told by attorneys assigned to prepare the state's case on Arnold's report that the BT system existed as alleged, White angrily asked if Estelle and TDC had been "lying" to him all along, and for the first time, like Whittington had done earlier, began to question his clients.

Early in the December 14 meeting with Reynolds, it became apparent that TDC's proposals would not provide a basis for settlement. On December 18, the parties presented their oral arguments to the appeals court. The state's attorney flatly denied that inmates possessed any "supervisory powers over other inmates."[55] Turner claimed that "the building tender system is the sorest reminder everyday that the court's order is being violated."[56] Reynolds, for the most part, spoke in support of Justice's reforms.

Almost immediately after the oral arguments on December 18, 1981, TDC and Fulbright and Jaworski attorneys turned their attention to the ongoing battle with the special master's office. As Nathan's assistants began to actively monitor the numerous areas of Justice's order and file reports, tension continued to build.[57] TDC's general counsel, Gerald Fall, was waging an almost-daily campaign of letter-writing, asking that Nathan's monitors "cease their intrusive and disruptive actions." For the next several months, Fulbright and Jaworski attorneys, working in concert with attorneys for the state, would keep busy preparing a strongly worded motion to discharge Nathan and his staff. At the same time, they prepared for the hearing on Arnold's report. In the process, the two issues became inextricably joined.

Frontal Assault on the Mastership

By December 1981, Nathan's elimination from the case was TDC's highest priority. Events that led to the attempted ouster were reminiscent of those that surrounded George Beto's efforts to rid the prison system of Frances Jalet ten years earlier. Like Jalet, Nathan and his monitors were collecting information adverse to the status quo. Just as Jalet had been accused of a revolutionary conspiracy, Nathan and his staff would stand accused of inciting prisoners to demonstrate against prison officials. George Beto's attempts to rid the prison system of Frances Jalet had ironically helped precipitate the changes she sought. With the same irony, the attempted ouster of Nathan would prove ill-advised when evidence emerged that TDC officials were guilty of the very allegations they leveled at Nathan.

By early January, inquiries made by TDC staff attorneys had provided enough information to prompt Fulbright and Jaworski attorneys to request a more thorough investigation of Arnold's allegations. In addition to Martin's confirmation that certain prisoners at Ramsey had access to riot batons and handcuffs, he also confirmed that one of the three building tenders involved in one of the rapes reported by Arnold[58] was still working as a BT, even though he had been charged with several disciplinary actions since the rape. Another staff attorney, Bruce Green, had received information from a reliable source that building tenders, armed with weapons, were used to assist guards in quelling the disturbance at Eastham in November.

When Justice scheduled the hearing on Arnold's charges for March 15, 1982, TDC staff attorneys, working with Fulbright and Jaworski lawyers, began to prepare their case, which included taking a deposition from Arnold. During the deposition Arnold was questioned at length about the weapons he had been shown by building tenders. TDC attorneys repeatedly demanded that Arnold furnish the names of the inmates so the weapons could be seized. These demands were initially refused, based on Arnold's promise to keep the names confidential. Within a few days, prison officials ordered a systemwide search for weapons in the possession of building tenders. Nathan, in turn, filed a request with the court that he be given information on all actions taken by TDC with regard to the systemwide search. TDC's response to this request was to accuse Nathan's office of withholding "vital information from TDC authorities at considerable risk to life and limb to both inmates and TDC employees."[59] It was also charged that Nathan and his monitors had "acted in concert with dangerous inmates to prevent prison authorities from carrying out the laws of the State of Texas."[60]

Arnold's failure to provide the information on the weapons was made, along with the wave of recent prison disturbances, the centerpiece of the state's motion to discharge Nathan, which was filed on January 25, 1982. In what proved to be a fatal error in judgment, the motion was filed by the state's attorneys while TDC staff attorneys were still investigating Arnold's allegations that prison officials had themselves made weapons available to BT's.[61] Estelle also disregarded the possible veracity of Arnold's claims when he announced the filing of the motion to his wardens (which was not unlike the letter written by Beto to Jalet some ten years earlier):

Dear Wardens:

Attached is a copy of our response to the officious and intrusive conduct of the mastership. We have tried to be tolerant and meet the demands of the court and its Master but reached a point where the security and safety of our units has been endangered. We have therefore felt it necessary to resort to the courts and ask for dissolution of the mastership.

It is important that all of your officers and staff understand that this action does not yet change their ongoing responsibility for fullfillment of obligations in the court's orders. We will continue to extend professional courtesy to the Master and comply with the law. To do otherwise would be self-defeating.

Let me take this opportunity to thank you and all of your officers and staff for your valiant efforts and support during these difficult times.

Sincerely,

/s/ W. J. Estelle, Jr.[62]

The motion, which was the most strongly worded pleading in the long history of the case, accused Nathan of "gross misconduct," which included "failing to report inmates' possessions of deadly weapons" and "undermining discipline and fostering unrest by spreading rumors, establishing a clandestine courier system, and scheming with inmates to thwart prison discipline." Nathan and his staff were also accused of engaging in activities that were "clearly the cause of inmate disturbances at TDC." In support of this charge, attorneys relied on statistics that linked the increase in disturbances to visits by staff from Nathan's office since the imposition of the mastership.

Regarding Arnold's failure to report the weapons, the state, with no shortage of zeal, stressed the seriousness of such an act: "It cannot be emphasized too strongly that the possession of weapons by an inmate within the TDC is perhaps *the* most egregious violation of prison rules, short of an assault itself, that can take place."

While possession of weapons was no doubt viewed as a quite serious offense, the state's motion, in the very next paragraph, through sworn affidavits from TDC officials, noted that this "most egregious violation of prison rules" had not been enforced [by department officials] due to the fear that they would be subjected to charges of "harassment of the inmate population." Nathan used the apparent lapse in enforcement to his own advantage in his response to the state's motion: "[T]he affidavits presented by the defendants themselves demonstrate that TDC officers failed to investigate for weapons when they admittedly had information that an inmate possessed weapons. [According to the affidavits of Warden Durbin, Assistant Warden Terell, and Major Gilliam], they knew on September 1, 1981 that at least one building tender possessed weapons. They took no action to confiscate the weapons until September 17, 1981, and only then because the inmate building tender was fortuitously 'arrested' on an unrelated matter." [63]

The same inconsistency was used to address the state's attempt to get Arnold indicted for failure to report the weapons: "In light of some rather well publicized efforts by Texas State officials and their representatives in seeking criminal investigations of the Special Master and his staff for allegedly failing to report weapons information to TDC authorities, the Court may wish to inquire whether TDC took any action to discipline or otherwise prosecute its own employees for failing to discharge their duty to search for weapons when they had information that such weapons existed." [64]

The state's attempt to have Arnold investigated had generated an angry exchange between Nathan and Governor Clements when the governor told the press that the "master and those monitors over there have been in a state of misbehavior and one of the reasons the master is refusing to comment is the master and those monitors are under grand jury investigation right now." Clements quickly retracted the charge when reporters verified with the United States attorney in Houston that no such investigation was under way, even though the state's attorneys had attempted to initiate one. However, when Nathan asked for an apology, Clements refused, though he did admit to being "a little premature" in releasing his information to the press.[65]

Within a few days of the widely publicized motion to fire Nathan,[66] the state filed another motion asking that payments of almost $100,000 to Nathan's office for monitoring expenses be withheld, arguing that "it would be unjust and inequitable to require them to pay the Special Master for his and his staff's time and expenses incurred while engaging in misconduct." The motion also noted that since the start of the mastership in April 1981, the state's bill over the ten-month period exceeded $350,000.[67] This motion, which was also widely reported by the press, prompted a biting response by Justice, in which he chided the state for filing a motion "laced with invective and innuendo." He also warned the state's attorneys that such an unwarranted attack reflected no credit on defendants, and such pleadings would not be countenanced, and further, that the state's attorneys would be held to a minimum standard of civility.[68]

The wave of publicity about the state's attack on the mastership included speculation that the motion was a diversionary tactic employed by state's attorneys intended to distract attention from Arnold's report on building tender abuses.[69] Such speculation was not entirely groundless, since Justice had already set a hearing on the building tender issue and there was some early indication that there were blatant violations of the state law on BT's and therefore of Justice's order. In addition, the state had requested that the motion to dismiss Nathan be considered before the hearing on the BT issue. Due to the "gravity" of the allegations against Nathan and his staff and the resulting statewide publicity, Justice was understandably receptive to a quick resolution of the matter. However, he also recognized the "paramount importance" of expeditiously resolving Arnold's equally serious observations of building tender abuses. In what proved to be a masterful strategic move, Justice consolidated the two matters for a single hearing and set the BT issue first in the order of proof. This order of proof gave Nathan a decided tactical advantage, since Arnold's observations, if proven, would irreparably damage the state's credibility.

After Justice's order consolidating the two issues, the state filed objections on February 12 laced with stinging criticisms of Justice. This set of objections also clearly reflected the import of Justice's tactical move.

Since the question of the mastership underlies the entire remedial phase of this litigation, that question may well be depositive of, and obviate any need to consider Monitor Arnold's report. Perhaps more importantly, it would be improper at worst and unseemly improprietous at best to have the Master and his monitors participate in a hearing on a monitor's report if the next order of business is to discharge the Master and his staff for acts of misconduct committed prior to that hearing.[70]

Justice responded with a stinging reply in which he overruled the objections, set a hearing date for March 15, and concluded with a stern warning to the state's attorneys.

It should be noted that defendants have apparently adopted the practice of challenging every order of this court by filing repetitive motions. They certainly are entitled to file such motions, in order to call to the attention of the court basic legal or factual matters which may have developed since the entry of a particular order, or, by inadvertence, escaped previous consideration. This mechanism for relief is not designed for endless reargument of matters which have been resolved by means of court order. Defendants' motions for reconsideration have been strikingly devoid of new factual and legal allegations. Instead, they typically have been increasingly contentious restatements of previously articulated positions. This improper abuse of process constitutes a substantial drain on the resources of the court, and will not be countenanced further. Future pleadings which have about them the air of dilatory intransigence which characterizes certain of defendants' recent pleadings will be rejected out of hand. Additionally sanctions may be imposed.[71]

It is ironic that while the state's attorneys, Nathan, and Justice were locked in this increasingly strident battle of pleadings, evidence was accumulating almost on a daily basis that would, within a matter of weeks, dramatically change the course of the litigation, and in turn start a revolution of change in TDC unequaled in its scope and magnitude.

Chapter Seven:
Prison Board Takes Control—
1982–83

Sed quis custodiet ipsos custodes*
Juvenal, Santines, vi, 1.347

*But who will watch the keepers themselves?

TDC Staff Attorneys Discover Damning Pattern
of Building Tender Abuses

After Justice issued his January 28 order consolidating the building
tender hearing with the state's motion to discharge Nathan, TDC staff
attorneys Bruce Green and Steve Martin, in coordination with Lee
Clyburn of Fulbright and Jaworski, began devoting most of their time
preparing for the March 15 hearing. Green and Martin had received independent information that the November riot at Eastham was triggered
when a group of predominantly Hispanic prisoners attacked a group of
building tenders in reprisal for the beating of a fellow prisoner. These
sources also reported the startling information that, once the assault had
escalated into a riotous situation, Eastham officials suppressed the riot
with the support of a "squad" of building tenders. This group of BT's,
armed with pipes, clubs, and knives, reportedly wore rag-like headbands
to distinguish themselves from the rioting prisoners. Since this information came to Green and Martin from separate sources (employees who
had been present during the riot), it was passed on to central administration officials with a request to investigate the disturbance fully.

Because of the information Martin had received within a few days of
the riot, he was anxious to review the official report filed by the Eastham
staff. However, the report was not forwarded to Estelle until almost a
month after it occurred. When Martin finally secured a copy, he found
no references to building tender involvement, either as a precipitating
factor or in suppressing the riot. The report simply stated that "officers,
under the supervision of Warden Turner and Assistant Warden Maples,
rushed into the area in an effort to quell the disturbance." In addition, the

report stated that a certain amount of force "was used on the rioting prisoners." Attached to the report were ten handwritten statements from prisoners who had witnessed the riot. For the most part, these statements supported the official version. However, buried in one of the statements was a barely legible paragraph consistent with the information received by Green and Martin: "Then a bunch of guards and inmates had to fight their way into the compound. They lined up along the north and east fences . . . At the fence there was guards and inmates with clubs lined up against this fence with room to get by. We was told to run down the fence and if we was not fast enough the clubs was used. This was when I was hit in the head."

In addition to this account, four of the other prisoner statements claimed that the disturbance was precipitated by an assault of a prisoner by building tenders. These statements were straightforward and to the point: "This is what I feel went down. They were trying to get [a BT] outside so they could kill him. Why, I really can't say. All I know was that it had something to do with someone [the BT] beat or let someone else beat or something."

Martin had also received information that an October disturbance at Retrieve was likewise triggered by the beating of a prisoner by building tenders and that a ranking unit official had resigned his position because of the incident. At the time Justice issued his January 28 order, neither of these incidents had been confirmed by the TDC administration, although information continued to reach agency officials that these reports were possibly accurate.

In early February, Martin received information that one of Nathan's monitors had visited the Retrieve Unit and reviewed a group of prisoner files. When Martin reviewed the same files, he learned that these prisoners had been involved in the October disturbance. Further investigation verified the presence of seven building tenders during the prisoner assault, not unlike the Gus Feist incident in 1979.

According to the incident report, the disturbance began when the seven building tenders became involved in an altercation with a prisoner who earlier in the day had argued with one of the seven. The altercation occurred during the noon feeding, when large numbers of prisoners were in the main hallway. Many of the prisoners who witnessed the assault refused to return to their cell blocks, and those in the cell blocks began breaking windows. Temporary quiet was achieved when assurances were given that the victim of the BT assault was safe. The following morning, when prisoners were released from their cells for work, they again began rioting. This continued for several hours until officials dispersed tear gas into the cell blocks.

Because the Retrieve disturbance was triggered by an altercation involving building tenders, Martin reported his findings to agency officials.

Further investigation of the incident revealed a very aggravated set of circumstances. The night before the initial disturbance, a prisoner was allegedly assaulted in solitary confinement by a building tender. The assault became the subject of discussion among prisoners and created a considerable degree of tension. The following morning, words were exchanged about the incident between a general-population inmate and a building tender. This exchange was observed by a lieutenant.

The lieutenant, who was concerned about the increasing tension and the possibility of retaliation by prisoners, especially the prisoner involved in the verbal exchange with the BT, spoke with a number of building tenders and gave them instructions to be on guard for trouble at the noon meal. Seven building tenders, some of whom were armed, were placed in the main hallway at noon, where they assaulted the troublesome prisoner just as he was about to enter the dining hall. When the lieutenant's supervisor learned that the lieutenant was responsible for placing the BT's in the hall, he recommended disciplinary action against the lieutenant. When the warden refused this recommendation, the supervisor resigned. After Estelle was advised of the supervisor's resignation, he met with him shortly thereafter to discuss the incident in an attempt to rehire him. The supervisor reported what he knew but would not retract his resignation.[1] No formal disciplinary action was ever initiated against the lieutenant, other than a letter of instruction from the warden suggesting that he should have maintained better communication with unit staff regarding potential unit disturbances.

While Martin was investigating the Retrieve disturbance, he and Bruce Green were asked to investigate another incident involving building tenders at the Ellis prison. While not nearly as serious as the Retrieve beating, the incident provided evidence that was in stark contrast to TDC's claim (so adamantly pleaded in the motion to discharge Nathan) that the possession of weapons by prisoners was "the most egregious violation of prison rules, short of an assault itself."

On February 24, the special master's office advised TDC's general counsel, Gerald Fall, that certain building tenders at Ellis and Ramsey were in possession of weapons. Upon their arrival at Ellis, Martin and Green learned that one of the building tenders had been transferred into federal custody at Nathan's request. Immediately after the transfer, a captain had gone to the BT's cell, where he found a screwdriver and a "billy club." The captain then asked the prisoner's cell partner, also a building tender, if there were other weapons in the cell. The cell partner revealed that his knife was in his cell locker and that his cellmate's knife was in the craft shop. The captain confiscated the "billy club" and screwdriver but, amazingly (given the publicity over Arnold's failure to report weapons), allowed the building tender to retain his knife.

After Martin and Green verified that the knife was still in the BT's cell,

they urged unit officials to seize it immediately. After briefing Fall on the
their findings, Martin and Green prepared a written report to Estelle. The
following day Martin was called into Estelle's office, where he was joined
by Fall, along with the captain and warden of the Ellis prison. The captain
denied telling Green and Martin that he had allowed the prisoner to keep
the knife. Immediately after this denial, Martin was excused from the
meeting, wondering how the matter would be handled. Within a matter
of months, Martin's curiosity was resolved when he learned that the captain had been promoted to the rank of major.

Within a few days of their investigation at Ellis, Green and Martin
received a list of Nathan's witnesses along with the anticipated testimony
at the upcoming hearing. Until then it was unknown whether Nathan's
office had developed information on the disturbances at Eastham or Retrieve. Not only was there to be testimony about these incidents, it also
became clear that Nathan and his staff had continued to gather information on building tender abuses, some of which were more aggravated
than any reported by Arnold in his October report.

One of these incidents was an extraordinarily enlightening episode of
building tender abuse that went to the very core of what the plaintiffs had
contended at trial was an inherent fault of a system that gave supervisory
authority to prisoners. This especially flagarant violation of both state law
and Justice's orders would be proven by TDC's own documents—a series
of disciplinary reports—which ironically were processed on the very day
Arnold filed his monitor's report on building tender abuses.

According to Nathan's witness, a former building tender who had
worked as the major's bookkeeper at the Central Unit, he was so inti-
mately involved in the administration of the prison that, other than the
warden, he possessed the only key to the major's office. This inmate was
prepared to testify that, upon orders from unit officials, he investigated
the destruction of a disciplinary report by a fellow bookkeeper. This investigation led to physical assaults of both the bookkeeper who destroyed
the report and the prisoner who was the subject of the disciplinary action
and who had paid the bookkeeper to remove the report.

The details of this incident provided overwhelming evidence that the
building tenders at Central exercised a high degree of control, not only
over other prisoners but even, albeit to a lesser extent, over staff as well.
According to the witness, the building captain at Central told the head
bookkeeper and a coworker that "they needed to do whatever they had to
do to find out which of the bookkeepers" had disposed of the disciplinary
report. The witness claimed he was told by the captain that "I can't help
it if an inmate comes in here where he doesn't belong and trips over a
trash can. . . . I've even known inmates to fall down stairs and get hurt
and since [the prisoner] is a cripple anyway, that wouldn't surprise
anybody."

After receiving these instructions, the head bookkeeper had a correctional officer send the prisoner who was the subject of the disciplinary charge to his office. There the prisoner was assaulted, prompting an admission that he had paid one of the other bookkeepers one carton of cigarettes to destroy the report. The enterprising bookkeeper was then called out and assaulted by the head bookkeeper and his coworker in plain view of the lieutenant, who was standing just outside the office. The witness also claimed that the lieutenant then entered the office and allegedly complimented the bookkeepers on their resolution of the matter.

The action taken by unit officials following these assaults provided documentary evidence that, in conjunction with the anticipated testimony, reflected an almost unbelievable disregard for Justice's orders by the ranking officials of Central. Because the incident had to "look good on paper," the head bookkeeper and his coworker were charged with fighting as was the errant bookkeeper.[2] The disciplinary reports, which were usually prepared by bookkeepers, were on this occasion drafted by staff and provided a surprisingly detailed account of the incident:

This incident had occurred at approximately 10:00, October 12, 1981. It was further revealed that this fight erupted when [the bookkeepers] discovered that [another bookkeeper] had been stealing officer's [sic] disciplinary reports; stealing other inmate's [sic] personal belongings . . . and selling rack [cell] assignments on the wings to pay gambling debts. The activities of [the bookkeepers] were causing suspicions to fall on all inmates working in the [major's office], therefore [the bookkeepers] took offense to these activities. Investigation further revealed that [the bookkeepers] met [the inmate] at the [major's office] where they accused him of the aforementioned activities.[3]

The head bookkeeper's statement to the disciplinary committee was equally revealing. "The fight was over him bringing heat down on all of us. We were all told that if we didn't find the case, we would lose our jobs." The disposition of the disciplinary cases also supported Arnold's conclusion in his monitor's report that building tenders were given favorable treatment. The head bookkeeper was given minimal punishment and transferred to the Darrington prison, where Warden Christian gave him a new building tender job as a turnkey.[4] The bookkeeper who had been stealing disciplinary reports (a subsequent search of his cell revealed numerous copies of other disciplinary reports) was placed in solitary confinement, reduced to a disciplinary status in which he received no good-time credits, and lost one year of accumulated credits.

The day after Martin had investigated the Central incident, he visited the Ramsey Unit to investigate allegations of another Nathan witness who claimed that Ramsey building tenders routinely appeared at the scene of disturbances armed with riot batons. Similar to the allegations involving Central Unit officials, this investigation provided undeniable evidence that prison officials were clearly violating Judge Justice's orders. The witness[5] had observed three BT's during one disturbance in possession of riot batons. One of these building tenders had befriended Martin ten years earlier when Martin was a guard at Ellis and the prisoner an inmate orderly. The former orderly was, at the time of Martin's visit, the major's head bookkeeper and therefore very knowledgeable about staff operations. When asked if he had access to riot batons, he proudly showed Martin a key to a large box containing riot equipment, in addition to various other keys, including a handcuff key and keys to locked filing cabinets and desks in the major's office. When asked if he and the other building tenders used the batons, he smiled and replied, "Boss you know we're going to take care of business if we need to."

Upon Martin's return to his office in Huntsville, the first week in March, he immediately briefed Gerald Fall and the Fulbright and Jaworski attorney, Lee Clyburn, of his findings. Martin had kept Clyburn fully briefed from the beginning of his investigations. Clyburn in turn had maintained frequent briefings with board member Harry Whittington. Even though Whittington was unaware of the evident and illegal action of building tenders in the three separate episodes at Eastham, Central, and Retrieve that took place just months before Estelle's December meeting with the governor, the attorney general and the prison board, Whittington was nonetheless beginning to suspect that Estelle was not being truthful when he continued to deny knowledge of systematic building tender abuses. As damaging evidence of building tender violations continued to mount, Whittington began his own independent investigation of the issue through interviews with prison employees and inmates. Ultimately, Whittington was successful in persuading key state officials that the building tender system did exist in Texas prisons, that it was wrong for the state to continue to support prison officials who engaged in such practices, and that it appeared to him that prison officials, including Estelle, had knowingly deceived the governor, the attorney general, the prison board, and their own attorneys about the existence of such an illegal system. Whittington also concluded that some of the prison officials who denied the existence of BT's at the trial must have given perjured testimony. Whittington's observation proved to be accurate in at least one instance: that of the Eastham captain who, during the trial, denied any knowledge of BT abuses. The captain later admitted in a national news magazine that he not only was aware of such abuses but also had personally used BT's illegally while employed as an officer at Eastham.

During this time, Martin, who had been on the TDC staff for less than six months, was called to attorney general Mark White's office for a briefing session on the upcoming hearing on the building tender issue and the state's motion to fire Nathan. Present at the meeting were Mark White, Fulbright and Jaworski attorneys Lee Clyburn and Pike Powers, David Herndon, Governor Clements's general counsel, and Harry Whittington. Early in this meeting, Martin was called upon to brief the attorney general on his assessment of Arnold's report. Even though Martin had not completed his investigation, he candidly advised the attorney general that the building tender system remained very much in place in TDC and that Arnold's "observations" could not be dismissed any longer by merely denying that the system existed. White, who had been in charge of the case for more than three years, dumbfoundedly asked why he had not been told by Estelle that the building tender system existed.

State Senator and TDC Board Member Prompt "Cease Fire"

By the first week of March, it was evident that the consolidated hearing would be quite lengthy, involving some one hundred and eighty witnesses and lasting a projected two to three months. On March 7, a Texas newspaper ran a feature story on the "more than $1 million" paid the Fulbright and Jaworski law firm and Nathan's office since April 1981.[6] This figure did not include the more than $1 million owed in attorneys' fees to plaintiffs' attorney Bill Turner, which the state had refused to pay.

Attorney general Mark White, in addressing the $1 million paid to Fulbright and Jaworski for nine months' work, said the "fees have been fair." On the other hand, White charged that the $1 million owed Bill Turner, which represented almost nine years of work on the case, was "an enormous amount."[7] State senator Ray Farabee, chairman of the State Affairs Committee of the Texas Senate and one of the most respected members of the Texas Legislature, wrote Estelle in early March complaining that TDC's "costly fight on all fronts" was being financed by money appropriated for implementing Justice's reforms and that the legislature had not intended that such funds be used to pay attorneys.[8] According to one observer, the letter from Farabee, who had supported Estelle throughout the litigation, "was like (Walter) Cronkite leaving LBJ over Vietnam."[9]

Farabee, as a member of the Senate's Committee on Criminal Justice, had developed considerable legislative expertise in areas of sentencing, parole, and prisons. Within the first month of the mastership, Farabee had arranged a meeting between Nathan and certain key legislators. Thereafter, one of Farabee's legislative assistants, Toni Hunter (who would later join the attorney general's office as cocounsel in *Ruiz* and play a key role in settlement of the crowding issue), maintained an ongoing dialogue with Nathan on a variety of *Ruiz* issues. Early on, Hunter had also prepared cost projections on the litigation, which at the time were considered unrealistically high. Later they proved to be quite accurate.

Farabee, through staff members like Hunter, remained fully briefed on developments in the case and recognized that little if any progress was being made toward compliance. Of particular concern was information that Hunter was gathering on the building tender issue. TDC's potential vulnerability in the face of Arnold's report, coupled with the costs of defending a client who refused to make concessions of any kind on this issue, led Farabee, in early March, to begin an effort "to bring this thing to a ceasefire situation." [10]

As Farabee was breaking ranks with TDC's costly litigation posture, Harry Whittington, as TDC board liaison with the state's attorneys, was continuing to receive briefings on preparations for the March 15 hearing. By the second week in March, Whittington had concluded that TDC would not enter Justice's court with "clean hands." Just prior to the hearing, Whittington met with Nathan and the plaintiffs' attorneys in an attempt to find common ground for settlement. Nathan took the position that he could not participate in settlement discussions unless the state was willing to withdraw its motion to end the mastership. Nathan also wanted to preserve the record of building tender activities made by Arnold. Whittington left the meeting abruptly, complaining that the question of illegal building tender activities had been lost in the mire of legal maneuvers by all parties.

On March 15, 1982, Justice began to take testimony on the building tender issue. Two of the witnesses put on the stand the first day by Nathan's attorney were former BT's at Ramsey who testified they were allowed to keep weapons such as a fifteen-inch knife and even a pair of "naun cheaucs" (a martial arts weapon). Each day of the hearing, former building tenders took the stand and provided testimony detailing a sensational pattern of alleged building tender abuses. Much of this testimony was reported in daily press accounts, such as an inmate's claim that he was given a knife by a correctional officer after the officer lost a dice game. [11] Another prisoner testified that he and other building tenders routinely gambled in a room adjoining a security office with the full knowledge of guards.

By the end of the first week of trial, some twenty inmate witnesses had testified to a wide variety of building tender abuses. On the fifth day of the trial, Harry Whittington had the first of a series of meetings over a five-day period that would change the course of the litigation. The first of these meetings brought Whittington and Farabee together for the first time to discuss their respective positions on litigation. Their discussion centered around the huge expenditures for the ongoing hearing, which at the time looked as though it would last for at least two months. Both men concluded that given the costs of trial and TDC's potential vulnerability on the building tender issue, an attempt at negotiated settlement should be made.[12] When the trial was recessed for the weekend, Nathan returned to his home in Toledo. The following morning, Farabee called Nathan to invite him back to Austin the next Monday to meet with various state officials about settlement prospects. After the hearing on Monday, Nathan flew to Austin, where he met with Whittington, Mark White, and Farabee. Prior to Nathan's arrival, Whittington advised a number of TDC board members of the impending settlement discussion. On Tuesday, Nathan met with Estelle, Farabee, Whittington, White, and others. In this meeting the decision was made to attempt a negotiated settlement on the building tender issue. Nathan and Estelle also worked out an agreement designed to reduce the costs of the mastership and to facilitate communication and cooperation between Nathan's office and TDC.

Hearings in Houston were reconvened to allow formal announcement of the settlement efforts and the decision to withdraw the motion to discharge Nathan. Richard E. Gray, III, attorney general Mark White's executive assistant and the attorney assigned to act as the chief negotiator for the state, made a brief opening statement of reconciliation between TDC and the special master.

Your Honor, this is a motion to withdraw the Motion for Reconsideration [discharge of master] that has been filed and has been under consideration by this court. The State and the parties have discussed the matter and the State is very pleased to announce to the Court that from our perspective we think we have resolved the matter internally and are prepared to proceed with negotiations on the building tender issue and are prepared to work cordially and in good faith with the master as we understand the master is prepared to work in the same respect with the State and for those reasons we ask leave of the Court to withdraw our motion with prejudice and proceed along some discussions as to the building tender issue for approximately two weeks until the fourteenth of April.[13]

With this thirty-second statement, a near-decade of open hostilities between Justice and TDC's attorneys ended. The motion to discharge Nathan, which had cost the state more than $300,000 in attorneys' fees and had been on file with the court less than sixty days, was permanently dropped. This proceeding also marked the end of Fulbright and Jaworski's role as counsel for the state, which meant an immediate savings to the state of monthly billings in excess of $100,000.

The announced willingness to withdraw the motion to oust Nathan, along with the willingness to negotiate the elimination of what prison officials had long denied even existed—the building tender system—reflected a dramatic change in TDC's litigation posture. Of equal importance, it marked the beginning of an eighteen-month period in which

Estelle would steadily lose control of the prison system to lawyers, legislators, and a board no longer willing to defer to his opinions and requests without question. Once these different factions began to ask questions and demand answers, Estelle and many top prison administrators, who had enjoyed near-total control over agency affairs for so many years, suddenly found themselves at the center of controversy over charges of mismanagement, guard brutality, and deception.

The state's newly adopted conciliatory posture was acknowledged by Judge Justice with a prepared statement of guarded optimism. "The defendant's application for withdrawal, it should be noted, terminates at least temporarily an unseemly campaign of vilification against the Special Master as well as the court. Hopefully, today's action by the defendants will provide more than a temporary respite from this behavior, thus changing the tone of this litigation. . . . While the history of this case prevents me from being overtaken by optimism, I nonetheless regard the withdrawal of the motion seeking dissolution of the mastership as promising."[14]

Although there had been only seven days of testimony on the building tender issue at the time of the recess, Justice placed the state on notice that he was especially concerned about the lack of compliance: "While the court, for the time being, will leave the parties to their own devices, it would seem imperative that if the pernicious effects of the preexisting system are to be effectively uprooted, those who are most entrenched in the system must be removed from their positions. It is most disturbing to learn that inmates about whom this court made express findings of abuse of authority are still seemingly functioning as building tenders, whatever their official job titles may be. This phenomenon should receive particular attention in the discussions among the parties."[15] This remark was prompted in part by testimony from one of the Eastham prisoners, who claimed that William "Butch" Ainsworth was still working as a building tender. It was not until this remark by Justice that Ainsworth, who had been the subject of so much testimony at trial, was finally transferred to a prison where he was not allowed to function as a building tender.

New Players Achieve Quick Settlement of Long-standing BT Issue

Immediately following the hearing, the plaintiffs' and state's attorneys met with Nathan to establish a negotiating format for the building tender issue. Noticeably absent from the state's side were the attorneys most closely associated with the now-abandoned posture of resistance—Ed Idar and Gerald Fall, TDC's general counsel. Richard Gray, who prior to March 22 had had very limited involvement in the *Ruiz* case, even though he was one of attorney general White's chief "troubleshooters,"[16] quickly assumed the role of lead counsel for the state at the March 29 meeting.

Gray was accompanied by Steve Martin and Brian Greig, a Fulbright and Jaworski attorney who would remain on the case through the negotiations. Greig and Martin would spend the next several days preparing Gray for the negotiations, since at the time he had had virtually no experience in prison litigation.

Joining Gray, Greig, and Martin on the TDC negotiating team was Jack Kyle, a veteran TDC administrator and liaison with the legislature. Nathan, whose reputation as a mediator would be enhanced by the building tender negotiations, recognized that even though TDC's new litigation posture was supported by state leadership, face-to-face negotiations between the parties would be difficult at best. He therefore kept the parties apart until their respective positions could be narrowed and incorporated into a single negotiation document prepared by Nathan and his monitor. This preliminary drafting period took two weeks and proved critical to settlement.

Late in the day on April 12, joint negotiations began, and by the end of the next day the parties had settled the most volatile issue in the case. The first section of the nineteen-page document provided definitions for each building tender position (referred to collectively as "support service" jobs) and was followed by a section that identified permissible job functions. There were more than forty prohibitions. First and foremost was that "no inmate possess any weapon." The agreement also required that TDC remove, reassign, or transfer 60 percent of the inmates assigned to building tender jobs. This realignment would be phased in over the first twelve months of the agreement. New building tenders were to be selected by criteria that eliminated inmates who had recent histories of assaults, escapes, possession of drugs, or aggressive sexual behavior. Once assigned, a prisoner could retain his job only as long as he maintained a record free of major disciplinary charges.[17]

Recognizing that the elimination of a substantial number of building tenders and their functions would require a concomitant increase in staffing, TDC agreed to conduct a staffing-needs analysis in conjunction with the National Institute of Corrections in order to determine the minimum level of staffing necessary to replace the building tenders. This analysis would also determine the deployment of staff in key positions within the cell blocks, dormitories, and at security doors, positions traditionally manned by building tenders.

On April 14, 1982, just over thirty-six hours after the face-to-face negotiations had begun, the "tentative" agreement was presented to Judge Justice. Rick Gray stated, "We are very pleased with the document and wholeheartedly endorse it and are in the process of calling a special meeting of the Board of Corrections to get it ratified as quickly as possible."[18] On April 16, 1982, the board met in Austin and "ratified without dissent [the] agreement to dismantle the building tender system."[19]

Because the agreement would require substantial appropriations from the legislature for increased staffing, the board asked that Governor Clements acknowledge his support of the agreement. Attorney general Mark White, who was in the midst of his campaign to unseat Governor Clements, had urged the board to seek Clements's approval because it "was important that the governor join in the unified front."[20] Immediately after the board meeting, White met with the press along with several board members and "in an apparent about-face from an attitude that prevailed only a few weeks ago had nothing but praise for Nathan."[21] White, who had been at the vanguard of opposition to Nathan and had just several months prior to this settlement denied the existence of the building tender system in oral arguments before the Fifth Circuit Court, all but acknowledged the invidious nature of the building tender system in response to a press inquiry.

Q: Isn't it a major problem to try to put the building tenders back in the general population?

A. That is one of the serious concerns. That is a problem for the [TDC] administration over there, and they are contemplating that in the negotiations.[22]

Ironically, Arnold's report, which had generated the move to oust Nathan and provided the impetus for settlement of the longstanding BT issue, is the only monitor's report of the thirty-two issued by Nathan's office (through 1985) that is not of official record in the case, because it was never filed with the court pursuant to an agreement by the parties.

Prison Closing Prompts Legislative Action

The reconciliation between TDC and Nathan and the resolution of the building tender issue kept the prison system in the news during the month of April. However, just as TDC was receiving some favorable press for ending the "ceaseless guerilla warfare" with the court, the Board of Corrections was forced to impose a freeze on accepting prisoners to avoid violation of population caps set by Judge Justice. The freeze, which set off a blitz of criticism from county jail officials directed at both TDC and Justice, was announced on May 10.[23]

The Texas Board of Corrections received a report this morning that shows the prison system is out of compliance with the square footage requirement of the Court's order. This is in spite of all the efforts of speeding construction and emergency housing. The prison population projections were wrong mainly because more prisoners have been sent to prison by the courts and fewer prisoners have been paroled than projected by the Board of Pardons and Paroles. Therefore, the Texas Board of Corrections, after considering all reasonable alternatives, hereby instructs the Director and his staff to accept no further inmates until the prison system can maintain compliance. The Director was also instructed to devise a plan to resume receiving prisoners in a manner to maintain compliance with the Court Order. Resumption of reduced admissions is anticipated within thirty days.[24]

Within twenty-fours of this board action, Harris County officials in Houston announced their decision to deliver eighty-two county prisoners to TDC in spite of the no-admissions policy. The Harris County Jail, also under a federal court order, was just as overcrowded as TDC. This created the unique situation of prisoners trying to "break-in" the Texas prisons. When the Harris County prisoners arrived at the TDC reception center, they were refused admission. The following morning Estelle was served with notice to appear before a state district judge in Houston to show cause why he should not be held in contempt of the order to accept the prisoners. Two days later Judge Justice entered a temporary restraining order preventing the state court "from conducting any proceedings" on the contempt issue. The potential head-on conflict between the federal and state courts was avoided by the immediate release on parole of 450 prisoners, followed over the next two months by the accelerated release of an additional 1,200 parole-eligible prisoners.

While TDC was embroiled in this storm of controversy with county officials, Governor Clements and attorney general Mark White were engaged in a series of angry exchanges. White claimed "he [had] consistently advised the governor, the Board of Corrections, and the TDC that Texas prisons should remain open."[25] David Dean, Clements's secretary of state and former general counsel, pointed out that White's "attorneys were present at the board meeting and participated in the decision to close the prison doors."[26] Clements responded by claiming, "the attorney general is lying about this [crowding crisis], just like he does about a lot of things."[27] Despite their hostility toward each other, both the governor and the attorney general publicly castigated the Board of Corrections for refusing to defy a court order. Clements also, in an unprecedented move, openly criticized Estelle after Clements "ordered" the Board of Corrections to reopen the prison doors.

Mr. Estelle is a small part of that system [probation, parole and prisons] and he is certainly not going to be the tip of the tail that wags the dog.

If he has some constructive suggestion to offer as how many prison beds we need and what kind of construction program then he needs to come forward with a plan, and I am positive that our legislative and our executive administrative branch of government will meet its responsibility. And if we can't get somebody down there who can come forward with a proper plan, we'll get someone else who can.[28]

Clements's criticism of Estelle prompted one news analyst to defend Estelle by pointing out that TDC had consistently identified overcrowding to the legislature in the 1970s and concluding that "Clements's call for intensive long-range planning underscores the failure of the Texas criminal justice system, lawmakers, and governors of years past to heed the warnings and recommendations of legislative and citizen studies which have spotlighted weaknesses not only in the TDC program but also in the criminal justice system as a whole."[29]

The temporary closing of the prison doors prompted almost immediate legislative action. In a special session the last week in May, the legislature appropriated $58 million to TDC for the construction of additional prison housing and staffing increases.[30] In addition, on June 10, 1982, Governor Clements issued an executive order creating the Blue Ribbon Commission for the Comprehensive Review of the Criminal Justice Corrections System. The non-partisan commission, made up of twenty prominent state officials, business leaders, and criminal justice professionals, was asked to produce a "master plan to carry the state's corrections system into the twenty-first century." Although the commission never produced a comprehensive master plan, their recommendations did help prompt the next regular session of the legislature to pass a series of laws aimed at reducing and controlling the flow of prisoners into TDC.[31]

Ruiz v. *Estelle*: Facts Affirmed, Relief Narrowed

Just as Clements's commission was getting under way to address overcrowding, the Fifth Circuit Court of Appeals issued its ruling on TDC's appeal of Justice's April 1981 order: "We affirm the district court's finding that TDC imposes cruel and unusual punishment on inmates in its custody as a result of the totality of conditions in its prisons. We also affirm the district court's finding that some of the TDC's practices deny inmates due process of law. We affirm its conclusion that remedial measures are necessary. . . . We also conclude that some of the remedial measures ordered are not demonstrably required to protect constitutional rights and intrude unduly on matters of state concern and we, therefore narrow the scope of the relief ordered."[32]

Throughout much of the *Ruiz* litigation, state officials had been more interested in who exercised control over the prison system than in the veracity of the factual findings. This posture was nowhere more apparent than in the reaction of state officials to the Fifth Circuit's ruling. Notwithstanding the circuit court's clear and unequivocal affirmation of Justice's findings of unconstitutionality and his authority to impose remedial measures, attorney general Mark White claimed that the ruling gave "the state of Texas a sweep on the issues that were before the court." Rick Gray, who had successfully negotiated the building tender agreement and was preparing for negotiations on other issues, also declared victory. "It appears to be a clean win for the state. It gives us a much stronger negotiating point. We have the hold cards and they don't." White, in later months, grew even stronger in his assessment on the ruling and, remarkably, in his public pronouncements seemed oblivious to the fact that the circuit court of appeals had affirmed Justice's findings of unconstitutionality: "Everyone knows that the district court was reversed and overruled on almost every major issue in the case. Had the plaintiffs succeeded in the case, the lower court's decision would have been affirmed and not reversed by the appellate court."[33]

Governor Clements also claimed that the ruling was a "significant victory" for the state, adding that it proved "Judge William Wayne Justice was wrong."[34] White, Clements, and other state officials were able to pass the ruling off as a victory for the state because of the Fifth Circuit's decision to vacate Justice's single-celling remedy, which the appeals court estimated would cost the state some $300 million.[35] However, even this "victory" was not clearly won. The decision to vacate the single-celling provision was based in part on the settlement of the building tender issue and the hoped-for effectiveness of other less costly remedies. The plaintiffs would be given another opportunity to seek relief twelve months after the effective date of the circuit ruling. "It has not been demonstrated that the provision of additional security guards and other measures required by the district court's decree and the two consent decrees will not remedy the constitutional deficiency. It appears desirable, therefore, first to undertake measures that will not be both costly and irreversible. If these measures do not work, then additional ones may be necessary. This 'wait and see' approach ensures that the intrusion into state processes will be no greater than that required to achieve compliance with the Constitution."[36] William Bennett Turner was more modest in his appraisal of the decision when he suggested the appeals court "gave each side half a loaf." He acknowledged that the plaintiffs had temporarily lost the the single-celling requirement, but upon expiration of the twelve-month "wait and see" period they would have another opportunity to present evidence for single-celling.

The circuit opinion had indeed modified and vacated numerous remedial measures in addition to the single-celling requirement, including the management reorganization of TDC's prisons. However, rulings involving the preremedy phase of the litigation remained intact without exception. TDC's challenge to the fairness of the trial and the challenges to the sufficiency of Justice's findings of fact, the intervention by the United States and the special master were all denied by the Fifth Circuit. Justice's findings of unconstitutionality, which Estelle had characterized as a "dimestore novel," had now been affirmed by a three-judge panel of the Fifth Circuit Court of Appeals. What the Fifth Circuit's decision did provide was a temporary reprieve in which the state could fashion and implement remedies to eliminate the unconstitutional deficiencies in the Texas prison system.

Estelle and the "Old Guard" Face Charges of Staff Brutality and Mismanagement

With the settlement of the building tender issue, Rick Gray began to play a prominent role in the TDC decisionmaking process. He had entered the case with a strong mandate from the state leadership. Through his skillful negotiations, he became inextricably involved almost overnight in key agency decisions because of the pressure Estelle and his staff were under to develop and implement compliance plans. Because of his close relationship with White, who won the gubernatorial election in November, Gray also became TDC's contact with key state officials in Austin.

Gray, with strong support from TDC's longtime assistant director Jack Kyle, took advantage of the momentum from the building tender negotiations to resolve other key areas of the case quickly. On November 10, 1982, Judge Justice granted preliminary approval to compliance plans in the areas of prisoner access to courts, administrative segregation, and occupational health and safety, which Gray, Kyle, and Martin had successfully negotiated in the months following resolution of the building tender issue.

That same month, Gray and Martin met with Nathan and his staff to discuss the general status of the litigation. Gray believed that an ongoing dialogue with Nathan was critical to the resolution of the many areas remaining in the case, such as classification, disciplinary hearings, and crowding, which remained problems despite the "clean win" for the state. The November status conference was the first of what would become routine bimonthly meetings with Nathan and his staff. At this first meeting, Nathan advised Gray and Martin that his office had started investigating allegations of excessive use of force by TDC staff. Preliminary findings prompted Nathan to warn that staff brutality could become an explosive issue in the case.

Estelle's vigorous denial of Justice's conclusion that staff brutality was nothing short of routine had been to this point unquestioned by agency attorneys, board members, and government leaders. However, given the preliminary evidence developed by Nathan's office and Estelle's tarnished credibility over the building tender issue, Gray began to monitor the issue closely. He also advised Estelle and other TDC administrators that instances of excessive force would have to be addressed within the agency in order to avoid further "explosive" findings by Nathan and Justice.

A set of standards for the use of force had been negotiated and then approved by Judge Justice on November 5, 1982. Justice was well aware that these changes, coupled with the "uprooting" of the building tender system, the cessation of the use of chemical agents, and the reform of disciplinary policies, could put the Texas prison system, which had come to rely heavily on these control devices, through a dangerous period. In concluding remarks to the participants in the November 5 hearing, Justice summarized his concerns: "The elimination of these policies, procedures, and practices, without more, will create nothing more than a vacuum with respect to the control of TDC's institutions and prisoners. Such a vacuum, if it is allowed to occur, will remain unfilled only briefly. Aggressive and predatory prisoners, disorganized or otherwise, will seize the opportunity to achieve control. As the experiences of other states have demonstrated, such illegal power structures, once they arise, take root quickly and defy the most vigorous efforts aimed at their elimination."[37]

Justice went on to note that when the Fifth Circuit vacated many of his specific remedies, it assigned the task of replacing unconstitutional practices squarely on the shoulders of prison officials. Through the negotiation process, important steps had been taken toward devising viable alternatives. However, Justice warned, the critical step of effective implementation was yet to come: "This court well remembers the case of *Morales* v. *Turman*. When an order was entered in that case which prohibited staff brutality against youths confined in Texas Youth Council facilities, the insufficiently trained guards stood idly by and permitted the youths in their charge to riot, not knowing any means to control the youths' behavior other than excessive force. To avoid such spectacles, all means should be used by TDC officials to improve and intensify the training of personnel having direct contact with inmates. If the necessary steps are not taken, TDC institutions could well dissolve into chaos."[38] These admonitions would take on prophetic significance when inmate violence began to rise dramatically in subsequent years. Before this happened, however, there would be substantial evidence that excessive use of force remained firmly entrenched some two years after Justice's memorandum opinion.

Just before the initial status conference with Nathan, Martin had completed an investigation involving allegations that on September 10, 1982, correctional officers had used excessive force on a handcuffed prisoner at Ellis after he had been transferred to solitary confinement. Martin had completed a preliminary investigation in late October that revealed that an altercation had occurred and injuries were sustained by the prisoner. Although there was evidence that the prisoner was assaulted by officers while handcuffed, Martin's preliminary report revealed an equally serious violation after the assault.

The prisoner had sustained several bruises and lacerations during the assault, one of which required sutures. The medical assistant, who had been called to solitary confinement after the assault, requested that the prisoner be moved to the unit hospital. Because of the head wounds, the medical attendant was fearful that the prisoner had sustained a concussion during the assault and therefore wanted him examined by a physician. The security captain refused the request, stating that treatment would have to be rendered on the scene. The captain explained that he did not want to transport the prisoner through the main hallway, where he might be seen by a representative from the special master's office.

After attending to the prisoner, the medical assistant wrote an injury report in which he noted the reason for not moving the inmate to the hospital—"due to the presence of the Special Master." Within a few hours, the medical assistant was ordered to retrieve all copies of the report. He was then ordered to rewrite his report without reference to the special master. He was also asked to amend the prognosis on the report from "unknown at this time" to "good." During the course of an interview with the medical assistant, Martin learned that one of Nathan's monitors had likewise interviewed the medical assistant and been given a copy of the original report.

Martin filed a final report on the incident in mid-November and briefed TDC's general counsel. In what was to become routine practice for the next eleven months regarding internal investigations of staff brutality, no action was taken by the TDC administration. When Gray met with Nathan in late November, he had been briefed on Martin's investigation. This investigation, coupled with Nathan's brutality report, caused Gray to become increasingly concerned over the extent and frequency of such incidents.

In the following two months (December and January), a series of events heightened Gray's concern, not only over the brutality issue, but also over TDC's hesitancy to support and implement the agreements he had recently negotiated. Once investigated, this series of events proved strikingly similar to violations of witness protection orders at the Ramsey prison in 1975–76. The parallel was accentuated by the fact that the assistant warden at the center of this controversy was considered a protégé of warden David Christian, the TDC official reprimanded for violation of the protective orders at Ramsey in 1976.

On December 3, 1982, nine prisoners, most of whom had been witnesses at the building tender hearing in March 1982, filed a complaint with Judge Justice alleging that TDC officials at the Wynne Unit were using the recently approved administrative segregation plan to punish and harass prisoners who had testified at the March hearing. Just before the beginning of the March hearing, TDC had entered into a protective order with Turner prohibiting TDC from punishing, threatening, or harassing any prisoner for testimony at the hearing. A number of the building tender witnesses had been transferred to Wynne pursuant to the protective order and placed in administrative segregation. Because of TDC's history of violating protective orders and the allegations that the recently approved plan was being violated during the first month of implementation, Justice asked, on December 20, 1982, that the allegations be investigated. The next day TDC's general counsel assigned the investigation to Martin and the chief of TDC's internal affairs division.

Martin and the internal affairs chief immediately verified that Assistant Warden Robert Lawson had imposed a series of especially onerous and punitive rules on prisoners who had testified at the building tender hearing shortly after the new administrative segregation plan was approved by Justice. These punishments were required, Lawson said, by the new plan. When Gray reviewed the rules, he concluded that they were in obvious violation of the court-approved plan and urged the Wynne officials to amend their practices, which they begrudgingly did.

Within the next week, three of the prisoners who had filed the December 3 complaint with Justice were involved in altercations with Assistant Warden Lawson and members of his staff. The first disturbance involved a prisoner who had been called to Lawson's office and, in the presence of six officers, "swung his fist at Mr. Lawson."[39] According to the incident report, the prisoner "violently fought" these officers but was finally subdued. Even though the prisoner had "violently fought" the officers, he was transferred to the hospital without restraints, where he "again began his assault on the officers." The prisoner was treated in the unit hospital for multiple bruises, given a forced shave, and charged with assaulting the officers.

The following day, a second administrative segregation prisoner, who had also been a building tender witness, was involved in an altercation with officers, which started when he inquired about the well-being of the prisoner involved in the altercation the previous day. The charging officer, who was later convicted and sentenced to prison for a beating and torture incident at Wynne,[40] claimed that the prisoner came out of his cell kicking the officer. According to the incident report, the officer and five other guards "were able to overcome [the inmate] after several blows had been exchanged." Later the same day, a third administrative segregation prisoner and building tender witness was struck repeatedly with riot batons by Lawson and other officers for his refusal to be moved from his cell.[41] After this assault, the prisoner was transferred by ambulance to the main prison hospital in Huntsville for head injuries received during the altercation.

A week later, Turner filed a motion for a hearing before Justice to offer testimony on the alleged violations of the administrative segregation plan and for further protection of the building tender witnesses. The day after Turner filed his motion, Martin and the chief of internal affairs were ordered to Wynne to investigate the altercations. At the end of the second day of the investigation, both these men had raised serious questions about the incidents.

A few days later, Justice held a hearing on the matter and took testimony from six of the Wynne prisoners, including the three who had been involved in the altercations. At the conclusion of the first day of testimony, Justice asked the parties to "work together towards a solution to the problems" at Wynne. It was agreed among Gray, Turner, and Nathan to transfer the prisoners to other TDC units. In addition, TDC agreed to expunge the disciplinary charges resulting from the temporarily imposed Wynne rules. In Justice's March order approving the transfers, he warned TDC against further violations of his orders: "The Court is not unmindful of the nine year history of the repeated necessity for the Court to enjoin the defendants from retaliation against plaintiffs and witnesses in this litigation. If the defendants prove themselves unmindful of the meaning of this history or unaware of the Court's continuing concern in this regard, the Court will not hesitate to entertain an application for further relief."

On March 24, 1983, Gray, Kyle, and Martin had their second meeting with Nathan and his staff to discuss the status of the litigation. By this time, Nathan's office had completed three investigations involving staff brutality that indicated serious abuses. Nathan expressed concern over TDC's increasing lack of cooperation with Paul Belazis, the monitor assigned to investigate and report on brutality allegations. TDC, Nathan noted, had taken no action on the investigations, which had been completed and forwarded to Estelle. On May 19, 1983, Gray and Martin had their third status conference with Nathan and were this time briefed on brutality investigations at seven different TDC prisons. Nathan advised Gray and Martin that his office was close to filing their report, which he felt could not be delayed much longer, given the seriousness of the findings and TDC's lack of action. Since no action had been taken on any of the investigations completed at this time, and a pattern was beginning to emerge that supported Justice's finding that staff brutality was "nothing short of routine," Gray requested that monitor Belazis meet with TDC officials to discuss the prospective findings of Nathan's office. This meeting, Gray hoped, would generate movement by Estelle and thus avoid another building tender–like confrontation.

After the briefing session, which was attended by D. V. "Red" McKaskle, assistant director in charge of security, and the director of internal affairs, Nathan agreed to give TDC time to initiate corrective measures. On June 8, 1983, Nathan expressed his optimism, which was to be short-lived, in a letter to Gray:

Until our general review of the case on May 19, 1983, I had little reason to believe that my efforts to avoid a confrontation would be successful. As early as September 28, 1982 monitors in my office began to share the results of use of force investigations with Director Estelle, but we received no indication that these investigative reports were resulting in any action by TDC. During the period that has since elapsed, I made it clear on a number of occasions that these reports, as well as interviews with inmates, former inmates, TDC staff members, and former TDC staff members, were producing substantial evidence of serious non-compliance with the use of force standards, at least at several institutions. In addition, increasing lack of cooperation by unit staff and, in some instances, departmental personnel confirmed my concern that it was TDC's intention to impede monitoring efforts in this area and to revert to litigation strategies that characterized the reaction to David Arnold's first building tender report.

By early May I had concluded that the only course of action open to my office was to prepare a report summarizing the substantial evidence of non-compliance that exists, to submit the report, and to defend it to the best of our ability. Your request, at our conference on May 19, for a meeting with persons principally responsible for compliance with the use of force standards provided a ray of hope.

Gray had successfully gained much-needed time for Estelle and TDC to initiate corrective measures that would at least demonstrate TDC's willingness to eliminate staff brutality. In an exchange of letters between Gray and Nathan in June and July, Gray, on Estelle's behalf, agreed to have TDC's internal affairs division review Nathan's investigations so that appropriate disciplinary action could be taken by Estelle. In order to reinforce TDC's commitment, recently elected attorney general Jim Mattox wrote Estelle a strongly worded letter on June 27, urging prompt action on these investigations.

Dear Mr. Estelle:

I am very concerned about allegations of excessive use of force by TDC personnel. I fully realize the need for some force to be used in a prison environment. I understand the need for reasonable force to be utilized upon occasion in subduing an inmate; however, the State cannot tolerate use of force for punishment purposes.

I believe it is most important that the TDC develop and implement a system whereby allegations of excessive use of force can be reported and thoroughly investigated by the TDC. It is absolutely essential that when the investigations reveal the use of excessive force that prompt action be taken so that we might show in litigation that the TDC does not and will not tolerate excessive force, particularly when used for punishment. . . .

/s/ Jim Mattox

During the summer months, TDC's recently created internal affairs division, staffed largely by untrained investigators who had worked as guards, devoted all its resources to following up investigations completed by the special master's office. By early August, more than half of fourteen investigations completed by Nathan's office had been confirmed. Most of these involved high-ranking unit officials who participated in especially brutal attacks on prisoners. As each investigation was confirmed, Gray grew more adamant in urging Estelle to initiate action against the offending guards. On August 17, 1983, Gray informed his former boss, now Governor White, that internal affairs had confirmed half of the investigations completed by the special master's office.

When it became evident that Estelle was unwilling to act on this growing body of evidence, Nathan advised Gray that he would file Belazis's report in September. In late August, with the filing of Belazis's report imminent, Estelle took disciplinary action against seven officers involved in three separate incidents. Each incident reflected clear instances of excessive brutality, illegal punishments administered by high-ranking officials, and falsification of agency documents. In the best possible light, they could be described as serious and willful violations.[42] The disciplinary actions, however, were nothing more than reprimands. One of the incidents involved warden Christian, who for the second time received a reprimand in which Estelle also reprimanded himself. This nominal disciplinary action only aggravated what had by this time evolved into the "explosive" issue to which Nathan had referred in his first meeting with Gray and Martin, ten months earlier. As with the building tender issue, Estelle and the TDC administration could no longer deny these abuses, many of which had been confirmed by TDC's own internal affairs division.

On September 13, 1983, in what would later be described as a "scathing report on violence in the Texas prison system," monitor Belazis hand-delivered copies of his draft Monitor's Report on Use of Force to Estelle and his lawyers. The eighty-three-page report, with more than four hundred pages of appendices, included fourteen separate brutality investigations. Each documented patterns similar to the findings of Judge Justice in his memorandum opinion almost three years earlier, findings that had been the subject of so much criticism by Estelle. In his report Belazis concluded:

> In summary, it is the Monitor's observation that physical abuse of inmates has continued to occur with alarming force and frequency. The instances of abuse identified by the Monitor's investigations go beyond over reactions to situations requiring the use of some physical force. In a great many instances, brutal, unprovoked beatings were inflicted upon inmates who were guilty of violating institutional rules but who posed no immediate threat to safety or security. Of critical significance is the fact that virtually all of these incidents involved the participation of officers with the rank of Sergeant and above. In many cases the physical abuse involved high ranking unit officials and staff . . .
>
> Moreover, all are characteristic of the improper force which the District Court found to be routine in the Texas prison system. Therefore, while the full extent of the magnitude of this phenomenon cannot be fully documented in this report, there is no question but that improper use of force continues to be routine in TDC.[43]

Like Arnold, Belazis began his report with a discussion of obstacles he encountered while monitoring staff brutality. Such impediments included refusal of staff to discuss use-of-force incidents, "altering or fabricating" agency reports to conceal incidents of excessive force, and the "failure of medical personnel to adequately document injuries sustained by inmates." Also cited was a general lack of cooperation by central administration officials in providing documents and access to TDC institutions. These impediments, Belazis concluded, reflected a "deliberate effort to impede" monitoring of staff brutality.

Also like Arnold, Belazis found evidence that prisoners who cooperated with the special master's office were later subjected to harassment or retaliation. As an example, he cited an incident that not only reflected harassment, but, like the Batts case (see Chapter 5), provided evidence that the enforcement of TDC's work ethic could be fatal to prisoners. Belazis had received allegations that a twenty-nine-year-old prisoner, who died after suffering an apparent heatstroke while working in the fields, had been kicked by a field officer when he complained of illness. It was alleged that when the prisoner fell to the ground, he was kicked as an inducement to get up and continue his work. Belazis noted that when the prisoners who witnessed the incident were interviewed by another monitor, they claimed that the officer who allegedly kicked the inmate had threatened them for their cooperation with the special master's office. The officer charged with kicking the inmate was also the subject of another particularly brutal incident set out in Belazis report. The officer resigned before the completion of TDC's investigation of the incident, in which he and others were found to have beaten two prisoners.[45]

After discussing TDC's "effort to cover up illegal use of force," the monitor identified several types of excessive force routinely employed by TDC staff. He provided vivid examples of each by drawing on the fourteen separate investigations set out in the appendices. Two of the fourteen investigations involved beatings on the Eastham Unit and illustrated how force was used as a form of disciplinary punishment.[46] One of the incidents was a classic example of an Eastham "tune-up." It was prompted by two prisoners' refusal to work. After they refused, the two were called to the building major's office, where they were beaten with nightsticks and a slapjack. Both prisoners sustained multiple injuries to their backs, legs, and ankles. The second incident at Eastham occurred after a fight broke out between several prisoners and building tenders over the volume of the television set in the cell block dayroom. After the fight, the prisoners who had fought with the building tenders were called one by one to the building major's office, where they were beaten by several officers in the presence of a major.

Another type of excessive force addressed in the Belazis report involved prisoners with mental handicaps. One of the investigations involved a prisoner who had "great difficulty in coping with the prison environment." Like James Batts, he "had displayed periodic agitation and a history of self-mutilation while in prison." The investigation revealed that the prisoner, who was mentally retarded, refused to work because his shirt had been torn. While arguing with a correctional officer, the prisoner became agitated and had to be restrained. The officer who restrained the prisoner claimed he hit the prisoner only three times in the midsection. However, Belazis visited the prisoner four hours after the altercation and observed "multiple bruises on his face, neck, chest, back, sides and arms." Belazis's investigation concluded that after he had been restrained and taken to a hallway leading to solitary confinement, the prisoner was beaten by correctional officers.

The report also cited examples of staff members' using weapons to assault prisoners. One of the more egregious instances involved a beating by several officers following a brief fight between two inmates. During the beating the inmate was allegedly hit in the eye with a pair of handcuffs wrapped around an officer's fist and was struck in the head by a hard object he believed was a nightstick. The prisoner charged that he had been hit several times after he was already handcuffed. The injuries to the prisoner were so severe that he was transported by helicopter to the emergency room of the prison hospital in Galveston. His prognosis was "guarded," and the attending nurse during the flight to Galveston noted that the prisoner had suffered inflammation in the ear; abrasions, including a linear vertical abrasion on the left side of his chest approximately six inches long and the width of a pencil; unequal pupils, which can indicate a blood clot on the brain; a swollen right eye showing the early signs of blackening; bilateral subconjunctival hemorrhage; and a very tender area over the left temple."[47]

Belazis also documented an incident that was indicative of TDC's practice of beating prisoners who attempted to escape. The prisoner, who was discovered hiding inside a storage barn within the prison compound, allegedly attacked four officers who had found him. All but one of the four officers denied striking the prisoner. However, medical records reflected multiple bruises on the face, chest, arms, shoulders, ribs, and back. He had lacerations on the back of his head and cheekbone, and both eyes were swollen. The attending medical assistant claimed that "the prisoner had been beaten more severely than any inmate that he had seen during his employment with TDC."[48] The official reports provided no explanation for the severe injuries.

Exactly two weeks after Belazis filed his report, an incident occurred that provided an even more graphic example of TDC's practice of beating prisoners who attempted to escape. On September 27, 1983, a prisoner attempted to escape at the Coffield prison but was apprehended by field officers within minutes after he ran from his work squad. When warden Cousins was notified that the prisoner had been recaptured, he issued an order over his car radio, which was heard by personnel at the three surrounding prisons, for the field officers to punish the prisoner. The actual order was, "Do something to his ass."[49] The prisoner was thereafter whipped with horse reins and trampled with a horse, which left imprints of a horse's hoof and rein marks on the prisoner's back. Since the illegal order had gone out over the prison radio, rumors of the assault spread quickly throughout the system. The matter was investigated, and on October 3, 1983, Estelle had to terminate his most senior warden.

Two weeks prior to the Cousins's firing, Estelle had announced his intention to resign within three to six months, citing his inability to secure adequate funding from the legislature and a refusal to compromise further on court-ordered prison changes as reasons for his decision.[50] What Estelle did not know on the day he fired Cousins was that Belazis's report, which had received statewide publicity in the preceding days, would be joined by charges of mismanagement that would force his own ouster only four days later.

Harry Whittington, who had begun to question Estelle's credibility over the building tender issue in 1981, had immersed himself in studying the management practices of Estelle's administration during the latter part of 1982. Whittington had already developed a reputation among agency officials and fellow board members as a maverick member who was unwilling to accept all of the staff explanations and recommendations. Prior to Whittington's tenure on the nine member board, votes were almost always unanimous. As early as January 1980, Whittington broke a longstanding tradition of unanimity on board votes when he cast the only dissenting vote to purchase land in the Rio Grande Valley for a new prison. (This purchase was not completed when Governor Clements and land commissioner Bob Armstrong failed to approve the board's decision.)

From January 1980 through July 1983, Whittington's dissenting vote became more frequent. At the January 1983 Board of Corrections meeting, Whittington questioned the payment of additional fees, which were almost one-third more than the contract amount, to the architect who designed the new Ellis II Unit. Later disclosures would reveal that substantial payments of fees above contract amounts had been paid to several architectural firms without any written amendments to show additional work. These questions were particularly disturbing to TDC officials, because the legislature had before it a budget request by TDC to construct nine new prisons using the Ellis II plans as a prototype.

In June and July 1983, just as the staff brutality issue was gaining momentum, evidence of questionable TDC management practices also began to solidify. Finally, at the July 1983 board meeting, Whittington's role as the lone dissenter ended when his motion to employ outside auditors to examine TDC construction practices passed by a vote of seven to one (one board member was absent).[51] The dissenting vote was cast by Bartell Zachry, who had worked closely with Estelle on construction projects and the employment of architects during the previous five years. At this meeting it was also confirmed that Estelle had entered into a $2.5 million construction management agreement with an architect without board knowledge or approval.

Whittington's motion came after his own six-month investigation into the construction project. His interest had been heightened after the January 1983 meeting when agency officials were unable to answer his questions about the fees paid on the Ferguson Unit to the same architect who designed the Ellis II Unit. The Ferguson project began at a cost of $4.7 million, but was raised to $21 million without board approval. By the March 1983 board meeting Whittington's inquiries prompted T. Louis Austin, chairman of the board, to request the state auditor to investigate TDC's spending practices on the project. Whittington had discovered, among other things, that within the first six months of the project, the estimated cost increased from $4.7 million to $12.4 million. During the second six months it rose to $16 million.[52] Neither of these increases had been brought to the board's attention, let alone approved. Within one month, on April 13, 1983, the state auditor, George McNeil, forwarded his report to the board, which absolved TDC of any wrongdoing.[53]

At the next board meeting, in May 1983, Whittington questioned one of the state auditor's representatives at length on what Whittington perceived were deficiencies in the report. Whittington was able to confirm that a number of conclusions reached by the state auditor were based on rank "assumptions."[54] Notwithstanding Whittington's questioning, during which a number of obvious deficiencies were clearly established, Estelle gave his unqualified endorsement to the state auditor's report,[55] and the board voted three to two, with two abstentions, to pay the architect an additional $500,000. Whittington then submitted a series of written follow-up questions,[56] and on June 15, 1983, the state auditor delivered a second report in which he retracted, corrected, and supplemented certain conclusions drawn in the first report.[57]

Whittington, however, was still not satisfied. In preparation for the July board meeting, he compiled a five-page analysis of spending abuses, which he read into the record prior to his motion for an independent outside investigation of the matter. He concluded his analysis with a strong indictment of both the auditor's reports and TDC's construction division:

> For four months this Board has been waiting for the State Auditor to examine the manner in which large sums of public money have been authorized to be spent and whether payments to the architect have been proper. After two conflicting written reports it is obvious that the State Auditor has been of no assistance in informing this Board of facts upon which it can rely and take action it deems appropriate . . . Both reports clearly indicate that the Construction Division has been completely out of control from the Board which is solely responsible for all construction expenditures and whose members are personally liable for waste and mismanagement.[58]

Not only did Whittington's motion carry with only one dissenting vote, but one of the majority voters, Robert Gunn, would become, with the careful orchestration of Whittington, the chairman of the board and Whittington's strongest ally within the next few months. These two men, both conservative Republicans, almost overnight found themselves in the unlikely roles of prison reformers.

Placebo Board Becomes Activist

Robert Gunn, a Wichita Falls geologist, appointed to the Board of Corrections in 1981 by Governor Clements upon the recommendation of Whittington, was by his own admission "duped" by Estelle and other prison officials during his first two years on the board.[59] He described himself as a "typical board member, letting the corrections administrators run the system and believing what they told him."[60] Gunn, a past president of the American Association of Petroleum Geologists and director of the Boys Clubs of Wichita Falls, had "never stepped into a prison or met anyone who had spent time there when he was appointed to the prison board." Because he was wholly lacking in prison experience, like most of his fellow board members, it was natural for him to defer to Estelle almost without question, hence his characterization that board members "were like placebos . . . medicine without any effect."[61] After Whittington read his five-page statement, Gunn responded with a short statement of his own, which reflected his transformation from a "placebo" board member to a proactive force who would eventually lead the Board of Corrections through its most tumultuous period. Given what was to follow in the months ahead, Gunn's conversion to an activist stance was reflected in a rather bland summary of his statement in the minutes of the board meeting. "Mr. Gunn stated that he thinks this [Whittington's proposal] points out a really serious problem that is much more important than simply an analysis of the Construction Division and that it is an analysis of the position of each Board member and the function of the Board. He stated that we, as Board members, have not taken enough time to keep ourselves informed and to be involved sufficiently in the operation of the Department."[62]

After the meeting, in response to press inquiries, Gunn stated his position more succinctly when he said, "I am damned if I want to be on a board and have a sense of no control."[63] One press account of the July meeting described Gunn as "shocked" when, in response to the issues raised by Whittington, Estelle supposedly told the board that TDC boards had always allowed him to "run the prisons as he wished."[64]

Gunn's transformation was not as sudden as it may have appeared at the time. When Whittington first raised questions of the construction project in January 1983, Gunn had already begun to doubt agency officials as a result of their handling of the building tender issue. A news story later recounted:

> In the spring of 1982 [Gunn] said, the board received proof of an instance in which prison officials had allowed favored inmates called building tenders to beat a prisoner. During the prison-reform trial before Justice, TDC officials denied that they allowed building tenders to discipline inmates.
> Gunn would not elaborate on the incident, but said details are in the monitor's report [David Arnold's report, see Chapter 6] that hasn't been made public. Gunn said he was upset over the way it was handled by prison officials. "It was pretty much of a hush-up, cover-up," he said.

Gunn said the episode created doubt in his mind about everything he had been told about TDC. "Once there's a crack in the dike, everything just pours in. And once the first crack appeared, you just couldn't stop the flow of all the abuses and excesses," Gunn said.[65]

With Gunn's transformation, Whittington now had a strong ally on the board. Primarily through Whittington, Gunn began to receive briefings from Rick Gray and other state officials who were convinced that serious "abuses and excesses" permeated the prison system.

In April 1983, Governor White had made his first appointments to the Board of Corrections to fill the three vacancies that occur every two years on the nine-member board. Joe LaMantia, an avid supporter of Estelle and a six-year veteran on the board, was reappointed for another six-year term. The other two vacancies were filled by the appointments of Tom McDade and Deralyn Davis. Although McDade was a partner in the Fulbright and Jaworski law firm, he had not participated in the firm's representation of TDC in the *Ruiz* litigation.

LaMantia became acting chairman, succeeding T. Louis Austin, who had been a board member since Estelle became director. Though the election was not to occur until September, Governor White began to lobby with members of the board for the selection of McDade as chairman. Whittington, who considered McDade and LaMantia to be supportive of past management at TDC, undertook a quiet campaign to elect Gunn as chairman. It was during this time that McDade became a key witness against attorney general Jim Mattox, which led to his criminal indictment for conspiracy over a dispute with the Fulbright & Jaworski law firm. This gave Whittington an additional reason to argue for a "conciliatory" chairman who could work with the attorney general in all legal matters affecting the agency. (Mattox was later acquitted by a Travis County jury.) Whittington was successful in gaining the support of Davis and all of the Clements appointees except Zachry, who had served with LaMantia on the board prior to Clements's election. On September 12, 1983, Gunn was named chairman by a six-to-three vote in the first split election of officers in the history of TDC; it was also a defeat for Governor White in his effort to influence the future direction of the board. The previous day, in a closed meeting of the board, Estelle had announced his intention to resign sometime during the next six months.

Later in the week, Estelle publicly announced that he would step down in three to six months. The same week, TDC attorneys were pouring through the ninth monitor's report on staff brutality, which was not yet public. On September 29, however, it became evident that the report had been leaked to a reporter for one of the state's larger newspapers, whose story led with the headline, "Texas prison brutality rampant."[68] The news article quoted heavily from the report and discussed several instances of brutality in detail.

The following day, Governor White, who had been advised by Rick Gray in mid-August that approximately half of the brutality claims had been confirmed by TDC's own investigators, answered press inquiries. As attorney general, White had represented TDC officials before Justice and the Fifth Circuit on the staff-brutality issue. In spite of the information from Gray and his own involvement with the case, White reacted with surprise at the monitor's findings. He denied that he had seen or heard of the report before its disclosure the previous day and issued a stern warning to department officials in the event the investigations were confirmed: "If there is any truth in those allegations that there has been any illegal conduct of any of our officials, I want it straightened out and straightened out now. It does very little good to try to practice rehabilitation, or really to effectively punish a prisoner, if members of the officials appointed there are violating the law. I hope they weren't. I trust they weren't. If they were, they're going to be dealt with harshly."[69]

In addition to the staff-brutality allegations and inquiries into TDC's management practices, state officials learned in late September that Estelle had given all TDC employees a pay raise earlier in the month that was not authorized by the legislature or approved by the board. The next week Governor White called a meeting to discuss the rapidly diminishing credibility of the prison system. Attending the meeting were Gunn, Whittington, and key state lawmakers. During the meeting a consensus emerged that the board should replace Estelle immediately and begin its search for a permanent director. Gunn was given the task of asking for Estelle's immediate resignation. Two days later the board met in a closed session and accepted Estelle's resignation. It was decided that Estelle, who left the meeting through a back door, would be retained through February as a consultant to assist in the transition to a new director.

After accepting Estelle's resignation, the board named D. V. McKaskle, Estelle's long-time assistant director in charge of security, as acting director. The board then issued a two-page statement that left no doubt that they intended to regain control of the Department of Corrections. The statement also reflected the prominent role that Rick Gray would play over the ensuing months.

> The Board plans immediately to initiate policies resulting in more complete control of all operations of the Department. Recent disclosures of financial and construction management problems, deteriorating communications with the legislature and State officials, and unfavorable reports of non-compliance in the *Ruiz* v. *Estelle* litigation leave the Board with no alternative but to adopt a plan for operating the Department to assure greater fiscal responsibility,

restore credibility with all State officials, improve relations with the Office of the Special Master, and increase the effort of TDC to provide inmates with greater opportunities for safety, productivity, education and rehabilitation.

The Board of the TDC is quite concerned with the Monitor's findings regarding the alleged use of excessive force within the TDC. The Board does not believe it is productive to enter into a period of "guerrilla warfare" with exchanges and counter exchanges, and accusations and denials, where little or no progress is made in resolving any problems that may exist.

The Board directs its legal counsel to pursue successful resolutions of this issue if at all possible. . . . It is the belief of the Board that compliance can be established in the area of use of force only after the Office of the Special Master is convinced (and ultimately the Court is convinced) that when allegations of excessive use of force are made the Department of Corrections thoroughly and completely investigates said allegations and takes appropriate disciplinary action when required.[70]

The following week McKaskle and Gray began negotiations with Turner on the use-of-force issue. McKaskle had worked over the years with many of the officers accused of brutality in Belazis's report and would be called upon to discipline a number of these officers during his seven-month tenure as acting director. Because of McKaskle's reluctance to "deal harshly" with correctional officers found guilty of staff brutality, a reluctance that became the subject of a subsequent monitor's report,[71] Gray would play an increasingly prominent role in administering the agency during McKaskle's tenure.

After several days of negotiations, a settlement was reached that included a provision adopting the monitor's observations on the use of force as factual findings without objections from the state. The state also acknowledged that "adequate disciplinary action [had] not been taken against all employees who engaged in excessive or unnecessary force and/or who engaged in retaliation and harassment of others for cooperation with investigation into such allegations, including some individuals named in the Monitor's Report."[72] As with the building tender issue, almost overnight TDC officials had been forced to abandon their deeply entrenched denials and admit to abuses documented by the special master's office.

Estelle, however, continued his refusal to abandon his long-standing denial of wrongdoing, even after the state had officially acknowledged these abuses. Over the ensuing months, Estelle became the subject of almost-daily news stories detailing allegations of mismanagement. On February 3, 1984, after four months of self-imposed silence, Estelle issued a press statement in which he denied any wrongdoing during his twelve-year tenure with the department.

I have been a public employee for thirty-one years. For the last twelve of those years, I have tried to serve Texas with competence, integrity and all the sense of duty I possess. I have never knowingly or willingly broken a law. I do not lie or steal. Any evidence that I have broken a law or that my conduct has constituted malfeasance should be taken immediately to an appropriate magistrate or grand jury. . . .

I regret having to make this statement because of some who would see it as a defensive effort. What I have done for twelve years needs no defense or apology; my job satisfaction has been infinitely greater than the frustrations. I understand my responsibilities and accountability to an employer. I also understand fairness and honor and recognize their absence. I have already been categorized by one potential employer as a "political liability" by reason of publicity surrounding my resignation. I bear no malice for such a finding; it was a value judgment to be made. I do resent, though, the unfair and unfounded insinuations and unwarranted attention to those insinuations. In my work, I have taken appropriate action when given facts and evidence. To do otherwise is not only a dereliction of duty, but cruel.[73]

Estelle had begun his tenure in Texas at the vanguard of a proud agency with a reputation as "one of the best." He had defined his task as continuing the tradition of efficiency and tight control established by Beto. Little did he know, when he accepted the directorship in 1972, that the small group of writ-writers, whom George Beto had segregated in the "eight-hoe squad" had begun a movement that would reveal the underbelly of this proud agency, and would eventually grow into the stream of events that would culminate in his own downfall as the unchallenged leader of the Texas prison system. With his departure, the Board of Corrections, the legislature, the governor, and the press coalesced, and decades of resistance to outside intervention in the affairs of the prison system drew to a close.

Chapter Eight:
A Changing of the Guard—
1984–87

*You never know exactly when something begins. The more you
delve and backtrack and think, the more it becomes that nothing
has a discrete, independent history.*

John Edgar Wideman,
Brothers and Keepers

Estelle's resignation in October 1983 served to heighten inquiries
into his administration by the press, legislators, and public-interest
groups. These inquiries produced almost-daily press accounts of charges
involving bid-rigging on TDC contracts, employee slush funds,
unaccounted-for TDC materials and commodities, and unethical business
relationships. One of the many charges brought during this time was the
result of questions raised by a former member of the "eight-hoe squad"
who, after his parole in June 1982, became a self-appointed watchdog of
TDC operations.

Lawrence Pope, one of the inmates when George Beto segregated on
the "eight-hoe squad" in 1971 and Turner's first witness during the *Ruiz*
trial, was a former bank employee who had spent his many years of
confinement attacking the Texas prison system in the courts. When he was
paroled to Austin, he became an active member of the Sullivans' prison
reform group, CURE. Because of his business background, Pope devoted
much of his time investigating TDC's management practices. His residence in Austin made it convenient to carry out inquiries by simply requesting and reading public agency documents. In April 1982 a Texas
magazine published a feature article on Estelle in which a rather innocuous reference was made to Estelle's financial interest in a small land-
holding company, Ten-K Inc. Pope had read this article when in later
months he began looking into a $2-million construction contract to build
a dairy facility at the Eastham prison. The contract had been awarded to
George Broxson, a Huntsville area contractor, who also happened to be

on the Board of Directors of Ten-K Inc. Once Pope learned of this connection, he began to write letters to the Board of Corrections and other interested parties. Among the recipients of Pope's information were board member Harry Whittington and state representative Ray Keller, chairman of the House Law Enforcement Committee.

Keller, who had been the first legislator openly to criticize Estelle's administration, demanded an independent investigation into the matter. In calling for the investigation, Keller claimed that the contract arrangement was "unethical" and suggested that it bordered on "graft and corruption." Whittington wanted the matter investigated on the question of whether state law prohibited a business partner of a public official from doing business or contracting with the state agency headed by the partner and official. Whittington characterized the relationship between Broxson and Estelle as "highly questionable."

Because the attorney general was already working with independent auditors hired by the board to determine the extent of mismanagement in TDC's construction division, an investigation was initiated on the dairy contract that revealed a number of "irregularities." The Ten-K corporation had been formed in the early 1970s for the purpose of investing in real estate. In addition to Broxson and Estelle, other shareholders included J. V. Anderson (see Chapters 3 and 4), Billy McMillan (a former warden at Eastham and Broxson's project supervisor on the construction of the dairy), wardens James Williamson and Bobby Morgan, and Fred Mote, a former director of TDC's employees' credit union who was later convicted of embezzling more than $100,000 from the credit union.

The attorney general's office learned that one of Broxson's competitors for the contract had protested the bidding and selection process, which was handled primarily by J. V. Anderson. Among the several other "irregularities" disclosed by the investigation, the most glaring was related to the requirement that the successful bidder have at least five years' experience in dairy operations and have successfully completed or overseen contracts of at least equal size and scope. Broxson did not submit any information on his experience with dairy operations nor did he submit information on other projects completed by his company that were of the size and scope of the $2-million dairy project. Projects listed by Broxson included construction of a truck stop, a service station, and a small bank.

The investigator for the attorney general's office concluded that a strict interpretation of the bid requirements would have probably disqualified Broxson. However, Anderson, the assistant director of agriculture for TDC, overlooked the faulty bid document and awarded the contract to Broxson. Although the investigation found no "direct evidence" that selection of Broxson's was influenced by his business relationships with Anderson and Estelle, the attorney general's report concluded that the entire matter was "particularly troublesome."

Just as the news broke on the dairy contract, chairman Gunn announced the firing of a TDC construction employee suspected of accepting kickbacks from construction companies that were seeking contracts with the TDC. In addition, the independent audit group hired by the prison board delivered a report in January 1984 that $1.8 million in equipment and supplies could not be accounted for by the construction division. Disclosures such as these continued to dominate the news with such front page headlines as "TDC Finances: Out of Control." The flood of reports documenting example after example of mismanagement did indeed reflect an agency out of control. One such disclosure, while serious in nature, produced the rather humorous news headline, "Where's the Beef," when it was discovered that more than 500,000 pounds of TDC meat could not be accounted for over a twelve-month period.

Within six months of Estelle's resignation in late 1983, four assistant directors resigned or retired. The first assistant director to come under fire after Estelle's departure was Jack Kyle, a twenty-six-year employee who had started as a guard under O. B. Ellis. He was promoted to warden and was later made assistant director of business by George Beto. Representative Keller, who at the time was devoting most of his staff resources to investigating TDC, called for Kyle's resignation in January, claiming that Kyle had mismanaged the business division of TDC. Kyle, who had been instrumental in reestablishing TDC's working relationships with the special master's office and in negotiating the building tender agreement, elected to retire in March 1984. Three other assistant directors, including TDC's general counsel, Gerald Fall, also resigned early in 1984.

In addition to this turnover of high-ranking administrators, five TDC wardens with more than 100 years' combined experience in running TDC prisons also resigned or retired within twelve months of Estelle's departure. Five additional wardens were removed during 1984 as a result of disciplinary actions based on findings of brutality and the fabrication of evidence against *Ruiz* inmate witness. Disciplinary action was also taken against several assistant wardens. Overall, approximately two hundred disciplinary actions were taken in 1984 against TDC officers for a variety of use-of-force violations.

Several months into acting director McKaskle's administration, board chairman Gunn asked Rick Gray to work as McKaskle's chief of staff. McKaskle, who had worked with many of the officers he was now being asked to discipline for brutality, found it increasingly difficult to punish officers, many of whom he had promoted over the years. Gray, who at one point had been offered the director's job, moved quickly to discipline guilty officers. As chief of staff, Gray virtually ran the department while McKaskle was acting director. Even though Gray was willing to take actions on behalf of the department to avoid further adverse findings from

Judge Justice over the brutality issue, McKaskle's reluctance to move aggressively in this area was documented in a report filed by the special master's office in August 1984. This report found that McKaskle and other central administrative staff "attempted to minimize or avoid disciplinary action with respect to some employees and to prevent certain misconduct from coming to the attention of the Special Master's Office."

Just as this administrative turmoil swept across TDC, prisoner violence escalated to new all-time highs. The Texas prison system had long taken pride in its low inmate homicide rate. In the late 1970s and early 1980s it compared quite favorably with other prison systems of comparable size. In 1984 and 1985 this changed. There were twenty-five inmate homicides in 1984 and twenty-seven in 1985. This more than doubled the previous highs of twelve inmate homicides in both 1981 and 1982. In addition, the nature of the homicides changed. Multiple-offender attacks became more prevalent, and more than half the assailants in both single-offender and multiple-offender incidents were identified with organized prison gangs. The rash of homicides came to an end in late August and early September 1985, when seven inmates were killed and prison officials responded by placing prisoners suspected of involvement with the organized nature of the killings in administrative segregation.

The increased attention focused on TDC due to administrative problems and escalating violence also mirrored a steep rise in the prison system's budget and operating costs. State appropriations for prisons in the two year biennium 1974–1975, the year *Ruiz* was certified as a class-action lawsuit, totated less than $100 million. In 1980, when Judge Justice issued his written opinion, state appropriations had risen to $300 million. By 1985, appropriations for the system totaled almost $1 billion. These figures reflected new construction expenditures, as well as day-to-day operating costs. It was estimated that the average daily operating cost per inmate increased almost ten times during this same time period, from just over $3 per day to more than $30 per day per inmate.

By mid-1985 questions were being raised about the counterproductive nature of the court-imposed reforms in the media. One article published in *Texas Monthly*[1] reviewed much of the post-*Ruiz* era and concluded, "The reformed Texas [prison] system is more difficult to control, more costly, and more dangerous to its occupants than ever before." The answer to the crisis of control and escalating costs, the article asserted, was to "run the jails the same way we did twenty years ago." This would mean a return to the building tender system and some routine practices that Judge Justice had labeled excessively brutal. The appeal for a return to an earlier era was attractive to many casual observers of the Texas prison system, who were quite willing to lay the blame for the prison system's problems on the doorstep of a meddling judge from Tyler and well-meaning but misguided liberal reformers.

Other observers attributed the heightened inmate violence during the post-*Ruiz* years to administrative resistance to court orders and flawed transition measures designed to decrease reliance on physical intimidation and inmate supervisory authority in the cell blocks. Throughout the *Ruiz* proceedings there was ample evidence that officials did engage in abusive practices and that many of these practices were systematically encouraged as a means to maintain order. It was also clear that, contrary to state law, inmates were given wide-ranging authority and on several units were placed in charge of cell blocks and dormitories. Denials by officials of the existence of the building tender system and of the allegation that staff engaged in abusive practices eventually backed prison officials into a corner where they could hardly agree to abandon practices that they denied existed. When the practices were finally acknowledged and terminated, the transition in mechanisms of control was abrupt.

The resulting instability was accentuated by a large increase in inexperienced staff. In 1979 there were slightly more than two thousand correctional officers, yielding an inmate-to-staff ratio of twelve to one. By the end of 1985, the number of correctional officers was approaching eight thousand, reducing the inmate-to-staff ratio to six to one. While available manpower was increased, the new correctional officers did not have the effective knowledge of day-to-day life in the cell blocks and dormitories that the former building tenders possessed. When prison officials failed, contrary to agreements in 1982, to hold unit officials accountable for their refusal to deploy correctional officers in housing areas in TDC prisons, the abrupt transition, coupled with inexperience and sparse ongoing contacts with inmates in the cell blocks and dormitories, meant that information between inmates and guards became less reliable. Sanctions became less certain, a struggle for position in the new power structure ensued, and violence escalated. These events seemed to confirm concerns expressed by Judge Justice in 1982 that elimination of unconstitutional policies, procedures, and practices, without careful attention to alternatives, would mean the increased influence of "aggressive and predatory prisoners, disorganized or otherwise."

After McKaskle announced his intention to retire and withdraw as candidate for the director's job, the board increased the pace of its search for a permanent director. In May 1984, Raymond Procunier was selected as the new director. As past director of four prison systems, including California's, Procunier had achieved a reputation as a tough but compassionate administrator capable of bringing the "quick fix" to problem-plagued systems. Ironically, just before assuming the directorship of the Texas prison system, Procunier had been retained by Turner to serve as an expert witness against TDC on the crowding issue. At the time, he was the deputy director of the New Mexico prison system, a position he had accepted after predicting the 1980 riot in New Mexico penitentiary in which thirty-three inmates died and approximately four hundred were injured. The Texas prison system, with its high turnover rate, increasing violence, and legal problems, not the least of which was overcrowding, would provide another stern test for Procunier's abilities.

In September 1983, the Fifth Circuit's one year "wait-and-see" period expired, and William Bennett Turner wasted no time in filing his motion for a hearing, in which he would attempt to show that the TDC had remained overcrowded. In his motion Turner acknowledged that new prisons had been built since the time of trial. He contended, however, that so many beds had been added that the system's support facilities, such as showers, toilets, infirmaries, gyms, and chapels, were inadequate to support the increased population. He charged that "the now gigantic size of several TDC units [had] produced significantly higher rates of suicides and deaths, and using jammed dormitories instead of cells [had] significantly increased prisoners' medical problems." He also cited the increase in violence using disciplinary infractions, which had increased from 6,500 in 1979 to 20,000 in 1982.

Just before Procunier assumed the directorship, state attorneys successfully negotiated a six-month delay on the overcrowding hearing by committing TDC to an ambitious experimental program intended to ameliorate the effects of crowding by increasing out-of-cell time for prisoners. Upon his arrival, Procunier moved aggressively on *Ruiz* compliance issues. Even though TDC had been ordered to file a classification plan in April 1981 to replace the outdated procedures initiated in the 1930s, no formally approved plan was on file when Procunier arrived. Within six months of his arrival, a new plan was filed. Procunier also addressed staffing problems and disciplinary and use-of-force procedures and ordered the immediate implementation of a policy and procedures manual, which amazingly had been nonexistent until his administration.

By putting in fourteen- to sixteen-hour days, Procunier also found time to visit most of the twenty-seven prison units shortly after assuming control. On one of his first visits he observed a large group of prisoners, returning from working in the fields, forced to wait in the nude on the outside yard due to a shortage of showers. After their showers, many of the prisoners were then forced to dry off with their underwear due to a shortage of towels. On subsequent visits Procunier observed similar conditions, leading him to conclude that prison units in the TDC were beyond their operational capacities by about 35 to 40 percent and in some cases as much as 50 percent. This assessment for the first time provided attorneys for the state with some concrete idea of the extent of overcrowding in the TDC. Since Procunier could very well have become Turner's most effective witness if he were called to testify at the overcrowding hearing, settlement of the issue gained momentum as the six month hearing delay negotiated by the state drew near.

Since Gray, Procunier, and others, such as board members Gunn and Whittington, realized that the state stood to lose what ground they had gained from the Fifth Circuit's ruling in 1982, the state began making settlement overtures late in 1984. In order to provide impetus for settlement, the board, led by Gunn and Whittington, voted to retain an outside consulting firm to conduct a capacity study which would result in recommendations for large expenditures, the board sought support from the legislature for the capacity study. In January 1985 legislative support was secured, and a consulting firm was directed to develop a ten-year facilities plan, including operational standards for realistically assessing the system's capacity, as well as a set of alternatives to control TDC's population.

The legislative resolution in support of the capacity study was passed just weeks before the overcrowding hearing was set to convene. In order to buy more time to develop support for settlement of the crowding issue, state attorneys negotiated a continuance of the hearing by offering the capacity study as a means to settlement. It was also agreed that the construction of a psychiatric facility would be expedited. The level of psychiatric services had been determined by an earlier agreement that was personally negotiated by then-attorney general Mark White. At the governor's weekly press conference held a few days following the announcement of the stipulation, Governor White criticized the commitment to expedite construction of the psychiatric facilities, claiming, "We are not going to have some psychiatrist sitting at the side of every prisoner. We are not running the world's biggest psychiatric hospital over there." Later in the day, reporters reminded Governor White that he had negotiated the very agreement that required the upgrading of psychiatric services in TDC. The reporters also pointed out that White's own budget submitted to the legislature called for restoring 360 psychiatric personnel who had been eliminated from the TDC budget by the Legislative Budget Board.

Even though Governor White was receiving reports from Gray, his former executive assistant, and Procunier, to the effect that TDC's deficient support systems would in all likelihood provide Turner and the plaintiffs a basis for further relief, he continued his criticism of efforts to settle the crowding issue. During this time, the consulting firm delivered a preliminary report, which was not inconsistent with Procunier's earlier estimate that in many areas TDC was 35 percent or more over capacity. The prison board voted to accept the preliminary findings, but White rejected the report's recommendations for more showers and toilets, claiming that he could not support "country club prisons." The deficiencies in TDC, White added, could be corrected with no more than "soap and water." Procunier and the board responded that the standards used to determine the capacity were conservative and fell below such nationally recognized standards as those advocated by the American Correctional Association. Procunier answered White's aversion to "country club prisons" rather succinctly when he commented that "it wouldn't be one that I would join."

A week after Governor White's criticism of the consultant's report, an environmental health and safety expert, who had been retained by TDC delivered his report, which clearly reflected that something more than "soap and water" was needed to correct deficiencies in TDC. "The environmental health and safety conditions of the institutions represent a systemic pattern of decades of neglect and mismanagement. . . . The substandard conditions are exacerbated by virtue of increases in population resulting in overtaxation of existing physical plants and support services."

Notwithstanding Governor White's hyperbolic comments and his apparent resistance, which was reminiscent of his rhetoric prior to settlement of the building tender issue (see Chapter 7), the potential for settlement remained intact through support of board members Gunn and Whittington and key legislators such as Senator Farabee and Representative Keller. However, just as the framework for settlement negotiations was developing, Whittington's six-year term on the board expired, and Governor White not only refused to reappoint him but even refused to allow him to remain on the board through what would be the most complex settlement talks in the history of the case. Governor White's refusal to reappoint Whittington quickly became the subject of controversy, since Whittington had been widely praised for his efforts to uncover abuses and mismanagement in Texas prisons. Whittington, a long-time Austin attorney, who prior to his appointment to the board had been characterized by Charles Sullivan of CURE as a "country club Republican," even received praise and support from one of Texas's most liberal senators, Craig Washington. Charles Sullivan, who over the years had become a staunch supporter of Whittington, charged that Governor White was "cutting the heart out of the prison reform movement" by not reappointing Whittington.

Whittington's loss at this juncture could not have been more ill-timed. No single board member was more knowledgeable on Texas prison operations. However, Gunn through his aggressive action as chairman, had developed a high degree of credibility with Turner, who agreed in March 1985 to entertain settlement discussions with Gunn, Procunier, and the state's lawyers.

With Nathan as the mediator, a settlement agreement was reached that required TDC to reduce the capacity of its prisons over a four-year period by five thousand inmates. It was also agreed that prison officials would place population caps at all units, also to be phased in over the four-year period. Many of the standards developed by the consulting firm were adopted by the board, such as minimum space requirements for cells, gyms, and dining facilities. Other areas of agreement included provisions for contact visiting, minimum staffing requirements, development of a preventive maintenance program, repair of major structural deficiencies (ventilation, roof leaks, heating), and minimum standards for new construction, one of which placed a population cap of 2,250 for new units. The agreement contained no minimum number of prisoners to be single-celled but did identify certain categories of prisoners, such as assaultive inmates, who, once identified, would be housed alone. Sanctions for failure to implement the settlement included depopulation to the extent necessary to bring the unit into compliance. With this agreement, the last outstanding issue, which was also potentially the most costly (had TDC been required to single-cell its entire population), was resolved, thirteen years after David Ruiz filed his original petition in 1972.

Within a few months of this settlement, Procunier, Martin, and Gunn all resigned. Gray also resigned as lead counsel. F. Scott McCown, an assistant attorney general, became the fourth lead counsel. Procunier was succeeded as director by his deputy director of operations, Lane McCotter. McCotter had come to TDC as deputy director of operations in 1984 after retiring from the military. He had been recommended by George Beto as a possible successor to McKaskle. Beto visited the military disciplinary barracks at Leavenworth when McCotter was commandant and was impressed with McCotter's operations. At Beto's suggestion, Governor White also visited the barracks and was likewise impressed. White had supported McCotter rather than Procunier for the directorship but agreed to back the more experienced Procunier if McCotter was appointed as deputy and successor after Procunier's two-year committment ended. McCotter's appointment stands as evidence of the indirect but important and continuing influence of George Beto, who had also referred W. J. Estelle to the Board of Corrections as a candidate to succeed him in 1972.

Six months after formal approval of the crowding settlement in July 1985, Turner filed a contempt motion, charging TDC with failure to implement major provisions of earlier settlements. Because TDC was in obvious noncompliance on certain issues, one of which was a long-standing refusal to deploy officers in cell blocks after removal of the building tenders, the new prison administration, backed by the board and the state's attorneys, worked out a settlement to avoid the potentially costly contempt hearing. (Turner had asked Justice to impose huge fines for noncompliance.) Governor White, however, prevailed on his board appointees to block the settlement, which contained a provision allowing prisoners to purchase televisions. Several commentators attributed White's intervention to election-year politics. Just before his intervention in the settlement, statewide polls indicated that White's Republican opponent, Bill Clements, had a substantial lead in the 1986 gubernatorial race.

On the first day of the contempt hearing, assistant attorney general F. Scott McCown, in his opening statement, claimed that TDC needed more time to make the complex transition from prisoner control to staff control in the cell blocks. Judge Justice, moving into the fifteenth year of the *Ruiz* litigation, understandably looked askance and replied, "Well, I can't help but recall that TDC heatedly denied that there was a building tender system in the first place, and it was only after the court's order had been in operation for a goodly period of time that it even started to dismantle it, so I'm having difficulty in accepting this explanation."

On December 31, 1986, Judge Justice issued a ninety-six-page opinion accompanied by a four-page order finding TDC in contempt of court. Justice's opinion left no doubt that he refused to accept the state's explanation for noncompliance with his court orders. "In numerous cases, TDC unquestionably has not reached compliance with particular orders—some dated as early as 1981—and it obviously will not be (in compliance) in the immediate future. It is also glaringly apparent that TDC made no effort whatsoever to comply with the orders in question for long periods of time and that in other instances attempts to observe them were extremely tentative. In sum, it is unmistakable that on the whole, TDC has been habitually and inexcusably dilatory in fulfilling its obligations in respect to the relevant orders."[2]

Justices' opinion was accompanied by a set of remedial orders in which he set out a series of coercive fines that, if triggered, could run as high as $800,500 a day or $24 million a month. The state appealed the findings of contempt to the Fifth Circuit Court of Appeals. The state's eighty-page appellate brief was in tone not unlike many briefs and charges made over the fifteen-year history of the case. Echoing charges made shortly after the trial began in 1978, the state's attorneys claimed that Judge Justice had "blithely [ignored] the safety and morale of the staff" when he ruled that the prison officials could not ban certain property in administrative segregation. Similarly, earlier claims that Justice's reasoning was confused were restated when the state's attorneys asserted that one of the contempt findings made "no sense whatsoever."

Justice's contempt ruling was issued shortly after Bill Clements defeated Mark White in a bitterly contested gubernatorial campaign. Just as they had done in their 1982 contest, each candidate criticized the other for an inability to resolve the prison issue. The day following the public disclosure of Justice's comtempt findings, and thirteen days before Clements was to replace Mark White as governor, White made a surprise visit to one of TDC's prisons and announced that TDC was operating "constitutional prisons" and characterized Judge Justice as "myopic" and certain TDC prisoners as "snapping dogs." Lane McCotter, who had announced his intention to resign as director of TDC after Clements had called for his resignation during the gubernatorial campaign, also fired a parting shot at Judge Justice during White's tour, characterizing the judge as "totally closed minded."

This rhetoric was quite consistent with postures taken by state leaders throughout the long history of the *Ruiz* case. In a sharp departure from previous practices, however, Governor-elect Clements initiated an unprecedented personal meeting with Judge Justice and attorneys for the plaintiffs to demonstrate his strong desire to address the prison issue in a more conciliatory manner. While most commentators acknowledged that such a meeting could prove to be a benchmark in the litigation, Mark White, still bitter from his election loss, stated doubts about whether Clements and Justice could come to a meeting of the minds. It would be impossible, White suggested, because "Clements gets confused with even inanimate objects."

The more optimistic assessment of the January 9 meeting proved to be correct. William Bennet Turner emerged from the meeting stating his belief that state officials recognized the "gravity of the problem" and that there had been an "unbelievably useful, productive exchange of views." Attorney general Mattox, a Democrat, thanked Clements, a Republican, for his leadership on the issue and suggested that the meeting might well prove to be a "watershed in resolving the case." Shortly after he took office, Clements in his State of the State address to the 70th Legislature: "Let me state clearly the facts of the *Ruiz* case. The lawsuit is over. Let me state clearly the facts of the contempt citation handed down by Judge Justice prior to my taking office: We must get in compliance as quickly as possible. We have no choice."

Governor Clements moved quickly to act on his commitment to move TDC toward compliance. Within thirty days after he took office, he successfully sought a $12.6 million emergency appropriation from the legislature to be applied toward bringing TDC in compliance with the issues that had been a basis for Justice's findings of contempt in his December opinion.

The emergency appropriation, which had been the first order of business of the new legislative session, had an almost immediate impact on the litigation. On March 13, 1987, just four days prior to oral arguments before the Fifth Circuit Court of Appeals on the state's appeal of the findings of contempt, Justice issued an order setting an evidentiary hearing on TDC's compliance efforts. Justice's order clearly acknowledged the swift action taken by Governor Clements and the legislature to move TDC toward compliance: "The court regards this action on the part of the Governor and Legislature as demonstrating the good faith pledged during the January 9 conference and is particularly interested in hearing evidence concerning the extent to which these newly appropriated funds will be used to ameliorate the elements of non-compliance described in the court's memorandum opinion of December 31, 1986."

More importantly, Justice ordered that the fines announced in the December order be suspended until the scheduled hearing on compliance. One week before Justice entered this order, he had taken an unannounced tour of two of TDC's prisons. Justice's visit, which was prompted by Governor Clements's invitation to view firsthand TDC's progress, was another first in the fifteen-year history of the case. Justice's suspension of the fines and his unprecendented tour of TDC prisons left little doubt that Governor Clements's initiatives had dramatically enhanced the state's litigation posture.

The two-day hearing on the changed conditions was followed by yet another order by Justice in which he vacated the contempt fines and praised TDC for its "remarkable progress toward complete compliance with the requirements of the court's order of December 31, 1986." The chairman of TDC's board, when advised of Justice's order, openly expressed his happiness by proclaiming it a "great day for TDC." He also revealed what in his opinion had emerged as an obstacle to compliance when he commented that "the great question in my mind was how are we ever going to get the judge to believe us, you know, after we lied to him for ten years."

Even though Justice vacated the potentially monstrous fines, which attorney general Jim Mattox characterized "as close to a pure victory as we could have hoped for," he set another compliance hearing for October 1, 1987. With the October hearing date, Justice ensured continuing pressure on the state to move aggressively toward compliance with his orders. In response to the order, Governor Clements's office was quick to note that "much still remains to be done."

Shortly after Justice's order was issued, the board of corrections selected a new director, whose first priority would be "complying with the court orders and running a safe and constitutional prison." The director's post, which prior to 1983 had seen just three directors in more than thirty years, had since 1983 gone through four directors in as many years. In addition, there was increasing instability on the board itself. The new director was selected with two of the nine board members absent and with three of the remaining seven members attending their first meeting. One of the newly appointed board members in a guest editorial in a Dallas newspaper shortly after his appointment advocated the establishment of a penal colony at a "remote location such as an island." The chairman, who had served little more than two years, announced that he was hoping to relinquish the chairmanship, noting that the "intensity" of the position was such that after two years "it's time to let somebody else get in." In announcing the new director to the press, the chairman acknowledged the tenuousness of the director's job when he suggested that "if the director stays three years, I'd be amazed."

The new director, James Lynaugh, an accountant with state comptroller's office for nineteen years before he became TDC's finance director in 1984, told the press after his appointment was announced that "the TDC is a $400 million-a-year operation. That is a business." He also indicated his reliance on unit-level management, much as Estelle had done when he suggested that "the director's job in TDC is really not one of administering correctional units. That is left up to the wardens."

As the litigation continues to dominate TDC, a few constants remain. State leadership continues to vacillate over prison issues. State politics continue to influence equally waffling gubernatorial decisions. The attorney generals' office continues to supply a stream of attorneys to represent TDC (more than fifty in the fifteen-year history of the case). Bill Turner continues to represent the prisoners. The prisoners, ever-growing in number, continue to file writs and exercise their constitutional rights. Board Members, none of whom are correctional professionals, continue their efforts to try to solve the litigation puzzle. George Beto continues to exert a quiet but significant influence over TDC, which proved to be a fertile hunting ground for the band of writ-writers he had confined to the "eight-hoe squad" fifteen years earlier. And finally, Judge Justice continues to be alternatively praised and condemned for the demise of what Austin MacCormick more than twenty years ago claimed was "one of the best" prison systems in the country.

Even though the reform of the TDC is not yet complete, a few lessons are clear. Prisons in Texas are much different places than they were when the reform efforts of Frances Jalet and Fred Cruz started in 1967. The process of change has been long, bitter, and costly. Many lives have been helped, others have been damaged, and some have been lost. On balance, the reforms have been for the good. Prison life in the future will be shaped by the reforms fashioned over the past two decades. If we allow our penal institutions to once again vanish from the public view, they could again develop into a law unto themselves. Above all else, the struggle over the past two decades demonstrates that prisons are an integral part of the broader social fabric. By resisting the temptation to push prisons from public view, we assure a more informed, continuous, and therefore less disruptive adjustment to evolving standards of decency.

Notes

Chapter 1

[1] *Cooper* v. *Pate* 378 U.S. 546 (1964).

[2] *Talley* v. *Stephans*, 247 F. Supp. 683, 687 (E.D. Ark. 1965).

[3] *Jackson* v. *Bishop* 404 F. 2d 571 (8th Cir. 1968).

[4] *Johnson* v. *Avery*, 393 U.S. 483 (1969).

[5] *Ruffin* v. *Commonwealth*, 62 Va. 790, 796 (1871). "A convicted felon, whom the law in its humanity punishes by confinement in the penitentiary instead of with death, is subject while undergoing that punishment, to all the laws which the Legislature in its wisdom may enact for the government of that institution and the control of its inmates. For the time being, during his term of service in the penitentiary, he is in a state of penal servitude to the State. He has, as a consequence of his crime, not only forfeited his liberty, but all his personal rights except those which the law in its humanity accords to him. He is for the time being the slave of the State. He is civiliter mortuus; and his estate, if he has any, is administered like that of a dead man."

[6] House Journal, March 15, 1875. Cited in "Texas Penitentiary Report of the Commission Appointed by The Governor of Texas, April 10, 1875, pp 67. Hereafter cited as Report to the Governor.

[7] Report to the Governor, 1875, p. 64.

[8] Ibid., p. 68.

[9] Ibid., p. 105.

[10] *Texas Department of Corrections: A Brief History* (Huntsville, Tex.: Texas Department of Corrections, 1970), p. 8.

[11] Ibid.

[12] Ibid., pp. 9–10.

[13] Correspondence between W. G. Pryor, prison commissioner, and Pat M. Neff, governor of Texas, May–July 1921.

[14] *Dallas Morning News,* February 11, 1925, p. 1.

[15] *Dallas Morning News,* February 10, 1925, p. 1.

[16] *Dallas Morning News,* February 12, 1925, p. 1.

[17] Lee Simmons, *Assignment Huntsville: Memoirs of a Texas Official* (Austin: University of Texas Press, 1957).

[18] F. G. Swanson, letter to Governor-elect Beauford Jester, December 31, 1946.

[19] *Assignment Huntsville,* p. 108–9. The idea took final shape one night when Simmons was visiting the "Bottoms," a prison farm: "Elder Griffin was a fine, sincere preacher, an old-timer interested in his work. I have heard him preach and pray; I have heard him soar into the very clouds as he warmed up. And I have seen his congregation warm up with him. Such singing! No white-skinned folks can equal it. I liked Elder Griffin. He made me think of the great Negro orator, Sin-Killer Griffin, who used to warm 'em up among his people when I was a boy. I decided the prison system should have its own music of its own making."

[20] *Adventures of a Ballad Hunter* (New York: Macmillan Co., 1947)

[21] Ibid., p. 173.

[22] *Assignment Huntsville,* pp. 77–79.

[23] Ibid., p. 67.

[24] Ibid., p. 64.

[25] Ibid.

[26] Ibid.

[27] 503 F. Supp. 1265 (1980).

[28] Carl Basland, *Classification in the Texas Prison System* (Austin: Bureau of Research in the Social Sciences, University of Texas, 1938), pp. 16–18.

29 Letter from Sam Sellers, chairman of the House Committee on Penitentiaries, to Governor Beauford Jester, August 28, 1947.

30 Letter from W. C. Windsor, chairman of the Texas Prison Board, to Governor Beauford Jester, November 18, 1947.

31 O. B. Ellis, report to the Texas Prison Board, February 20, 1948.

32 Interview, August 23, 1985, Huntsville, Texas.

33 James B. Jacobs, *Stateville: Penitentiary in Mass Society* (Chicago: University of Chicago Press, 1977), p. 29.

34 Ibid., p. 29.

35 Ibid., p. 28.

36 Ibid., p. 50.

37 *Employees' Manual of Rules and Regulations,* revised June 1970.

38 "Standing on the wall" was a punishment that required the offending prisoner to stand motionless with his nose touching the wall. This punishment could be made more severe by requiring the prisoner to stand on a small box or gallon bucket. There were reports that some prisoners were even required to hold small objects, such as a peanut, between their nose and the wall.

39 Article 6184K-1, Vernon's Annotated Statutes.

40 *Rules and Regulations of the Texas Department of Corrections,* revised January 1968, pp. 13–14.

41 *Texas Department of Corrections: 30 Years of Progress* (Huntsville, Tex.: Texas Department of Corrections, 1977), p. 11.

Chapter 2

1 *Banning* v. *Looney,* 213 F. 2nd 771 (10th Cir. 1954).

2 *Monroe* v. *Pape,* 365 U.S. 167 (1961).

3 Section 1983 of the Civil Rights act of 1871 provides: "Every person who, under color of any statute, ordinance, regulation, custom, or usage of any State or Territory subjects, or causes to be subjected, any citizen of the United States or other person within the jurisdiction thereof to the deprivation of any rights, privileges, or immunities secured by the Constitution and laws shall be liable to the party injured in an action at law, suit in equity, or other proper proceeding for redress."

[4] Annual Reports of Director of Administrative Office of U.S. Courts.

[5] U.S. Court Clerk, Southern District of Texas, Houston Division.

[6] *Austin American-Statesman*, September 14, 1967.

[7] *Dreyer* v. *Jalet*, 349 F. Supp. 452 (1972).

[8] He was eventually involved in numerous landmark cases in California, New York, and Texas. For example, *Sostre* v. *McGinnis*, 442 F. 2d 178 (1971), amici curiae. *Younger* v. *Gilmore*, 404 U.S. 15 (1971), amici curiae. *Procunier* v. *Martinez*, 416 U.S. 396 (1974). *Cruz II* v. *Beto*, 453 F. Supp 905,910 (1977).

[9] *Carswell* v. *Wainwright*, 413 F. 2d 1044 (1969) and *Granville* v. *Hunt*, 411 F. 2d 9 (1969).

[10] *Holland* v. *Beto*, 309 F. Supp. 784 (1970) and *Bailey* v. *Beto*, 313 F. Supp. 918 (1970).

[11] *Novak* v. *Beto*, 320 F. Supp. 1206, 1209 (1970).

[12] *New York Times*, December 4, 1969.

[13] *Corpus* v. *Estelle*, 551 F. 2d 68, 71 (1977).

[14] *Johnson* v. *Avery*, 393 U.S. 483, 490 (1969)

[15] *Corpus* v. *Estelle*, 409 F. Supp. 1090 (1975).

[16] *Novak* v. *Beto*, 320 F. Supp. 1206, 1212 (1970).

[17] Ibid., at 1213.

[18] *Novak* v. *Beto*, 453 F. 2d 661 (1971).

[19] Ibid., at p. 685.

[20] 456 F. 2d 1303 (1972).

[21] The dissents of Tuttle and Wisdom reflected their involvement in a national trend toward a more active judiciary. They, along with John Brown and Richard Rives, were credited with providing the leadership necessary for the implementation of the Supreme Court's decision in *Brown* v. *Board of Education* in the southern states. Burke Marshall is quoted in *Unlikely Heroes* (New York: Simon and Schuster, 1981), p. 17. as saying: "Those four judges, I think, have made as much an imprint on American Society and American law as any four judges below the Supreme Court have ever done on any court . . . If it hadn't been for judges like that on the Fifth Circuit, I think *Brown* would have failed in the end." Having observed the pernicious effects of segregation policies, these judges believed strongly that the judiciary had a duty to seek change in order to correct social injustices. This applied as much to

the traditionally insulated world of prison administration as to the policies governing schools.

[22] Interview, Huntsville, Texas, August 23, 1985.

[23] 329 F. Supp. 443, 446 (1970).

[24] 445 F. 2d 801 (1971).

[25] *Bogard* v. *Cook,* 586 F. 2d 399, 420 (1978).

[26] 449 F. 2d 741 (1971).

[27] See *Patsy* v. *Florida Board of Regents,* 457 U.S. 496 (1982), for discussion of exhaustion requirements in Section 1983 cases.

[28] *Granville* v. *Hunt,* 411 F. 2d 9 (1969).

[29] *Cruz* v. *Beto II,* unreported opinion 71-H-1371, SD/Tex, Houston Division, William Bennett Turner's opening arguments, trial transcript.

[30] *Dreyer* v. *Jalet,* 349 F. Supp. 452 (1972).

[31] *Ruiz* v. *Estelle,* 503 F. Supp. 1265 (1980).

[32] Articles from *U.S. News and World Report,* September 27, 1971, pp. 19–21, 37–39 were cited for evidence of the national wave of prison violence then being experienced. These articles cited disturbances and killings in California, Florida, Illinois, Indiana, Kentucky, New Jersey, New York, North Carolina, Ohio, Oregon, Texas, and Wisconsin.

[33] *Dreyer* v. *Jalet,* trial transcript, Fred Cruz.

[34] *Houston Post,* September 14, 1971.

[35] In a letter to Professor Howard Lesnick at the University of Pennsylvania Law School, Jalet wrote of her activities and frustrations:

Dear Howard,

Should I still be addressing you at regional Heber Smith Headquarters or the law school, because actually you are, as they say, wearing two hats. Thank you for returning my call today. It is always good to talk with you. When I got home there was a letter from Professor Amsterdam, a copy enclosed. I had to type it as our copy machine has broken down. It is a very nice message, and I am grateful for it. Will keep you apprised of my developments.

To return to my basic problem, am still terribly frustrated and unhappy about Beto's prohibition made by Mr. Taylor's cooperation. I want so much to lash out at him or both of them and the whole prison system here, but need to do things the most effective way.

It really tears at my heart and conscience to think of the poor prisoners I have been trying to help still in solitary. It's over a month now they have been held incommunicado from me and from others in the outside world. I pray that it would end soon and that you will do your utmost to bring Mr. Taylor around to doing it. That is, what must be done to rectify the damage he has done.

I fear you are getting tired of this problem, and I am sorry, but it's ever-present for me, weighing me down.

All the best.

Sincerely yours.

This letter was taken in testimony in *Cruz* v. *Beto II*, C.A. 71-H-1371, SD/Tex. It reveals not only Jalet's anger and frustration but also the fact that George Beto was not the only one with strong support.

[36] Deposition of Frances Freeman Jalet Cruz in *Cruz* v. *Beto II*.

[37] *Dreyer*, trial transcript, Fred Cruz.

[38] Ibid.

[39] Ibid.

[40] Ibid., trial transcript, George Beto.

[41] *Cruz* v. *Beto II*, trial transcript, George Beto.

[42] Beto had been offered the services of prominent Houston attorney Joseph Jamail, but other trial commitments prevented him from representing Beto in the *Cruz* v. *Beto II* litigation.

[43] *Dreyer* v. *Jalet*, trial exhibit no. 7.

[44] Ibid., trial transcript, George Beto.

[45] Frances Jalet and Fred Cruz were married shortly after Cruz's release from prison.

[46] *Cruz* v. *Beto II*, C.A. 71-H-1371, SD/Tex, trial transcript, R. M. Cousins.

[47] *Dreyer*, trial transcript, George Beto.

[48] Ibid.

[49] Ibid.

[50] 349 F. Supp. 452, 474 (1972).

[51] Ibid., at p. 475.

[52] *Dreyer*, trial transcript, George Beto.

[53] TDC Incident Report, Statement of fact re: Melvin Austin, June 4, 1970.

[54] Incident Report, re: Melvin Austin.

[55] "TDC Failed to Investigate Prison Death," *Dallas Times Herald*, February 21, 1982.

[56] *Dreyer*, trial transcript, George Beto.

[57] *Ruiz* v. *Estelle*, "First Monitor's Report of Factual Observations to the Special Master," October 1981, p. 39.

[58] *Dreyer*, trial transcript, Frances Jalet.

[59] Mayberry's unexplained death prompted one prisoner, Lawrence Pope, to write a local district attorney providing information on the circumstances on Mayberry's death. Pope's letter never reached the district attorney, as it was seized by unit officials and Pope was charged with "giving unauthorized information." As a result, Pope was placed in solitary confinement and lost all earned good time. As a result of his loss of good time, Pope filed a writ of *habeus corpus*, contending that prison officials improperly censored his correspondence with government officials. This type of censorship was later ruled impermissable in *Guajardo* v. *Estelle*, a class action in which Pope was one of the original coplaintiffs.

[60] Confidential source.

[61] TDC disciplinary report, Harvey Mayberry, May 13, 1971.

[62] *Dreyer* v. *Jalet*, 349 F. Supp. 452, 488 (1972).

[63] Ibid.

[64] Ibid., Plaintiffs' Exhibit.

[65] *Cruz* v. *Beto II*, 71-H-1371, unreported opinion, SD/Tex (1976).

[66] *Cruz* v. *Beto II*, 603 F. 2d 1178, 1180 (1979).

[67] Ibid., unrebutted testimony of plaintiff prisoners.

[68] Prior to the creation of the eight-hoe squad, James Baker, Fred Cruz, Lorenzo Davis, Ernest L. Ivey, Richard Jimenez, and Edward Mauricio were participating in college programs. Felipe Barbosa, James Bilton, and O'Neal Browning were enrolled in the Windham Independent School District. Lorenzo Davis, Richard Jimenez, Allen Lamar, and Arturo Rocha participated in an Alcoholics Anonymous program. Once assigned to the eight-hoe squad, prisoners were not allowed to participate in these programs.

[69] The eight-hoe prisoners were earning an average of 72.3 points in the Point Incentive Program (PIP) in the three quarters prior to segregation in 1971. Among those who remained in segregation for the first

full three quarters of 1972, the average was 47.2, thus making them ineligible for parole.

[70] Unreported opinion 71-H-1371, SD/Tex., at p. 9.

[71] Pursuant to the Texas Statute, Article 6252–26, regarding the state's liability of claims for conduct of state officers and employees, TDC was prohibited from paying the judgment on behalf of Beto due to the finding of bad faith. TDC circumvented the statute and paid the judgment for Beto by allowing forfeiture of $40,704.53 of the $50,000 bond posted by TDC upon appeal of the district court's finding. The prevailing statute seemed clearly to prohibit the posting of the bond. "No payment by the state may be made under this Act if damages are found by the trial court to have been proximately caused by the officers, employees, or member's willful and wrongful act or gross negligence," 6252–26 Sec 1(b), 64th Legislature, Effective May 27, 1975, amended 65th Legislature, August 29, 1977. Under any construction of the relevant law, once the personal liability based on bad faith by Beto was affirmed by the circuit court, the judgment clearly should not have been satisfied by payment of state monies. Upon forfeiture of the bond, the attorney general's office should have initiated action against Beto to recoup the money. For whatever reason, the attorney general, Mark White, elected not to pursue the matter, and the debt remains outstanding.

[72] *Cruz v. Beto II,* 603 F. 2d 1178, 1186 (1979).

[73] Ibid., at p. 1185.

[74] *Jimenez v. Beto,* 70-H-843, SD/Tex.

[75] Ibid.

[76] 405 U.S. 910 (1972).

[77] 468 F. 2d 616 (1972).

[78] TDC records, Richard Jimenez.

[79] Ibid.

[80] *Dreyer,* trial transcript, Fred Cruz.

[81] Ibid., George Beto transcript.

[82] The *Guajardo* plaintiffs were represented by one of Houston's oldest and most prestigious law firms, Vinson and Elkins.

[83] This lawsuit resulted in a settlement in 1977 requiring the TDC to implement an affirmative action plan to eliminate segregation in housing and job assignments. The prison system has had difficulty implementing the requirements of the settlement. In August 1985, the Department

of Justice filed a motion for the TDC to show cause why they should not be held in contempt for not implementing certain requirements of the plan such as integration of cells, cell blocks, and job assignments.

After Allen Lamar filed the desegregation suit in 1972, he remained very active as a writ-writer until his transfer to a federal prison pursuant to a protective order in the *Ruiz* case in 1979. In 1982 Lamar won a judgment against a TDC correctional officer, having filed suit alleging that the officer in 1975–76 burned his legal materials, asked another prisoner to kill him, and threatened to send him home "in a pine box." These actions took place while he was a prisoner at the Ellis unit, where Fred Cruz had also allegedly been given the "pine box" warning. *Lamar* v. *Steele*, 693 F. 2d 559 (1982). Civil Action 72-H-1393. SD/Tex, Houston Div., Motion for Issuance of Order to Show Cause and for Contempt Judgment, August 1985.

84 *Corpus* v. *Estelle*, 409 F. Supp. 1090 (1975).

Chapter 3

1 "Lifer," *Houston City Magazine*, April 1982, p. 81.

2 *Cruz* v. *Beto II*, transcript of testimony of W. J. Estelle, Jr., pp. 62–63.

3 "Lifer," *Houston City Magazine*, April 1982, p. 79.

4 Kevin Krajick, "Profile Texas," *Corrections Magazine*, March 1978, p. 5.

5 Ibid., p. 5.

6 Ibid., p. 21.

7 *TDC, A Brief History*, January 1974.

8 TDC: 30 Years of Progress, 1977.

9 *Austin American-Statesman*, "CURE: Poor, yes, but determined," February 21, 1977.

10 Fred Cruz, Testimony before Committee on Criminal Jurisprudence, House of Representatives, 63rd Legislature, March 28, 1973.

11 Ibid., Charles Sullivan.

12 W. J. Estelle, Jr., testimony before Joint Committee on Prison Reform, 63rd Legislature, January 24, 1974.

13 *Guajardo* v. *Hudgens*, C.A. 73-H-672, SD/Tex; Houston Division.

[14] Ibid.

[15] Ibid.

[16] First Monitor's Report of Factual Observations to the Special Master.

[17] IOC, Attorney General's Office, Tom Pollan to Harrell Moore, June 15, 1973.

[18] *Ruiz* v. *Estelle*, testimony of A. R. Schwartz.

[19] *McMillan* v. *Estelle*, C.A. 73-H-1108, SD/Tex, Houston Division, testimony of W. J. Estelle, Jr. and Bobby Taylor.

[20] Ibid.

[21] *McMillan* v. *Estelle*, Findings of Fact and Conclusion of Law.

[22] Ibid., testimony of Bobby Taylor.

[23] Ibid., testimony of W. J. Estelle, Jr.

[24] TDC Memorandum No. 201, June 29, 1973.

[25] Statement to the Press, Joint Committee on Prison Reform, July 20, 1973.

[26] Joint Committee on Prison Reform, Hearings of November 15, 1973, Testimony of Lt. Lon Glenn.

[27] While employed at the Ellis Unit in 1972–73, one of the coauthors was chastised by a lieutenant for referring to an inmate as a "black" rather than a "nigger" or "ol thang."

[28] Ibid., testimony of Lt. Lon Glenn.

[29] *McMillan* v. *Estelle*, testimony of W. J. Estelle, Jr.

[30] Ibid., Findings of Fact and Conclusions of Law.

[31] Ibid.

[32] Ibid., testimony of W. J. Estelle, Jr.

[33] Ibid., testimony of Bobby Taylor.

[34] Joint Committee on Prison Reform, Survey of Prisoner Correspondence, August 15, 1974.

[35] Joint Committee on Prison Reform, "Building Tender System, Supplemental Report."

[36] *Ruiz* v. *Estelle*, 503 F. Supp. 1265 (1980). Footnote 77.

[37] Joint Committee on Prison Reform, "Report on Investigation of Incident at Ramsey I, Thursday, November 8, 1973. J. V. Anderson told

the investigators that "the Federal Government required him to give every inmate, no matter who they have hurt or what they have done, access to the writ room to work on their legal matters." This type of distorted analysis of legal issues was routinely employed by prison officials. In essence it allowed them to blame their problems on the federal courts. This practice became a dominant theme during the course of the *Ruiz* v. *Estelle* litigation.

[38] The dilemma articulated by this TDC building tender in 1973 was not unlike that facing convict guards in an Australian penal colony 133 years earlier: "If a convict constable [guard] failed to report some insubordination, word of his cover-up would usually get back to the military command and he would be flogged. If he did report it, and the disobedient convict was flogged, the other prisoners would hate him all the more." Hughes, Robert, *The Fatal Shore*, Alfred A. Knopf, N.Y. 1987, pp. 377-8.

[39] *Ward* v. *Estelle*, C.A. 73-H-1721, SD/Tex, Houston Division.

[40] Ibid., Complaint filed December 19, 1973.

[41] *Ruiz* v. *Estelle*, Testimony of Janet Stockard p. 85. Ms. Stockard's personality mannerisms produced one of the more curious interchanges between counsel and the court in the *Ruiz* v. *Estelle* trial:

> Ed Idar (lead counsel for TDC): Ms. Stockard, would you agree with me that your style is somewhat abrasive?
>
> Ms. Stockard: Yes, sir, I would.
>
> The Court: You resemble Mr. Idar in that respect. (laughter)
>
> Ms. Stockard: I would take that as an insult, your honor.
>
> Mr. Idar: Well I hope I'm not that way in person outside the courtroom, Your Honor. I guess I am sometimes.

[42] *Austin American-Statesman*, July 4, 1974.

[43] *Ruiz* v. *Estelle*, 550 F. 2d 238, 1977.

[44] Final Report of Joint Committee on Prison Reform, p. 47.

[45] Ibid., p. 44.

[46] Citizens Report, p. 65.

[47] *Stipulation Modifying Crowding Provisions of Amended Decree*, May 1985.

[48] Citizens Report, p. 20.

[49] *Austin American-Statesman* November 11, 1985.

[50] See "Psychiatric Services Plan" and "MROP Plan" on file in *Ruiz* v. *Estelle*.

[51] John Irwin, in *Prisons in Turmoil*, (Boston: Little Brown and Co., 1980), especially pp. 133–52, provides a useful summary of how "movement activists" and prison officials clashed between 1970 and 1975.

> Some of the persons drawn to the prison during the prison movement did intentionally violate prison rules and laws in their contacts with prisoners. It appears that in at least two events in California—the escape of Ron Beaty from Chino and the attempted escape of George Jackson from San Quentin—outside activists help plan and execute incidents that resulted in the homicides of guards. But many guards and prison administrators tended to see conspiracies everywhere, and their reaction to this type of threat was disproportionate (p. 136).

[52] Ibid., p. 141.

Chapter 4

[1] *Holt* v. *Sarver* 309 F. Supp. 362, 374 (1971).

[2] Undoubtedly, the findings in *Holt* and *Gates* regarding the abuses of inmates in administrative and disciplinary positions influenced the Texas Legislature in 1973 when it passed H.B. 1056 prohibiting such practices in the Texas prison system. It is testimony to the insulated nature of prison life and the tenacity of informal arrangements between prison staff and inmates that the building tender system in Texas continued for almost a decade in the face of court cases and statutory provisions to the contrary. Such insulation gives ample reason for the intrusive measures taken by many courts when implementing institutional reforms. See, for example, Note, "Implementation Problems in Institutional Reform Litigation," 91 *Harvard Law Review* 428; "Judicial Intervention and Organization Theory: Changing Bureaucratic Behavior and Policy," 89 *Yale Law Review* 513; and "The Judge as Political Powerbroker: Superintending Structural Changes in Public Institutions," 65 *Virginia Law Review* 43.

[3] N. Glazer, "Towards an Imperial Judiciary," *Public Interest* 41 (1975), 104; D. Horowitz, *The Courts and Social Policy* (Washington, D.C.: Brookings Institution, 1977).

[4] One such judge was Frank M. Johnson, Jr. See *Wyatt* v. *Stickney*, 325

F. Supp. 781 (1971)–mental health institution; *Newman* v. *Alabama,* 349 F. Supp. 278 (1972)–medical care in Alabama prisons; *Pugh* v. *Locke* 406 F. Supp. 318 (1976)–Alabama prisons declared unconstitutional. Judge Johnson was later elevated to the Fifth Circuit Court of Appeals. Looking back on his experience with institutional reform cases involving both prison and mental health institutions in Alabama, Judge Johnson characterized his stance as activism by default: "Judges are trained in the law. They are not penologists, psychiatrists, public administrators, or educators, and, in most cases, do not wish to assume such roles. Faced with defaults by government officials, however, a judge does not have the option of declaring that litigants have rights without remedies. The judge has no alternative but to take a more active role in formulating appropriate relief." "The Role of the Federal Courts in Institutional Litigation," 32 *Alabama Law Review* 271 (1981).

5 "When Prisoners Sue: A Study of Prisoner Section 1983 Suits in the Federal Courts," 92 *Harvard Law Review* 610, 631 (1979).

6 "Justice," PBS, aired January 3, 1986, Austin, Texas.

7 *U.S.* v. *Tatum ISD,* 306 F. Supp. 285 (1969).

8 *U.S.* v. *Texas,* 321 F. Supp. 1043 (1970).

9 *U.S.* v. *Texas,* 330 F. Supp. 235 (1971), 447 F. 2d 441 (1971).

10 *Landsdale* v. *Tyler Junior College,* 318 F. Supp. 529 1970, aff'd 470 F. 2d 659 (1972).

11 "The Real Governor of Texas," *Texas Monthly,* June 1978, p. 189.

12 *Austin American-Statesman,* March 12, 1978.

13 "The Real Governor of Texas."

14 *Dallas Times Herald,* May 18, 1977.

15 *Austin American-Statesman,* March 12, 1978.

16 "The Real Governor of Texas," p. 192.

17 Ibid.

18 Ibid.

19 Michael J. Churgin, "Mandated Change in Texas: The Federal District Court and the Legislature," in *Neither Angels Nor Thieves: Studies in Deinstitutionalization of Status Offenders,"* Appendix G, (Washington, D.C.: National Academy Press), 1982.

20 "Senator Says TYC Reform Politics Victim," *Austin American-Statesman,* December 6, 1973.

[21] Churgin, "Mandated Change in Texas," p. 874.

[22] "The Real Governor of Texas," p. 199.

[23] *Houston Chronicle*, September 13, 1973.

[24] Earlier in the century, prison officials had offered similar arguments when the legislature abolished the use of the "strap." *Report of the Penitentiary Investigating Committee*, 1913, p. 29. The same charge would resurface during the implementation of the court's orders in *Ruiz*.

[25] "Was the Uprising Supposed to Halt Reforms?", *National Observer*, September 29, 1973.

[26] Churgin, "Mandated Change in Texas," p. 882.

[27] "Was the Uprising Supposed to Halt Reform?"

[28] "Reforming the Reform School," *Texas Observer*, October 5, 1973.

[29] "Reforming the Reform School," p. 5.

[30] Churgin, "Mandated Change in Texas," p. 884.

[31] *Austin American-Statesman*, "The TYC Rejects Court's Timetable," September 10, 1974.

[32] *Morales* v. *Turman*, 383 F. Supp. 53 (1974). See also 562 F. 2d 993 (1977), in which the Fifth Circuit found the order excessively detailed.

[33] Ibid., p. 121.

[34] Ibid., p. 122.

[35] In addition to Ruiz, six other Eastham prisoners filed petitions selected by Judge Justice for consolidation: L. D. Hilliard, Amado Soto, Arthur Winchester, Herman Randall, Amado Pardo, and Ernesto Montana. The seventh petition was filed by O. D. Johnson, who was confined at the Coffield Unit, which was the second prison located in the Eastern District.

[36] *Ruiz* v. *Estelle*, Civil Action No 5523, ED/Tex., Order of April 12, 1974. On May 20, 1974, Judge Justice entered an order consolidating an eighth suit, *Montana* v. *Beto*, with the other seven suits. Montana had actually filed his suit prior to David Ruiz's.

[37] *Hoptowit* v. *Ray*, 682 F. 2d 1237, 1260 (1982).

[38] *Ruiz* v. *Estelle*, Oral arguments of John Hill, 516 F.2d 480 (1975).

[39] Two of the the original plaintiffs had been released from prison since consolidation and were therefore not named in the amended complaint.

[40] Memorandum in Support of Defendant's Motion That the U.S. Be Dismissed from the Case, January 30, 1975.

[41] *Ruiz* v. *Estelle,* 550 F. 2d 238 (1977).

[42] TDC Newsletter, December 1978, draft of letter to TDC employees from Robert DeLong, general counsel, TDC.

[43] *Graves* v. *Barnes,* 343 F. Supp. 704 (1972), 378 F.Supp. 640 (1974). See also *White* v. *Regester,* 412 U.S. 755 (1973).

[44] Interview with Ed Idar, January 31, 1986.

[45] See Chapter 3, note 41.

[46] Interview with Ed Idar, January 31, 1986, in which Mr. Idar characterized the Department of Justice attorneys when commenting on early settlement discussions.

[47] Correspondence from Justice to William Bennett Turner, David Vanderhoof (Justice Department), Ed Idar, dated July 11, 1977. In one letter written in early 1977, Idar set out in excruciating detail problems he had with Justice Department attorneys over microfilming records and concluded that the problem could have been avoided "if the attorneys for the U.S. had exercised any common sense" (correspondence from Idar to Vanderhoof, March 17, 1977.)

[48] In a later letter to then-attorney general Mark White, Turner took exception to the "ludicrous" assertion made by AG attorneys that counsel for the U.S., including Drew Days, were guilty of obstructing justice. Turner went on to note, "I do not believe any settlement discussions can be fruitful unless you take charge of your trial team and put an end to their childish and irresponsible litigation posturing" (letter from William Bennett Turner to Mark White, March 23, 1979).

[49] "Legislative Action Urged to Forestall Court Prison Order," *Austin American-Statesman,* February 6, 1975.

[50] "Changes Bring Pressure for More Prison Funds," *Dallas Morning News,* December 12, 1974.

[51] The writ of certiorari is the procedural vehicle used to seek review of a lower court's decision. Four of the nine Supreme Court Justices must vote in favor of review before the writ is granted.

[52] *Estelle* v. *Justice,* 426 US 925 (1976).

[53] *Ruiz* v. *Estelle,* Record of Proceedings on Plaintiff's Motion to Punish for Contempt and for Further Relief, May 22 and 23.

[54] *Ruiz* v. *Estelle,* 550 F.2d, 239 (1977).

[55] Order Granting Future Relief, December 30, 1975.

[56] *Ruiz* v. *Estelle,* Brief of Appellants, Fifth Circuit, No. 76–1948.

[57] *Ruiz* v. *Estelle,* 550 F. 2d 238 (1977).

[58] Orders of June 20, 1974; January 20, 1975; December 30, 1975.

[59] Motion for Further Preliminary Relief, May 24, 1976. The witnesses included David Ruiz, Ernesto Montana, Joe Traylor, and L. D. Hilliard.

[60] One of these disciplinary reports (January 20, 1976) was signed by three Ramsey officials, all of whom were later fired or disciplined for brutality by Estelle's successors. David Christian, Robert Lawson (who was later convictd of two counts of civil rights violations in Federal District Court in Houston in February 1986) and N. K. Ramsey.

[61] Record of Proceedings on Plaintiff's Motion for Further Preliminary Relief, July 15 and 16, 1976, Testimony of L. D. Hilliard. During Hilliard's testimony regarding a cell search, an exhibit was entered into evidence that reflected a clear violation of the statute prohibiting building tenders from acting in a supervisory capacity. An officer had left Hilliard a note on his bunk after a cell search, ordering him to get instructions from a building tender as to how to leave his cell while at work.

[62] Correspondence from W. J. Estelle to David Christian, July 1, 1976.

[63] See Sec K.2 of Order Granting Further Relief, December 30, 1975.

[64] Ibid., Estelle to Christian correspondence, July 1, 1976.

[65] Record of Proceedings, July 15 and 16, 1976, Testimony of Freddy B. Parker, Tommy L. Dovia, Johnny Haynes, and John W. Johnson.

[66] Ibid.

[67] Record of Proceedings, Oral Hearing to Establish Schedule for Discovery Completion and Set Trial Date on Merits, December 16, 1976. A few months following this hearing, Justice awarded attorneys' fees to Turner. The state thereafter appealed the order to the Fifth Circuit and for the third time in as many tries failed to overturn a Justice order. See *Ruiz* v. *Estelle,* 609 F. 2d 118 (1980).

[68] Expert Report Security, Arnold Pontesso, Prepared for U.S., Plaintiff-Intervenor, filed February 18, 1977; Inspection of Security and Control Procedures in all Institutions, Fred T. Wilkinson, prepared for the TDC, filed March 10, 1977.

[69] Ibid., Pontessa Report.

[70] Ibid.

[71] Record of Proceedings, Preliminary Pretrial Conference, February 3, 1978, p. 79.

[72] Record of Proceedings, Oral Hearing on Discovery Matters, July 22, 1977.

[73] *Ruiz* v. *Estelle*, U.S. Court of Appeals for Fifth Circuit, Brief of the Appellants, N0 81-2224, October 1981, pp. 21, 79, and 89.

[74] Memorandum and Order, July 31, 1978.

[75] 1975 Annual Statistical Report, Texas Department of Corrections.

Chapter 5

[1] *Corrections Magazine,* March 1978, p. 14.

[2] Interview with Richel Rivers, August 9, 1985.

[3] Interview with Ed Idar.

[4] *Houston Post,* October 3, 1978.

[5] Record of Proceedings, October 2, 1978.

[6] Ibid.

[7] See, for example, Transcribed Testimony of Dr. Kenneth Babcock, October 19, 1972, p. 177; Transcribed Testimony of Oliver Lee Davis, November 28, 1978, pp. 63–66.; Transcribed Colloquy Between Court and Counsel, June 7, 1979, pp. 18–20.

[8] It had been eight years since *Holt* v. *Sarver* (see Chapter 4) had initiated the trend toward an examination of the cumulative effect of prison conditions. This innovation in the application of the cruel and unusual punishment section of the Eighth Amendment had been emulated in a number of subsequent cases. By October 2, 1978, it was clear that while a single factor, taken by itself, might not rise to a constitutional violation, a number of conditions assessed for their total impact could. This growing body of law often involved assessments of such things as physical facilities, crowding, classification systems, segregation cells, medical facilities and treatment, food service, personal hygiene and sanitation, protection from violence, staffing, rehabilitation programs, and numerous other prisoners' rights, such as lack of procedural due process and unreasonable searches and seizures. See Ira P. Robbins and Michael B. Buser, "Punitive Conditions of Prison

Confinement: An Analysis of *Pugh* v. *Locke* and Feʊɪ.. vision of State Penal Administration Under the Eighth Amendment," 29 *Stanford Law Review* 893 (1977).

9   *Texas Department of Corrections: A Brief History,* (Huntsville, Tex.: Texas Department of Corrections, 1974); *30 Years of Progress,* (Huntsville, Tex.: Texas Department of Corrections, 1977).

10   Transcript of Testimony of Salvador Gonzales, October 6, 1978, p. 129. This same pattern was noted by a witness testifying on the last day of Turner's presentation. "There was [under Christian] a much larger number of people working in the hall as enforcers as there was when Warden Savage and Warden Turner were there. At that time they weren't even considered by many of the other inmates as enforcers. We didn't look at them as such at that time." Transcribed Testimony of Steve Stevens, October 17, 1978, p. 187. See also Transcribed Testimony of Lawrence C. Pope, October 2 and 3, 1978, p. 212.

11   Transcribed Testimony of Don Costilow, July 2, August 20–21, 1979, p. 103.

12   Ibid.

13   Note 60, Memorandum Opinion, December 1980.

14   Transcribed Testimony of David A. Christian, May 23–24, 1979, p. 37. The "truth" that Justice perceived was made explicit in his Memorandum Opinion (note 77): The violent propensities of Warden David Christian . . . were repeatedly underscored by the evidence. One inmate stated that violence follows Warden Christian 'like a shadow', an observation that is borne out by the record. A high percentage of the reported incidents of brutality by officers and building tenders occurred at units under Warden Christian's supervision."

15   *Houston Post,* October 17, 1978.

16   Affidavit sworn to by Robert E. DeLong, Jr., October 9, 1978.

17   Ibid.

18   Ibid.

19   "Release to any media question regarding a work stoppage on TDC Units on October 5, 1978."

20   *Huntsville Item,* October 5, 1978.

21   Interoffice communication from S. K. Little to Warden Turner, October 11, 1978.

22   Letter to Judge Justice from Ellis Inmates, October 30, 1978. It read, in part, "To be brief and concise the Administration is trying its best

to force us into a violent confrontation. They won't let us return to work, they won't let us shower, and we are being fed only twice a day, that being sack lunches. . . . We wish you to know that the Administration by its very actions is pushing us into a dangerous situation . . . by not allowing us to return to work, and with the constant inhuman treatment, they realize its only a matter of time before somebody's temper explodes, which would cause a chain reaction. We are ready and willing to return to work and to *Stop* the *Work Stoppage.*"

[23] Letter from David Vanderhoof to Judge Justice, November 3, 1978.

[24] *Houston Post,* November 7, 1978.

[25] Between 1971 and 1974, the prisoner population fluctuated between sixteen and seventeen thousand inmates. In 1975 it rose to nineteen thousand and increased in a linear fashion until the end of trial, when it was just over twenty-six thousand inmates. *Annual and Fiscal Reports,* Texas Department of Corrections.

[26] For example, American Public Health Association (60 sq. ft./inmate); National Advisory Commission on Criminal Justice Standards and Goals (80 sq. ft./inmate); National Sheriff's Association (70 sq. ft./inmate).

[27] See note 49, Memorandum Opinion. Summarized from the testimony of James Williamson, August 17, 1979, and Lester H. Beaird, August 28–29, 1979. Also illustrative is testimony referred to above, where an officer testified about a brutal attack by one inmate on another with two pipes. In his report about the incident, the officer wrote, "Due to our employee shortage, there was no officer working the cell block at the time of the incident."

[28] For examples, see Transcribed Testimony of Arnold Pontesso, December 4–6, 1978, pp. 26–30, 40–43, 56–57, 189–90; Oscar Turner, October 27, 1978, pp. 22, 25–34; Walter Harvey Ballard, November 27, 1978, pp. 45–48, 50–51, 52–60, 128–47, 164–65; Harvey Allen Smith, December 1 and 4, 1978, pp. 17–18, 23–32, 70–79, 152–58; Jesse Joseph Deters, December 7,8, and 11, 1978, pp. 78, 85–87, 93–94, 116–36, 142–45; Michael Conroy, December 4 and 11, 1978, pp. 7–14, 19–20, 30–38, 43–45, 50–53; Roger Pirkle, April 5, 1979, pp. 14–16, 25–32; James Lagermaier, December 21, 1978, and April 3, 1979, pp. 11–12, 16–18, 45–46, 49–57, 60–62, 188–97.

[29] Transcribed Testimony of Keith Price, June 8, 1979, p. 11. This same officer would later change his story when he took over the internal affairs division of the department and was assigned the task of investigating events similar to those he denied existed at trial. See Chapter 6.

[30] For additional examples see transcribed testimony of David A. Chris-

30-33, 38-41, 54-65; Ernesto Carranza, June 11-12, 1979, pp. 24-27, 31-54; Robert Lawson, June 25, 1979, pp. 35-70, 75-94, 115-291, 145-51, 158-59, 159-61; Don Costilow, July 2 and August 20-21, pp. 73-74; Norman Kent Ramsey, July 13, 16, 1979, pp. 22-24, 26-31, 46-48, 55-59.

[31] Transcribed Testimony of James A. Williamson, August 17, 1979, p. 41.

[32] "Charges Against Convict Called Fragile, Unusual," *Austin American-Statesman,* December 18, 1978.

[33] Ibid.

[34] See, for example, Testimony of Walter Harvey Ballard, November 27, 1978, pp. 39-43, 46-48, 118-142, 164-165; Harvey Allen Smith, December 1 and 4, 1978, pp. 36-66, 148-54; Michael Conroy, December 4 and 11, 1978, pp. 17-20; Jesse Joseph Deters, December 7, 8, and 11, 1978, pp, 66-87, 142-45, 150-51, 194-97; James Lagermaier, December 21, 1978, April 3, 1979, pp. 11-12, 48-53, 94-98, 126-31, 211-14; Roger Pirkle, April 5, 1979, pp. 20-24, 29-32, 49-59.

[35] See for example, testimony of Oscar Savage, May 22, 1979, pp. 36-38, 47-50, 54-65, 78-87, 101-8, 115-17, 120-23; David A. Christian, May 23-24, 1979, pp. 11-27, 32-34, 71-73, 121-22, 141-53, 179-81, 267-68, 273-82, 287-99, 305-7; Ernesto Carranza, June 11-12, 1979, pp. 14-20, 48-54, 68-84, 96-111, 118-21, 132-63, 175-78; Robert Lawson, June 25, 1979, pp 21-28, 97-106, 121-40, 155-56; Don Costilow, July 2, August 20-21, pp. 68-71, 78-80, 104-7, 113-23, 138-40, 151-52, 158-59; Norman Kent Ramsey, July 13 and 16, 1979, pp. 22-29, 33-37, 48-52, 61-75, 101-7, 121-24, 129-43, 150-54, 160-66; John Maples, July 25-26, 1979, pp. 30-37, 86-89, 98-99, 133-36, 150-52, 161-68, 184-89, 193-95, 205-6; William J. Estelle, Jr., August 27-28, 1979, pp. 67-73, 89, 165, 175-78, 181.

[36] "TDC Witness Killed in Prison Knife Fight," *Dallas Morning News,* October 24, 1981.

[37] Quoted in "Slain Inmate Had Feared For Life at Prison Unit," *Dallas Times-Herald,* October 17, 1979.

[38] Ibid.

[39] Ibid.

[40] Interoffice communication, Texas Department of Corrections, from R.M. Lawson and G.H. Stricklin, October 25, 1978.

[41] "Inquiry ordered into death of Angleton inmate," *Austin American-Statesman*, November 25, 1979. Notes taken in preparation for Mr. and Mrs. Gus Feist, Sr., v. D. A. Christian, Robert M. Lawson and Texas Department of Corrections, C.A. G-80-96, by Kenneth W. Lewis.

[42] TDC Incident Report, October 24, 1979.

[43] Official Certificate of Death, October 24, 1979.

[44] "Inquiry ordered into death of Angleton inmate," *Austin American-Statesman*, November 25, 1979. Interview with Kenneth W. Lewis, May 14, 1986.

[45] C.A. No. G-80-96.

[46] Farm manager Billy Mack Moore and warden Wallace M. Pack were killed in an altercation with Eroy Brown at the "river bottoms" of the Ellis Unit on April 4, 1981. Brown claimed that he killed the two officials in self-defense after Moore beat him and Pack threatened him with a gun. The first trial on the charge that Brown murdered warden Pack resulted in a hung jury, when ten of the twelve jurors voted to acquit Brown on March 4, 1982. The second trial, in November 1982, resulted in Brown's acquittal in the Pack death. In May 1984, Brown was acquitted on the charge that he murdered farm manager Moore.

[47] Statement from Haynes and Fullenweider to Jack Kyle, June 9, 1980. Purchase Voucher, Texas Department of Corrections, payable to Haynes and Fullenweider, July 3, 1980. There were no details provided on what services were rendered. According to the voucher, the $10,000 fee was paid for "professional services" rendered on April 16, 1980. In a letter dated May 30, 1980, which was more than a month after Haynes rendered his "professional services," attorney general Mark White approved TDC's employment of Haynes to represent employees "relative to the investigation by federal grand juries." Whether the attorney general can authorize an agency to pay state funds to outside counsel to represent state employees in criminal matters is certainly subject to question and at least represents a dubious expenditure of state funds.

[48] Section 504 of the Rehabilitation Act of 1973 and the Architectural Barriers Act of 1968.

[49] See Testimony of Ronald Dean Goforth, October 23–24, 1978; Lewis McDonald, October 25, 1978; Dean F. Pustejovsky, Jr., October 26–27, 1978; Marjorie Mae Vickers, October 26, 1978.

50 See, for example, Transcribed Testimony of Kenneth Babcock, October 19, 1978, pp. 20–27, 35–40; Ronald Dean Goforth, October 23–24, pp. 27–32, 70–74, 76–91, 142–65; Marjorie Mae Vickers, October 26, 1978, pp. 24–25, 52–54; Dean F. Pustejovsky, Jr., October 26–27, 1978, pp. 12–14, 35–51, 81–93,105–7, 122–23; Dr. Luke L. Nigliazzo, October 31, 1978, pp 13–24, 30–72, 78–101, 107–12, 136–67, 271–93, 308–12, 386–90, 411–16; Dr. Richard Della Penna, November 29–30, 1978, pp. 26–38, 50–53, 60–85, 110–29, 133–98, 407–29; Dr. Ralph Gray, August 21–24, 27, 30–31, and September 1 and 5, 1979.

51 See notes 84–139 in Memorandum Opinion.

52 Autopsy Report, Office of the Medical Examiner of Harris County, James Elton Batts, PA-77-118, September 22, 1977.

53 See note 72 in Memorandum Opinion.

54 "State opposes moving prison reform suit," *Dallas Morning News,* January 4, 1979.

55 "Prison reform trial winds down quietly," *Dallas Times Herald,* September 21, 1979.

Chapter 6

1 *Ruiz* v. *Estelle,* Hearing on First Monitor's Report on Factual Observations and Defendant's Motion for Reconsideration of the Amended Order of Reference, March 29, 1982.

2 "Estelle Refutes Judge's Charges of Guard Brutality," *Dallas Times Herald,* December 17, 1980.

3 Ibid.

4 "Lifer," *Houston City Magazine,* April 1982.

5 Ibid.

6 "Prison Director Lambasts Judge Justice's Partiality, Literary Skills," *San Antonio Express,* February 21, 1982.

7 *Morales* v. *Turman,* 383 F. Supp. 53 (1974).

8 430 U.S. 322 (1977).

9 562 F. 2d 993 (1977).

10 See Dick Reavis, "How They Ruined Our Prisons," *Texas Monthly,* May 1985.

[11] "The Roar of the Crowd," *Texas Monthly,* July 1985.

[12] *Corrections Yearbook* (South Salem, N.Y.: Criminal Justice Institute, 1981).

[13] Order of Reference, April 20, 1981.

[14] See "Special Masters in Institutional Litigation," *ABF Research Journal* 1979: 543.

[15] Ibid., p. 553.

[16] Ibid., p. 543.

[17] Defendant's Nominees for Special Master, February 1981.

[18] "Prison vs Court in Texas," *Newsweek,* February 22, 1982.

[19] "The Use of Special Masters in Institutional Reform Litigation," 10 *Tol. L. Rev.* 419, 439 (1979).

[20] Transcript of April 22, 1981, meeting with W. J. Estelle, Jr., Gerald Fall, Jr., Ed Idar, Jr., Ken Petersen, Leonard Peck, Vincent Nathan, and Pat Trujillo.

[21] "The Use of Masters in Institutional Reform Litigation."

[22] Transcript of April 22, 1981, meeting.

[23] Transcript of July 14, 1981, meeting with W. J. Estelle, Jr., Gerald Fall, Jr., Ed Idar, Jr., Ken Petersen, Vincent Nathan, David Arnold, Bill Babcock, Jackie Boney, p. 12.

[24] "Troubleshooting for Texas," *American Lawyer,* January 1981.

[25] Ibid., p. 578. On September 28, 1981, the state filed a second motion to stay certain provisions of the Amended Decree. On January 14, 1982, the Fifth Circuit rendered a decision granting some relief on staffing, housing, and inmate turnkeys; see 666 F. 2d 854 (1982).

[26] "Houston Firm Bills State $1 Million in Prison Suit," *Austin American Statesman,* July 2, 1982.

[27] TDC Business Department Records through Fiscal Year 1984. Fulbright & Jaworski Monthly Statements, July 1981–March 1982.

[28] Fulbright & Jaworski Monthly Statements; Gray, Allison and Becker Monthly Statements.

[29] Fulbright & Jaworski Monthly Billings.

[30] Brief of Appellants, pp. 26–27, citing *Rhodes.*

[31] "Judicial Reform and Prisoner Control: The Impact of *Ruiz* v. *Estelle* on a Texas Penitentiary, 19 *Law & Society Review,* 1985, p. 568.

[32] Ninth Monitor's Report, Appendix P

[33] See Appendices A and B, First Monitor's Report.

[34] Ibid.

[35] For example, "TDC Monitor Says Inmates Still Play Role in Maintaining Order, Authority, *Houston Chronicle,* October 20, 1981.

[36] See First Monitor's Report, p. 25, for similar response made to Arnold during the course of an interview with a building tender.

[37] Report and Recommendations Concerning Status of Huntsville Unit Hospital, August 19, 1981.

[38] "State Report Assails TDC Hospital Care," *Houston Chronicle,* October 15, 1981.

[39] "A Rough Year for TDC, and No Relief in Sight," *Houston Chronicle,* December 6, 1981.

[40] "Special Master Accuses TDC of Harassment," *Huntsville Item,* October 18, 1981.

[41] *Houston Chronicle,* December 6, 1981.

[42] TDC began adding tents as temporary housing to ease overcrowding in July and August 1981. By the end of 1981, 241 tents, which contained just over five hundred square feet of living area, had been added and allocated to thirteen of the prison units. Ninety-eight additional tents were added in 1982. By the end of 1983, all but ten of these tents (at the Diagnostic Unit) had been removed, and the inmates had been reassigned to permanent housing made available by new construction.

[43] "Overseer Denies Charges by TDC," November 24, 1981.

[44] "Special Master Defends Role in Prison Reform," *Dallas Times Herald,* November 24, 1981.

[45] "Texas Officials Blame Prison Rioting on Judge's Reform Order," *Houston Chronicle,* November 23, 1981.

[46] *San Antonio News,* November 23, 1981.

[47] "Special Master Defends Role in Prison Reform."

[48] "Texas Officials Blame Prison Rioting on Judge's Reform Order."

[49] "Reynolds: Not Gone and Not Forgotten," *New York Times,* October 3, 1985.

[50] Office of Governor, Memo: David Herndon to Governor Clements, October 29, 1981.

51 Transcript of Executive Meeting with Governor William P. Clements, Jr., David Herndon, Mark White, Ed Idar, Pike Powers, Lee Clyburn, Brian Greig, Louis Austin, Joe LaMantia, T. L. Roach, Robert Gunn, Clifford Smith, Lindsey Waters, Harry Whittington, Bartell Zachry, W. J. Estelle, Gerald Fall, Richard Hartley, Governor's Conference Room, December 11, 1981.

52 Interview with Harry Whittington, March 13, 1986.

53 Interview with Harry Whittington, April 16, 1986.

54 Transcript of December 11, 1981 meeting, p. 38.

55 "Prison Negotiations Aim for Compromise," *Houston Chronicle*, December 9, 1981.

56 "Justice Lawyer Stands Behind Prison Order," *Dallas Times Herald*, December 19, 1981.

57 See, for example, Second Monitor's Report of Factual Observations (Disciplinary Procedures and Administrative Segregation), November 9, 1981.

58 First Monitor's Report, p. 60.

59 Letter from Fall to Nathan, January 28, 1982.

60 Ibid.

61 The filing of the motion happened to coincide with the opening of Mark White's campaign for the Democratic gubernatorial nomination.

62 Interoffice communication, Estelle to All Wardens, January 25, 1982.

63 Response of Special Master to Defendants' Motion for Reconsideration of the Amended Order of Reference, February 22, 1982, p. 7. Warden Durbin was in fact terminated in November 1984, when a TDC internal investigation found that he had knowledge that officers at Ramsey had planted a weapon in the cell of a *Ruiz* witness and he failed to take any corrective action, See Twenty-ninth Monitor's Report of Factual Observations, July 23, 1985.

64 Ibid.

65 "Clements Says He's Wrong on Monitor Probe," *Houston Chronicle*, January 29, 1982.

66 For example, see *Houston Chronicle*, January 26, 1982; *Dallas Times Herald*, January 26, 1982; and *Austin American Statesman*, January 26, 1982.

67 It is interesting to note that the state had paid Fulbright and Jaworski,

the law firm that filed this motion, in excess of $750,000 for just seven months' work. Further, one of the Fulbright and Jaworski attorneys noted Nathan's expenses such as telephone, postage, etc. for the month of November 1981 (see "Freeze on TDC Monitor's Funds Asked," *Houston Chronicle,* February 5, 1982). Those combined expenses did not equal the $3,261.82 for copying alone paid to Fulbright and Jaworski the same month.

[68] Order, February 15, 1982.

[69] "Prison-Master Debate Seen as Diversion," *Austin American Statesman,* January 27, 1982.

[70] Defendant's Motion to Vacate Order of Consolidation, February 12, 1982.

[71] Order, February 23, 1982.

Chapter 7

[1] The supervisor was later rehired as a correctional officer and was promoted through the ranks to become one of three regional directors of TDC.

[2] Monitor's Witness List.

[3] TDC Disciplinary Report, No. 14626, October 16, 1981.

[4] Inmate Records.

[5] In the following months this witness would be charged with a disciplinary offense after unit officials planted a weapon in his cell, see Chapter 6, note 63.

[6] "Cost of prison suit soaring above $1 million," *Fort Worth Star-Telegram,* March 7, 1982.

[7] Ibid.

[8] "State drops jail master objections," *Austin American Statesman,* March 30, 1982.

[9] Ibid.

[10] Ibid.

[11] "Prisoner testifies TDC inmates armed with riot batons patrolled dormitory," *Houston Chronicle,* March 16, 1982; "Inmate tells judge he kept weapons in cell," *Houston Post,* March 18, 1982; testimony of

Robert White, March 15, 1982. The officer who was allegedly gambling with White was in later years fired for excessive use of force on prisoners. See Ninth Monitor's Report, Factual Observations.

[12] Interview with Harry Whittington, April 29, 1986.

[13] Record of Proceedings, March 29, 1982.

[14] Ibid.

[15] Ibid.

[16] "Troubleshooting for Texas," *American Lawyer*, 1985.

[17] Stipulated Modification of Section IID, and Section IIA, of Amended Decree, April 14, 1982.

[18] Record of Proceedings, April 14, 1982.

[19] "TDC Board votes to dismantle BT system," *Houston Post*, April 17, 1982.

[20] Ibid.

[21] Ibid.

[22] Ibid.

[23] "State shuts prison doors to new inmates," *Dallas Times Herald*, May 11, 1982; "TDC announces freeze on taking new prisoners," *Houston Chronicle*, May 11, 1982; TDC bars new inmates from counties, *Dallas Morning News*, May 11, 1982.

[24] Texas Board of Corrections, Board Motion, May 10, 1982.

[25] "Clements orders TDC to take inmates," *Houston Chronicle*, May 14, 1982.

[26] "State prison wrangle has that tinge of politics," *Dallas Times Herald*, May 14, 1982.

[27] "Clements calls White liar, newspaper reports," *Dallas Morning News*, May 11, 1982.

[28] "Clements tells TDC to admit more prisoners," *Houston Post*, May 14, 1982.

[29] "Prison mandate perplexing," *Houston Chronicle*, May 14, 1982.

[30] General and Special Laws, Texas, 67th Legislature, 2nd Called Session, May 28, 1982.

[31] General and Special Laws, Texas, 68th Legislature, Regular Session. See Texas Prison Management Act, Chapter 233 and Good Conduct Time, Chapter 375.

[32] *Ruiz* v. *Estelle*, 679 F. 2d 1115, 1126 (June 23, 1982).

[33] "State told to pay 'modest' $1.6 million in prison suit fees," *Houston Chronicle*, November 20, 1982.

[34] "Appeals court overturns single celling," *Dallas Morning News*, June 24, 1982; "Single-cell issue rejected in prison victory for the state," *Austin American Statesman*, June 24, 1982.

[35] 679 F. 2d 1115, 1146 (1982).

[36] Ibid., p. 1148.

[37] Record of Hearing, November 5, 1982.

[38] Ibid.

[39] TDC incident report, Wynne Unit, January 11, 1983.

[40] *U.S.* v. *Robert Lawson, et al.*, SD/Tex, Cr. H-85-160, March 11, 1986.

[41] TDC incident report, Wynne Unit, January 12, 1983.

[42] Ninth Monitor's Report, Appendices F, I, and P.

[43] Ninth Monitor's Report, pp. 50–51.

[44] Ibid., p. 23.

[45] TDC Disciplinary Log, June 19, 1984.

[46] Ninth Monitor's Report, Appendices E and K.

[47] Ibid., Appendix O, p. 7.

[48] Ibid., p. 30, Appendix O.

[49] TDC Incident Report, September 29, 1983.

[50] "Problems toppled TDC chief," *Dallas Morning News*, December 4, 1983. Estelle actually announced his intention to resign on September 15, two days after Belazis filed his report on use of force.

[51] Texas Board of Corrections, Minutes, July 1983.

[52] Ibid., March 1983.

[53] Correspondence, George McNiel to Members of the Texas Board of Corrections, April 13, 1983.

[54] Texas Board of Corrections, Minutes, May 1983.

[55] Ibid.

[56] Correspondence, Harry Whittington to George McNiel, May 19, 1983.

[57] Correspondence, George McNiel to Harry Whittington, June 15, 1983.

[58] Texas Board of Corrections, Minutes, July 1983.

[59] "TDC Chairman riding high," *Fort Worth Star-Telegram,* June 24, 1984.

[60] "Tumultuous year transforms Chief of Prisons Board," *Dallas Morning News,* July 29, 1984.

[61] Ibid.

[62] Texas Board of Corrections, Minutes, July 1983.

[63] "Problems toppled TDC Chief."

[64] Ibid.

[65] Ibid.

[66] "Tumultuous year transforms Chief of Prison Board."

[67] "TDC chairman riding high."

[68] *Dallas Times Herald,* September 29, 1983.

[69] "White vows action of report if abuse in TDC confirmed," *Houston Post,* September 30, 1983.

[70] Statement of the Board of the State Department of Corrections, October 7, 1983.

[71] Nineteenth Monitor's Report of Factual Observations, August 30, 1984.

[72] Stipulation, November 17, 1983.

[73] "Letters to the Editor," *Huntsville Morning News,* February 3, 1984.

Chapter 8

[1] Dick J. Reavis, "How They Ruined Our Prisons," *Texas Monthly,* May 1985.

[2] *Ruiz* v. *McCotter,* Memorandum Opinion and Order, December 31, 1986.

Names Index

Subject Index

Cases Index

T

U

V

W

Y